Quantum Computing Concepts

Fundamentals, circuits, and code

Sudeep Satheesan

Sri Mounica Kalidasu

bpb

www.bpbonline.com

First Edition 2025

Copyright © BPB Publications, India

ISBN: 978-93-65895-049

LIMITS OF LIABILITY AND DISCLAIMER OF WARRANTY

To View Complete
BPB Publications Catalogue
Scan the QR Code:

Dedicated to

Schrödinger's Cat
and
The Next Generation of Quantum Pioneers

About the Authors

- **Sudeep Satheesan** is an Enterprise Architect with over two decades of experience in machine learning, cloud, distributed computing, Generative AI and quantum computing. He began exploring quantum computing six years ago and has conducted sessions at reputed institutes such as NIT Raipur and SRM University.

  Sudeep has co-authored a research paper related to quantum computing titled *A Scalable 5,6-Qubit Grover's Quantum Search Algorithm*. He recently published an article exploring the application of the Bernstein-Vazirani algorithm to the classic household game 'Chor-Police.'

  Outside of his professional pursuits, Sudeep is deeply passionate about football and chess. In addition to his love for strategy and sports, he channels his creativity into storytelling and is the author of two fiction books.

- **Sri Mounica Kalidasu** is a software engineer with 8 years of experience specializing in Data Science, Generative AI, cloud technologies and quantum computing. She has 6 months of experience in quantum computing and holds a bachelor's degree in Physics from IIT Guwahati. She further pursued a postgraduate degree in Business Analytics and Applications from IIM Trichy.

  She has co-authored a research paper related to quantum computing titled *A Scalable 5,6-Qubit Grover's Quantum Search Algorithm*. With a strong foundation in both classical and quantum computing paradigms, she actively explores advancements in quantum algorithms, machine learning applications, and cloud-based quantum computing platforms.

About the Reviewers

❖ **Dr. Tahir Manzoor** is working as an Assistant Professor at JBIET, Hyderabad. His areas of expertise are Mathematics and Quantum Technology. He is engaged in applying the Clifford algebra approach in quantum computing, quantum information theory, and quantum cryptography. Additionally, he participates in the review process of books and research articles related to his field of expertise. He has recently been awarded the title of Excellent Reviewer by a peer-reviewed journal. He is continuously exploring new subdomains of quantum technology.

❖ **Madhuri Konnur** is a Freelancer, quantum enthusiast, and hackathon activist. She has over 14 years of IT experience in various domains like Retail, Energy, EdTech, Transport, and Supply Chain, among others. Her recent focus has been on research related to real-time implementations of quantum computing in areas like Security **quantum key distribution (QKD)**, **Quantum Secure Direct Communication (QSDC)**, Quantum Sensors, and Quantum AI. Having had opportunities to solve complex problems in Data Science and machine learning like Replenishment Optimization in SCM, customer churning in EdTech marketing, X-ray prediction during Covid, etc., it is more promising to work on Quantum real-time problem solving. She has also been part of Womanium Global Quantum, **Women in Optics and Photonics (WOPI)**. She has authored various technical articles on Medium and LinkedIn. She enjoys networking with Research scientists and startup enthusiasts in various events organized by companies, to understand the latest trends/innovations/ideas and where the IT market is heading.

Acknowledgements

Quantum computing may be a field of probabilities, but one thing we are certain of is that this book would not have been possible without the invaluable support of many individuals and organizations.

We extend our deepest gratitude to BPB Publications for their guidance and expertise in bringing this book to life. The journey of refining and structuring this work has been an adventure, made possible by the insightful collaboration of reviewers, technical experts, and editors who contributed their time and knowledge to ensure the highest quality content.

Writing about quantum computing has felt at times like wielding an Infinity Gauntlet, each concept adding a new dimension of power but requiring immense precision to avoid unintended paradoxes. We sincerely appreciate the pioneers in this field whose research has laid the groundwork for this book, making it possible for others to explore and understand the quantum realm.

Finally, to the readers, whether you are enthusiasts, students, researchers, or future quantum computing superheroes, thank you for your curiosity and passion. The quantum revolution is just beginning, and much like the Avengers assembling to face challenges beyond imagination, the collective effort of bright minds will shape the future of computation.

Preface

Quantum computing is ushering in a new era of computational capabilities, challenging the fundamental limitations of classical computing and opening doors to unprecedented possibilities. As researchers, engineers, and enthusiasts navigate this rapidly evolving landscape, a solid understanding of quantum principles, algorithms, and applications is essential.

This book serves as a comprehensive guide to the core concepts of quantum computing, from foundational quantum mechanics to practical implementations using contemporary tools such as Qiskit and IBM Q. By exploring topics such as superposition, entanglement, quantum gates, quantum error correction, and quantum communication, this book aims to provide readers with the knowledge required to grasp the nuances of quantum information processing and computation.

Throughout this book, we cover various aspects of quantum computing, starting with the fundamental principles that distinguish it from classical computing. We examine the different types of quantum computers and their architectures, ensuring readers understand the diverse approaches taken in the field. Moving forward, we explore quantum gates and circuits, their mathematical representations, and their role in quantum computation. Practical tools such as Qiskit and IBM Q are introduced to help readers experiment with quantum algorithms and gain hands-on experience. Additionally, the book covers crucial topics like quantum communication, error correction, and the design of classical gates using quantum gates, offering a holistic perspective on the potential and challenges of quantum computing.

Chapter 1: Principles of Quantum Computing- Introduces the fundamental concepts of quantum computing, including the nature of subatomic particles, fundamental quantum mechanics principles, and key quantum phenomena such as superposition and entanglement.

Chapter 2: Types of Quantum Computers- Provides an overview of different types of quantum computers, their architectures, and how they differ from classical computing paradigms.

Chapter 3: Superposition and Entanglement- Explores the key quantum principles that distinguish quantum computing from classical computing and their implications for computational efficiency.

Chapter 4: Quantum Gates and Circuits- Covers the basic building blocks of quantum circuits, including various quantum gates and their mathematical representations.

Chapter 5: Introduction to Qiskit and IBM Q- Introduces readers to the Qiskit framework and IBM Q, providing hands-on experience in running quantum experiments.

Chapter 6: Design of Classical Logic Gates Using Quantum Gates- Examines how classical logic gates can be designed using quantum gates and their implications in computational models.

Chapter 7: Quantum Communication- Discusses key aspects of quantum communication, including superdense coding, quantum teleportation, and quantum key distribution.

Chapter 8: Quantum Error Correction- Explains the necessity of error correction in quantum computing and various techniques used to mitigate errors.

Chapter 9: Quantum Algorithms- Introduces fundamental quantum algorithms such as Grover's search and Shor's algorithm, demonstrating how quantum computing can outperform classical methods in specific problem domains.

Chapter 10: Applications of Quantum Computers Across Industries- Explores how quantum computing is revolutionizing various industries, including cryptography, optimization, healthcare, material science, and artificial intelligence.

This book is designed for students, researchers, and professionals who are eager to understand and apply quantum computing principles. Whether you are new to the field or seeking to deepen your knowledge, this book provides structured guidance with theoretical insights, mathematical foundations, and practical examples to bridge the gap between theory and application.

By the end of this book, readers will have a strong foundation in quantum computing concepts, an appreciation for the current state of the technology, and a clear vision of the transformative impact quantum computing may have on fields such as cryptography, optimization, artificial intelligence, and beyond. I hope this book serves as a valuable resource in your journey into the fascinating world of quantum computing.

Code Bundle and Coloured Images

Please follow the link to download the
Code Bundle and the *Coloured Images* of the book:

https://rebrand.ly/8a7jd7a

The code bundle for the book is also hosted on GitHub at
https://github.com/bpbpublications/Quantum-Computing-Concepts.
In case there's an update to the code, it will be updated on the existing GitHub repository.

We have code bundles from our rich catalogue of books and videos available at
https://github.com/bpbpublications. Check them out!

Errata

We take immense pride in our work at BPB Publications and follow best practices to ensure the accuracy of our content to provide with an indulging reading experience to our
subscribers. Our readers are our mirrors, and we use their inputs to reflect and improve
upon human errors, if any, that may have occurred during the publishing processes involved. To let us maintain the quality and help us reach out to any readers who might be
having difficulties due to any unforeseen errors, please write to us at :

errata@bpbonline.com

Your support, suggestions and feedbacks are highly appreciated by the BPB Publications'
Family.

Did you know that BPB offers eBook versions of every book published, with PDF
and ePub files available? You can upgrade to the eBook version at www.bpbonline.
com and as a print book customer, you are entitled to a discount on the eBook copy.
Get in touch with us at :

business@bpbonline.com for more details.

At www.bpbonline.com, you can also read a collection of free technical articles,
sign up for a range of free newsletters, and receive exclusive discounts and offers
on BPB books and eBooks.

Piracy

If you come across any illegal copies of our works in any form on the internet, we would be grateful if you would provide us with the location address or website name. Please contact us at business@bpbonline.com with a link to the material.

If you are interested in becoming an author

If there is a topic that you have expertise in, and you are interested in either writing or contributing to a book, please visit www.bpbonline.com. We have worked with thousands of developers and tech professionals, just like you, to help them share their insights with the global tech community. You can make a general application, apply for a specific hot topic that we are recruiting an author for, or submit your own idea.

Reviews

Please leave a review. Once you have read and used this book, why not leave a review on the site that you purchased it from? Potential readers can then see and use your unbiased opinion to make purchase decisions. We at BPB can understand what you think about our products, and our authors can see your feedback on their book. Thank you!

For more information about BPB, please visit www.bpbonline.com.

Join our Discord space

Join our Discord workspace for latest updates, offers, tech happenings around the world, new releases, and sessions with the authors:

https://discord.bpbonline.com

Table of Contents

CHAPTER 1
Principles of Quantum Computing

Introduction

Quantum computing is a groundbreaking field that challenges classical computing paradigms by leveraging the principles of quantum mechanics. Unlike traditional computers that process data in binary form (0s and 1s), quantum computers utilize quantum bits (qubits) that can exist in multiple states simultaneously due to properties such as superposition and entanglement. These fundamental principles enable quantum computers to solve complex problems exponentially faster than their classical counterparts.

This chapter explores the foundational concepts of quantum computing, including the nature of subatomic particles, fundamental quantum mechanics principles, and key quantum phenomena such as superposition, entanglement, and quantum wave theory. By understanding these core principles, readers will gain insight into the mechanisms that power quantum computers and their vast potential in fields such as cryptography, optimization, and artificial intelligence.

Structure

The following topics are covered in this chapter:

- Fundamental principles of quantum behavior
- Electrons

- Discoveries about photons in the field of quantum mechanics
- Evolution of quantum mechanics
- Superposition
- Quantum entanglement for computational advantage
- Quantum wave theory
- No-cloning theorem
- Heisenberg's uncertainty principle
- Copenhagen interpretation
- Double-slit experiment

Objectives

This chapter aims to provide readers with a solid foundation in quantum computing principles by exploring the key concepts and theories that define the field. By the end of this chapter, readers will understand the fundamental building blocks of quantum mechanics, including electrons, photons, and subatomic particles. They will also gain insight into the historical evolution of quantum mechanics and its impact on modern computing. Additionally, the readers will be able to comprehend key quantum principles such as superposition, entanglement, and quantum wave theory, and their implications in quantum computation. We will learn about crucial quantum theories, including the No-cloning theorem and Heisenberg's uncertainty principle, and their significance in quantum information processing. Also, we will explore major interpretations of quantum mechanics, such as the Copenhagen interpretation and the double-slit experiment, to understand how quantum behaviors are observed and analyzed.

By mastering these topics, readers will be well-equipped to delve deeper into quantum computing technologies and their applications in scientific and industrial domains.

Fundamental principles of quantum behavior

At the subatomic scale, particles exhibit behaviors that diverge significantly from classical expectations. Quantum mechanics governs this domain, where principles such as superposition, entanglement, and wave-particle duality dictate the dynamics of elementary entities. Understanding these foundational phenomena is crucial for exploring quantum computing, as the operation of quantum systems relies on the non-classical properties of quantum bits (qubits). This chapter introduces the essential quantum mechanical concepts that form the basis for quantum information processing.

Quantum stage

Picture a stage, not with grandiose curtains and dazzling lights, but one where the theatre of existence unfolds at scales inconceivably small. At this quantum stage, entities such as electrons, photons, and quarks emerge as protagonists in a narrative that challenges the very fabric of reality. These entities, far from the billiard ball simplicity of classical particles, embody the dual nature of waves and particles—a paradox encapsulated in the wave-particle duality.

The process is represented in the following figure:

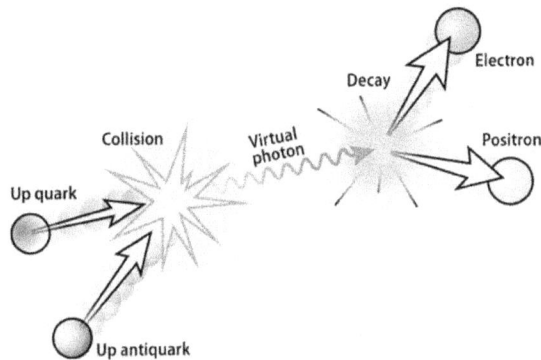

Figure 1.1: The collision of an up quark and an up antiquark

A virtual photon can violate some laws of physics, as long as its lifetime is less than a value determined by the photon's energy and a physical constant (called **Planck's constant**). This *loophole* is related to something called **Heisenberg's uncertainty principle**. A virtual photon briefly lives and then decays into new particles. This process shows how particles interact and transform, revealing the fascinating ways nature works at the smallest scales.

Virtual photons are important because they act as carriers of force between particles, helping us understand interactions in particle physics, virtual photons are essential as they mediate electromagnetic interactions between charged particles, even though they exist only briefly and cannot be directly observed. Their role helps explain processes like particle annihilation, scattering, and decay, revealing the underlying forces and interactions that govern the quantum world. For example, when a quark and an antiquark collide, they can briefly create a virtual photon, which then decays into other particles like an electron and a positron. (*Figure 1.1*)

Here is one simple example of a quark-antiquark interaction:

- An up quark (electric charge +2/3) interacts with a down antiquark (charge: 2/3).
- They form a virtual photon, which has no charge but does have a mass. (A photon with mass is a violation of the laws of physics).

- The virtual photon decays within the time limit allowed by Heisenberg's uncertainty principle, sometimes into an electron (charge −1) and an anti-electron, called a positron (charge +1).

- A quark and antiquark that annihilate each other can form other quark pairs and other elementary particle pairs such as a muon and an anti-muon. Nature provides many other ways that quarks can combine.

Imagine electrons gracefully surfing probability waves, their trajectories uncertain until the moment of observation. The quantum dance introduces an indeterminacy that fuels the excitement of discovery and innovation in the realm of quantum computing. It is within this dance that the promise of qubits, the quantum bits that power quantum computers, materializes.

Quantum ensemble and the role of subatomic particles

As the curtain rises on the quantum stage, subatomic particles take center stage. Quarks, the elemental constituents of protons and neutrons, showcase their vibrant personalities, each with distinct **flavors** that contribute to the symphony of matter. Gluons, the glue holding quarks together, emphasize the interconnectedness of the quantum world, much like the intricate choreography of a ballet. Refer to the following figure:

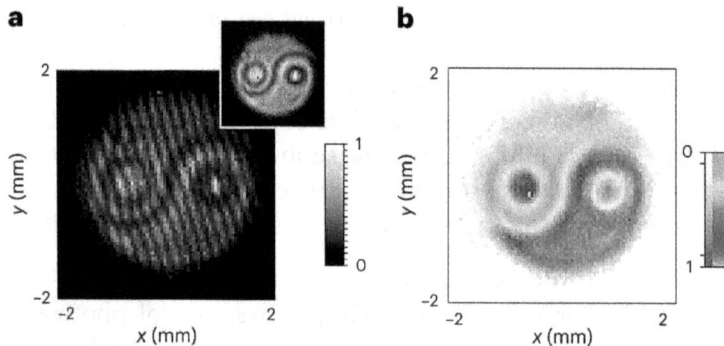

Figure 1.2: Biphoton state holographic reconstruction

Photons, the carriers of light and electromagnetic force, waltz through space and time, transcending classical limitations. Meanwhile, neutrinos, the elusive particles with almost negligible mass, play hide-and-seek, traversing the cosmos without much interaction. Together, these subatomic actors form an ensemble that orchestrates the quantum mechanics spectacle, captivating scientists and enthusiasts alike. *Figure 1.2* depicts the quantum entanglement of photons observed for the first time by researchers at the *University of Ottawa*, in collaboration with *Danilo Zia* and *Fabio Sciarrino* from the Sapienza University of Rome, who recently demonstrated a novel technique that allows the visualization of the wave function of two entangled photons, the elementary particles that constitute light, in real-time.

Entanglement and quantum synchronization

As we explore the quantum narrative, the concept of entanglement emerges, a phenomenon that Einstein famously referred to as **spooky action at a distance**. Entanglement is the quantum sync, where particles become entwined in such a way that the state of one instantaneously influences the state of the other, regardless of the physical distance separating them. This connection underpins the potential for quantum computers to perform complex computations exponentially faster than their classical counterparts. In this unfolding quantum drama, the entities and subatomic particles showcase a dance that challenges our understanding of reality. As we peer into the intricacies of the quantum world, the promise of harnessing these phenomena for computation beckons, promising a revolution that transcends the boundaries of classical computing.

Imagine you have two identical dice that are magically connected. You roll one dice in India, and the moment it lands on a number, the dice in New York instantly shows the same number, even though no one touched it. This mysterious connection happens faster than any signal could travel between them, it is as if the dice knew what the other rolled, no matter how far apart they are. That is how quantum sync, or entanglement, works in the quantum world.

Electrons

In the quantum realm, where classical limits dissolve into the limitless possibilities of quantum superposition and entanglement, one entity stands as the true author of this groundbreaking narrative—the electron (e− or β−). Electrons, those elementary particles that whiz around atomic nuclei, reveal their true prowess in the quantum domain and their distribution is described by atomic orbitals. These orbitals are three-dimensional regions around the nucleus where electrons are likely to be found (*Figure 1.3*). Atomic orbitals come in different types, each denoted by a unique set of quantum numbers. The primary types of atomic orbitals include:

- **S orbitals (spherical):** S orbitals are spherical in shape and are characterized by the principal quantum number (n). As the principal quantum number increases, the size of the spherical region increases. Each energy level (shell) in an atom can have one or more S orbitals.
- **P orbitals (dumbbell-shaped):** P orbitals have a dumbbell or figure-eight shape and come in sets of three (px, py, and pz), each oriented along one of the three coordinate axes. They are associated with the azimuthal quantum number ($l = 1$) and can exist in different planes within a given energy level.
- **D orbitals (cloverleaf-shaped):** D orbitals have more complex shapes, including cloverleaf and double-dumbbell configurations. There are five D orbitals (dxy, dyz, dzx, dx2-y2, and dz2), corresponding to $l = 2$. They appear in higher energy levels than S and P orbitals.

- **F orbitals (intricate shapes):** F orbitals have even more intricate shapes, and there are seven different F orbitals (and 14 electrons in total), corresponding to $l = 3$. These orbitals appear in even higher energy levels than D orbitals.

The number of orbitals in each subshell is determined by the magnetic quantum number (ml), which can take values from -l to +l. For example, in an S orbital ($l = 0$), there is only one orbital (ml = 0). In a P orbital ($l = 1$), there are three orbitals (ml = -1, 0, +1).

These orbitals provide a framework for understanding the distribution of electrons in an atom and play a crucial role in chemical bonding and the overall behavior of atoms in chemical reactions. The **Pauli Exclusion Principle** and the **Aufbau Principle** guide the filling of these orbitals with electrons, ensuring the stability and energy minimization of the atom. Their quantum states, governed by the laws of quantum mechanics, form the foundation upon which quantum bits or qubits, the fundamental units of quantum information, are built. The book aims to shed light on the electron's role, exploring how its spin, charge, and quantum states contribute to the creation of quantum gates—the building blocks of quantum algorithms. It is shown in the following figure:

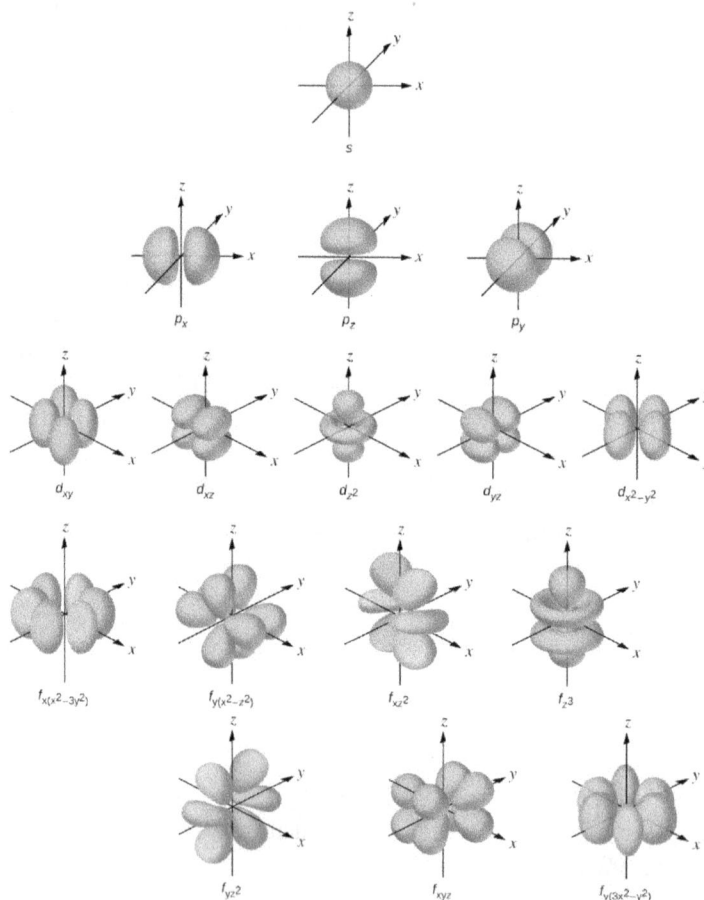

Figure 1.3: Shapes of atomic orbitals

In his groundbreaking 1924 dissertation *Recherches sur la théorie des quanta* (Research on quantum theory), French physicist *Louis de Broglie* proposed a revolutionary hypothesis, suggesting that all matter possesses both particle and wave-like characteristics. This wave-particle duality, akin to the behavior of light, indicated that under specific conditions, electrons and other matter could exhibit properties of both particles and waves. Experimental confirmation of this dual nature emerged in 1927 when *George Paget Thomson, Alexander Reid, Clinton Davisson*, and *Lester Germer* demonstrated interference patterns in beams of electrons, mirroring the wave-like behavior observed in light. *De Broglie's* wave hypothesis inspired *Erwin Schrödinger* to formulate a wave equation for electrons within atoms, leading to the development of quantum mechanics. Schrödinger's equation, established in 1926, not only successfully described the propagation of electron waves but also introduced the concept of probability distribution, emphasizing the likelihood of finding an electron at a particular position. The evolution of quantum mechanics continued in 1928 with *Paul Dirac's* Dirac equation, incorporating relativity theory and predicting the existence of the positron—the antimatter counterpart of the electron. The subsequent discovery of the positron in 1932 by *Carl Anderson* validated Dirac's theory. Further advancements, such as *Willis Lamb* and *Polykarp Kusch's* findings in 1947, revealed the Lamb shift and anomalous magnetic dipole moment of the electron, challenging existing theories. The resolution to these anomalies came with the development of **quantum electrodynamics (QED)** in the late 1940s by *Sin-Itiro Tomonaga, Julian Schwinger*, and *Richard Feynman*. Their groundbreaking work not only explained these phenomena but also marked a significant leap forward in our understanding of quantum mechanics, laying the foundation for subsequent quantum advancements. We will cover the intriguing world of superposition, where electrons can exist in multiple states at once, challenging our classical intuition and paving the way for exponentially faster computations. We explore the concept of entanglement, where electrons become entwined across vast distances, sharing information instantaneously, an ability that holds the key to quantum communication and the development of quantum networks. As we disentangle the complexities of quantum algorithms and their applications, the electron takes center stage, guiding us through the maze of quantum gates, quantum circuits, and the promise of solving problems exponentially faster than classical computers.

Discoveries about photons in the field of quantum mechanics

The history of discoveries about photons in the field of quantum computing is a fascinating journey marked by key milestones that have shaped our understanding and applications of quantum phenomena. Here is a concise overview of some significant events:

- **1920s wave-particle duality:** The concept of wave-particle duality, initially proposed by *Louis de Broglie*, laid the foundation for understanding the dual nature of particles, including photons. In 1927, experiments by *Clinton Davisson* and *Lester*

Germer demonstrated the wave-like behavior of electrons, extending the wave-particle duality principle to particles beyond light.

- **Quantum electrodynamics:** The development of QED in the late 1940s by renowned physicists such as *Sin-Itiro Tomonaga, Julian Schwinger,* and *Richard Feynman* provided a theoretical framework for understanding the behavior of photons and electrons in quantum systems. QED became an essential tool for describing the interaction between light and matter.

- **Quantum entanglement (1935):** The concept of quantum entanglement, where particles become interconnected regardless of distance, was introduced by *Albert Einstein, Boris Podolsky,* and *Nathan Rosen* in a 1935 paper. Though initially a subject of debate between *Einstein* and *Niels Bohr*, entanglement later became a key resource in quantum computing, including the entanglement of photons as shown in *Figure 1.4*. The spontaneous parametric down-conversion process can split photons into type II photon pairs with mutually perpendicular polarization.

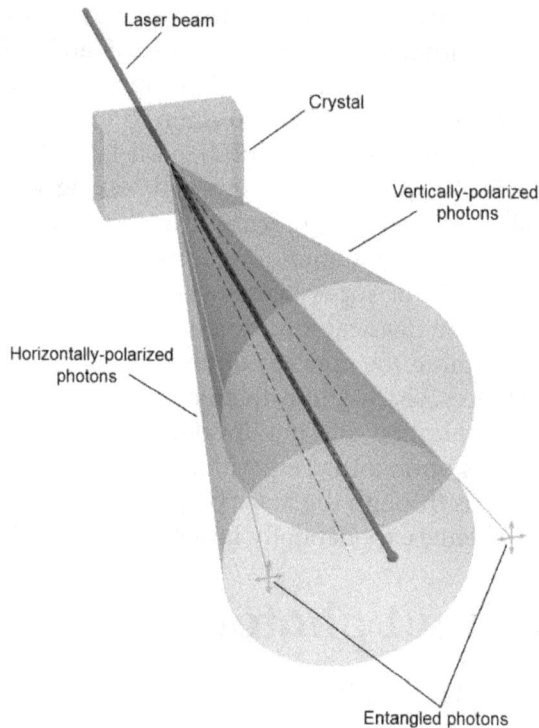

Laser beam

Crystal

Vertically-polarized photons

Horizontally-polarized photons

Entangled photons

Figure 1.4: Entanglement of photons

- **Quantum cryptography (1984):** Physicist *David Deutsch* proposed the concept of quantum cryptography, leveraging the principles of quantum mechanics for secure communication. In **quantum key distribution (QKD)** protocols, the transmission of photons is used to establish secure cryptographic keys, exploiting the unique properties of quantum states.

- **Quantum computing algorithms (1990s):** The 1990s saw the development of groundbreaking quantum algorithms, including *Peter Shor's* algorithm for factoring large numbers exponentially faster than classical algorithms and Lov Grover's algorithm for searching unsorted databases. Photons played a crucial role in these algorithms, especially in implementations of quantum parallelism and quantum interference.

- **QKD experiments (2000s):** Experimental implementations of QKD became a reality in the 2000s, with researchers achieving secure communication using the principles of quantum entanglement and the transmission of individual photons.

- **Quantum teleportation (1997):** The successful demonstration of quantum teleportation, transferring the quantum state of a photon to another photon at a distant location, by a team of scientists including *Anton Zeilinger*, showcased the potential of quantum communication using entangled photons.

- **Photonic quantum computing (Current era):** Contemporary research focuses on the development of photonic quantum computing platforms. Various technologies, such as linear optics, photon detectors, and integrated photonics, are being explored to manipulate and measure the quantum states of photons for quantum information processing.

The history of discoveries related to photons in quantum computing reflects the continuous evolution of our understanding of quantum mechanics and the innovative applications of these principles in emerging technologies.

The narrative extends beyond the confines of quantum computing, touching upon the implications of photon-driven quantum technologies for cryptography, sensing, and secure communication. Through the pages of this book, readers gain a profound understanding of how photons, as the radiant scribes of quantum computing, are shaping the future of information processing.

Evolution of quantum mechanics

The evolution of quantum mechanics is a captivating journey marked by groundbreaking discoveries and paradigm shifts in our understanding of the fundamental nature of the quantum world. Here is a brief overview of key evolutions in the field.

In the nascent years of the 20th century, the landscape of physics underwent a revolutionary transformation with the birth of quantum mechanics. Pioneered by *Max Planck* and propelled forward by *Albert Einstein*, this epoch marked the emergence of a groundbreaking paradigm shift. Planck's daring **quantum hypothesis** in 1900 and Einstein's groundbreaking work on the **photoelectric effect** in 1905 collectively set the stage for the unraveling of a new understanding of the fundamental nature of energy and light. As we delve into the foundational years of quantum mechanics (1900-1925), we witness the birth of concepts that would redefine the very fabric of physics, challenging classical notions and laying the groundwork for a quantum revolution.

Birth of quantum mechanics

In the vibrant intellectual ferment of the 1920s, the realm of quantum mechanics witnessed a profound revelation—wave-particle duality. Spearheaded by the visionary insights of *Louis de Broglie* and further crystallized through the ingenious formulations of *Erwin Schrödinger* and *Werner Heisenberg*, this transformative era reshaped our understanding of the fundamental nature of particles. *De Broglie's* audacious proposal of matter waves for particles like electrons challenged conventional wisdom, ushering in an era where particles defied the constraints of classical categorizations. As we traverse the landscape of the 1920s, we encounter pivotal contributions—from de Broglie's conceptual breakthrough to *Schrödinger* and *Heisenberg's* complementary formulations—forming the cornerstone of wave-particle duality and laying the groundwork for the enigmatic and exhilarating world of quantum mechanics:

- **Planck's quantum hypothesis (1900):** *Max Planck* introduced the concept of quantized energy, laying the foundation for quantum theory by suggesting that energy is emitted or absorbed in discrete packets called quanta.

- **Einstein's photoelectric effect (1905):** *Albert Einstein* extended quantum theory by proposing that light consists of quantized particles called photons, explaining the photoelectric effect.

Wave-particle duality

In the crucible of quantum exploration during the pivotal year of 1927, the foundations of quantum mechanics were further solidified with *Werner Heisenberg's* uncertainty principle and *Paul Dirac's* unifying synthesis of wave and matrix mechanics. *Heisenberg's* groundbreaking principle introduced a fundamental limit to our precision in simultaneously measuring certain pairs of properties, challenging classical notions of determinism. Concurrently, the profound work of *Paul Dirac* harmoniously melded the disparate realms of wave and matrix mechanics into a singular, comprehensive framework. As we delve into the quantum landscape of 1927, *Heisenberg* and *Dirac's* contributions not only unveiled the inherent limits of our understanding but also forged the path toward a more profound and nuanced comprehension of the quantum realm:

- **De Broglie's matter waves (1924):** *Louis de Broglie* suggested that particles, like electrons, exhibit both wave and particle properties.

- **Wave mechanics and matrix mechanics (1925):** *Erwin Schrödinger* formulated wave mechanics, while *Werner Heisenberg* developed matrix mechanics, providing two equivalent formulations of quantum mechanics.

Uncertainty principle and matrix mechanics

In the annals of quantum physics, the year 1935 bore witness to the emergence of quantum entanglement—a phenomenon that both perplexed and captivated the minds of physicists.

It was a time when *Albert Einstein, Boris Podolsky,* and *Nathan Rosen,* in their landmark paper on the *EPR Paradox,* illuminated the seemingly paradoxical nature of particles entangled in quantum states. Concurrently, *Erwin Schrödinger's* enigmatic thought experiment, famously known as *Schrödinger's Cat,* introduced a feline paradox that would become emblematic of the bizarre and counterintuitive facets of quantum mechanics. As we delve into this era of quantum entanglement, we explore the intellectual conundrums posed by EPR and the whimsical paradox of Schrödinger's Cat—two thought experiments that challenged the very fabric of our classical intuitions and propelled the exploration of the quantum world into uncharted territories:

- **Heisenberg's uncertainty principle:** Werner Heisenberg proposed the uncertainty principle, stating that certain pairs of properties (like position and momentum) cannot be simultaneously known with arbitrary precision.

- **Dirac's quantum mechanics (1927):** Paul Dirac unified wave and matrix mechanics into a single, comprehensive formulation.

Quantum entanglement

In the post-war scientific renaissance of the 1940s and 1950s, the quantum realm experienced a profound maturation with the birth of QED. The collaborative endeavors of visionaries such as *Richard Feynman, Julian Schwinger,* and *Sin-Itiro Tomonaga* heralded a transformative era in theoretical physics. QED emerged as a comprehensive and elegant framework, providing unparalleled insight into the intricate dance between matter and electromagnetic fields. As we delve into this period, we witness the crystallization of QED as a cornerstone in the edifice of quantum field theory, marking a watershed moment where theory and experiment converged to unveil the intricate tapestry of the quantum world:

- **Einstein-Podolsky-Rosen (EPR) paradox:** *Albert Einstein, Boris Podolsky,* and *Nathan Rosen* presented a thought experiment highlighting the apparent paradoxes of quantum entanglement.

- **Schrodinger's Cat (1935):** *Erwin Schrödinger* introduced a thought experiment involving a cat in a superposition of states, illustrating the peculiar aspects of quantum mechanics.

Birth of quantum electrodynamics

Embarking on a trajectory of innovation that transcends the boundaries of classical computation, the realm of quantum information and computing has unfolded as a captivating frontier since the 1980s. At its genesis, *David Deutsch's* groundbreaking proposal in 1984 introduced the concept of quantum cryptography, harnessing the unique properties of quantum systems to forge a new era of secure communication. The momentum of this quantum revolution gained further impetus with *Peter Shor's* seminal contribution in 1994—Shor's algorithm—a computational marvel capable of factoring large numbers exponentially faster than classical counterparts, laying bare the transformative potential of quantum computers. As the theoretical foundations solidified, the 21st century witnessed experimental endeavors in QKD, where the application of quantum principles emerged as a practical avenue for securing communication channels. In the unfolding narrative of quantum information and computing, these milestones not only illuminate the past but also cast a brilliant light on the ever-expanding horizons of the quantum landscape, where the interplay of theory and experimentation continues to redefine the possibilities of information processing and secure communication:

- **Quantum electrodynamics (QED):** The development of QED by *Feynman, Schwinger,* and *Tomonaga* provides a complete framework for understanding the interactions between matter and electromagnetic fields.

Quantum information and computing

Venturing into the awe-inspiring realm of quantum phenomena, the 1990s marked an epoch of remarkable strides with the advent of quantum teleportation and ongoing experiments probing the mysteries of quantum entanglement. In the year 1997, a pivotal breakthrough unfolded as scientists achieved the seemingly miraculous feat of quantum teleportation—transferring quantum states between particles with unprecedented precision. This remarkable achievement not only captivated the imaginations of physicists but also laid the groundwork for a future where the instantaneous transmission of quantum information could redefine the boundaries of communication. Simultaneously, the scientific community embarked on a sustained journey of exploration, delving deeper into the enigmatic realm of quantum entanglement. Rigorous experiments were conducted to scrutinize and verify these intricate quantum phenomena, including meticulous tests of Bell's inequalities. As we navigate through the evolving narrative of quantum teleportation and entanglement experiments, we witness a saga of scientific ingenuity unraveling the mysteries of quantum mechanics and pushing the boundaries of our understanding of the fundamental nature of reality:

- **Quantum cryptography (1984):** *David Deutsch* proposed quantum cryptography, utilizing quantum properties for secure communication.
- **Shor's algorithm (1994):** *Peter Shor* developed an algorithm for factoring large numbers exponentially faster than classical algorithms, showcasing the potential of quantum computers.
- **Quantum key distribution (QKD):** Experimental implementations of QKD protocols for secure communication.

Quantum teleportation and quantum entanglement experiments

In the current era, the landscape of quantum technologies has evolved into a realm where scientific innovation converges with practical applications, propelling us into a new frontier of computational possibilities. At the forefront of this evolution is the rapid advancement of photonic technologies for quantum information processing, offering unprecedented potential for harnessing the unique properties of quantum systems. Concurrently, a watershed moment in the field occurred in 2019 when Google's Sycamore processor achieved quantum supremacy. This groundbreaking achievement marked a pivotal juncture as the quantum processor outpaced the most sophisticated classical supercomputers in performing a specific task. As we navigate the unfolding developments in quantum technologies and witness the realization of quantum supremacy, we find ourselves at the threshold of a transformative era where the fusion of theoretical innovation and practical applications redefines the landscape of computation and ushers in a new era of technological possibilities:

- **Quantum teleportation (1997):** The successful teleportation of quantum states between particles is achieved.
- **Quantum entanglement experiments:** Continued exploration and verification of quantum entanglement phenomena, including tests of Bell's inequalities.

Quantum technologies and quantum supremacy

The field of quantum mechanics has witnessed continuous evolution, from its early conceptual foundations to the emergence of practical quantum technologies. Ongoing research continues to unveil new facets of quantum phenomena, promising revolutionary advancements in computation, communication, and information processing:

- **Photonic quantum computing:** Advancements in photonic technologies for quantum information processing.
- **Quantum supremacy (2019):** Google's Sycamore processor achieves quantum supremacy by performing a specific task faster than the most advanced classical supercomputers.

Superposition

Quantum superposition is a fundamental principle in quantum mechanics that describes a quantum system's ability to exist in multiple states or configurations simultaneously. It is a key feature that differentiates quantum systems from classical systems, where objects typically exist in well-defined states.

Schrödinger's wave mechanics

In the midst of the quantum revolution during the early 20th century, a radical departure from classical physics was underway, spearheaded by groundbreaking contributions that would redefine our understanding of the microscopic world. Among these pivotal advancements, *Erwin Schrödinger's* wave mechanics emerged as a cornerstone, unveiling a new mathematical framework that elegantly described the behavior of particles at the quantum scale. As we delve into the narrative of Schrödinger's wave mechanics, we embark on a journey through the intricacies of wave-particle duality and the profound implications of superposition. This transformative period not only challenged the conventional tenets of classical physics but also laid the groundwork for a comprehensive and nuanced understanding of quantum mechanics, setting the stage for a paradigm shift that continues to shape our comprehension of the quantum realm:

- **Formulation:** *Erwin Schrödinger* developed wave mechanics in 1926, introducing a wave equation that describes the behavior of quantum systems. Erwin Schrödinger crafted a thought experiment that has since become an iconic symbol of the peculiarities inherent in the quantum world—the paradox of Schrödinger's Cat. Imagine a sealed box containing a curious amalgamation of elements: a cat, a vial of poison, a Geiger counter, and a radioactive substance as shown in *Figure 1.5:*

Figure 1.5: A cat is placed inside a sealed box along with a radioactive substance, a Geiger counter, and a vial of poison

- **Superposition in wave mechanics:** The Schrödinger equation allows for the superposition of quantum states. A particle's wavefunction is a combination of multiple possible states, and the actual state is determined upon measurement. Schrödinger's hypothetical scenario delves into the conundrums of superposition, entangling the fate of the cat with the unpredictable decay of a radioactive particle. As we peer into the confines of this conceptual box, we enter a realm where the traditional boundaries of classical reality blur, challenging our intuitions and beckoning us to contemplate the perplexing nature of quantum states and the paradoxes they present as depicted in the *Figure 1.6:*

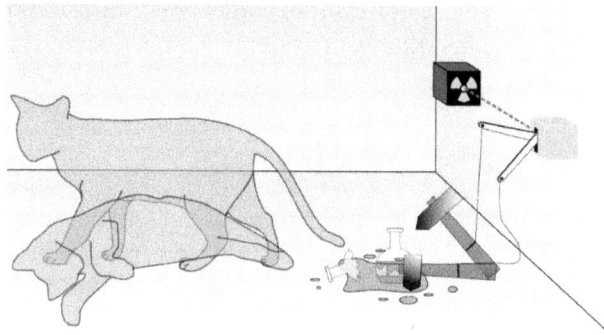

Figure 1.6: Schrödinger's Cat

Matrix mechanics

In the crucible of quantum innovation during the mid-1920s, a profound divergence in the mathematical formulations of quantum mechanics unfolded, giving rise to *Werner Heisenberg's* matrix mechanics. Introduced as an alternative to *Erwin Schrödinger's* wave mechanics, matrix mechanics presented a novel approach to describing the behavior of particles at the quantum scale. Within the framework of matrix mechanics, the concept of superposition emerged, mirroring its counterpart in wave mechanics. Quantum states found expression through matrices, and the superposition principle allowed the seamless combination of these states, portraying a quantum world defined by inherent uncertainties. As the mathematical foundations of quantum mechanics solidified, *Paul Dirac*, in the late 1920s and 1930s, introduced **Dirac notation** and the abstract concept of **Hilbert space**. This formalization not only provided a rigorous mathematical language for quantum mechanics but also emphasized the ubiquitous role of superposition, wherein quantum states are represented as vectors in Hilbert space—a realm where the linear combinations of these vectors illuminate the intricacies of quantum superposition:

- **Formulation:** *Werner Heisenberg* independently formulated matrix mechanics in 1925 as an alternative to Schrödinger's wave mechanics.

- **Superposition in matrix mechanics:** Matrix mechanics also supports the concept of superposition. Quantum states are represented by matrices, and the superposition principle allows for the combination of different states.

- **Dirac notation and Hilbert space:** *Paul Dirac*, in the late 1920s and 1930s, introduced Dirac notation and the concept of Hilbert space to formalize quantum mechanics mathematically.

- **Superposition in Hilbert space:** Quantum states are represented as vectors in Hilbert space, and superposition is expressed through the linear combination of these vectors.

Copenhagen interpretation

In the labyrinth of quantum mechanics, where the rules defy classical intuition, the Copenhagen interpretation emerges as a cornerstone, shaping our conceptualization of the quantum realm. Propounded by the visionary minds of *Niels Bohr* and *Werner Heisenberg*, this interpretative framework places a unique emphasis on the interplay between measurement and the observer's influence within quantum systems. Within the confines of the Copenhagen interpretation, the enigmatic concept of superposition takes center stage, portraying a quantum reality where a system exists in a simultaneous confluence of multiple states until subjected to measurement. As we unravel the tenets of this interpretative paradigm, we delve into a philosophical and theoretical exploration that underscores the profound impact of observation on the very nature of quantum entities, offering both insight and intrigue into the intricate dance between particles and perception:

- **Interpretation:** The Copenhagen interpretation, championed by *Niels Bohr* and *Werner Heisenberg*, emphasizes the role of measurement and observer effects in quantum systems.

- **Superposition in Copenhagen interpretation:** Superposition is a fundamental aspect of the Copenhagen interpretation, where a quantum system is considered to exist in a superposition of states until measured.

Many-worlds interpretation

In the expansive landscape of quantum interpretations, the many-worlds interpretation stands as a provocative and audacious proposition, challenging our conventional understanding of reality. Conceived by *Hugh Everett III* in 1957, this interpretative framework ventures into the realm of the extraordinary, suggesting that every conceivable outcome of a quantum measurement unfolds across distinct branches of a vast and ever-expanding multiverse. As we delve into the intricacies of the many-worlds interpretation, the very fabric of quantum superposition reveals itself as a natural consequence within this paradigm. Within the tapestry of the multiverse, all potential states coexist, each in their own branch, presenting a quantum reality that transcends the confines of a singular, deterministic outcome. Embarking on a journey through the theoretical corridors of many-worlds, we explore a cosmos where the quantum possibilities are not merely potentialities but tangible and concurrent realities within the infinite expanse of parallel universes:

- **Interpretation:** Proposed by *Hugh Everett* III in 1957, the many-worlds interpretation suggests that all possible outcomes of a quantum measurement occur, each in a separate branch of the universe.

- **Superposition in many-worlds interpretation:** Superposition is a natural consequence of this interpretation, as all possible states coexist in different branches of the multiverse.

Quantum field theory

Quantum field theory (QFT), developed in the mid-20th century, extends quantum mechanics to include fields and particles. Quantum fields can exist in superpositions of states, and particles are excitations of these fields, exhibiting superposition properties.

These theories collectively form the foundation of quantum mechanics and provide a conceptual framework for understanding and applying the principle of superposition in diverse quantum phenomena. Superposition is a central feature in the quantum world, contributing to the unique and often counterintuitive behavior observed at the quantum scale.

Quantum entanglement for computational advantage

Quantum entanglement is a phenomenon in quantum mechanics where two or more particles become correlated and instantaneously affect each other's properties, regardless of the physical distance that separates them. These particles, often referred to as entangled particles, exhibit a strong, non-local connection that cannot be explained by classical physics.

Analyzing the fundamental properties of quantum entanglement, we elucidate the distinctive characteristics that underscore its role as one of the most profound and non-classical phenomena in quantum mechanics. These features redefine the boundaries of classical physics, inviting us to explore the entangled states, non-local correlations, and the instantaneous influence between particles. As we navigate through the fundamental principles of quantum entanglement, we embark on a journey that transcends the conventional notions of physical reality, revealing a tapestry woven with threads of entangled connections and opening new dimensions of inquiry into the very nature of the quantum universe.

Key features of quantum entanglement

Despite its seemingly paradoxical nature, quantum entanglement has been experimentally observed and verified, making it a central and fascinating aspect of quantum mechanics. Understanding and harnessing entanglement is crucial for the development of quantum technologies with transformative implications for communication, computing, and information processing:

- **Correlation beyond classical limits:** Entangled particles exhibit correlations that surpass classical limits. Changes in the state of one particle are immediately reflected in the state of the entangled partner, violating the principle of local realism.

- **Non-locality:** The influence between entangled particles occurs instantaneously, regardless of the spatial separation between them. This apparent "spooky action at a distance," as Einstein called it, challenges classical notions of causality.

- **Entangled states:** Entanglement is typically described using quantum states called entangled states. These states cannot be factored into independent states for each particle, emphasizing the inseparability of their properties.

- **Entanglement creation:** Entanglement can be created through various processes, such as spontaneous parametric down-conversion or the decay of certain particles. Once entangled, the properties of the particles are interdependent.

  Enter the realm of the *quantum entanglement and measurement image*, a visual abstraction that seeks to capture the elusive nature of entangled particles and the intricate dance between measurement and quantum states. In this visual exploration, we navigate the complexities of rendering a snapshot of entangled particles at the moment of measurement, where the act of observation precipitates a collapse of quantum probabilities into tangible realities as shown in *Figure 1.7*:

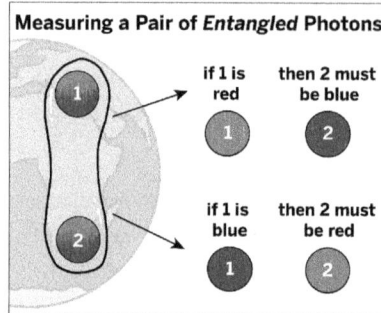

Figure 1.7: Quantum entanglement and measurement

- **Quantum measurement:** When a measurement is performed on one entangled particle, it instantaneously determines the state of the other, regardless of the distance between them. This phenomenon persists even if the measurement is made before the particles can communicate through any known means.

- **Quantum entanglement and information:** Quantum entanglement is essential for quantum information processing and quantum computing. Entangled particles can be used as qubits, the basic units of quantum information, enabling the creation of quantum gates and circuits.

- **Bell's theorem:** Physicist *John Bell* formulated Bell's theorem, which provides a way to test the predictions of quantum entanglement against classical models. Experiments based on Bell's theorem support quantum predictions and challenge local realistic theories.

- **Applications:** Quantum entanglement has practical applications in quantum communication, where it can be used for secure communication channels through QKD. It is also explored for its potential role in quantum teleportation and quantum cryptography.

Quantum wave theory

Quantum wave theory, also referred to as wave mechanics, constitutes a pivotal aspect of quantum mechanics, elucidating the conduct of particles at the quantum scale. Originating to surmount the constraints of classical physics in explicating phenomena on minute scales, particularly observable in electrons and other subatomic entities, this theory incorporates key principles.

It introduces the concept of wave-particle duality, positing that particles like electrons and photons can manifest both wave-like and particle-like attributes. Described by a mathematical expression termed the wave function, this dual nature encapsulates the probability amplitude of locating a particle in a specific state. Governed by the Schrödinger equation, the evolution of wave functions over time characterizes the behavior of quantum systems. The square of the wave function produces the probability density, signifying the inherently probabilistic nature of a particle's location—a departure from classical determinism.

Each quantum system aligns with a distinctive evolving wave function, constituting a complete orthonormal basis of potential states. Quantum superposition allows particles to exist in multiple states concurrently, contrasting classical physics. Localized disturbances in a wave function, termed wave packets, illustrate wave-particle duality and the uncertainty principle. Quantum tunneling, where particles traverse energy barriers deemed impenetrable in classical physics, is explained by the wave function. Finally, quantum entanglement, wherein the wave functions of entangled particles instantaneously correlate, regardless of distance, is a foundational concept. This potent framework challenges classical determinism, paving the way for quantum technological advancements.

Quantum leap

It suggests a sudden and profound shift, akin to the instantaneous and discontinuous jumps observed at the quantum level. For example, one might say there has been a **quantum leap in technology** to highlight a rapid and groundbreaking advancement in technological capabilities.

Quantum tunneling

Quantum tunneling is a phenomenon in quantum mechanics where particles, such as electrons, can pass through energy barriers that classical physics would predict as impenetrable. In classical physics, particles are confined by potential energy barriers and cannot move through them unless they possess sufficient energy to overcome the barrier.

However, in the quantum realm, particles exhibit wave-particle duality. According to the principles of quantum mechanics, particles can exist in multiple states simultaneously, and their behavior is described by a wave function. Quantum tunneling occurs when a particle's wave function extends into a region beyond the energy barrier, allowing the particle to pass through it, even if its energy is technically lower than the energy of the barrier. Refer to the following figure:

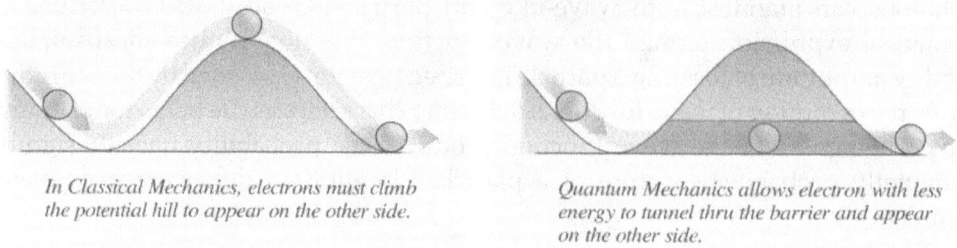

In Classical Mechanics, electrons must climb the potential hill to appear on the other side.

Quantum Mechanics allows electron with less energy to tunnel thru the barrier and appear on the other side.

Figure 1.8: *Classical vs. quantum tunneling*

This phenomenon challenges classical intuitions and underscores the probabilistic nature of quantum mechanics. Quantum tunneling has been observed in various contexts, such as in nuclear fusion processes within stars and in the operation of tunnel diodes in electronics.

The probability of tunneling decreases exponentially with the thickness and height of the barrier. Despite its counterintuitive nature, quantum tunneling has practical applications, including in the development of tunneling microscopes and certain electronic devices. The concept plays a crucial role in understanding the behavior of particles at the quantum level, where traditional notions of barriers are redefined by the probabilistic nature of quantum wave functions.

No-cloning theorem

The no-cloning theorem is a fundamental concept in quantum mechanics that states an arbitrary unknown quantum state cannot be duplicated exactly. Proposed by physicist *Wootters* and *Zurek* in 1982, this theorem has significant implications for quantum information theory and the nature of quantum systems.

In classical information theory, one can make a perfect copy of any information. However, in the quantum realm, the situation is different due to the principles of superposition and measurement disturbance.

The no-cloning theorem can be succinctly stated as follows: It is impossible to create an identical copy of an arbitrary unknown quantum state. Mathematically, if $|\psi\rangle$ represents an arbitrary quantum state, there is no unitary operation U and a blank state $|0\rangle$ such that $U(|\psi\rangle \otimes |0\rangle) = |\psi\rangle \otimes |\psi\rangle$.

This has profound implications for quantum computing and quantum communication. In classical computing, copying information is a routine operation (like copying a file on a computer). However, the no-cloning theorem implies that quantum information cannot be copied in the same straightforward manner.

This principle is crucial for the security of quantum communication protocols. For example, QKD relies on the fact that any eavesdropping attempt will inevitably disturb the quantum states being transmitted, providing a detectable trace of interference.

In summary, the no-cloning theorem is a foundational concept in quantum mechanics, setting a fundamental limit on the replication of quantum information and influencing the design of quantum information processing systems.

Heisenberg's uncertainty principle

Heisenberg's uncertainty principle is a fundamental concept in quantum mechanics, formulated by German physicist *Werner Heisenberg* in 1927. This principle establishes a fundamental limit on the precision with which certain pairs of properties, such as a particle's position and momentum, can be simultaneously known.

The uncertainty principle challenges the classical notion of definite, simultaneous values for all physical properties of a particle. Specifically, it states that the more precisely the position of a particle is known, the less precisely its momentum can be known, and vice versa. Mathematically, the principle is expressed as:

$$\Delta x \cdot \Delta p \geq \hbar/2$$

where:

- Δx is the uncertainty in position
- Δp is the uncertainty in momentum
- $\hbar$ is the reduced Planck constant $(h/2\pi)$

This principle introduces an inherent fuzziness or uncertainty into the nature of quantum systems. It implies that there are intrinsic limits to the precision with which certain pairs of properties can be simultaneously measured. This is not due to limitations in measurement devices but is a fundamental aspect of the quantum nature of particles.

In this intricate snapshot, we witness the interplay of particles—incident photons, scattered photons, and recoiling electrons—capturing a moment that reflects the inherent uncertainties governing the quantum realm. Werner Heisenberg's revolutionary principle, etched into the very fabric of this visual tableau, comes to life as the simultaneous measurement of position and momentum unravels, revealing the fundamental limitations imposed by quantum mechanics as depicted in the image *Figure 1.9*:

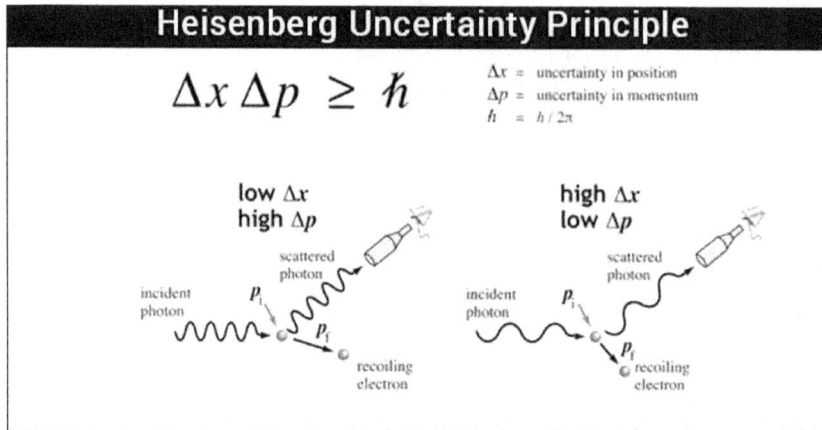

Figure 1.9: Heisenberg's uncertainty principle

The uncertainty principle has profound implications for our understanding of quantum mechanics. It underscores the probabilistic nature of quantum systems and challenges the deterministic worldview of classical physics. Additionally, it has practical consequences, influencing the design and interpretation of experiments in the quantum realm.

Copenhagen interpretation

The Copenhagen interpretation, a pivotal stance in quantum mechanics, traces its roots to discussions held in the 1920s among luminaries such as *Niels Bohr* and *Werner Heisenberg* in Copenhagen. This interpretation furnishes a theoretical framework, emphasizing the central role of observation and measurement in understanding quantum phenomena.

At its core, the Copenhagen interpretation acknowledges the dual nature of particles, recognizing their ability to exhibit both wave-like and particle-like characteristics. The crux lies in the notion that a quantum system exists in a superposition of states until subjected to measurement. The act of measurement precipitates the system's **collapse** into a specific state, and the outcome is inherently probabilistic.

A distinctive feature is the emphasis on the observer's role in quantum systems. The interpretation posits that the conscious act of observation or measurement significantly influences and determines the properties of a particle. This aligns with Werner Heisenberg's uncertainty principle, a key tenet stating inherent limits to simultaneously knowing certain pairs of properties, such as position and momentum.

The concept of complementarity, introduced by *Niels Bohr*, adds another layer. Complementarity asserts that particles may exhibit seemingly contradictory behaviors depending on the experimental conditions, highlighting the contextual nature of quantum phenomena.

While the Copenhagen interpretation has significantly shaped quantum theory, it remains a subject of philosophical discourse. Debates persist around the role of consciousness, the nature of measurement, and the concept of wave function collapse. Nevertheless, its enduring influence underscores its status as a cornerstone in the understanding of the intricate and perplexing realm of quantum mechanics.

Double-slit experiment

The double-slit experiment shows that particles, like electrons, can behave like waves, creating interference patterns similar to those seen with light or water. This surprising result reveals the dual nature of particles; they can act as both particles and waves, depending on how they are observed. The experiment involves shining a beam of particles through two closely spaced slits onto a screen. The resulting pattern on the screen provides insights into the nature of particles and waves.

The interference pattern observed on the screen is a key feature of the experiment. This pattern is analogous to the interference patterns observed when waves, such as light waves, interact with each other. Mathematically, this interference pattern can be described using the following formula:

$$I(\theta) = I_0 cos(\pi dsin\theta/\lambda)$$

In this formula:

- $I(\theta)$ represent the intensity of the pattern at a particular angle θ.
- I_0 is the maximum intensity of the pattern.
- d is the distance between the two slits.
- λ is the wavelength of the particles.

This formula demonstrates the wave-like nature of particles, where the interference pattern depends on the wavelength and the geometry of the experiment.

In the captivating interplay of light and matter, this visual representation encapsulates one of the most profound experiments in the history of quantum physics. As we uncover this image, we enter the realm where particles exhibit both wave and particle properties, challenging our classical intuitions. The double-slit configuration, a simple yet profound setup, becomes a stage for the manifestation of quantum behaviors that defy our everyday understanding of reality as shown in *Figure 1.10*:

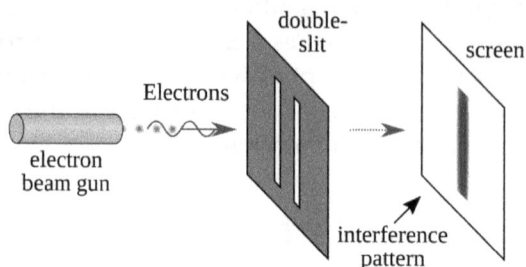

Figure 1.10: Double-slit experiment

However, the experiment becomes more intriguing when particles are sent through one at a time. Even with individual particles, over time, an interference pattern still emerges. This suggests that each particle is behaving as a wave and interfering with itself. The mathematical formalism for this scenario involves probability amplitudes and is described by the quantum mechanics formalism, including wavefunctions and superposition.

The experiment takes a dramatic turn when attempts are made to determine which slit a particle passes through. The introduction of measurement or observation collapses the wave function, erasing the interference pattern. The act of measurement disrupts the delicate quantum state, showcasing the dual nature of particles and the role of observation in quantum phenomena.

Conclusion

Our exploration of quantum computing has taken us through the fascinating world of quantum mechanics, where we have learned about the tiny particles, like electrons and photons, that form the basis of this groundbreaking field. We have seen how these particles behave in strange and surprising ways, which is essential to understanding how quantum computers work.

In the next chapter, we will look at different approaches to building quantum computers. We will explore technologies like quantum annealing, developed by D-Wave, and trapped-ion systems from companies like IonQ and Honeywell. We will also dive into exciting innovations, like Microsoft's topological quantum computing, Xanadu's work with photons, and Atom Computing's focus on neutral atoms. Additionally, we will examine superconducting chips, used by companies like IBM, Google, and Rigetti, and their potential to achieve powerful, universal quantum computing. As we continue our journey, we will also discuss the concept of **Noisy Intermediate-Scale Quantum computers** (**NISQs**) and how they fit into the current state of quantum computing. Finally, we will explore how we measure the performance of quantum computers through a metric called **quantum volume**, which takes into account factors like the number of qubits, error rates, and coherence.

Multiple choice questions

1. **What are the fundamental building blocks of quantum computing often referred to as?**

   a. Protons

   b. Subatomic entities

   c. Neutrons

   d. Atoms

2. **In the context of quantum mechanics, which term describes the simultaneous existence of multiple states in a particle?**

   a. Superposition

   b. Entanglement

   c. Quantum leap

   d. Quantum tunneling

3. **Which of the following phenomena challenges classical notions by allowing particles to exhibit interconnectedness over large distances?**

   a. Quantum tunneling

   b. Wave theory

   c. Entanglement

   d. Copenhagen interpretation

4. **The concept of wave-particle duality is experimentally exemplified by which iconic experiment?**

   a. Quantum leap

   b. No-cloning theorem

   c. Double-slit experiment

   d. Heisenberg's uncertainty principle

5. **Which principle, introduced by Werner Heisenberg, states that certain pairs of properties cannot be simultaneously known with arbitrary precision?**

   a. Quantum tunneling

   b. Superposition

   c. Heisenberg's uncertainty principle

   d. Quantum leap

Answer key

1. b

2. a

3. c

4. c

5. c

Questions

1. Explain the concept of superposition and its significance in the realm of quantum computing.

   Answer: Superposition allows quantum bits (qubits) to exist in multiple states simultaneously, forming the basis for quantum parallelism and potential computational advantages.

2. How does the phenomenon of entanglement challenge classical intuitions about particle behavior?

   Answer: Entanglement involves a correlation between particles that surpasses classical limits, and changes in the state of one particle are immediately reflected in the state of the entangled partner, challenging classical notions of local realism.

3. Compare and contrast the wave and particle aspects of electrons in the context of quantum mechanics.

   Answer: Electrons exhibit both wave and particle properties. In wave theory, electrons are described by wavefunctions, and in certain situations, they behave like particles.

4. Discuss the implications of Heisenberg's uncertainty principle on the precision of measurements in quantum systems.

   Answer: Heisenberg's uncertainty principle imposes a fundamental limit on the precision with which certain pairs of properties (for example, position and momentum) can be simultaneously known. It introduces inherent uncertainties in measurements.

5. Elaborate on the experimental setup and observations of the double-slit experiment, emphasizing its relevance in quantum mechanics.

   Answer: The double-slit experiment involves shining light or particles through two slits, creating an interference pattern. It demonstrates the wave-particle duality of particles, showing that they can exhibit both wave and particle behaviors.

6. Explore the philosophical implications of the Copenhagen interpretation in the context of quantum mechanics.

Answer: The Copenhagen interpretation raises questions about the role of observation in determining reality, challenging the classical notion of an objective and independent reality.

7. Provide a detailed explanation of the no-cloning theorem and its significance in quantum information theory.

   Answer: The No-cloning theorem states that an arbitrary unknown quantum state cannot be perfectly copied. This has implications for quantum communication and quantum cryptography.

8. Analyze the practical applications of quantum tunneling and its potential impact on future technologies.

   Answer: Quantum tunneling is crucial in technologies such as tunnel diodes and scanning tunneling microscopes. Its potential impact includes advancements in electronics and nanotechnology.

9. Discuss the role of quantum leap in the energy transitions of particles and its consequences in quantum systems.

   Answer: Quantum leap refers to an abrupt transition of a particle between energy levels. It is fundamental to the emission and absorption of quantized energy and plays a key role in quantum systems.

10. Evaluate the importance of subatomic entities in the foundational principles of quantum computing, considering their unique behaviors and characteristics.

    Answer: Subatomic entities, such as electrons and photons, are essential in quantum computing as they exhibit quantum properties like superposition and entanglement, forming the basis for quantum information processing.

Join our Discord space

Join our Discord workspace for latest updates, offers, tech happenings around the world, new releases, and sessions with the authors:

https://discord.bpbonline.com

CHAPTER 2
Types of Quantum Computers

Introduction

Quantum computers represent a revolutionary approach to computing that leverages the principles of quantum mechanics to perform calculations. Unlike classical computers, which use bits as the fundamental unit of information (either 0 or 1), quantum computers use quantum bits or qubits, which can exist in multiple states simultaneously thanks to a property known as **superposition** (where qubit exists in combinations of 0 and 1 at the same time allowing faster computations). This ability to exist in multiple states simultaneously enables quantum computers to perform certain calculations much more efficiently than classical computers.

Structure

The topics to be covered in this chapter are as follows:

- Quantum annealing and D-Wave
- Trapped-ion and IonQ, Honeywell
- Quantum topological computers and Microsoft
- Quantum photonics-based computers and Xanadu
- Neutral atoms and Atom Computing
- Superconducting chips and IBM, Google, Rigetti

- Universal quantum computers
- Noisy Intermediate-Scale Quantum computers
- Performance comparison of quantum computers

Objectives

By the end of this chapter, you will have a comprehensive understanding of various quantum computing technologies and the companies leading their development. You will explore quantum annealing through D-Wave's approach, and delve into trapped-ion methods as employed by IonQ and Honeywell, gaining insight into their unique advantages and challenges. The chapter will also cover Microsoft's work on topological quantum computing, highlighting the potential for error resistance and stability in these systems. You will learn about quantum photonics-based computing, focusing on Xanadu's use of photonic qubits, as well as neutral atom quantum computing, with Atom Computing's innovative approaches at the forefront. Additionally, the chapter will provide an analysis of superconducting chips used by industry giants like IBM, Google, and Rigetti, and explain the concept of universal quantum computers and their capabilities. You will also explore **Noisy Intermediate-Scale Quantum** (**NISQ**) computers, which represent the current generation of quantum devices, and assess the performance of various quantum computing technologies by understanding the key metrics and benchmarks used to evaluate their effectiveness. Through these topics, the chapter aims to equip you with a solid understanding of the diverse landscape of quantum computing.

Quantum annealing and D-Wave

Quantum annealing is a computational technique that leverages quantum mechanics to solve optimization problems. It is a specific approach to quantum computing, distinct from gate-based quantum computing, and is designed to address a class of problems known as **combinatorial optimization problems**. Quantum annealers, like those from D-Wave, are particularly well-suited for solving problems described by the **Ising model**, a mathematical model of interacting spins. The Ising model describes how magnetic spins interact, with each spin being either up or down. It is used to simulate how particles in a material behave, especially during phase transitions. In quantum annealing, the Ising model helps find the lowest energy state of a system, which is key for solving optimization problems. Quantum annealers use this model to explore multiple solutions at once, offering faster solutions than classical methods.

The following are key aspects of quantum annealing:

- **Annealing process:** The term **annealing** is borrowed from classical physics, where it refers to a process of slowly cooling a material to remove defects and optimize its structure.

- **Quantum annealing:** In the quantum context, annealing involves initializing a quantum system in a simple, known state and then gradually evolving it toward the desired solution to an optimization problem. Refer to the following figure:

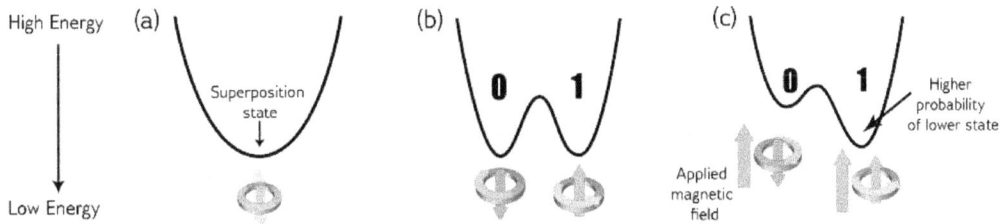

Figure 2.1: Energy diagram changes over time as the quantum annealing process runs and a bias is applied

The physics underlying this process can be visualized through an energy figure, as depicted in *Figure 2.1*, which evolves, as illustrated in panels (a), (b), and (c). The annealing process can be considered to find the lowest point in a bumpy landscape. Imagine a ball rolling across the surface, it wants to settle into the lowest valley. Initially, there is only one valley (a) with a clear lowest point. As the process continues, a barrier forms, creating two valleys (b). These valleys represent the two possible states of the qubit: 0 and 1. At the end of the annealing process, the qubit **settles** into one of these valleys, corresponding to its final state.

Under identical conditions, the probability of the qubit ending in either the 0 or 1 state is equal (50 percent). However, by applying an external magnetic field to the qubit (c), the likelihood of it assuming the 0 or 1 state can be controlled. This field inclines the double-well potential, heightening the probability of the qubit occupying the lower well. Termed a bias, this programmable parameter governs the qubit's response to the external magnetic field.

Yet, the bias term alone lacks utility. The true efficacy of qubits emerges when they are interconnected to influence each other, achieved through a device known as a **coupler**.

Biases and couplers help control how qubits behave. A bias is like tilting a hill so that a ball (the qubit) rolls to one side, encouraging it to choose a particular state. Couplers, on the other hand, connect qubits and make them influence each other, similar to springs pulling or pushing between two balls. These connections can make qubits adopt the same state or opposite states. By programming these biases and couplings, we define the problem that the D-Wave quantum computer solves.

Refer to the following figure:

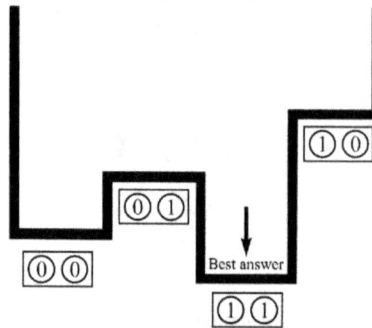

Figure 2.2: Energy diagram showing the best answer

The employment of a coupler entails harnessing another quantum phenomenon termed entanglement. When two qubits are entangled, they form a singular entity with four potential states. Illustrated in *Figure 2.2*, this concept manifests as a potential with four states corresponding to various combinations of the two qubits: (0,0), (0,1), (1,1), and (1,0), that the valleys represent possible states that the qubit can settle into. The energy of each state is contingent upon the biases of the qubits and the coupling between them. Throughout the annealing process, the qubit states undergo potential delocalization within this landscape before ultimately converging to (1,1) upon completion of the anneal.

Each qubit possesses a bias, and interactions between qubits are mediated by couplers. When formulating a problem, users specify values for these biases and couplers, collectively defining an energy landscape. Quantum annealing in the D-Wave quantum computer entails identifying the minimum energy state within this landscape.

As qubits are incrementally added, system complexity escalates: two qubits afford four potential states for defining an energy landscape, while three qubits yield eight. With each additional qubit, the number of states for defining the energy landscape doubles, resulting in exponential growth with the qubit count.

In summation, the system initiates with qubits in a superposition state of 0 and 1, devoid of coupling. Through quantum annealing, the introduction of couplers and biases precipitates qubit entanglement. Consequently, the system enters an entangled state, harboring numerous potential solutions. By the anneals conclusion, each qubit attains a classical state representing the problem's minimum energy state or a closely proximate one. Remarkably, these operations transpire within microseconds within D-Wave quantum computers.

The following section provides a detailed overview of D-Wave quantum annealers, exploring their approach to quantum computing, the technology behind their systems, and the innovations they bring to the field:

- **D-Wave quantum annealers:**
  - **Function of D-Wave:** D-Wave focuses on quantum computing, recognizing the limitations of classical systems in addressing intricate problems arising from the exponential growth of data. Quantum computing offers a novel solution to the world's most challenging problems.

  - **Approaches in quantum computing:** Two prominent approaches in quantum computing are gate-model and quantum annealing. Gate-model quantum computing employs quantum gates to implement algorithms, similar to classical Boolean gates. In contrast, quantum annealing initializes the system in a low-energy state, gradually introducing problem parameters to reach an optimal solution.

  - **Quantum annealing at D-Wave:** D-Wave employs quantum annealing in its quantum computers, like the Advantage™ system. This scalable approach enables the creation of **quantum processing units (QPUs)** with over 5000 qubits, surpassing the state of the art for gate-model quantum computing.

  - **D-Wave quantum computer systems:** D-Wave's quantum computer includes a QPU that operates at cryogenic temperatures near absolute zero. Achieving these temperatures involves a closed-loop cryogenic dilution refrigerator system. The QPU, composed of superconducting metal loops, becomes quantum-mechanical below 9.2 kelvin. The advantage system, with over 5,000 qubits and 35,000 couplers, is the most complex superconducting integrated circuit, as shown in *Figure 2.3*:

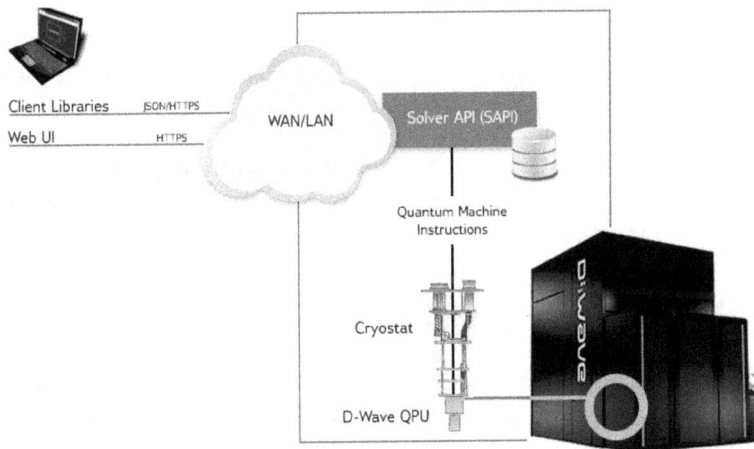

Figure 2.3: D-Wave environment

  - **D-Wave software environment:** Users interact with the D-Wave quantum computer through a web user interface and open-source tools communicating with the **Solver API (SAPI)**. SAPI handles user interaction, authentication, and work scheduling. It connects to back-end servers, routing problems to QPUs and additional solvers in different geographical regions.

- o **Leap™ quantum cloud service:** Leap™, D-Wave's quantum cloud service, allows users to explore problem-solving capabilities, run demos, contribute ideas, and engage with a community of users. It provides an accessible entry point to quantum computing.

- o **Ocean SDK:** D-Wave's Python-based open-source **software development kit (SDK)**, Ocean, streamlines quantum application development and facilitates collaboration. It offers a range of tools for quantum computing projects.

In summary, D-Wave pioneers quantum computing with a focus on quantum annealing, utilizing superconducting QPUs operating at cryogenic temperatures. The company provides accessible interfaces like Leap™ and collaborative tools like the Ocean SDK, contributing to the evolution of quantum computing technology.

- • **Applications and limitations:**
  - o **Optimization applications:** Quantum annealing has applications in finance, logistics, machine learning, and cryptography.
  - o **Limitations:** Quantum annealing machines are sensitive to noise, and their effectiveness depends on factors such as the specific problem being solved, the machine's coherence time, and the nature of the quantum states involved.

- • **Quantum advantage:**
  - o **Potential speedup:** Quantum annealers have the potential to provide speedup over classical algorithms for certain optimization problems.
  - o **Quantum supremacy:** While not yet demonstrated for practical problems, quantum annealers contribute to the broader goal of achieving quantum supremacy over classical computers in certain domains.

Quantum annealing represents a specialized and promising approach to quantum computing. It addresses specific classes of optimization problems by exploiting the principles of quantum mechanics.

Trapped-ion and IonQ, Honeywell

Trapped-ion quantum computers use individual ions, held in electromagnetic traps, as qubits to perform quantum information processing. Certain ions, like calcium or ytterbium, are chosen because they are highly stable and their quantum states can be precisely controlled using lasers. This stability and controllability make them ideal for maintaining coherence and performing accurate operations, which are critical for reliable quantum computation. Trapped-ion quantum computers have gained attention for their potential to address challenges faced by other quantum technologies, with companies like IonQ and Honeywell leading the way.

Here are the key aspects of quantum-trapped-ion computers:

- **Qubits and ion traps:**
  - **Qubits:** The fundamental units of quantum information in trapped-ion computers are individual ions, usually of elements like calcium, magnesium, or ytterbium.
  - **Ion traps:** Electromagnetic traps confine individual ions in a **three-dimensional** (**3D**) space. These traps create stable environments for the qubits to be manipulated and measured.

- **Quantum gates and operations:**
  - **Quantum gates:** Quantum operations, or gates, are performed on the qubits to manipulate their quantum states. This is typically achieved using laser pulses and magnetic fields to induce transitions between different quantum states of the ions.
  - **Entanglement:** Quantum gates are used to create entanglement between qubits, a fundamental property for quantum computing.

- **IonQ architecture:**
  - IonQ employs stable and identical trapped atomic ions as qubits, forming a chain of qubits using ion trap chips. The key advantage lies in achieving all-to-all connectivity among the qubits, enabling efficient quantum algorithm execution. Refer to the following figure:

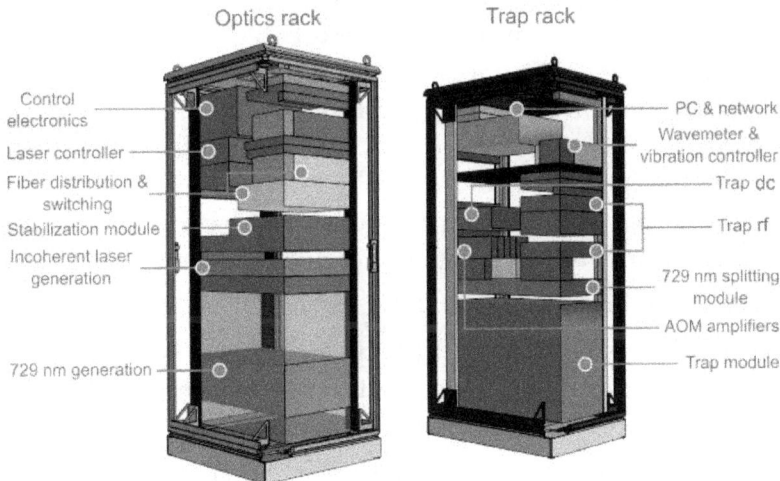

Figure 2.4: Scale model of quantum computing demonstrator in two 19-inch racks

  - As shown in *Figure 2.4*, modules are color-coded for easy identification: red signifies optical systems, green denotes communication and readout, blue represents electronics and amplifiers, yellow indicates fiber routing and switching, and purple is reserved for miscellaneous core modules. The **optics rack** primarily hosts light generation, switching, and routing modules, along with associated electronics. It also accommodates the coherent **radio frequency (RF)** and digital signal generation module. The *trap rack* houses the main trap module, complete with associated drive electronics, and serves as the communications and remote-control hub. Interconnections between modules and racks are facilitated by both electrical and optical patch cords. A semi-transparent red module is designated for the planned 729 nm light generation.

o   Similar to classical CPUs, IonQ faces limitations in the size of individual QPUs due to the complexity of entangling gates. To overcome this, IonQ plans to implement multicore QPUs using a **Reconfigurable Multicore Quantum Architecture (RMQA)**. This approach involves dynamically forming quantum computing cores by manipulating multiple ion chains, exponentially increasing computational power. The demonstration showcases configurations combining chains into cores, allowing parallel quantum operations. IonQ anticipates integrating RMQA into its systems, paving the way for triple-digit qubit counts on a single chip and Parallel Multicore QPUs in the future.

- **Quantinuum architecture:**

o   **Quantum Charge-Coupled Device (QCCD)** architecture, the H1 system is highlighted as a 20-qubit universal quantum computer with high two-qubit gate fidelities (99.87%). The hardware allows mid-circuit measurement, enabling the measurement of select qubits during algorithm execution without inadvertently measuring others. This feature is crucial for fault-tolerant quantum computing and facilitated the first-ever demonstration of real-time quantum error correction. Additionally, the hardware's capability to move and regroup qubits into arbitrary pairs during a circuit provides **all-to-all connectivity**, reducing computational steps and overhead in near-term quantum computing applications, resulting in higher-fidelity results.

- **Decoherence and error correction:**

o   **Decoherence:** Trapped ion systems are known for having relatively long coherence times, which refer to the time when quantum information is preserved before being affected by external factors.

o   **Error correction:** While trapped-ion systems inherently exhibit low error rates, error correction techniques are still explored to enhance the fault tolerance of quantum computations.

- **Quantum parallelism:**
  - o **Parallel processing:** Trapped ion computers leverage the principles of quantum superposition to perform computations in parallel, potentially enabling them to solve certain problems more efficiently than classical computers.

- **Scalability:**
  - o **Challenges:** Scaling up trapped-ion systems to a large number of qubits presents challenges, such as addressing and controlling individual ions within larger arrays.
  - o **Advancements:** Researchers and companies are actively working on addressing scalability challenges and improving the overall performance of trapped-ion quantum computers.

- **Research and development:**
  - o **Companies and institutions:** Several companies and research institutions, including IonQ, Honeywell, and the University of Maryland, are actively involved in the research and development of trapped-ion quantum computers.
  - o **Benchmarking:** Trapped ion systems are assessed by comparing their performance against various metrics, including gate fidelities, coherence times, and error rates.

- **Applications:**
  - o **Optimization and simulation:** Trapped ion quantum computers hold promise for applications in optimization problems, quantum simulation, and potentially in solving problems in quantum chemistry and materials science.

Quantum-trapped-ion computers represent a promising avenue in the field of quantum computing, offering unique advantages and capabilities that contribute to the broader goal of realizing scalable and fault-tolerant quantum information processing.

Quantum topological computers and Microsoft

Quantum topological computers, as pursued by Microsoft, represent a distinct approach to quantum computing that relies on the principles of topological quantum computing. Microsoft's quantum computing division is actively researching and developing this quantum computing architecture, aiming to create a scalable and fault-tolerant quantum computer using topological qubits.

Here are the key aspects of Microsoft's quantum topological computers:

- **Topological qubits:**
  - **Unique properties:** Topological qubits are based on anyons, exotic particles with nontrivial braiding properties that can exist in certain **two-dimensional (2D)** materials.
  - **Braiding operations:** The key to topological quantum computing is the manipulation and braiding of anyons, which induces quantum gates and allows for quantum computation.

- **Majorana fermions:**
  - **Particle type:** Microsoft's approach involves using a type of anyon known as Majorana fermions, which are expected to exhibit topological properties that make them more robust against certain errors.
  - **Braiding Majoranas:** The braiding of Majorana fermions forms the basis for implementing quantum gates in Microsoft's topological qubit architecture.
  - **Majorana zero modes**: MZMs are a pivotal feature of topological qubits, which are constructed by positioning a semiconductor nanowire in close proximity to a superconductor. When brought into proximity with the superconductor, the semiconductor nanowire acquires superconductivity. Under specific conditions—such as an appropriate magnetic field along the wire and the application of voltages to the device—the semiconductor nanowire transitions into a topological phase. In this topological phase, MZMs emerge at each end of the wire, accompanied by an energy gap throughout the rest. This gap refers to a region devoid of allowed quantum mechanical states. The appearance of MZMs in the topological phase is attributed to the presence of Majoranas, which carry current in the wire and are notable for being their antiparticles. MZMs facilitate the unhindered flow of current in the wire and manifest as heightened conductance without voltage. Moreover, the energy gap, often termed the *topological gap,* shields the current-conducting Majoranas from local noise and disruptions. Microsoft has developed a **topological gap protocol (TGP)** designed to detect these phenomena in device measurements, thereby enabling the characterization and utilization of MZMs in topological qubits.

- **Topological quantum computation:**
  - **Fault tolerance:** Topological qubits have the potential for increased fault tolerance due to their inherent protection against certain types of errors through their topological properties.
  - **Quantum error correction:** Microsoft is exploring techniques for quantum error correction within the topological quantum computing framework.

- **StationQ project:**
  - o **Dedicated research initiative:** Microsoft's quantum computing division initiated the StationQ project, which focuses on developing topological qubits for quantum computation.
  - o **Collaborations:** Microsoft collaborates with various institutions and researchers globally to advance the understanding and implementation of topological quantum computing.
- **StationQ and Microsoft Quantum Development Kit:**
  - o **Development tools:** Microsoft provides the Quantum Development Kit, a set of tools and resources for researchers and developers to experiment with quantum algorithms and programming languages, including the Q# programming language, as shown in *Figure 2.5*:

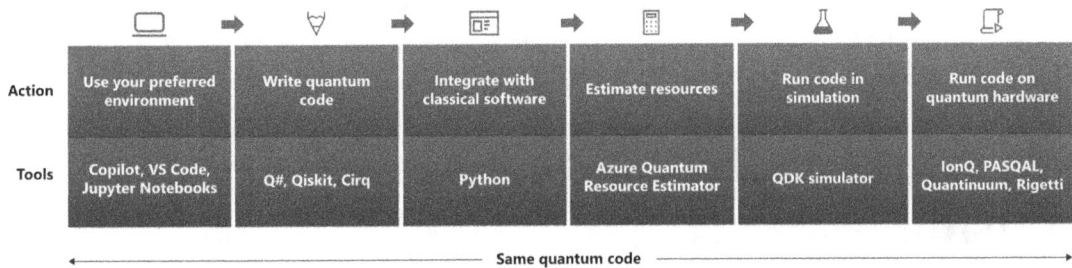

	Use your preferred environment	Write quantum code	Integrate with classical software	Estimate resources	Run code in simulation	Run code on quantum hardware
Action	Use your preferred environment	Write quantum code	Integrate with classical software	Estimate resources	Run code in simulation	Run code on quantum hardware
Tools	Copilot, VS Code, Jupyter Notebooks	Q#, Qiskit, Cirq	Python	Azure Quantum Resource Estimator	QDK simulator	IonQ, PASQAL, Quantinuum, Rigetti

Same quantum code

Figure 2.5: Stages of a quantum program

  - o Azure aims to make scaled quantum computing a reality and deliver its benefits seamlessly to customers. Microsoft's unique topological qubit design enhances fault tolerance, but stable operation requires advanced software and significant compute power. The quantum machine will be integrated with Peta scale classical compute in Azure, enabling bandwidths between quantum and classical systems exceeding 10–100 terabits per second. Continuous interactions between the quantum and classical computers, occurring at every logical clock cycle, ensure the quantum computer remains operational and produces reliable output solutions. Azure is positioned as a key enabler and differentiator in Microsoft's strategy to bring quantum computing at scale to the world.
  - o **Integration with Azure:** Microsoft is integrating quantum computing resources into its cloud computing platform, Azure, to provide users with access to quantum computing capabilities.

- **Challenges and progress:**
  - o **Technical challenges:** Implementing topological qubits poses technical challenges, including the requirement for stable and precisely controlled physical systems.
  - o **Progress:** Microsoft has made strides in the understanding and control of Majorana fermions, marking progress toward the realization of topological qubits.
- **Applications:**
  - o **Quantum algorithms:** Microsoft's topological quantum computing efforts aim to enable the execution of quantum algorithms for solving complex problems in areas such as cryptography, optimization, and materials science.

Microsoft's pursuit of topological quantum computing reflects a commitment to exploring innovative approaches to quantum information processing, with the goal of creating robust and scalable quantum computers that can tackle problems beyond the reach of classical computers.

Quantum photonics-based computers and Xanadu

Photonic quantum computers use particles of light, called photons, as qubits to perform quantum computations. Photonic qubits are particularly useful for transmitting information over long distances, making them ideal for applications like quantum communication and secure networks. Quantum photonics, as pursued by **Xanadu Quantum Technologies**, represents an innovative approach to quantum computing that leverages the properties of photons (quantum particles of light) for quantum information processing. Xanadu is a Canadian quantum technology company that focuses on developing and commercializing quantum computing and quantum communication technologies.

The following are the key aspects of Xanadu's quantum photonics approach:

- **Photonic qubits:**
  - o **Encoding information:** Xanadu's quantum computing architecture is built on the use of photonic qubits, where quantum information is encoded in properties of individual photons, such as polarization and path.
  - o **Superposition and entanglement:** Photonic qubits can exist in superposition states and can be entangled, allowing for quantum parallelism and the creation of quantum correlations between distant photons.

- **Continuous-variable quantum computing:**
  - o **Quantum states in phase space:** Xanadu explores continuous-variable quantum computing, where quantum states are represented in the phase space of position and momentum variables.
  - o **Gaussian states:** Xanadu's approach characteristically uses Gaussian states, which are states with Gaussian distributions in phase space.
- **Integrated photonics:**
  - o **On-chip components:** Xanadu's quantum photonic processors are implemented using integrated photonic circuits, where beam splitters, phase shifters, and detectors are miniaturized onto a chip.
  - o **Precision and scalability:** Integrated photonics provides a platform for precise control of quantum states and scalability for building larger quantum processors. Refer to the following figure:

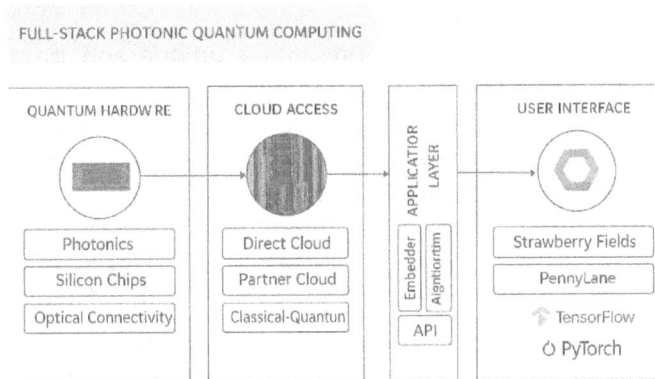

FULL-STACK PHOTONIC QUANTUM COMPUTING

QUANTUM HARDW RE	CLOUD ACCESS	APPLICATION LAYER	USER INTERFACE
Photonics	Direct Cloud	Embedder / Algorithm	Strawberry Fields
Silicon Chips	Partner Cloud		PennyLane
Optical Connectivity	Classical-Quantun	API	TensorFlow / PyTorch

Figure 2.6: Full-stack photonics quantum computing XANADU

- **Quantum algorithms and quantum machine learning:**
  - o **Applications:** Xanadu focuses on developing quantum algorithms for solving specific problems, including applications in quantum machine learning, optimization, and simulation.
  - o **Variational quantum algorithms:** Xanadu has contributed to the development of variational quantum algorithms, where the quantum processor is trained to find optimal solutions to problems. The Full-Stack photonics architecture is provided in *Figure 2.6*.
- **PennyLane software:**
  - o **Quantum software platform:** Xanadu provides PennyLane, an open-source platform designed for quantum computing using photonic qubits. It enables users to program and simulate quantum algorithms.

- o **Integration with other quantum devices:** PennyLane supports the integration of quantum processors from various quantum computing platforms, fostering collaboration and comparison.
- **Quantum communication:**
  - o **Quantum key distribution (QKD):** In addition to quantum computing, Xanadu is involved in developing quantum communication technologies, including quantum key distribution for secure communication.
- **Collaborations and research partnerships:**
  - o **Industry collaborations:** Xanadu collaborates with industry partners and research institutions to advance the development and applications of quantum photonics.
  - o **Quantum community engagement:** Xanadu actively engages with the broader quantum computing community to contribute to the field's collective understanding and progress.

Xanadu's focus on quantum photonics represents a unique and promising approach to quantum computing, where the use of photons allows for efficient processing of quantum information and integration with existing telecommunication infrastructure. The company's efforts aim to push the boundaries of quantum technology for practical applications in computation and communication.

Neutral atoms and Atom Computing

Quantum computing using neutral atoms, as explored by Atom Computing, represents a novel approach to quantum information processing. Atom Computing is a company dedicated to advancing quantum computing technologies, and its work with neutral atoms involves manipulating individual atoms to perform quantum computations.

The following are the key aspects of quantum neutral atoms as pursued by Atom Computing:

- **Neutral atom qubits:**
  - o **Neutral atom qubits:** In contrast to ions, which are charged atoms, neutral atom qubits involve manipulating neutral atoms for quantum information processing.
  - o **Alkaline earth atoms:** Atom Computing uses alkaline earth atoms, such as strontium or calcium, as the basis for their neutral atom qubits.
- **Optical tweezers and traps:**
  - o **Individual atom manipulation:** Atom Computing uses advanced techniques such as optical tweezers and magnetic traps to precisely trap and manipulate individual neutral atoms.

o **Lattice configurations:** Neutral atoms are often arranged in optical lattice configurations, allowing for controlled interactions between neighboring atoms.

- **Quantum gate operations:**

o **Quantum gates:** Quantum gates are implemented by using lasers to induce controlled interactions between neutral atoms, allowing for the creation of entanglement and execution of quantum algorithms.

o **Entanglement:** Neutral atom qubits can be entangled, forming a critical component for quantum computation.

- **High-fidelity operations:**

o **Fidelity:** Atom Computing aims for high fidelity in quantum operations, ensuring that the quantum states of neutral atoms are manipulated with precision and minimal errors.

o **Coherence time:** The coherence time of neutral atom qubits, which measures the time during which quantum information is preserved, is an important parameter for the performance of quantum computations.

- **Scalability and connectivity:**

o **Scalability:** Neutral atom qubits hold promise for scalability due to their potential for precise control and manipulation, allowing for the creation of larger quantum processors.

o **Connectivity:** The ability to establish and control interactions between distant neutral atom qubits is crucial for building practical and powerful quantum computers.

- **Quantum error correction:**

o **Error correction techniques:** Atom Computing will likely explore quantum error correction techniques to enhance the fault tolerance of quantum computations using neutral atoms.

- **Applications and algorithms:**

o **Quantum algorithms:** Atom Computing's work involves developing quantum algorithms that efficiently execute their neutral atom quantum processors.

o **Potential applications:** Quantum chemistry simulations, optimization problems, and machine learning are among the applications that may benefit from quantum computing using neutral atoms.

- **Research and development:**

o **Ongoing research:** Atom Computing is actively engaged in research and development efforts to advance the capabilities of quantum computing using neutral atoms.

- o **Industry collaboration:** Collaboration with research institutions and industry partners to pool resources and expertise is common in the quantum computing landscape.

Atom Computing's pursuit of quantum computing with neutral atoms represents a cutting-edge approach that leverages the unique characteristics of neutral atoms for quantum information processing. This approach contributes to the broader landscape of quantum computing technologies with the potential for scalability and enhanced control.

Superconducting chips and IBM, Google, Rigetti

Quantum superconducting chips are a key technology in the field of quantum computing. Several leading companies, including IBM, Google, and Rigetti, are actively working on developing and implementing quantum processors based on superconducting circuits. Superconducting qubits, the fundamental units of quantum information in these systems, exhibit unique quantum properties when operated at extremely low temperatures.

The following is an overview of quantum superconducting chips from IBM, Google, and Rigetti:

- **IBM Quantum processors:**
  - o **Qubit technology:** IBM uses transmon qubits, a type of superconducting qubit, in their quantum processors, as shown in *Figure 2.7*:

Figure 2.7: IBM superconducting quantum computer setup

  - o **Gate-model quantum computing:** IBM's approach is based on gate-model quantum computing, where quantum gates are used to manipulate qubits and perform quantum operations.
  - o **Open quantum system:** IBM provides access to its quantum processors through the IBM Quantum Experience, allowing researchers and developers

to run quantum experiments on real hardware. It also provides a software experience via the Qiskit library and IBM Quantum Composer.

o **IBM Quantum scalability:** IBM Quantum is making significant strides in the scalability of quantum computing with its advanced infrastructure and hardware innovations. With two global data centers, IBM Quantum supports a network of quantum systems that provide access to cutting-edge quantum technology. The quantum systems run 3 trillion circuits, demonstrating their capability to handle extensive quantum workloads. IBM Quantum operates over ten utility-scale quantum systems globally, making quantum computing more accessible and enabling a wide range of research and development opportunities. Notably, the Heron chip, which houses 133 qubits, showcases IBM's achievement in developing high-qubit processors with real-time classical communication capabilities between processors, as shown in *Figure 2.8*. This advanced architecture represents a major milestone toward realizing scalable, practical quantum computing for a variety of applications across industries.

Figure 2.8: IBM Heron chip, which houses 133 qubits

- **Google quantum processors:**
  - o **Architecture and achievements:**
    - **Superconducting qubits:** Google's quantum processors use superconducting qubits, which are based on the principles of superconductivity and Josephson junctions. These qubits are typically implemented as transmon qubits, which are a type of superconducting qubit known for their long coherence times and relative ease of control.
    - **2D and 3D architectures:** Google has explored both 2D and 3D architectures for arranging qubits on a chip. The qubits are typically arranged in a grid pattern, allowing for connections between neighboring qubits. This configuration enables entanglement and other quantum operations necessary for quantum computing.

- **Control and measurement:** Google's quantum processors use microwave pulses to control qubit states and manipulate quantum information. The measurement of qubit states is typically done using resonators and amplifiers to detect changes in the qubits' quantum states.

- **Noise and error mitigation:** Google Quantum AI has developed advanced error correction techniques and noise mitigation strategies to improve the performance and reliability of its quantum processors. These efforts are essential for achieving higher fidelity operations and scalability.

- **Bristlecone and Sycamore processors:** Google's quantum processors include Bristlecone and Sycamore as shown in *Figure 2.9.*, both based on superconducting qubits.

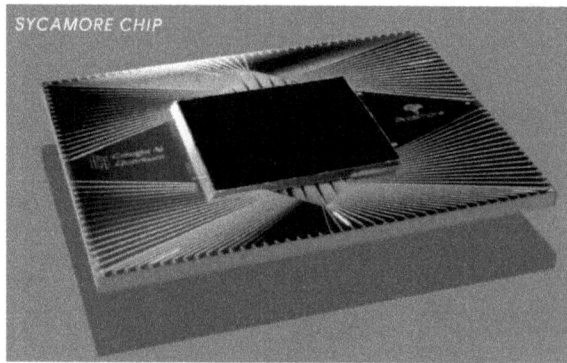

Figure 2.9: Google Sycamore Chip

- **Quantum supremacy:** In 2019, Google announced that it had achieved quantum supremacy with its 53-qubit processor, named Sycamore. This milestone demonstrated that a quantum processor could perform a specific calculation faster than the world's fastest classical supercomputers. This achievement marked a significant breakthrough in the field of quantum computing.

- **Quantum error correction:** Google is actively researching and developing quantum error correction techniques to improve the reliability and scalability of their quantum processors.

- **Rigetti quantum processors:**
  - **Hybrid quantum-classical computing:** Rigetti employs a hybrid quantum-classical computing model, integrating superconducting qubits with classical computing resources.
  - **Forest Quantum Cloud Services:** Rigetti offers access to their quantum processors, as shown in *Figure.2.10*, through the Forest Quantum Cloud Services platform, allowing users to run quantum algorithms and experiments.

- o **Full-stack quantum computing:** Rigetti focuses on providing a full-stack quantum computing solution, including quantum hardware, control software, and cloud services.

- o **Qiskit integration:** Rigetti's quantum processors are compatible with Qiskit, a popular open-source quantum computing framework. This integration provides developers with a seamless experience for designing and executing quantum algorithms.

- o **Architecture:**

    - **Superconducting qubits:** Rigetti's quantum processors use superconducting qubits, based on circuits that exhibit quantum properties when cooled to near absolute zero. These qubits can be controlled and manipulated using microwave pulses.

Figure 2.10: The Rigetti 19Q superconducting processor

    - **Transmon qubits:** The company primarily uses transmon qubits, a type of superconducting qubit known for its long coherence times and robust performance. These qubits offer good stability and coherence, making them ideal for quantum computing.

    - **Circuit connectivity:** Rigetti's quantum processors feature various connectivity architectures, allowing qubits to interact and perform entanglement operations. These architectures range from linear chains to more complex grid-like topologies, enabling a higher degree of qubit interaction.

    - **Control and readout:** The quantum processors are controlled using microwave pulses that manipulate the qubits' quantum states. The qubits' states are typically read out using resonant circuits that convert the quantum information into classical signals.

- **Superconducting qubit properties:**

    - o **Coherence time:** Coherence time measures how long a qubit can maintain its quantum state without significant information loss. In superconducting qubits, coherence times can range from microseconds to milliseconds. Achieving longer coherence times is crucial for the practical implementation of quantum computing, as it allows qubits to perform more complex operations and calculations before losing their quantum state.

o **Josephson junctions:** Josephson junctions are critical components in superconducting qubit circuits. They consist of two superconductors separated by a thin insulating barrier, allowing quantum tunneling of Cooper pairs (pairs of electrons) across the junction. This quantum mechanical effect gives the circuit unique properties, such as nonlinearity and the ability to oscillate at specific frequencies. Josephson junctions enable the creation and control of qubits by allowing for precise manipulation of the qubit's quantum state through microwave pulses and magnetic fields.

In addition to these properties, superconducting qubits often have other notable characteristics, such as:

o **Energy levels:** Superconducting qubits usually have a set of quantized energy levels, with the lowest two levels representing the qubit's states (0 and 1). By manipulating these levels, qubits can perform various quantum operations.

o **Control and measurement:** Superconducting qubits can be controlled using microwave pulses, allowing for precise manipulation of their quantum states. Measurement is typically done using resonant circuits or amplifiers to detect changes in the qubit's state.

o **Scalability and connectivity:** Superconducting qubits can be interconnected using various circuit architectures, such as transmon qubits or flux qubits, allowing for the construction of more complex quantum processors.

Overall, superconducting qubits hold great promise for the development of practical quantum computers due to their potential for scalability and their compatibility with existing microwave and electronic control technologies. However, researchers are continually working to overcome challenges related to coherence times and qubit control to make large-scale quantum computing a reality.

Cryogenic cooling in superconducting qubits

This sub-section outlines the critical aspects of cryogenic cooling in superconducting qubits and explores the quantum advantage and challenges associated with superconducting quantum processors:

- **Cryogenic cooling:**

  o **Operation at low temperatures:** To maintain their superconducting states, superconducting qubits operate at temperatures close to absolute zero, typically around a few millikelvins.

- o **Dilution refrigeration:** Quantum processors are housed in sophisticated cryogenic systems, such as dilution refrigerators, to achieve low temperatures.
- **Quantum advantage and challenges:**
  - o **Quantum advantage:** Superconducting quantum processors have demonstrated a quantum advantage for certain tasks, showcasing their potential impact on specific computational problems.
  - o **Challenges:** Challenges include addressing quantum errors, improving qubit connectivity, and increasing the number of qubits for more complex computations.

IBM, Google, and Rigetti are at the forefront of the quantum computing industry, actively contributing to the development and advancement of superconducting quantum processors. Their efforts aim to unlock quantum computing's potential for practical applications and scientific discovery.

Universal quantum computers

Universal quantum computers are a type of quantum computing architecture designed to perform various quantum algorithms and computations. Unlike specialized quantum computing approaches, such as quantum annealing or specific quantum processors tailored for certain tasks, universal quantum computers are intended to be programmable and capable of executing a broad set of quantum applications.

The following are the key features and aspects of universal quantum computers:

- **Qubits and quantum gates:**
  - o **Quantum bits (qubits):** Universal quantum computers use qubits as the basic units of quantum information. Qubits can exist in superposition states, allowing them to represent multiple classical bits simultaneously.
  - o **Quantum gates:** Quantum gates are the basic building blocks of quantum circuits. They perform operations on qubits, manipulating their quantum states to execute quantum algorithms.
- **Gate-model quantum computing:**
  - o **Universal quantum gates:** In gate-model quantum computing, a universal set of quantum gates is used to construct any quantum algorithm. Common universal gates include single-qubit gates and entangling two-qubit gates.
  - o **Quantum circuit model:** Quantum algorithms are represented as sequences of quantum gates in a quantum circuit.
- **Quantum entanglement:**
  - o **Entanglement:** Universal quantum computers leverage entanglement, a quantum phenomenon in which qubits become correlated so that the state

of one qubit is dependent on the state of another, even if separated by large distances. Entanglement is crucial for quantum parallelism.

- **Quantum error correction:**
  - **Error correction:** Universal quantum computers face challenges due to quantum errors caused by environmental noise and imperfections in quantum hardware. Quantum error correction techniques are essential for mitigating errors and preserving the integrity of quantum information.

- **Algorithms and applications:**
  - **Shor's algorithm:** Universal quantum computers can potentially execute algorithms that offer exponential speedup over classical counterparts, such as Shor's algorithm for factoring large numbers.
  - **Grover's algorithm:** Another significant algorithm is Grover's algorithm, which provides a quadratic speedup for searching unsorted databases.

- **Superposition and parallelism:**
  - **Superposition:** Universal quantum computers utilize superposition to explore multiple computational paths simultaneously. This feature enables parallelism, allowing quantum algorithms to process information in parallel and potentially solve certain problems faster than classical computers.

- **Physical implementations:**
  - **Superconducting qubits:** Many universal quantum computers are based on superconducting qubits, implemented using superconducting circuits operating at extremely low temperatures.
  - **Trapped ions:** Another approach involves using trapped-ions as qubits, where individual ions are manipulated using electromagnetic fields.

- **Challenges and scalability:**
  - **Decoherence and noise:** Maintaining quantum coherence is challenging due to environmental factors and noise. Quantum computers need to operate in highly controlled environments to minimize these effects.
  - **Scalability:** Universal quantum computers face a significant challenge in achieving scalability, which means increasing the number of qubits while maintaining low error rates.

Leading companies and research institutions, including IBM, Google, Microsoft, and others, are actively pursuing the development of universal quantum computers to unlock the potential for solving complex problems currently intractable for classical computers.

Noisy Intermediate-Scale Quantum computers

NISQ stands for Noisy Intermediate-Scale Quantum computers. These are a class of quantum computers characterized by Intermediate-Scale Quantum processors with many qubits but with limitations such as higher error rates and challenges in maintaining quantum coherence. NISQ devices are considered noisy due to errors in quantum operations and intermediate-scale because they fall short of the large-scale, fault-tolerant quantum computers envisioned for the future.

The following are the key characteristics and considerations related to NISQ:

- **Intermediate-Scale Quantum processors:**
  - **Number of qubits:** NISQ devices typically have tens to hundreds of qubits, representing an intermediate scale between small-scale quantum processors and large, fault-tolerant quantum computers.
  - **Quantum volume:** Quantum volume is a metric that combines factors like the number of qubits, gate fidelities, and connectivity, providing a measure of the computational power of a quantum processor.

- **Higher error rates:**
  - **Noisy quantum operations:** NISQ devices exhibit higher error rates in quantum operations compared to the fault-tolerant quantum computers that are envisioned for the future.
  - **Decoherence and noise:** Factors such as decoherence, which is the loss of quantum information due to interactions with the environment, contribute to errors and noise in NISQ devices.

- **Challenges in error correction:**
  - **Quantum error correction:** Implementing robust quantum error correction is challenging in NISQ devices due to their higher error rates. This limits the ability to perform fault-tolerant quantum computations.
  - **Variational quantum algorithms:** Some approaches in the NISQ era involve using variational quantum algorithms that mitigate the impact of errors by optimizing quantum circuits.

- **Applications and quantum advantage:**
  - **Demonstrating quantum advantage:** Despite limitations, NISQ devices aim to demonstrate quantum advantage, solving certain problems more efficiently than classical computers. This could include applications in optimization, quantum chemistry simulations, and machine learning.

- o **Quantum supremacy:** Quantum supremacy, achieved by demonstrating a quantum computer's ability to perform a specific task faster than the best classical supercomputers, is a milestone associated with NISQ devices.
- **Contributions to quantum research:**
  - o **Quantum algorithms and software development:** NISQ devices provide a platform for researchers to develop and test quantum algorithms, as well as explore the potential applications of quantum computing.
  - o **Quantum software ecosystem:** The development of a quantum software ecosystem, including quantum programming languages and algorithms, is a significant aspect of the NISQ era.
- **Industry and research initiatives:**
  - o **Leading companies:** Various companies, including IBM, Google, Rigetti, and others, are actively working on NISQ devices and exploring their potential applications.
  - o **Research institutions:** NISQ devices are the focus of research and development efforts in both industry and academia, contributing to advancements in quantum computing.

The NISQ era represents a transitional phase in the development of quantum computing, providing a glimpse into the potential of quantum processors with intermediate-scale qubit counts. While NISQ devices have limitations, they play a crucial role in advancing quantum research and paving the way for the eventual realization of fault-tolerant quantum computers.

Performance comparison of quantum computers

This section introduces key concepts and techniques fundamental to understanding quantum computing. These topics encompass quantum hardware, error correction, measurement mitigation, benchmarking, and quantum state representation:

- **Quantum hardware using quantum circuits:**
  - o Quantum hardware refers to the physical implementation of quantum bits (qubits) and the components necessary for quantum computation.
  - o Quantum circuits are sequences of quantum gates that manipulate qubits to perform specific quantum algorithms.
  - o Quantum hardware includes elements like superconducting qubits, trapped-ions, topological qubits, and other technologies, each with its own advantages and challenges.

- **Introduction to quantum error correction via the repetition code:**
  - **Quantum error correction** (**QEC**) is crucial for mitigating errors in quantum computations caused by noise and decoherence.
  - The repetition code is a simple quantum error correction code where a logical qubit is encoded into multiple physical qubits, and the information is redundantly stored.
  - Errors can be detected and corrected by comparing the redundant copies of the information.
  - The repetition code involves encoding a logical qubit $|\psi\rangle$ into a physical qubit state $|0\rangle$ or $|1\rangle$ using multiple copies. For example, for a 3-qubit repetition code:

  $$|0\rangle_L = |000\rangle_P, \; |1\rangle_L = |111\rangle_P$$

  - The decoding process involves majority voting or other techniques to correct errors.
- **Measurement error mitigation:**
  - Measurement errors can occur due to imperfections in quantum devices or environmental noise during measurements.
  - Measurement error mitigation techniques aim to correct or mitigate the impact of errors in the outcomes of quantum measurements.
  - This involves using additional measurements or calibration procedures to improve the reliability of the obtained results.
  - Error mitigation involves using a calibration matrix M to correct the measured probabilities p according to the formula:

  $$\mathbf{p}_{corrected} = M \cdot \mathbf{p}$$

  - The calibration matrix is determined through additional measurements and calibration procedures.
- **Randomized benchmarking:**
  - Randomized benchmarking is a technique used to assess the overall error rates of quantum gates in a quantum processor.
  - It involves applying random sequences of quantum gates and measuring the fidelity of the output compared to an ideal (error-free) scenario.
  - The results provide a benchmark for the overall performance of the quantum processor.
  - The average gate fidelity F_{avg} can be calculated using the formula:

  $$F_{avg} = (d+1)/d \cdot (1 - p_{gate})/d$$

- o Where d is the Hilbert space dimension (2 for a qubit) and p_{gate} is the average gate error rate.
- **Measuring quantum volume:**
  - o Quantum volume is a metric developed by IBM to assess the capabilities of a quantum computer, taking into account factors like gate errors, connectivity, and qubit coherence.
  - o It provides a single-number quantification of the potential computational power of a quantum device.
  - o Think of quantum volume like the horsepower of a car—just as higher horsepower indicates a more powerful and capable vehicle, a higher quantum volume means a more powerful and reliable quantum computer, capable of solving more complex problems.
- **The density matrix and mixed states:**
  - o In quantum mechanics, the density matrix is a mathematical representation of a quantum system's state.
  - o For a pure state $|\psi\rangle$, the density matrix ϱ is given by:

$$\varrho = |\psi\rangle\langle\psi|$$

  - o For a mixed state with probabilities pi and corresponding pure states $|\psi_i\rangle$ the density matrix is:

$$\varrho = \sum_i p_i |\psi_i\rangle\langle\psi_i|$$

  - o These formulas provide a foundation for understanding and implementing the respective concepts in quantum computing. However, practical applications may involve additional considerations and adaptations based on the specific quantum computing hardware and experimental conditions.
  - o Mixed states describe situations where a system is in a statistical mixture of pure states, reflecting uncertainty or lack of knowledge about the exact state.
  - o The density matrix is a powerful tool for describing quantum states in both pure and mixed scenarios.

These concepts collectively form a foundational understanding of quantum computing, addressing aspects of hardware, error correction, measurement mitigation, benchmarking, and quantum state representation. Further exploration and study of each topic can provide a deeper understanding of the complexities and challenges in quantum computing.

Conclusion

This chapter has provided a comprehensive overview of the different types of quantum computers and their underlying technologies. We have explored various approaches to quantum computing, each with its unique advantages and challenges. From annealing with D-Wave to trapped-ions with IonQ and Quantinuum, and from topological qubits with Microsoft to photonics with Xanadu, each technology offers a distinct pathway toward advancing quantum computing. Additionally, we examined neutral atoms with Atom Computing and superconducting chips with industry leaders such as IBM, Google, and Rigetti.

The chapter also highlighted the concept of universal quantum computers and the current state of **near-term intermediate-scale quantum (NISQ)** devices, which offer promising applications while quantum hardware continues to evolve. In the performance comparison section, we discussed critical metrics such as quantum volume, which encompasses the number of qubits, error rates, qubit connectivity, and crosstalk, as well as coherence. These factors play a pivotal role in assessing the capabilities and potential of different quantum computing architectures.

Overall, as quantum computing progresses, the ongoing research and development across these diverse technologies will drive the field closer to realizing scalable and practical quantum computing solutions. This chapter has laid the groundwork for understanding the multifaceted landscape of quantum computers and their impact on the future of computation.

In the next chapter, we will look at the foundational quantum principles of superposition and entanglement in detail. These phenomena are central to the power and potential of quantum computing, providing the basis for many advanced quantum algorithms and applications. We will begin with an in-depth examination of superposition, which allows qubits to exist in multiple states simultaneously. This property enables quantum computers to perform complex computations more efficiently than classical computers, as they can process many possibilities at once. Next, we will explore the concept of entanglement, which describes the strong correlation between qubits that share a quantum state. Entanglement enables qubits to interact in ways that give quantum computers extraordinary capabilities, such as teleportation and quantum communication. A key focus of the chapter will be on Bell states, which are specific entangled states that serve as a fundamental building block for many quantum communication and computation protocols. We will discuss how these states can be prepared and manipulated in quantum systems and their significance in demonstrating the non-classical nature of quantum mechanics. To understand these complex concepts, we will present analogies and illustrative examples throughout the chapter. These analogies will help bridge the gap between the abstract nature of superposition and entanglement and more familiar classical concepts.

Multiple choice questions

1. **Which quantum computing approach uses qubits based on superconducting circuits?**

    a. Trapped ion

    b. Annealing

    c. Photonics

    d. Superconducting chips

2. **Which company is known for its research in topological qubits?**

    a. D-Wave

    b. IonQ

    c. Microsoft

    d. Xanadu

3. **What is a key characteristic of neutral atom-based quantum computers?**

    a. They use photons to carry information.

    b. They trap ions in electromagnetic fields.

    c. They manipulate individual atoms with lasers.

    d. They are based on superconducting circuits.

4. **Which term describes the intermediate stage of quantum computers with limited capabilities?**

    a. Universal quantum computers

    b. NISQs (Near-term intermediate-scale quantum computers)

    c. Classical computers

    d. Quantum annealers

5. **Quantum volume is a metric that measures:**

    a. The speed of quantum processors

    b. The overall performance of a quantum computer

    c. The number of quantum gates in a circuit

    d. The size of quantum data storage

Answer key

    1. d

    2. c

    3. c

    4. b

    5. b

Questions

1. Explain the key differences between the trapped-ion and superconducting chip approaches to quantum computing. What are the advantages and challenges of each method?

2. Describe the concept of quantum volume and discuss how it is used to compare the performance of different quantum computers.

3. Compare and contrast the annealing approach of D-Wave with the neutral atom approach of Atom Computing. Include the types of problems each approach is best suited for.

4. Discuss the potential of universal quantum computers and how they differ from NISQ devices. What are the challenges in developing universal quantum computers?

5. How do qubit connectivity and crosstalk impact the performance of a quantum computer? Provide examples from different types of quantum computer architectures.

6. Fill in the blank: D-Wave is known for its _____ approach to quantum computing.

   Answer: Annealing

7. **True or False**: Photonics-based quantum computers use lasers and other optical components to manipulate qubits.

   Answer: True

8. Fill in the blank: The term _____ refers to the interaction between qubits that can cause unwanted interference and errors.

   Answer: Crosstalk

9. **True or False**: Neutral atom quantum computers manipulate ions using electromagnetic fields.

   Answer: False (Neutral atom quantum computers manipulate atoms with lasers)

10. Fill in the blank: _____ is a key factor in determining the overall coherence time of a quantum computer.

    Answer: Error rates

Join our Discord space

Join our Discord workspace for latest updates, offers, tech happenings around the world, new releases, and sessions with the authors:

https://discord.bpbonline.com

CHAPTER 3
Superposition and Entanglement

Introduction

In quantum computing, the phenomena of superposition and entanglement are the bedrock upon which revolutionary advancements are built. While exploring the fundamentals of quantum computing, we will look at these concepts comprehensively in this chapter.

This chapter serves as a guide to understanding the intricacies of quantum states and their pivotal role in shaping the landscape of quantum information processing. From delineating the distinctions between classical and quantum states to unraveling the mathematical underpinnings of superposition and entanglement, each section looks at the essence of these phenomena. As we go through the definition, representation, and significance of superposition, we uncover its profound implications for quantum algorithms and computational paradigms. Similarly, our expedition into the realm of entanglement unveils its enigmatic nature, transcending classical intuition and opening pathways to quantum communication and information processing.

Furthermore, we illuminate the experimental endeavors that have materialized these theoretical constructs, paving the way for groundbreaking advancements in quantum computing. Through meticulous examination, we confront the challenges posed by decoherence while also envisaging the boundless possibilities that lie ahead in the quantum computing landscape. Ultimately, this chapter serves as a beacon of knowledge, guiding readers through the foundational concepts, applications, and future prospects of superposition and entanglement in the realm of quantum computing.

Structure

The topics covered in the chapter are as follows:

- Introduction to quantum states
- Superposition as the basis of quantum computing
- Entanglement and quantum correlations beyond classical intuition
- Experimental realization of superposition and entanglement
- Limitations and challenges
- Future directions and applications

Objectives

By the end of this chapter, you will have a solid understanding of the foundational concepts and experimental aspects of quantum computing. The topics covered will guide you through an introduction to quantum states, where you will learn about the essential nature of quantum systems. You will explore superposition, the core principle that allows quantum computers to process information in ways classical computers cannot. Additionally, the chapter discusses entanglement, a phenomenon that creates quantum correlations beyond classical intuition, providing insights into the power of quantum computing. You will also examine the experimental realization of superposition and entanglement, showing how these abstract concepts are brought to life in the lab. The chapter will address the limitations and challenges facing quantum computing today, preparing you to understand the hurdles that must be overcome for further advancement. Finally, you will look at future directions and applications of quantum computing, exploring how this technology may evolve and impact various fields. Through these topics, you will build a comprehensive understanding of both the theoretical and practical aspects of quantum computing.

Introduction to quantum states

Quantum mechanics, the theoretical framework governing the behavior of particles on the smallest scales, introduces a profound departure from classical physics. At the heart of quantum mechanics lies the concept of quantum states, which are mathematical descriptions representing the properties of physical systems. This chapter is a foundational introduction to quantum states, elucidating their significance, mathematical formalism, and relevance to quantum computing.

Classical vs. quantum states

In classical physics, the state of a system is fully determined by precisely specifying its properties, such as position and momentum. This deterministic worldview is fundamentally challenged by quantum mechanics, where the state of a system is described probabilistically. Quantum states embody the inherent uncertainty and indeterminacy of quantum systems, reflecting the wave-particle duality and the uncertainty principle. Wave-particle duality refers to the idea that particles, like electrons or photons, can behave as both waves and particles, depending on how they are observed. For example, light can act like a wave when it creates interference patterns, such as in the double-slit experiment, but it also behaves like a particle when it is detected as individual photons, like tiny packets of energy. This dual behavior is a key concept in quantum mechanics and helps us understand the strange nature of the quantum world.

Representation of quantum states

Quantum states are represented by vectors in a complex vector space known as a **Hilbert space**. These vectors encapsulate all possible configurations of a quantum system, each corresponding to a different combination of properties. The state of a quantum system evolves over time according to the Schrödinger equation, which describes how the state vector changes in response to the system's Hamiltonian.

Importance of superposition and entanglement

Two fundamental phenomena in quantum mechanics, superposition and entanglement, play a central role in shaping quantum states. Superposition allows a qubit to exist in a combination of both 0 and 1 states simultaneously, unlike classical bits, which are either 0 or 1. This unique property enables quantum computers to process many possibilities at once, greatly enhancing their computational power for specific problems. A concept famously illustrated by Schrödinger's Cat, which is both alive and dead until observed. Entanglement, on the other hand, describes the intricate correlations between particles that defy classical intuition, influencing each other's states instantaneously across vast distances. It is like having a pair of magic gloves, if you put one on in New York and it is a right glove, the other glove in Tokyo will instantly be a left glove, even though they are separated by thousands of miles. This mysterious connection is what makes entanglement so fascinating and useful in quantum computing.

Understanding quantum states lays the groundwork for exploring the profound implications of superposition and entanglement, which are crucial for harnessing the power of quantum computing.

Mathematical formalism

Quantum states are represented mathematically using ket notation, where a state vector $|\psi\rangle$ corresponds to a unique ket in the Hilbert space. These vectors can be manipulated using linear algebra operations, such as addition, scalar multiplication, and inner products. The inner product of two ket vectors yields a complex number known as the probability amplitude, providing the basis for probabilistic predictions in quantum mechanics.

Key concepts

Several key concepts elucidate the properties and behavior of quantum states. They are as follows:

- **Normalization:** Quantum states must be normalized to ensure that the sum of their probabilities equals one, reflecting the certainty that the system exists in some state.

- **Orthogonality:** Orthogonal states are mutually exclusive, with no overlap in their probability distributions. Orthogonal states form a basis for the Hilbert space, allowing any quantum state to be expressed as a linear combination of basis states.

- **Measurement:** Measurement collapses the quantum state onto one of its possible outcomes, resulting in a probabilistic outcome consistent with the probabilities encoded in the state vector. This collapse is unique to quantum systems and differs from classical systems, where the state of a system is well-defined and unaffected by observation. In quantum mechanics, the act of measuring directly influences the system, forcing it into a specific state, unlike in classical physics where measurements do not alter the state in such a fundamental way, projecting it onto a specific eigenstate of the measured observable.

Quantum states in quantum computing

Quantum computing harnesses the unique properties of quantum states to perform computational tasks with unprecedented speed and efficiency. Quantum bits, or qubits, represent the fundamental units of information in quantum computing, embodying the principles of superposition and entanglement. By exploiting these quantum phenomena, quantum algorithms can outperform their classical counterparts in tasks such as factorization, optimization, and simulation.

To summarize, quantum states form the bedrock of quantum mechanics, embodying the probabilistic nature and wave-particle duality of quantum systems. Understanding quantum states is essential for comprehending the profound phenomena of superposition and entanglement, which underpin the revolutionary potential of quantum computing. As we proceed, a solid grasp of quantum states provides the necessary foundation for exploring the frontiers of quantum technology and computation.

Superposition as the basis of quantum computing

Superposition is a fundamental principle of quantum mechanics that allows quantum systems to exist in multiple states simultaneously. Unlike classical systems, where the state is uniquely determined, quantum systems can be in a linear combination of different states. This means that a quantum system can occupy a state of being both **here** and **there**, **up** and **down**, or any other combination of possible states until measured.

The concept of superposition challenges our classical intuition, as it implies a departure from the notion of definite properties and locations for particles. Instead, particles can exhibit a wave-like behavior, spreading out and existing in a multitude of states simultaneously. Superposition lies at the heart of many quantum phenomena and technologies, including quantum computing, quantum cryptography, and quantum communication.

Mathematical representation of superposition

In quantum mechanics, superposition is mathematically represented using ket notation within the framework of Hilbert spaces. A quantum state vector $|\psi\rangle$ can be expressed as a linear combination of basis states $|0\rangle$ and $|1\rangle$ as shown in *Figure 3.1*, representing the two possible states of a qubit:

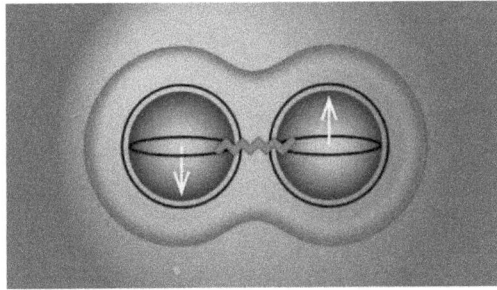

Figure 3.1: *Quantum superposition*

Mathematically, this is written as:

$$|\psi\rangle = \alpha\,|0\rangle + \beta\,|1\rangle$$

Here, α and β are complex probability amplitudes, reflecting the probability of finding the qubit in the $|0\rangle$ or $|1\rangle$ state, respectively. The coefficients α and β satisfy the normalization condition $|\alpha|^2 + |\beta|^2 = 1$, ensuring that the total probability adds up to one.

This mathematical formalism captures the essence of superposition, allowing us to describe and manipulate quantum states with precision. By controlling the coefficients α and β, we can engineer complex superposition states tailored to specific quantum algorithms and applications.

Examples of superposition in quantum systems

Superposition manifests in various quantum systems, from individual particles to composite systems. One of the most famous examples is the double-slit experiment, where a single particle, such as an electron or photon, exhibits interference patterns indicative of being in a superposition of multiple paths simultaneously.

Another example is the state of a qubit in a quantum computer, which can be prepared in a superposition of the $|0\rangle$ and $|1\rangle$ states. This superposition allows quantum algorithms to explore multiple computational paths in parallel, potentially leading to exponential speedups over classical algorithms for certain problems.

A great example of this is Grover's algorithm, which uses superposition to search through an unsorted database faster than any classical algorithm. While a classical computer would check each item one by one, a quantum computer can evaluate multiple possibilities at once, drastically reducing the time needed to find the correct answer. This makes superposition a powerful resource for solving certain computational problems more efficiently.

Additionally, superposition plays a crucial role in quantum cryptography protocols, where qubits are manipulated to encode information in superposition states, providing security against eavesdropping and tampering.

Importance of superposition in quantum algorithms

Superposition lies at the heart of quantum algorithms, enabling quantum computers to perform computations in parallel across a vast array of possible states. Quantum algorithms exploit superposition to explore multiple computational paths simultaneously, leveraging interference effects to amplify the correct solution and suppress incorrect ones.

For example, in Shor's algorithm for integer factorization, quantum superposition allows the algorithm to simultaneously evaluate multiple candidate factors of a composite number, exploiting interference to extract the correct factors efficiently. Similarly, Grover's algorithm for unstructured search harnesses superposition to search through a database of N items in $\sqrt{N}$ steps, offering a quadratic speedup over classical algorithms.

The ability to encode and manipulate superposition states is essential for realizing the full potential of quantum computing. By harnessing the power of superposition, quantum algorithms promise to revolutionize fields such as cryptography, optimization, machine learning, and simulation, paving the way for a new era of computational capabilities.

In conclusion, superposition is a foundational concept in quantum mechanics, allowing quantum systems to exist in multiple states simultaneously. Mathematically represented using ket notation, superposition enables the exploration of parallel computational paths and underpins the operation of quantum algorithms. Understanding and controlling superposition states are essential for realizing the transformative potential of quantum computing and unlocking new frontiers in technology and science.

Entanglement and quantum correlations beyond classical intuition

Entanglement is one of the most intriguing phenomena in quantum mechanics. It describes the intricate correlations between particles that defy classical intuition. When two or more particles become entangled, their states become inseparably linked, such that the state of one particle instantaneously influences the state of the other(s), regardless of the distance between them. This phenomenon, famously referred to by Einstein as *spooky action at a distance*, challenges our classical understanding of locality and realism.

Entanglement arises from the superposition of composite quantum systems, where the individual states of the particles cannot be described independently. Instead, the entangled states of the particles exhibit correlations that cannot be explained by classical theories, highlighting the fundamentally non-classical nature of quantum mechanics.

Mathematical representation of entangled states

Entangled states are mathematically represented using tensor products within the framework of Hilbert spaces. For a system of two qubits, the general form of an entangled state can be expressed as:

$$|\Psi\rangle = \alpha\,|00\rangle + \beta\,|01\rangle + \gamma\,|10\rangle + \delta\,|11\rangle$$

Here, α, β, γ, and δ are complex probability amplitudes that determine the entanglement properties of the system. The entangled state $|\Psi\rangle$ cannot be factored into separate states for each qubit, illustrating the inseparable nature of entanglement.

Entanglement is quantified mathematically using measures such as entropy and concurrence, which capture the degree of correlation between the entangled particles. These measures provide insights into the strength and structure of entanglement, allowing researchers to characterize and manipulate entangled states effectively. Refer to the following figure:

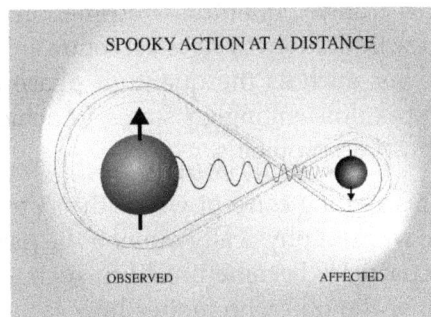

Figure 3.2: Quantum entanglement

Examples of entanglement in quantum systems

Entanglement manifests in various quantum systems, ranging from simple two-particle systems to complex multipartite systems. One of the most well-known examples is the phenomenon of spin entanglement in pairs of particles, such as electrons or photons. When two particles are prepared in an entangled state, measuring the spin of one particle instantaneously determines the spin of the other particle, regardless of the distance between them, as shown in *Figure 3.2*.

Another example is the phenomenon of **Einstein-Podolsky-Rosen (EPR)** pairs, where two particles are prepared in a special type of entangled state exhibiting strong correlations in position and momentum. EPR pairs played a pivotal role in Einstein's critique of quantum mechanics and later became a cornerstone of quantum information theory.

Entanglement also arises in systems of multiple particles, where complex interactions give rise to intricate patterns of correlation. Quantum many-body systems, such as those studied in condensed matter physics and quantum chemistry, exhibit emergent phenomena driven by entanglement, leading to novel phases of matter and exotic quantum states.

Entanglement in quantum communication and processing

Entanglement plays a central role in quantum communication and information processing protocols, enabling secure communication and enhanced computational capabilities. In quantum cryptography, entangled particles can be used to establish secure cryptographic keys through protocols such as **quantum key distribution (QKD)**. By encoding information in the entangled states of particles, quantum cryptography ensures that any eavesdropping attempts are immediately detected, preserving the integrity and confidentiality of the communication channel.

In quantum information processing, entanglement is a valuable resource for performing tasks such as teleportation, superdense coding, and quantum error correction. Entangled states can be manipulated to transfer quantum information between distant locations instantaneously, surpassing the limitations of classical communication channels. Moreover, entanglement-based algorithms, such as the quantum phase estimation algorithm and quantum Fourier transform, exploit entangled states to achieve exponential speedups over classical algorithms for certain problems.

Quantum teleportation is a fascinating concept where the state of a particle is transferred from one location to another, without physically moving the particle itself. This is possible through entanglement: two particles become linked in such a way that the state of one can instantly affect the state of the other, no matter how far apart they are. In quantum teleportation, information about the state of one particle is sent to another particle at a distant location, using a combination of classical communication and entanglement. This allows the original state to be *teleported* to the other particle, even though the particles never physically move. It is important to note that this does not mean faster-than-light travel or communication, but it does demonstrate the power of quantum entanglement and could have applications in secure communication and quantum networking.

In conclusion, entanglement represents a fundamental aspect of quantum mechanics, illustrating the non-local correlations that defy classical intuition. Mathematically represented using tensor products, entangled states exhibit inseparable connections between particles, enabling novel applications in quantum communication and information processing. Understanding and harnessing entanglement are essential for realizing the transformative potential of quantum technologies and unlocking new frontiers in communication, computation, and cryptography, which have a great potential for secure communication because any attempt to intercept or measure the entangled particles would immediately disturb the system, revealing the presence of eavesdropping. This makes quantum entanglement a promising foundation for unbreakable encryption and highly secure communication networks.

Experimental realization of superposition and entanglement

Experimental verification of superposition and entanglement lies at the heart of quantum mechanics research, providing empirical evidence for the theory's counterintuitive predictions. Experimentalists employ various techniques to manipulate and measure quantum systems, ranging from precision control of individual particles to complex setups involving entangled states of multiple particles.

One common technique is laser cooling and trapping, which allows researchers to cool atoms to ultra-low temperatures and confine them in optical traps. This enables precise control and manipulation of individual atoms, essential for studying quantum phenomena such as superposition and entanglement. Other techniques include cavity **quantum electrodynamics (QED)**, ion traps, superconducting qubits, and photonic systems, each offering unique advantages and challenges for experimental quantum research.

Key experiments demonstrating superposition and entanglement

Numerous groundbreaking experiments have demonstrated the reality of superposition and entanglement, providing compelling evidence for the quantum nature of the universe. One of the earliest and most famous experiments is the double-slit experiment, which demonstrates the wave-particle duality of quantum particles. By observing interference patterns produced by individual particles passing through two slits, researchers confirmed the existence of superposition at the microscopic scale.

Another seminal experiment is the EPR experiment, which tests the entanglement of pairs of particles. In this experiment, two particles are prepared in an entangled state, and measurements of their properties reveal instantaneous correlations, violating classical notions of locality and realism. The success of the EPR experiment provided strong support for the concept of entanglement and sparked intense debate about its implications for the nature of reality.

More recent experiments have demonstrated increasingly complex forms of superposition and entanglement, including multipartite entanglement and quantum teleportation. These experiments push the boundaries of our understanding of quantum mechanics and pave the way for practical applications in quantum communication, computation, and cryptography.

Challenges and advances in experimental quantum computing

Despite the remarkable progress in experimental quantum computing, significant challenges remain on the path towards practical quantum technologies. One major challenge is decoherence, the loss of coherence due to interaction with the environment. Decoherence introduces errors and limits the lifetime of quantum states, posing a significant obstacle to building reliable quantum computers.

To address decoherence, researchers have developed techniques such as quantum error correction, which redundantly encodes quantum information to protect against errors. Quantum error correction codes enable fault-tolerant quantum computation, allowing quantum computers to perform reliable calculations even in the presence of noise and imperfections.

Another challenge is scalability, as current experimental platforms are limited in the number of qubits they can reliably control and manipulate. Scaling up quantum systems requires overcoming technical barriers related to precision control, noise mitigation, and inter-qubit connectivity. Advances in fabrication techniques, materials science, and engineering are driving progress toward scalable quantum technologies, with efforts focused on improving qubit coherence times, minimizing crosstalk, and developing scalable architectures.

Despite these challenges, recent advances in experimental quantum computing have been promising, with demonstrations of small-scale quantum processors capable of executing simple quantum algorithms. As experimental techniques continue to improve and mature, researchers are increasingly optimistic about the prospects of realizing large-scale, fault-tolerant quantum computers capable of solving practical problems beyond the reach of classical computers.

In conclusion, the experimental realization of superposition and entanglement represents a cornerstone of quantum mechanics research, providing empirical validation of the theory's predictions. Key experiments have demonstrated the existence of superposition and entanglement, confirming the non-classical nature of quantum systems. Challenges such as decoherence and scalability remain but advances in experimental techniques and quantum engineering offer hope for the eventual realization of practical quantum technologies with transformative capabilities.

Harnessing superposition and entanglement in quantum computing

Harnessing superposition and entanglement is fundamental to the power of quantum computing. Superposition allows quantum bits (qubits) to exist in multiple states simultaneously, enabling quantum computers to process vast amounts of information at once. Entanglement, conversely, creates strong correlations between qubits, allowing them to influence each other instantly, even when separated by large distances. Together, these phenomena enable quantum computers to perform complex computations more efficiently than classical computers, offering potential breakthroughs in areas like cryptography, optimization, and materials science.

Quantum gates and circuits using superposition

Quantum computing harnesses the unique properties of superposition and entanglement to perform computational tasks with unprecedented speed and efficiency. Central to quantum computing are quantum gates, analogous to classical logic gates, which manipulate qubits to perform quantum operations. Quantum gates exploit superposition and entanglement to process information in parallel across a vast array of possible states, enabling exponential speedups over classical computing for certain problems.

Quantum gates operate on qubits by applying unitary transformations to the quantum state vector. Common quantum gates include the Hadamard gate, which creates superposition states, and the CNOT gate, which entangles pairs of qubits. By combining these basic gates into quantum circuits, researchers can construct complex algorithms capable of solving problems that are intractable for classical computers.

Quantum algorithms leveraging superposition and entanglement

Quantum algorithms leverage the power of superposition and entanglement to solve computational problems with remarkable efficiency. One of the most famous quantum algorithms is Shor's algorithm for integer factorization, which exploits the quantum Fourier transform and modular exponentiation to efficiently factor large composite numbers. Shor's algorithm demonstrates the potential for exponential speedups over classical algorithms for certain problems, posing a significant threat to classical cryptographic schemes such as RSA.

Another influential quantum algorithm is Grover's algorithm for unstructured search. This algorithm leverages amplitude amplification to search through a database of N items in √N steps, offering a quadratic speedup over classical search algorithms. Grover's algorithm has applications in various domains, including database search, optimization, and machine learning, where it promises to revolutionize computational tasks that are computationally intensive for classical computers.

Quantum algorithms also enable advances in areas such as quantum simulation, quantum chemistry, and quantum machine learning. Quantum computers can efficiently simulate complex quantum systems, discover new materials and drugs, and train powerful quantum neural networks. These applications leverage the inherent parallelism and computational power of quantum systems, offering transformative capabilities for scientific research and technological innovation.

Superposition and entanglement in quantum networks

Classical networks facilitate the transmission of data from sender to receiver, forming the backbone of modern communication systems. However, quantum networks introduce a paradigm shift by offering the generation of end-to-end quantum entanglement between endpoints, paving the way for novel applications in quantum computing, communication, and cryptography. At the heart of many quantum networking protocols lie Bell pairs, which play a fundamental role in enabling quantum entanglement-based operations. In this discussion, we will look at the history and significance of Bell pairs, as well as their applications in quantum networking protocols.

EPR paradox and origins of Bell pairs

The EPR paradox, proposed by *Albert Einstein, Boris Podolsky,* and *Nathan Rosen* in 1935, challenged the principles of quantum mechanics by describing a scenario that seemingly violated the principle of locality. According to locality, no object can influence another object instantaneously, implying that there must be a hidden-variable theory underlying quantum mechanics to reconcile this violation. However, in the 1960s, *John S. Bell* demonstrated that such a hidden-variable theory was not necessary and introduced Bell pairs as a means to understand and exploit quantum entanglement.

Bell pairs, also known as EPR pairs, are a specific set of entangled quantum states that defy classical intuition. These pairs serve as a cornerstone in the study of quantum mechanics, revealing the non-local correlations that emerge between entangled particles. *Bell's* formulation of the EPR paradox showcased the inherent strangeness of quantum entanglement and laid the foundation for developing quantum information theory.

Quantum bits, superposition, and entanglement

Quantum bits, or qubits, are the fundamental units of information in quantum computing, analogous to classical bits in classical computing. Unlike classical bits, which can exist in either a 0 or 1 state, qubits can exist in a superposition of both states simultaneously. This superposition enables quantum computers to perform parallel computations and explore multiple computational paths simultaneously.

Measurement of a qubit collapses its superposition into a definite state, with probabilities determined by the initial superposition. Additionally, entanglement allows for the correlation of quantum states across multiple qubits, resulting in non-local correlations that defy classical intuition. Bell pairs exemplify this entanglement, serving as maximally entangled states that exhibit unique properties under measurement.

Bell pairs

Bell pairs encompass four entangled two-qubit quantum states, collectively known as the four **Bell states**. These states exhibit distinct patterns of entanglement, with two pairs resulting in both qubits sharing the same state upon measurement and the other two pairs resulting in opposite states. The properties of Bell pairs enable them to serve as fundamental resources in quantum networking protocols and algorithms.

Bell states, also known as EPR pairs, are a set of maximally entangled quantum states involving two qubits. These states are of great importance in quantum information theory, as they exhibit perfect correlations and form the basis for many quantum communication and computation protocols.

Mathematically, the Bell states are represented using the tensor product of two-qubit states. There are four possible Bell states, often denoted ny $|\Phi+\rangle$, $|\Phi-\rangle$, $|\Psi+\rangle$, and $|\Psi-\rangle$. Each of these states is a superposition of the two-qubit basis states $|00\rangle$ and $|11\rangle$ for the Φ states, or $|01\rangle$ and $|10\rangle$ for the Ψ states.

The following are the mathematical representations of the Bell states:

1. $|\Phi+\rangle$: This state is a superposition of the $|00\rangle$ and $|11\rangle$ states:

$$|\Phi+\rangle = 1/\sqrt{2}((|00\rangle + |11\rangle))$$

2. $|\Phi-\rangle$: This state is a superposition of the $|00\rangle$ and $|11\rangle$ states, with a minus sign in front of the $|11\rangle$ state:

$$|\Phi-\rangle = 1/\sqrt{2}((|00\rangle - |11\rangle))$$

3. $|\Psi+\rangle$: This state is a superposition of the $|01\rangle$ and $|10\rangle$ states:

$$|\Psi+\rangle = 1/\sqrt{2}((|01\rangle + |10\rangle))$$

4. $|\Psi-\rangle$: This state is a superposition of the $|01\rangle$ and $|10\rangle$ states, with a minus sign in front of the $|10\rangle$ state:

$$|\Psi-\rangle = 1/\sqrt{2}((|01\rangle - |10\rangle))$$

These Bell states are orthonormal, meaning they are mutually orthogonal and normalized. They are also maximally entangled states, as they exhibit perfect correlations between the two qubits. In other words, measuring one qubit instantly determines the state of the other qubit. This property makes Bell states fundamental to quantum teleportation, QKD, and other quantum information protocols.

Each Bell pair exhibits unique properties that make them suitable for various quantum networking applications. For instance, the entanglement between qubits in Bell pairs enables instantaneous correlations across vast distances, making them valuable resources for quantum teleportation and secure communication protocols.

Bell pairs in quantum networks

Quantum teleportation relies on the consumption of Bell pairs to transmit quantum states between distant parties. By sharing a Bell pair and performing measurements, two parties can effectively teleport quantum information from one qubit to another, leveraging the principles of entanglement to achieve secure and efficient communication.

QKD, a cornerstone of quantum cryptography, also uses Bell pairs to establish secure communication channels between parties. Protocols such as the E91 protocol utilize entanglement-based techniques to generate cryptographic keys with enhanced security properties, leveraging the non-local correlations inherent in Bell pairs.

Going beyond Bell pairs

While Bell pairs serve as essential resources in quantum networking, some applications require the generation of entanglement across multiple qubits. States such as the **Greenberger-Horne-Zeilinger (GHZ)** and W states offer entanglement across three or more qubits, enabling advanced quantum network functionalities. Future research in quantum networking will explore the generation and utilization of multipartite entangled states for enhanced communication, computation, and cryptography.

Analogies to explain

Understanding Bell states, with their complex quantum properties, can be daunting. However, analogies offer valuable tools to grasp their significance and behavior more intuitively:

- **Dancing partners analogy:** Imagine two dancers executing a choreographed routine. In the $|\Phi+\rangle|\Phi+\rangle$ state, both dancers move synchronously, performing identical steps simultaneously. Conversely, in the $|\Phi-\rangle|\Phi-\rangle$ state, the second dancer executes the routine in reverse, mirroring the first dancer's steps but in an inverted order. Transitioning to the $|\Psi+\rangle|\Psi+\rangle$ state, the dancers perform complementary steps, synchronized but with one performing the opposite movement of the other. Lastly, in the $|\Psi-\rangle|\Psi-\rangle$ state, the second dancer mirrors the first but inversely, creating a complementary yet reversed sequence of movements.

- **Twin telepathy analogy:** Picture a pair of twins with an uncanny telepathic connection. In the $|\Phi+\rangle|\Phi+\rangle$ state, both twins share the same thoughts simultaneously, as if reading each other's minds effortlessly. Conversely, in the $|\Phi-\rangle|\Phi-\rangle$ state, the second twin experiences contrasting thoughts, diverging from the first twin's mental state. Transitioning to the $|\Psi+\rangle|\Psi+\rangle$ state, the twins' thoughts complement each other, one thinking the opposite of the other yet in perfect harmony. Finally, in the $|\Psi-\rangle|\Psi-\rangle$ state, the second twin's thoughts mirror the first's, but in reverse, creating a complementary yet inverse mental dialogue.

- **Coin flipping analogy:** Envision two coins entangled in their outcomes when flipped simultaneously. In the $|\Phi+\rangle|\Phi+\rangle$ state, both coins land on the same side, exhibiting a synchronous outcome. Conversely, in the $|\Phi-\rangle|\Phi-\rangle$ state, the second coin lands on the opposite side, creating a reverse outcome compared to the first coin. Moving to the $|\Psi+\rangle|\Psi+\rangle$ state, the coins land on opposite sides, presenting a complementary outcome—one head and one tail. Finally, in the $|\Psi-\rangle|\Psi-\rangle$ state, the second coin lands on the opposite side of the first coin, but the outcomes are reversed, leading to a complementary yet inverted result.

These analogies offer tangible scenarios to visualize the behavior of Bell states, capturing their intricacies and non-local correlations in a relatable manner. While they may simplify the complexity of quantum mechanics, they provide valuable insights into the entangled nature of quantum systems, aiding in comprehending quantum phenomena and their applications in quantum networking protocols.

In conclusion, Bell states represent a cornerstone of quantum mechanics, demonstrating the intricate correlations that arise in entangled quantum systems. Analogies such as the dancing partners, twin telepathy, and coin flipping help to elucidate the properties of Bell states and their significance in quantum information processing. Understanding and harnessing Bell states are essential for realizing the potential of quantum technologies and unlocking new frontiers in computation, communication, and cryptography.

Potential speedups and advantages of quantum computing

The potential speedups and advantages of quantum computing stem from its ability to explore exponentially large computational spaces in parallel. Classical computers rely on binary bits to represent information, limiting their computational power to linear scaling with the number of bits. In contrast, quantum computers employ qubits, which can exist in superposition states, allowing them to explore 2^n possible states simultaneously for n qubits.

This exponential scaling enables quantum computers to tackle problems that are intractable for classical computers, such as integer factorization, discrete optimization, and quantum simulation. Quantum algorithms exploit this parallelism to efficiently solve these problems, offering exponential speedups over classical algorithms and fundamentally changing the landscape of computation.

Moreover, quantum computers offer advantages beyond speedups, including enhanced security through quantum cryptography, improved accuracy in quantum sensing and metrology, and novel approaches to machine learning and artificial intelligence. Quantum computing has the potential to revolutionize industries ranging from finance and healthcare to materials science and cybersecurity, unlocking new opportunities for innovation and discovery.

In conclusion, harnessing superposition and entanglement for quantum computing offers unparalleled computational capabilities with the potential for exponential speedups and transformative applications across various domains. Quantum gates and circuits exploit the principles of superposition and entanglement to manipulate qubits and perform quantum operations, while quantum algorithms leverage these phenomena to solve computational problems with remarkable efficiency. The potential speedups and advantages of quantum computing promise to revolutionize computation, offering unprecedented opportunities for scientific discovery, technological innovation, and societal impact.

Limitations and challenges

Quantum computing holds immense promise for revolutionizing various fields with its unparalleled computational power. However, several limitations and challenges hinder the realization of practical quantum technologies. This chapter delves into the primary obstacles hindering the development of quantum computing, including decoherence, error correction, fault tolerance, scalability issues, and practical constraints.

Decoherence is the enemy of superposition and entanglement

Decoherence arises from the interaction of quantum systems with their environment, leading to the loss of coherence and the destruction of superposition and entanglement states. Quantum systems are extremely sensitive to their surroundings, making them prone to decoherence from factors such as temperature fluctuations, electromagnetic interference, and material imperfections.

Decoherence poses a significant challenge to quantum computing, as it limits the coherence time of qubits and degrades the performance of quantum algorithms. Mitigating decoherence requires careful engineering of quantum hardware and developing error correction techniques to protect against environmental noise.

Error correction and fault tolerance in quantum computing

Error correction is essential for overcoming the detrimental effects of noise and errors in quantum systems. Unlike classical computers, which employ redundancy and error-correction codes to mitigate errors, quantum error correction faces unique challenges due to the fragile nature of quantum states and the No-cloning theorem, which prohibits perfect replication of arbitrary quantum states.

Quantum error correction codes, such as the surface code and the Shor code, encode quantum information redundantly to detect and correct errors caused by decoherence and other noise sources. Fault-tolerant quantum computation relies on the redundancy introduced by error correction to ensure the reliable operation of quantum algorithms, even in the presence of errors.

Achieving fault-tolerant quantum computation requires stringent error thresholds, typically on the order of 10^{-3} to 10^{-4}, which necessitate high-fidelity quantum gates, long coherence times, and low error rates in physical qubits. Overcoming these challenges is essential for realizing fault-tolerant quantum computers capable of solving practical problems.

Scalability issues and practical constraints

Scalability is another critical challenge facing the development of quantum computing. Current experimental quantum systems are limited in the number of qubits they can reliably control and manipulate, making it difficult to scale up to large-scale quantum processors capable of solving complex problems.

Scalability issues arise from technical limitations such as inter-qubit connectivity, crosstalk, and fabrication constraints. Quantum architectures must address these challenges to achieve the necessary qubit density and connectivity for performing meaningful computations.

Moreover, practical constraints such as cost, power consumption, and physical footprint impose additional challenges on the development and deployment of quantum computing technologies. Building and operating quantum computers require substantial resources and expertise, limiting their accessibility and widespread adoption.

Addressing scalability issues and practical constraints requires interdisciplinary collaboration between physicists, engineers, materials scientists, and computer scientists. Advances in quantum hardware, error correction techniques, and system integration are essential for overcoming these challenges and realizing quantum computing's full potential.

In conclusion, limitations and challenges such as decoherence, error correction, fault tolerance, scalability issues, and practical constraints pose significant obstacles to developing practical quantum computing technologies. Overcoming these challenges requires innovative approaches to quantum hardware, error correction techniques, and system integration, as well as interdisciplinary collaboration and investment in research and development.

Despite these challenges, the potential of quantum computing to revolutionize computation, communication, and cryptography motivates ongoing efforts to overcome these obstacles and realize the transformative promise of quantum technologies. By addressing the limitations and challenges discussed in this chapter, researchers aim to unlock the full potential of quantum computing and usher in a new era of computational capabilities.

Future directions and applications

Quantum computing has the potential to transform various fields, offering unprecedented computational power and capabilities. As researchers continue to push the boundaries of quantum technologies, new directions and applications emerge with far-reaching implications for science, industry, and society. This section explores the future directions and potential applications of quantum computing, including emerging technologies, research areas, and their implications.

Emerging technologies and research areas

Advances in quantum computing research have led to the emergence of several promising technologies and research areas. Quantum hardware development remains a focal point, with efforts focused on improving qubit coherence times, reducing error rates, and scaling up qubit counts. Novel approaches to quantum control and manipulation, such as topological qubits and error correction schemes, hold promise for achieving fault-tolerant quantum computation.

Quantum networking and communication represent another exciting research area, aiming to leverage quantum entanglement for secure communication and distributed computing. Quantum repeaters, QKD, and quantum internet protocols enable the establishment of secure communication channels resistant to eavesdropping and hacking, with applications in cryptography, finance, and national security.

Quantum simulation and optimization offer transformative capabilities for solving complex problems in physics, chemistry, materials science, and finance. Quantum simulators can accurately model quantum systems that are computationally intractable for classical computers, enabling advances in drug discovery, materials design, and energy optimization. Quantum optimization algorithms promise to revolutionize fields such as logistics, supply chain management, and financial modeling by efficiently solving large-scale optimization problems with quantum speedups.

Potential applications beyond computing

The impact of quantum computing extends beyond traditional computational tasks, with potential applications in diverse fields. Quantum sensing and metrology leverage quantum principles to achieve unprecedented levels of precision and sensitivity, enabling advances in medical imaging, environmental monitoring, and navigation systems. Quantum sensors can detect minute changes in magnetic fields, gravitational waves, and electromagnetic radiation, offering insights into fundamental phenomena and practical applications.

Quantum machine learning and artificial intelligence represent another frontier of research. Quantum algorithms and quantum neural networks promise to outperform classical counterparts in pattern recognition, data analysis, and optimization tasks. Quantum machine learning holds potential applications in fields such as drug discovery, image recognition, and autonomous vehicles, where computational efficiency and accuracy are paramount.

Quantum materials and quantum sensing technologies are poised to revolutionize the electronics industry, offering novel materials with unique electronic, optical, and magnetic properties. Quantum devices, such as quantum dots, superconducting qubits, and spintronics devices, enable advances in quantum computing, quantum communication, and quantum sensing applications, with implications for information technology, telecommunications, and renewable energy.

Implications for science, industry, and society

The widespread adoption of quantum technologies has profound implications for science, industry, and society. Quantum computing promises to accelerate scientific discovery by enabling simulations of complex quantum systems, elucidating fundamental physical phenomena, and solving longstanding computational challenges. Quantum cryptography and secure communication protocols enhance data privacy and cybersecurity, protecting sensitive information and critical infrastructure from cyber threats and attacks.

In industry, quantum computing offers competitive advantages in areas such as optimization, logistics, finance, and drug discovery, where computational efficiency and accuracy drive innovation and cost savings. Quantum technologies also enable advances in materials science, renewable energy, and environmental monitoring, addressing pressing global challenges such as climate change, resource depletion, and pollution.

On a societal level, quantum technologies have implications for education, workforce development, and economic competitiveness. Investment in quantum research and education programs prepares the next generation of scientists, engineers, and innovators to harness the potential of quantum technologies and drive future advancements. Quantum literacy and awareness initiatives raise public understanding of quantum principles and their impact on everyday life, fostering a culture of innovation and collaboration.

In conclusion, the future of quantum computing is bright, with emerging technologies, research areas, and potential applications poised to transform science, industry, and society. Advances in quantum hardware, algorithms, and applications promise to unlock unprecedented computational power and capabilities, revolutionizing fields such as materials science, cryptography, and machine learning. By embracing the opportunities presented by quantum computing and investing in research, education, and infrastructure, we can harness the transformative potential of quantum technologies to address global challenges and drive innovation in the 21st century.

Conclusion

Throughout this study of quantum computing, we have explored its fundamental principles, applications, challenges, and future directions. From the foundational concepts of superposition and entanglement to the practical considerations of error correction and scalability, we have uncovered its potential and limitations.

Key points highlighted include the probabilistic nature of quantum states, represented mathematically through ket notation within Hilbert spaces. Superposition allows quantum systems to exist in multiple states simultaneously, while entanglement creates intricate correlations between particles, defying classical intuition.

In quantum computing, harnessing superposition and entanglement enables exponential speedups over classical computing for certain problems. Quantum gates and circuits exploit these phenomena to perform operations on qubits, and quantum algorithms leverage them to solve complex computational tasks efficiently.

However, quantum computing faces significant challenges, including decoherence, error correction, and scalability issues. Decoherence, arising from interaction with the environment, disrupts quantum states, while error correction techniques are essential for protecting quantum information from noise and errors. Scalability constraints limit the size and complexity of current quantum systems, necessitating advances in hardware and architecture.

In the next chapter, we will explore the foundational elements of quantum computing, focusing on the building blocks that enable the execution of quantum algorithms: quantum gates and circuits. The next chapter will provide a comprehensive overview of various topics that are essential for understanding and manipulating quantum information.

Multiple choice questions

1. **Which of the following represents the superposition of a qubit state?**

   a. $|0\rangle$

   b. $|1\rangle$

   c. $\alpha|0\rangle + \beta|1\rangle$

   d. $0\rangle \oplus |1\rangle$

2. **What is the primary use of Bell pairs in quantum communication?**

   a. Quantum simulation

   b. Quantum error correction

   c. Quantum teleportation

   d. Quantum gates

3. **Which term describes the process of collapsing a quantum state to a definite state during measurement?**

   a. Coherence

   b. Entanglement

   c. Decoherence

   d. Superposition

4. **What is the mathematical representation of the Bell state $\Psi-$?**

   a. $1/\sqrt{2}((|00\rangle+|11\rangle))$

   b. $1/\sqrt{2}((|00\rangle-|11\rangle))$

   c. $1/\sqrt{2}((|01\rangle+|10\rangle))$

   d. $1/\sqrt{2}((|01\rangle-|10\rangle))$

5. **Which analogy best describes entanglement?**

   a. A coin flip

   b. Twins sharing the same thoughts

   c. Dancers performing identical steps

   d. A spinning top

Answer key

1. c

2. c

3. c

4. d

5. b

Questions

1. Explain the concept of superposition in quantum mechanics and provide a mathematical representation of a qubit in superposition.

   Answer: Superposition is a fundamental principle where a qubit exists in a linear combination of both basis states $|0\rangle$ and $|1\rangle$ simultaneously:

   $|\psi\rangle = \alpha|0\rangle + \beta|1\rangle$, where α and β are complex numbers satisfying $|\alpha|^2 + |\beta|^2 = 1$.

2. Discuss the role of Bell pairs in quantum teleportation. How do Bell pairs enable the transmission of quantum information over a distance?

   Answer: Bell pairs are maximally entangled qubit pairs used in quantum teleportation to share quantum information; they act as a quantum channel between sender and receiver.The sender performs a joint measurement on their qubit and one half of the Bell pair, collapsing the receiver's qubit into the desired state after classical communication and correction.

3. Define entanglement and explain its significance in quantum communication. Provide an example of a quantum protocol that relies on entanglement.

   Answer: Entanglement is a quantum correlation where the state of one particle instantly influences another, regardless of distance.**Quantum key distribution (QKD)**, such as Ekert's protocol (E91), relies on entanglement to detect eavesdropping and ensure secure communication.

4. Describe how quantum states can be measured and how measurement affects the state of a qubit.

   Answer: Quantum measurement collapses a superposed qubit state to one of the basis states, $|0\rangle$ or $|1\rangle$, with probabilities $|\alpha|^2$ and $|\beta|^2$, respectively.This process irreversibly changes the state, destroying any superposition or entanglement it had.

5. Provide an analogy to explain the concept of Bell states and their different types. How can this analogy help in understanding the properties of Bell states?

   Answer: Bell states can be analogized as perfectly synchronized coin flips between two distant players — if one gets heads, the other always gets tails (or the same, depending on the state).

   This analogy helps illustrate their perfect correlations and mutual dependence, despite spatial separation, which is key to understanding quantum entanglement.

6. **Fill in the blank:** The process of collapsing a quantum state to a definite state during measurement is known as _____.

   Answer: decoherence

7. **True or False:** Quantum entanglement allows for instantaneous correlations between qubits regardless of distance.

   Answer: True

8. **Fill in the blank:** Quantum teleportation relies on _____ to transmit quantum states between two parties.

   Answer: Bell pairs

9. **True or False:** In quantum mechanics, a qubit can exist in both states $|0\rangle$ and $|1\rangle$ simultaneously due to superposition.

   Answer: True

10. **Fill in the blank:** The mathematical representation of the Bell state $|\Phi+\rangle$ is _____.

    Answer: $1/\sqrt{2}((|00\rangle+|11\rangle))$

CHAPTER 4
Quantum Gates and Circuits

Introduction

This chapter explores the fundamental components of quantum computing, known as quantum gates. We will delve into the various types of quantum gates and their mathematical representation using matrices, as well as the use of Kronecker product in quantum gate operations. Additionally, this chapter will cover the concept of unitary matrix and representation of qubits on the Bloch sphere.

Structure

The chapter covers the following topics:

- Quantum gates
- Unitary matrix
- Bloch sphere
- Types of quantum gates
- Representation of gates as matrices
- Kronecker product

Objectives

In this chapter, we will learn the concept of quantum gates, its mathematical representation as matrices, and its significance in quantum computing. We will also familiarize with the unitary matrix, its properties, and how it differs from classical gates. This chapter aims to help the reader gain an understanding of the Bloch sphere and how it is used to visualize quantum states and operations. Additionally, we will learn about the different types of quantum gates and their specific functions. This chapter will also help the reader to become proficient in using the Kronecker product to represent composite quantum operations.

Mastering these topics is crucial for executing quantum algorithms effectively, as a deep understanding of quantum gates and their operations forms the foundation of quantum computation. By grasping the nuances of quantum gate operations and their mathematical underpinnings, readers will be better equipped to design and implement sophisticated quantum algorithms.

Quantum gates

Quantum gates are fundamental components in the realm of quantum computing and play a crucial role in manipulating and processing information in a quantum system. Unlike classical gates which operate on bits (0s and 1s), quantum gates operate on quantum bits or **qubits**, which are the fundamental units of quantum information. One of the key differences between quantum and classical gates is the principle of superposition, where a qubit can exist in multiple states simultaneously, whereas a classical bit can only hold one value at a time. This property allows quantum gates to perform computations and operations on a vast number of possible states simultaneously, making them much more powerful and efficient than classical gates. Additionally, quantum gates also exhibit a phenomenon called **entanglement**, where two or more qubits can become correlated, allowing for highly complex computations to be performed in parallel. This is in contrast to classical gates, which can only process information sequentially. Quantum gates are designed to manipulate qubits in specific ways, such as flipping their state, rotating their phase, or creating superpositions. These operations are essential for executing quantum algorithms, which are different from classical algorithms and utilize the unique properties of qubits. While classical gates are limited in their ability to process and manipulate information, quantum gates open a whole new realm of possibilities and have the potential to solve problems that are practically impossible for classical computers to tackle. In essence, quantum gates represent a significant advancement in the field of computing and hold promise for revolutionizing various industries and fields, such as cryptography, pharmaceuticals, artificial intelligence, and many more.

Unitary matrix

Before we get into quantum gates, let us see what makes them different from classical gates. A quantum gate is reversible. If an input generates a certain output, that output when passed through the quantum gate will generate the original input. This is not true for all classical gates. An output of the OR gate, when passed back as input to the gate will not generate the original inputs. An example of reversibility in classical gates is the NOT gate. An input value of 1 will generate 0, and when that 0 is passed through the NOT gate as input, the original 1 will be the output. So, what makes a quantum gate reversible? It is because of the property of unitary matrix.

> Note: **Quantum gates are operations, while unitary matrices are their mathematical representation. All quantum gates are represented by unitary matrices, but not all unitary matrices necessarily represent useful quantum gates.**

A unitary gate is a quantum gate that is represented by a unitary matrix. It is a fundamental building block in quantum computing that performs a unitary transformation on a quantum state. It performs a specific logical operation on one or more input signals to produce one or more output signals. A unitary gate is considered an ideal gate, as it does not introduce any loss or noise into a circuit. It is also reversible, which means that it can be undone by feeding the output signal back into the gate, resulting in the original input signal. Unitary gates have two main properties that distinguish them from other gates: they preserve the normalization of quantum states, and they are linear, meaning that the output is a linear function of the input. In simple terms, this means that the sum of probabilities of all possible combinations of outputs (e.g. 0 and 1) must come up to 1, and the output must be directly proportional to the input. These gates are commonly used in quantum computing to manipulate qubits and perform logical operations such as flipping or swapping qubit states. Unitary gates can be implemented in various physical systems, including optical systems, quantum circuits, and even classical electronic circuits. They are an integral part of quantum computing and play a crucial role in enabling quantum algorithms and protocols.

Quantum gates are represented by unitary matrices. In mathematical terms, a matrix is unitary if the conjugate transpose is also its inverse. The **conjugate transpose**, also known as the **Hermitian transpose**, is a fundamental concept in linear algebra, particularly in the context of complex matrices. For a given complex matrix U, the conjugate transpose is denoted by U^* in the given equations. It is obtained by taking complex conjugate of each element and the transpose of the matrix.

That is, for a unitary matrix:

$$U^*U = UU^* = UU^{-1} = I,$$

where I is the identity matrix.

As quantum gates are essentially matrices, it is important to understand the concept of unitary matrices when building new types of gates or matrices. Let us look at an example of a unitary matrix.

Let us first understand what a conjugate is. To find the conjugate of a given matrix, replace each element of the matrix with its complex conjugate. In simple terms, a conjugate of a matrix can be derived by reversing the signs of the imaginary element. Let us look at a

2-dimensional matrix → $\begin{bmatrix} 0 & -i \\ i & 0 \end{bmatrix}$

Complex conjugate:

$$\begin{bmatrix} 0 & -i \\ i & 0 \end{bmatrix} \qquad \rightarrow \qquad \begin{bmatrix} 0 & i \\ -i & 0 \end{bmatrix}$$
(U)

Transpose:

$$\begin{bmatrix} 0 & i \\ -i & 0 \end{bmatrix} \qquad \rightarrow \qquad \begin{bmatrix} 0 & -i \\ i & 0 \end{bmatrix}$$
(U*)

UU* becomes,

$$\begin{bmatrix} 0 & -i \\ i & 0 \end{bmatrix} \qquad \times \qquad \begin{bmatrix} 0 & -i \\ i & 0 \end{bmatrix} \qquad = \qquad \begin{bmatrix} 1 & 0 \\ 0 & 1 \end{bmatrix}$$
(I)

The matrix is unitary and can represent a quantum gate. Incidentally, this is a *Pauli-Y* quantum gate (covered in a later section).

Let us look at another matrix and apply conjugate transpose on it → $\begin{bmatrix} 0 & i \\ -i & 1 \end{bmatrix}$

Complex conjugate:

$$\begin{bmatrix} 0 & i \\ -i & 1 \end{bmatrix} \qquad \rightarrow \qquad \begin{bmatrix} 0 & -i \\ i & 1 \end{bmatrix}$$
(U)

Transpose:

$$\begin{bmatrix} 0 & -i \\ i & 1 \end{bmatrix} \qquad \rightarrow \qquad \begin{bmatrix} 0 & i \\ -i & 1 \end{bmatrix}$$
(U*)

UU* becomes,

$$\begin{bmatrix} 0 & i \\ -i & 1 \end{bmatrix} \qquad \times \qquad \begin{bmatrix} 0 & i \\ -i & 1 \end{bmatrix} \qquad = \qquad \begin{bmatrix} 1 & i \\ -i & 2 \end{bmatrix}$$
(≠I)

The result is not an Identity matrix. Hence, it cannot be used for a quantum gate.

Bloch sphere

The Bloch sphere, named after physicist *Felix Bloch*, serves as a geometric illustration of the pure states within a two-state quantum mechanical system.

It is a three-dimensional unit sphere representing the pure states of the quantum system, where the north pole represents state 0 and the south pole represents state 1. The equator of the sphere represents equal probability superposition states of 0 and 1. The points located on the surface of the sphere represent the pure states of the system, while the points inside the sphere represent the mixed states.

The Bloch sphere is commonly used to represent the state of a qubit, which is the smallest unit of quantum information. A qubit can exist in a superposition of states, and is depicted as a point on the surface of the Bloch sphere. The north pole corresponds to the state $|0\rangle$, while the south pole corresponds to the state $|1\rangle$. The equator represents superpositions of these two states. The Bloch sphere also allows for the visualization of quantum operations, such as rotations and measurements. Any operation on a qubit can be illustrated with a point on the sphere's surface, and the result of the operation is a new point on the sphere.

The Bloch sphere represents both the amplitude and the phase of the qubit. Phase is an important concept in quantum mechanics that describes the state of a system at a particular point in time. It can be understood by considering interference. When two waves combine, their amplitudes can either add constructively (in-phase) or destructively (out-of-phase), resulting in a different overall amplitude. Similarly, in a quantum system, the combination of two basis states with different phases can lead to interference effects, affecting the probability of measuring a particular state. Phase is essential in quantum computing and quantum communication. In quantum computing, the ability to control and manipulate the phase of a system is crucial for performing quantum operations and algorithms. In quantum communication, the phase of a system can be used to encode information and ensure its secure transmission.

In Bloch sphere (*Figure 4.1*), phase is represented by the angle of rotation ϕ around the Z-axis, where ϕ ranges from 0 to 2π radians. The probability amplitude of finding a particle in a specific state is determined by the angle θ made with respect to the Z-axis, where θ ranges from 0 to π radians. The amplitude of the $|0\rangle$ state is $\cos\frac{\theta}{2}$ and the amplitude of the $|1\rangle$ state is $e^{i\phi} \sin\frac{\theta}{2}$. At the equator, θ is $\pi/2$. Therefore, the amplitudes of states $|0\rangle$ and $|1\rangle$ on the positive X-axis (where $\phi = 0$) will be $\frac{1}{\sqrt{2}}$, and corresponding probabilities will be the square of amplitudes, that is 0.5.

The Bloch sphere is a powerful tool for understanding and visualizing quantum states and operations, making it a fundamental concept in the study of quantum mechanics.

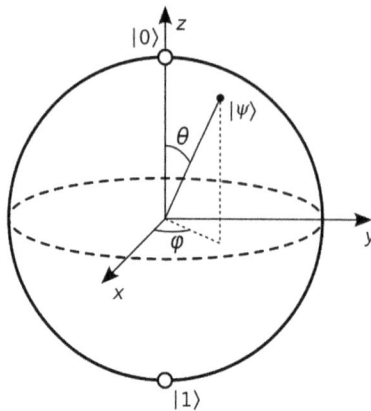

Figure 4.1: *Bloch sphere*

Let us look at how to read the Bloch sphere. If the qubit is at positive Z-axis, it denotes the state $|0\rangle$. If it is at negative Z-axis, it denotes the state $|1\rangle$. Anywhere else represents the state of superposition.

The matrix representation of state $|0\rangle$ at positive Z-axis is $\begin{bmatrix} 1 \\ 0 \end{bmatrix}$. The matrix representation of state $|1\rangle$ at negative Z-axis is $\begin{bmatrix} 0 \\ 1 \end{bmatrix}$.

The positive X-axis represents a superposition state where the amplitude of qubit is equal to $\frac{1}{\sqrt{2}}$ and phase 0. When there is a phase shift of π radians, the qubit is at negative X-axis.

At positive X-axis, the superposition state is represented as $|+\rangle$, and matrix representation is $\frac{1}{\sqrt{2}} \begin{bmatrix} 1 \\ -1 \end{bmatrix}$.

At negative X-axis, the superposition state is represented as $|-\rangle$, and matrix representation is $\frac{1}{\sqrt{2}} \begin{bmatrix} 1 \\ i \end{bmatrix}$.

The Y-axis represents the complex phase of the quantum state. At positive Y-axis, the superposition state can be represented as $|i\rangle$, and matrix representation is $\frac{1}{\sqrt{2}} \begin{bmatrix} 1 \\ -i \end{bmatrix}$.

At negative Y-axis, the superposition state can be represented as $|-i\rangle$, and matrix representation is .

The state of superposition of a qubit can be represented by the following equation:

$$|\psi\rangle = \cos\frac{\theta}{2} \, |0\rangle \; + \; e^{i\phi} \, \sin\frac{\theta}{2} \, |1\rangle$$

Equation 4.1: *Qubit superposition state*

Where, θ is the angle with respect to positive Z-axis and ϕ is the angle in the XY plane from the positive X-axis.

Different kinds of quantum gates can be applied to observe the states and phases of qubit on the Bloch sphere. One can try these various states at the following link: **https://javafxpert.github.io/grok-bloch/**.

Types of quantum gates

There are several categories of quantum gates. In this section, we will look at the functions of all such gates. In a later section, we will go through the matrix values of the gates and their manipulations.

Here are the different categories of gates along with their specific function and operation:

- **Single-qubit gates:** These gates manipulate one qubit at a time to change its state. These gates can be represented as 2x2 unitary matrices and are used to rotate the state of a qubit on the Bloch sphere. Few examples of single-qubit gates are the Pauli gates (X, Y, Z), Hadamard gate, and phase gate.

- **Multi-qubit gates:** These gates manipulate two or more qubits at the same time and change the joint state of the qubits. These gates can be represented as larger unitary matrices with dimensions that depend on the number of qubits they act on. Some examples of multi-qubit gates include the **Controlled-NOT** (**CNOT**) gate, **Controlled-Z** (**CZ**) gate, and SWAP gate.

- **Entangling gates:** These gates are a type of multi-qubit gate that create entanglement between qubits. Entanglement is a phenomenon in quantum mechanics where the state of one qubit becomes correlated with that of another, even if they are physically separated. Some examples of entangling gates include the CNOT gate, CZ gate, and **Controlled-U** (**CU**) gate.

- **Measurement gates:** These gates are used to measure the state of a qubit. These gates collapse the qubit's superposition state into one of its basis states (0 or 1) and provide a classical output. It performs a measurement along a specific basis (axis) and projects the state of a qubit onto that basis. Since measurement changes the qubit's state, these gates can only be used once in a quantum circuit.

- **Phase gates:** These gates are single-qubit gates that introduce a phase shift to a qubit's state. This phase shift can be either a rotation or a multiplication of the qubit's state by a complex number. Phase gates are used in quantum algorithms to manipulate the phase of a qubit's state and perform quantum phase estimation.

- **Universal gates:** These are a set of gates that can be used to implement any quantum operation on a qubit. A universal gate set can include single-qubit gates, multi-qubit gates, and measurement gates. They form the building blocks from which any quantum circuit can be constructed. A common universal set includes Hadamard, CNOT and T gates. For example, repeatedly applying the T gate enables the construction of any Z-axis rotation. Another example would be the combination of Hadamard and CNOT that enables the creation of superposition and entanglement, which are essential for many quantum computing operations.

There are several types of quantum logical gates, and they are as follows:

- **Pauli gates:** These gates are the basic building blocks of quantum circuits, which are used to manipulate and transform quantum states. Their function includes flipping the state of a qubit, flipping the phase of a qubit, or a combination of the two. The following are three types of Pauli gates:

    o **Pauli X:** The X gate flips the state of the qubit and is equivalent to the NOT gate in classical computing. If the input state is $|0\rangle$, it is flipped to $|1\rangle$, and vice-versa. When applied to a superposition of states, the Pauli X gate has the effect of flipping the amplitudes of the $|0\rangle$ and $|1\rangle$ states. For example, if the input state is a superposition of $|0\rangle$ and $|1\rangle$ with higher amplitude for $|0\rangle$ with respect to $|1\rangle$, the output state will be a superposition of $|1\rangle$ and $|0\rangle$ with $|1\rangle$ having the higher amplitude. This is because the X gate flips the amplitudes of the two basis states, effectively switching their roles in the superposition.

    o **Pauli Z:** This gate operates on a single qubit, executing a π radians rotation around the Z-axis on the Bloch sphere. This gate is commonly used to introduce a phase shift of either 0 or π (180°) to a qubit, depending on the state of the qubit before the gate is applied. If the qubit is in the state $|0\rangle$, the gate will not change the state. If the qubit is in the state $|1\rangle$, the gate will introduce a phase shift of π radians to change the state to $-|1\rangle$. The Pauli Z gate is valuable in quantum computing because it introduces a phase shift into the quantum state. This phase shift is an important parameter in various quantum algorithms, such as the *Deutsch-Jozsa algorithm* and the *Grover's algorithm*. It is also used in quantum error correction codes to detect and correct errors in quantum states.

    o **Pauli-Y:** The Y gate rotates the state of the qubit around the Y-axis by an angle of π radians. This gate will introduce a phase shift of $\pi/2$ radians around the Z-axis, landing the qubit state on the imaginary plane, which is the Y-axis. If the qubit is in the state $|0\rangle$, the gate will change the state to $i|1\rangle$. If the qubit is in the state $|1\rangle$, the gate will change the state to $i|0\rangle$. The gate is equivalent to a bit and phase flip. This gate is often used in quantum algorithms for quantum state manipulation and quantum error correction.

    These gates find use in most of the use cases such as quantum error correction, quantum teleportation, various quantum algorithms etc.

- **Hadamard gate:** The **Hadamard gate (H gate)** is a single qubit gate that is used to create superposition states. It maps the basis state $|0\rangle$ or $|1\rangle$ to a superposition of $|0\rangle$ and $|1\rangle$. It is a 2 x 2 matrix that rotates the qubit around the X and Z axes of the Bloch sphere, resulting in a state that is equally likely to collapse into either $|0\rangle$ or $|1\rangle$ when measured. It takes a qubit as input in either the state $|0\rangle$ or $|1\rangle$, and outputs a superposition state, denoted as $|+\rangle$ or $|-\rangle$.

$$|+\rangle \text{ state is } \frac{(|0\rangle + |1\rangle)}{\sqrt{2}} \text{ , and } |-\rangle \text{ is } \frac{(|0\rangle - |1\rangle)}{\sqrt{2}}.$$

Let us see how this happens:

Hadamard gate rotates the qubit at state $|0\rangle$ around Y-axis by 90^0 and it lands on positive X-axis. So, θ is 90^0 (refer *Figure 4.1*). The rotation around Z-axis is 0. So, ϕ is 0. Let us look at the equation: $|\psi\rangle = \cos\frac{\theta}{2}\,|0\rangle + e^{i\phi}\,\sin\frac{\theta}{2}\,|1\rangle$

If we substitute the values,

$$|\psi\rangle = \cos\frac{90}{2}\,|0\rangle + e^{i.0}\,\sin\frac{90}{2}\,|1\rangle \;\blacktriangleright\; |\psi\rangle = \tfrac{1}{\sqrt{2}}(|0\rangle + |1\rangle)$$

$$(\,|+\rangle\,)$$

If the qubit is at $|1\rangle$, the same operation by Hadamard gate will land the qubit on negative X-axis. θ is still 90^0, but ϕ is 1800. Substituting the values in the equation:

$$|\psi\rangle = \cos\frac{\theta}{2}\,|0\rangle + e^{i\phi}\,\sin\frac{\theta}{2}\,|1\rangle,$$

we get:

$$|\psi\rangle = \cos\frac{90}{2}\,|0\rangle + e^{i.\pi}\,\sin\frac{90}{2}\,|1\rangle$$

Now, $e^{i.\pi} = \cos\pi + i.\sin\pi = -1$

This will yield $\blacktriangleright\;\; |\psi\rangle = \tfrac{1}{\sqrt{2}}(|0\rangle - |1\rangle)$

The Hadamard gate is pivotal in creating entangled states in quantum computing. When combined with a Controlled-NOT (CNOT) gate, the Hadamard gate can entangle two qubits. Th gate is often employed in a variety of quantum algorithms, including quantum cryptography, quantum Fourier transform, amplitude amplification, among others.

- **CNOT gate (CX):** The Controlled-NOT gate (CNOT or CX gate) is a two-qubit gate that flips the target qubit's state if the control qubit is $|1\rangle$ and does nothing if the control qubit is $|0\rangle$. It is a controlled operation that changes the target qubit's state only when the control qubit is 1. This gate is essential for entangling two or more qubits, and is used in use cases such as quantum teleportation, quantum error correction, etc.

- **CY gate:** The CY gate, also known as the controlled-Y gate, is a two-qubit quantum gate that performs a conditional phase shift operation on the target qubit, based on the state of the control qubit. The CY gate works by applying a phase shift of π radians around the Y-axis to the target qubit if the control qubit is in the state $|1\rangle$. No phase shift is applied to the target qubit if the control qubit is in the state $|0\rangle$. In simple words, it applies Pauli Y operation on the target qubit only when the control qubit is 1. This gate is useful for creating entangled states, performing certain types of quantum algorithms, and correcting errors in quantum algorithms.

- **CZ gate:** The CZ gate performs a controlled phase shift operation on the target qubit, based on the state of the control qubit. It leaves the control qubit unchanged and applies a phase of π to the target qubit if the control qubit is in the state $|1\rangle$. However, it does nothing if the control qubit is $|0\rangle$. This gate is commonly used in quantum algorithms such as quantum error correction and quantum teleportation. It is also a building block for more complex multi-qubit gates.

- **SWAP gate:** As the name suggests, this gate swaps the states of two qubits. This gate is useful for reordering qubits in a quantum circuit, and it is also used in quantum algorithms such as quantum phase estimation and quantum search.

- **Toffoli gate (CCNOT):** The Toffoli gate is a three qubit gate that is also known as the **Controlled-Controlled-NOT (CCNOT)** gate. When both the control qubits are $|1\rangle$, this gate performs a NOT operation on the target qubit. Otherwise, it leaves the target qubit's state unchanged. Thus, it creates entanglement among three qubits. This gate is useful in implementing reversible classical logic operations without loss of information, which is essential for implementing classical logic in quantum systems, seamless integration between quantum and classical systems and robust error correction.

- **CCZ gate:** The quantum **Controlled-Controlled-Z (CCZ)** gate is a three qubit gate that executes a controlled phase shift operation on the third qubit based on the state of the two control qubits. The state of the target gate will remain unchanged except when the two control qubits are both in the state $|1\rangle$, in which case the third qubit will be phase shifted by π. This property makes the CCZ gate a crucial component in various quantum algorithms such as quantum error correction, reversible logic, and quantum teleportation.

- **Phase gates (S, T):** Phase gates allow manipulation of the phase of qubits and are used for precise control of the quantum state in quantum algorithms. They are single-qubit gates that introduce a phase shift of $\frac{+\pi}{n}$ to the qubit state, where 'n' is 4 for S gate and 8 for T gate. There are custom phase gates as well where 'n' can take any integer value. Phase gates are essential for implementing quantum algorithms such as the quantum Fourier transform and quantum phase estimation.

- **Rotation phase gates (RX, RY, RZ):** These are phase gates that induce a phase shift by rotating the state of qubit around X, Y and Z axis respectively. Unlike S and T gates, the phase angle is not pre-determined. It can be set to custom values by appropriate rotation around different axes.

- **Controlled phase gates (CRX, CRY, CRZ):** Controlled phase gates operate on multiple qubits simultaneously. The control qubit determines whether target qubit's phase has to be rotated or not. If the control qubit is $|1\rangle$, rotation is applied. These gates are essential in implementing algorithms such as quantum error correction and quantum information processing.

- **Inverse phase gates (S†, T†):** These are quantum gates that operate by applying a phase shift of $\frac{-\pi}{n}$ to qubits, as opposed to the usual $\frac{+\pi}{n}$ shift applied by regular phase gates. They are typically denoted as S† or T† and are the inverse operation of S and T gates. They are important components in quantum computing as they allow for the manipulation of the quantum state by applying different relative phases to the qubits. This, in turn, enables a wider range of operations and calculations to be performed, making them crucial in quantum algorithms and protocols.

- **Identity gate:** Quantum identity gate, also known as the I gate or the identity operator, is a basic quantum gate used in quantum computing. It is a single-qubit gate that leaves the state of the qubit unchanged. In other words, it performs the identity operation on the qubit, hence the name. Mathematically, the quantum identity gate is represented by the 2x2 identity matrix, which is a diagonal matrix with 1's on the main diagonal and 0's elsewhere. In a quantum circuit, the identity gate is typically used as a placeholder or a control for other gates. It can also be used to synchronize multiple qubits in a circuit. One of the key properties of quantum identity gate is that the gate is its own inverse. This makes it a useful component in quantum algorithms that require reversible operations.

To summarize, this list represents some of the most common types of quantum gates, each with its unique functionality and purpose. While the Pauli, Hadamard, and phase gates are used for preparing states and rotations, the C-series and Toffoli gates are crucial for implementing complex quantum operations and entangling qubits. Understanding these gates and their operations is essential for designing and implementing quantum circuits and algorithms.

Representation of gates as matrices

Unitary matrices serve as mathematical representations of quantum gates, and ensure that the total probabilities of all possible quantum state outcomes always sum to 1. This characteristic makes the quantum gate reversible; this is one of the defining properties of quantum gates. This means that the operation performed by the gate can be undone by applying the same gate again. In other words, the input and output states of the gate can be reversed, allowing the initial state to be recovered.

Let us look at the matrix representation of commonly used quantum gates:

- **Pauli gates:** All Pauli gates are represented by a 2-dimensional matrix.
    - **Pauli X:**

      Matrix:

      $$\begin{bmatrix} 0 & 1 \\ 1 & 0 \end{bmatrix}$$

      Symbol:

    - **Pauli-Y:**

      Matrix:

$$\begin{bmatrix} 0 & -i \\ i & 0 \end{bmatrix}$$

Symbol:

Y

o **Pauli Z:**
    Matrix:

$$\begin{bmatrix} 1 & 0 \\ 0 & -1 \end{bmatrix}$$

Symbol:

Z

- **Hadamard gate:**
    Matrix:

$$\frac{1}{\sqrt{2}} \begin{bmatrix} 1 & 1 \\ 1 & -1 \end{bmatrix}$$

Symbol:

H

- **CNOT gate:**
    Matrix:

$$\begin{bmatrix} 1 & 0 & 0 & 0 \\ 0 & 1 & 0 & 0 \\ 0 & 0 & 0 & 1 \\ 0 & 0 & 1 & 0 \end{bmatrix} \quad \text{or,} \quad \begin{bmatrix} 1 & 0 & 0 & 0 \\ 0 & 0 & 0 & 1 \\ 0 & 0 & 1 & 0 \\ 0 & 1 & 0 & 0 \end{bmatrix}$$

Symbol:

- **CY gate:**
    Matrix:

$$\begin{bmatrix} 1 & 0 & 0 & 0 \\ 0 & 1 & 0 & 0 \\ 0 & 0 & 0 & -i \\ 0 & 0 & i & 0 \end{bmatrix} \quad \text{or,} \quad \begin{bmatrix} 1 & 0 & 0 & 0 \\ 0 & 0 & 0 & -i \\ 0 & 0 & 1 & 0 \\ 0 & i & 0 & 0 \end{bmatrix}$$

Symbol:

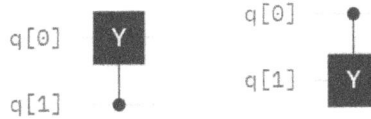

- **CZ gate:**
  Matrix:

$$\begin{bmatrix} 1 & 0 & 0 & 0 \\ 0 & 1 & 0 & 0 \\ 0 & 0 & 1 & 0 \\ 0 & 0 & 0 & -1 \end{bmatrix}$$

  Symbol:

- **SWAP gate:**
  Matrix:

$$\begin{bmatrix} 1 & 0 & 0 & 0 \\ 0 & 0 & 1 & 0 \\ 0 & 1 & 0 & 0 \\ 0 & 0 & 0 & 1 \end{bmatrix}$$

  Symbol:

- **Toffoli gate (CCNOT):**
  Matrix:

$$\begin{bmatrix} 1 & 0 & 0 & 0 & 0 & 0 & 0 & 0 \\ 0 & 1 & 0 & 0 & 0 & 0 & 0 & 0 \\ 0 & 0 & 1 & 0 & 0 & 0 & 0 & 0 \\ 0 & 0 & 0 & 1 & 0 & 0 & 0 & 0 \\ 0 & 0 & 0 & 0 & 1 & 0 & 0 & 0 \\ 0 & 0 & 0 & 0 & 0 & 1 & 0 & 0 \\ 0 & 0 & 0 & 0 & 0 & 0 & 0 & 1 \\ 0 & 0 & 0 & 0 & 0 & 0 & 1 & 0 \end{bmatrix} \text{ or, } \begin{bmatrix} 1 & 0 & 0 & 0 & 0 & 0 & 0 & 0 \\ 0 & 1 & 0 & 0 & 0 & 0 & 0 & 0 \\ 0 & 0 & 1 & 0 & 0 & 0 & 0 & 0 \\ 0 & 0 & 0 & 0 & 0 & 0 & 0 & 1 \\ 0 & 0 & 0 & 0 & 1 & 0 & 0 & 0 \\ 0 & 0 & 0 & 0 & 0 & 1 & 0 & 0 \\ 0 & 0 & 0 & 0 & 0 & 0 & 1 & 0 \\ 0 & 0 & 0 & 1 & 0 & 0 & 0 & 0 \end{bmatrix}$$

  Symbol:

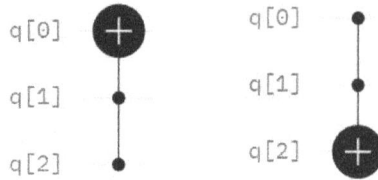

- **CCZ gate:**
  Matrix:

$$\begin{bmatrix} 1 & 0 & 0 & 0 & 0 & 0 & 0 & 0 \\ 0 & 1 & 0 & 0 & 0 & 0 & 0 & 0 \\ 0 & 0 & 1 & 0 & 0 & 0 & 0 & 0 \\ 0 & 0 & 0 & 1 & 0 & 0 & 0 & 0 \\ 0 & 0 & 0 & 0 & 1 & 0 & 0 & 0 \\ 0 & 0 & 0 & 0 & 0 & 1 & 0 & 0 \\ 0 & 0 & 0 & 0 & 0 & 0 & 1 & 0 \\ 0 & 0 & 0 & 0 & 0 & 0 & 0 & -1 \end{bmatrix}$$

  Symbol:

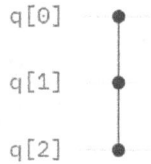

- **Phase gates:**
  - **S gate:**
    Matrix:

$$\begin{bmatrix} 1 & 0 \\ 0 & i \end{bmatrix}$$

    Symbol:

  - **T gate:**
    Matrix:

$$\begin{bmatrix} 1 & 0 \\ 0 & e^{i\Pi/4} \end{bmatrix}$$

    Symbol:

- **Identity gate:**
  Matrix:

$$\begin{bmatrix} 1 & 0 \\ 0 & 1 \end{bmatrix}$$

  Symbol:

$$\boxed{I}$$

Kronecker product

The Kronecker product is a mathematical operation that plays a crucial role in the field of quantum computing. This concept is named after *Leopold Kronecker*, a renowned mathematician, in the 19th century. Its application in the world of quantum computing has been revolutionary. In quantum computing, the basic building blocks are qubits, which exist in a state of superposition. This feature enables quantum computers to execute complex calculations at an exponentially faster rate than classical computers. The Kronecker product comes into play when we need to represent a system with multiple qubits. Similar to how classical computers use bits to represent information, quantum computers use qubits to encode data. However, in quantum computing, qubits can be entangled with each other, meaning that the state of one qubit can affect the state of another qubit. This entanglement is key to quantum computing's power, as it allows for more efficient calculations. To represent a system with two or more qubits, we need to use the Kronecker product to combine the states of individual qubits into a single, larger state. This process allows for the representation of more complex and larger quantum systems, making it an essential tool in quantum computing algorithms. Moreover, the Kronecker product is also used in quantum gates, which are operations that manipulate the state of qubits. These gates are the fundamental operations that enable quantum computers to perform calculations. The Kronecker product helps in constructing gates that act on multiple qubits simultaneously, making quantum computation even more efficient. In addition to its use in quantum gates and representing qubit states, the Kronecker product is also essential in designing quantum error correcting codes, which are crucial for maintaining the delicate quantum states and protecting them from noise and unwanted interactions. In effect, the Kronecker product is a powerful tool in quantum computing that has enabled the development of revolutionary algorithms and technologies. Its ability to combine qubits and represent the state of multiparticle quantum systems has helped pave the way for the advancement of this cutting-edge field. As quantum computing continues to evolve and push the boundaries of traditional computing, the Kronecker product remains a fundamental concept in its development.

Kronecker product is denoted by the symbol $\otimes$ and is also called tensor product in quantum theory. It is a product of two matrices or vectors. In Kronecker product, each element from the first matrix is multiplied with the entire second matrix. Let us look at an example of how it is applied to combine states of multiple qubits:

Consider two qubits, one having a state $S1 = \begin{bmatrix} S11 \\ S12 \end{bmatrix}$ and the other having the state $S2 = \begin{bmatrix} S21 \\ S22 \\ S23 \end{bmatrix}$. The Kronecker product of the two states is as follows:

$$S1 \otimes S2 \;=\; \begin{bmatrix} S11 \begin{bmatrix} S21 \\ S22 \\ S23 \end{bmatrix} \\ \\ S12 \begin{bmatrix} S21 \\ S22 \\ S23 \end{bmatrix} \end{bmatrix} \;=\; \begin{bmatrix} S11S21 \\ S11S22 \\ S11S23 \\ S12S21 \\ S12S22 \\ S12S23 \end{bmatrix}$$

Let us take an example where S1 is in state $|0\rangle$ and S2 is $|00\rangle + |01\rangle + |10\rangle + |11\rangle$.

The ket state is represented in matrix form in the follow way: the top row in matrix represents the first state, the second row represents the second state, and so on. Therefore, S1 in matrix form will be:

$\begin{bmatrix} 1. |0\rangle \\ 0. |1\rangle \end{bmatrix}$, where 1 and 0 are amplitudes corresponding to the states $|0\rangle$ and $|1\rangle$. Since S1 has just state $|0\rangle$, hence, the amplitude for state $|1\rangle$ is 0.

Similarly, S2 can be represented as $\begin{bmatrix} |00\rangle \\ |01\rangle \\ |10\rangle \\ |11\rangle \end{bmatrix}$.

Their Kronecker product will be:

$$\begin{bmatrix} 1. |0\rangle \\ 0. |1\rangle \end{bmatrix} \otimes \begin{bmatrix} |00\rangle \\ |01\rangle \\ |10\rangle \\ |11\rangle \end{bmatrix} \;=\; \begin{bmatrix} 1. |000\rangle \\ 1. |001\rangle \\ 1. |010\rangle \\ 1. |011\rangle \\ 0. |100\rangle \\ 0. |101\rangle \\ 0. |110\rangle \\ 0. |111\rangle \end{bmatrix} \;=\; \begin{bmatrix} |000\rangle \\ |001\rangle \\ |010\rangle \\ |011\rangle \\ 0 \\ 0 \\ 0 \\ 0 \end{bmatrix}$$

The same result can be achieved by multiplying the two states arithmetically using ket notations.

If S1 is $|0\rangle$ and S2 is $(|00\rangle + |01\rangle + |10\rangle + |11\rangle)$, then S1 x S2 is $(|00\rangle + |01\rangle + |10\rangle + |11\rangle)$.

Let us look at another example of how Kronecker product is applied to combine multiple quantum gates to form composite gates, which then manipulates the quantum state of qubits.

Assume two qubits, both at state $|0\rangle$. Pauli X gate and Pauli Z gate are respectively applied to the two qubits.

$$\text{Pauli X} \otimes \text{Pauli Z} = \begin{bmatrix} 0 & 1 \\ 1 & 0 \end{bmatrix} \otimes \begin{bmatrix} 1 & 0 \\ 0 & -1 \end{bmatrix} = \begin{bmatrix} 0 & 0 & 1 & 0 \\ 0 & 0 & 0 & -1 \\ 1 & 0 & 0 & 0 \\ 0 & -1 & 0 & 0 \end{bmatrix}$$

The combined state of the two qubits is $|00\rangle$, which in matrix form is $\begin{bmatrix} 1.|00\rangle \\ 0.|01\rangle \\ 0.|10\rangle \\ 0.|11\rangle \end{bmatrix}$

Apply the composite gate on the two qubits using standard matrix multiplication.

Note: Standard matrix multiplication is employed to manipulate qubit state by quantum gates.

$$\begin{bmatrix} 0 & 0 & 1 & 0 \\ 0 & 0 & 0 & -1 \\ 1 & 0 & 0 & 0 \\ 0 & -1 & 0 & 0 \end{bmatrix} \times \begin{bmatrix} 1.|00\rangle \\ 0.|01\rangle \\ 0.|10\rangle \\ 0.|11\rangle \end{bmatrix} = \begin{bmatrix} 0.|00\rangle \\ 0.|01\rangle \\ 1.|10\rangle \\ 0.|11\rangle \end{bmatrix} \Rightarrow |10\rangle$$

The preceding result is correct. Pauli X on the first qubit flips the state from to . Meanwhile Pauli Z has no effect on , and so the state will continue to be .

Therefore, the final state is .

Conclusion

This chapter has provided a comprehensive overview of quantum gates and their significance in the realm of quantum computing. By delving into the mathematical representation of quantum gates as matrices, the use of unitary gates, and the visualization of qubits on the Bloch sphere, a deeper understanding of the fundamental components of quantum computing has been achieved. Furthermore, the discussion on the different types of quantum gates and the use of Kronecker product has equipped readers with the necessary knowledge to perform composite quantum operations. With this knowledge, readers can now begin to explore more advanced topics in quantum computing. The upcoming chapter focuses on the IBM Q cloud and its associated tools and frameworks, including the GUI-based composer and the Qiskit SDK.

Multiple choice questions

1. **What is the primary function of quantum gates in a quantum system?**

   a. To store information like classical bits.

   b. To operate strictly on 0s and 1s.

   c. To solve only problems that classical computers can handle.

   d. To manipulate qubits for executing quantum algorithms.

2. **What is the mathematical definition of a unitary matrix U?**

   a. A matrix U is unitary if its determinant is zero.

   b. A matrix U is unitary if its transpose is equal to its inverse.

   c. A matrix U is unitary if its conjugate transpose (U*) is also its inverse, meaning U*U=UU*=I, where I is the identity matrix.

   d. A matrix U is unitary if it only contains real numbers.

3. **On the Bloch sphere, what do the points located on the surface represent?**

   a. Mixed states of the system

   b. Superposition states of 0 and 1

   c. Pure states of the quantum system

   d. Quantum operations and algorithms

4. **Which of the following statements about quantum gates is incorrect?**

   a. Single-qubit gates are represented as 2x2 unitary matrices and rotate the state of a qubit on the Bloch sphere.

   b. Measurement gates can be used multiple times in a quantum circuit to repeatedly check a qubit's state.

   c. Entangling gates are a type of multi-qubit gate that create correlations between qubits.

   d. Universal gates are a set of gates that can be used to implement any quantum operation.

5. **What is the primary function of the Kronecker product in representing a system with multiple qubits in quantum computing?**

   a. To combine the states of individual qubits into a single, larger state.

   b. To separate the states of individual qubits.

   c. To convert qubits into classical bits.

   d. To reduce the number of qubits in a system.

Answer key

1. d
2. c
3. c
4. b
5. a

Questions

1. Explain the key advantage that quantum gates have over classical gates.

   Answer: The key advantage that quantum gates have over classical gates is their ability to perform computations on multiple states simultaneously (quantum superposition) and to enable complex parallel computations through entanglement. This allows quantum computers to process and manipulate vastly larger amounts of information in parallel than classical gates, unlocking new computational possibilities.

2. What makes a quantum gate reversible?

   Answer: A quantum gate is reversible because of the property of the unitary matrix that represents it.

3. In the Bloch sphere, what does the angle of rotation ϕ around the Z-axis represent?

   Answer: The Phase.

4. Explain why Measurement gates can only be used once in a quantum circuit.

   Answer: Measurement gates collapse the qubit's superposition state into one of its basis states (0 or 1) and project the qubit's state onto a specific basis. Because this process changes the qubit's state, it can only be performed once.

5. What is the fundamental difference in function between single-qubit gates (like Pauli, Hadamard, Phase) and multi-qubit controlled gates (like CNOT, Toffoli) in quantum computing?

   Answer: Single-qubit gates act on individual qubits, performing arbitrary unitary operations such as rotations and phase shifts, thereby changing the state of a single qubit without reference to others. In contrast, multi-qubit-controlled gates (like CNOT and Toffoli) apply operations on one or more qubits conditional on the state(s) of one or more other "control" qubits, thus enabling entanglement and essential quantum logic operations.

Join our Discord space

Join our Discord workspace for latest updates, offers, tech happenings around the world, new releases, and sessions with the authors:

https://discord.bpbonline.com

CHAPTER 5

Introduction to Qiskit and IBM Q

Introduction

Quantum computing is revolutionizing how we approach complex computational problems, offering unprecedented capabilities that transcend classical computing limitations. Power frameworks and tools developed by industry leaders such as IBM and Google are central to this revolution. This chapter discusses two pivotal components of the quantum computing ecosystem: Qiskit and IBM Q. We will explore how these tools, alongside essential technologies such as Python and Jupyter Notebook, empower researchers, developers and enthusiasts to harness the potential of quantum computing.

Structure

The following topics are covered in this chapter:

- Tools in quantum computing
- Introduction to programming with Qiskit
- Building quantum circuits
- Overview of Quantum Composer

Objectives

This chapter aims to provide readers with a thorough understanding of the tools and frameworks critical to quantum computing, including Python, Jupyter Notebook, Qiskit, and IBM Q. By the end of the chapter, readers will be able to set up Python and Jupyter Notebook environments for quantum computing development. Also, they will be able to use Qiskit to create, simulate, and optimize quantum circuits. The reader will understand the components of IBM Q, such as Quantum Composer and Quantum Lab, and their applications in quantum programming. Additionally, you will gain knowledge on building and analyzing quantum circuits using a variety of gates and operations, and learn to leverage the **Composer Operations Glossary** to utilize quantum gates and non-unitary operations effectively.

These outcomes will empower readers to develop quantum algorithms, experiment with quantum circuits, and engage with IBM's quantum computing platforms to solve real-world problems.

Tools in quantum computing

Quantum computing tools provide an accessible way to develop and test quantum algorithms. Python, Jupyter Notebooks, and Qiskit enable users to write and simulate quantum circuits, while IBM Quantum Composer offers a visual interface to design and run them on real quantum hardware.

Python in quantum computing

Python, renowned for its simplicity and versatility, serves as the backbone of quantum computing development. Its extensive library ecosystem, readability, and ease of integration make it the preferred language for implementing quantum algorithms and managing quantum circuits. Beyond just programming, Python plays a crucial role in quantum research, enabling tasks such as quantum optimization, quantum machine learning, and quantum data analysis. It provides the foundation for frameworks like Qiskit and Cirq, allowing seamless interaction with quantum simulators and real hardware.

Jupyter Notebook in quantum computing

Jupyter Notebook is an interactive web application that enhances the quantum computing experience by integrating live code execution, rich text, and visualizations into a single document. It provides an ideal environment for experimenting with quantum circuits, documenting research, and sharing results. IBM Q seamlessly integrates with Jupyter, enabling users to write, test, and execute Qiskit code efficiently. This hands-on approach simplifies debugging, enhances visualization of complex quantum algorithms, and fosters an interactive learning experience.

IBM Qiskit open-source quantum framework

Qiskit is IBM's open-source quantum computing framework, designed to make quantum computing accessible to researchers, developers, and educators. It provides a robust set of tools for developing, simulating, and executing quantum programs on both simulators and real quantum hardware via IBM Q.

Qiskit consists of four key components:

- **Qiskit Terra:** For building and optimizing quantum circuits.
- **Qiskit Aer:** For high-performance simulation of quantum computations.
- **Qiskit Ignis:** For error correction and noise mitigation in quantum systems.
- **Qiskit Aqua:** For implementing quantum algorithms across various domains, including **drug discovery, financial modeling, optimization problems, and machine learning**.

By integrating with IBM Q, Qiskit allows users to test and execute their quantum algorithms on actual quantum processors, bridging the gap between theoretical research and real-world applications. Its versatility and comprehensive toolset make it an essential resource for quantum computing development.

IBM Q cloud-based quantum computing access

IBM Q is IBM's quantum computing platform that provides cloud-based access to real quantum processors, enabling users to design, test, and execute quantum circuits. The platform supports both **free-tier access for beginners** and **paid access for advanced users** requiring greater computational power.

IBM Q grants access to **cutting-edge quantum hardware**, including processors built on architectures like **Falcon (27 qubits), Hummingbird (65 qubits), and Eagle (127 qubits)**, with more powerful systems under development.

The platform includes two key tools:

- **Quantum Composer:** A user-friendly graphical interface that allows users to construct and visualize quantum circuits using a drag-and-drop approach, making quantum computing more accessible to beginners and educators.
- **Quantum Lab:** An integrated development environment powered by Jupyter Notebooks, offering advanced capabilities for writing, testing, and running quantum algorithms on IBM's quantum systems.

This chapter provides an in-depth exploration of these tools and frameworks, demonstrating how they collectively advance quantum computing. By understanding the roles of **Python, Jupyter Notebook, Qiskit, and IBM Q**, readers will gain the knowledge needed to navigate and contribute to this rapidly evolving field.

Getting started with Qiskit and IBM Quantum

You can write your Qiskit code in a Jupyter Notebook, where you can design and simulate quantum circuits. Once ready, you can execute these circuits on IBM Q's real quantum hardware or simulators via Qiskit's **application programming interface (API)**.

For further learning, you can explore:

- IBM Quantum Experience for hands-on access to real quantum systems.
- Qiskit textbook for structured learning materials and tutorials.
- Qiskit documentation for API references and example projects.

Introduction to programming with Qiskit

Qiskit is designed to be accessible to both quantum computing novices and experts, offering a Python-based interface for quantum circuit construction, execution, and optimization.

Python setup for Qiskit and Quantum Lab

To start with Qiskit and Cirq, you need to have Python installed in your system along with a few essential packages. The following is a step-by-step guide to help you set up your environment for using these powerful quantum computing frameworks:

1. **Install Python:**
   a. **Download Python:**
      i. Go to the official Python website(**https://www.python.org/**).
      ii. Navigate to the **Downloads** section.
      iii. Download the latest stable version of Python for your operating system (Windows, macOS, or Linux).
   b. **Install Python:**
      i. Run the downloaded installer.
      ii. During installation, ensure you check the box that says **Add Python to PATH**. This makes it easier to run Python from the command line.
2. **Install a virtual environment (optional but recommended):** Creating a virtual environment helps to manage dependencies and avoid conflicts between different projects. The steps are:
   a. **Install virtualenv:** Open your command prompt (Windows) or terminal (macOS or Linux) and run:

      ```
      pip install virtualenv
      ```
   b. Create a virtual environment

    c. **Navigate to your project directory**:

```
cd /path/to/your/project
```

    d. **Create a virtual environment:**

```
virtualenv venv
```

    e. **Activate the virtual environment:**

- **On Windows:**
  - ```
    venv\Scripts\activate
    ```
- **On macOS or Linux:**
  - ```
    source venv/bin/activate
    ```

3. **Install Jupyter Notebook:** Jupyter Notebook provides an interactive environment to write and run your code.

    a. **Install Jupyter:**

```
pip install jupyter
```

    b. **Start Jupyter Notebook:**

```
jupyter notebook
```

This command will open the Jupyter Notebook interface in your default web browser.

4. **Install Qiskit:** Qiskit is IBM's open-source quantum computing framework. To install Qiskit, follow these steps:

    a. **Install Qiskit:**

```
pip install qiskit
```

    b. **Verify Qiskit installation:**

Open a Jupyter Notebook and run the following code to ensure Qiskit is installed correctly:

```
import qiskit
print(qiskit.__version__)
```

    c. If you plan to run jobs on quantum hardware, also install Qiskit Runtime.

```
pip install qiskit-ibm-runtime
```

    d. If you intend to use visualization functionality or Jupyter Notebooks, it is recommended to install Qiskit with the extra visualization support ('qiskit[visualization]').

```
pip install qiskit[visualization]
```

Components of Qiskit

Qiskit consists of several modules, as shown in *Figure 5.1*, each serving a distinct purpose within the framework. The following are the components of Qiskit:

- **Qiskit Terra:**
  - **Description:** Qiskit Terra is the core module of Qiskit, providing foundational tools for quantum circuit construction, optimization and execution.
  - **Key features**:
    - Quantum circuit construction using a high-level Python interface.
    - Simulation of quantum circuits on local and remote backends (simulators and real quantum devices).
    - Optimization tools for compiling quantum circuits to target specific quantum hardware architectures.
    - Integration with classical computing for hybrid quantum-classical algorithms.
- **Qiskit Aer:**
  - **Description:** Qiskit Aer is a high-performance simulator framework for quantum circuits in Qiskit. It supports noiseless and noisy simulations, essential for understanding the impact of errors in quantum computations.
  - **Key features:**
    - Various simulation backends including state vector simulators, unitary simulators, and noise models.
    - Support for parallel execution to accelerate large-scale quantum circuit simulations.
- **Qiskit Ignis:**
  - **Description:** Qiskit Ignis focuses on quantum error correction and mitigation techniques. It provides tools for studying and improving the performance of quantum systems through error characterization and correction.
  - **Key features:**
    - Implementation of quantum error correction codes (e.g., surface codes, repetition codes).
    - Error mitigation techniques to reduce the impact of noise and errors on quantum computations.
- **Qiskit Aqua:**
  - **Description:** Qiskit Aqua is dedicated to quantum applications in domains such as optimization, chemistry, finance and machine learning. It offers

high-level tools and algorithms for solving specific problems using quantum computing techniques.

- o **Key features:**
  - ▪ Quantum algorithms including **Variational Quantum Eigensolver** (**VQE**), **Quantum Approximate Optimization Algorithm** (**QAOA**) and Grover's algorithm.
  - ▪ Domain-specific modules for tasks such as quantum chemistry simulations and portfolio optimization.

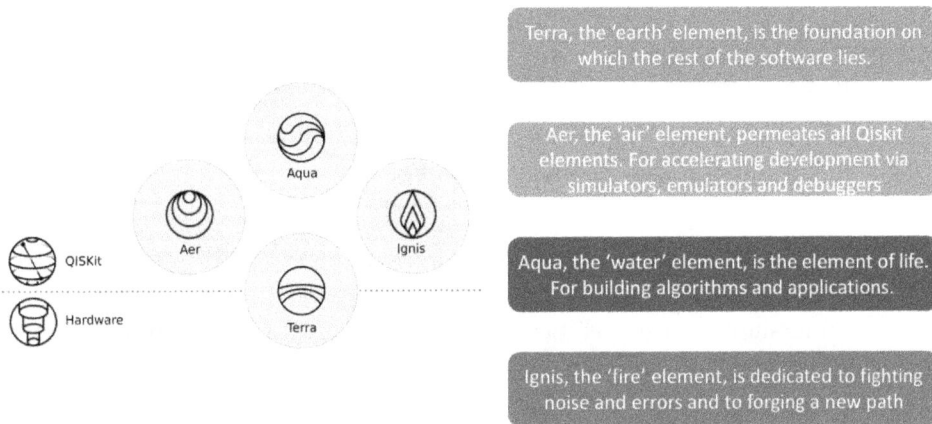

Figure 5.1: *Qiskit elements*

Running Hello World in Qiskit

Once Qiskit is installed, you can run a simple **Hello World** program to verify the setup. Following is an example:

- **Map the problem to a quantum-native format:** In quantum programming, quantum circuits are used to represent quantum instructions, while operators correspond to the observables to be measured. Typically, you create a new quantum circuit object and add instructions to it sequentially. The following example demonstrates how to create a Bell state, a fully entangled state of two qubits:

  o **Note on bit ordering:** The Qiskit framework adopts a **least significant bit** (**LSb**) convention for bit numbering. **Let us look at LSb notation in Qiskit and its impact on quantum computation.**

  The Qiskit framework adopts a **LSb convention** for bit numbering, meaning that qubit indices are ordered from right to left. This notation is important for understanding measurement results and how quantum circuits map onto classical registers.

Example: Bit ordering in quantum computation

Consider a simple **Bell state** circuit using two qubits:

```
from qiskit import QuantumCircuit, Aer, execute


qc = QuantumCircuit(2)
qc.h(0)  # Apply Hadamard gate to qubit 0
qc.cx(0, 1)  # Apply CNOT gate with qubit 0 as control and qubit 1
as target
qc.measure_all()
qc.draw('mpl')
```

In Qiskit's LSb convention, qubit *0* is the rightmost bit when measured. This affects how results are interpreted. For example, if the output is *01*, it means qubit 1 is in state $|0\rangle$ and qubit 0 is in state $|1\rangle$).

This ordering differs from other frameworks that use **most significant bit (MSb) notation**, where the leftmost bit represents the lowest-indexed qubit. Understanding this distinction helps avoid confusion when comparing results or working across different quantum computing platforms.

○   In this system, the nth bit corresponds to the value $2\text{\textasciicircum}n$ or $1 \ll n$.

```
from qiskit import QuantumCircuit

from qiskit.quantum_info import SparsePauliOp

from qiskit.transpiler.preset_passmanagers import generate_preset_
pass_manager

from qiskit_ibm_runtime import EstimatorV2 as Estimator


# Initialize a QuantumCircuit with two qubits
circuit = QuantumCircuit(2)


# Add a Hadamard gate to the first qubit (qubit 0)
circuit.h(0)


# Add a controlled-X (CNOT) gate targeting the second qubit (qubit
1), with the first qubit (qubit 0) as the control
circuit.cx(0, 1)


# Visualize the circuit using Matplotlib
```

```
circuit.draw('mpl')
```

The following is the output:

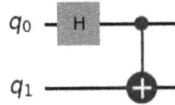

Figure 5.2: *Bell state quantum circuit*

When designing quantum circuit, you need to decide the type of data you want to retrieve post-execution.

```
# Qiskit provides two approaches for retrieving results: # either as a
probability distribution of the measured qubits
```

```
# or as the expectation value of a given observable.
```

```
# Design your circuit's measurement tasks accordingly using Qiskit primitives.
```

```
# Define six distinct observables
```

```
from qiskit.quantum_info import SparsePauliOp
```

```
observable_labels = ["IZ", "IX", "ZI", "XI", "ZZ", "XX"]
```

```
observables = [SparsePauliOp(label) for label in observable_labels]
```

The example measures expectation values using the qiskit.quantum_info submodule with operators (mathematical objects representing actions or processes that change a quantum state). This code creates six two-qubit Pauli operators: IZ, IX, ZI, XI, ZZ, and XX.

Here, the ZZ operator represents the tensor product Z⊗Z, which means measuring the Z observable on both qubit one and qubit zero simultaneously, providing information about their correlation. Expectation values like this are typically denoted as ⟨Z1Z0⟩.

If the state is entangled, the measurement of ⟨Z1Z0⟩ should yield 1. This indicates a strong correlation between the two qubits, characteristic of entanglement.

> **Note: When running quantum circuits on a device, it is crucial to optimize the instructions and minimize the circuit's overall depth (number of instructions) to reduce error and noise. Furthermore, the circuit's instructions must conform to the device's instruction set architecture (ISA), including its basis gates and qubit connectivity.**

The following example demonstrates how to set up a real quantum device for job execution and adjust the circuit and observables to be compatible with the device's ISA:

```
from qiskit_ibm_runtime import QiskitRuntimeService
```

```
# If your credentials are not already saved, you can use this line instead:
```

```
#service   =   QiskitRuntimeService(channel="ibm_quantum",   token="<MY_IBM_
QUANTUM_TOKEN>")

service = QiskitRuntimeService()


# Select the least busy operational backend that is not a simulator

backend = service.least_busy(simulator=False, operational=True)


# Optimize the circuit and map observables to the selected backend's ISA

pass_manager = generate_preset_pass_manager(backend=backend, optimization_
level=1)

isa_circuit = pass_manager.run(qc)
```

In Qiskit, the **pass manager** is responsible for optimizing quantum circuits before execution on a backend. It applies a series of transformations to improve circuit efficiency, reduce gate count, and account for hardware constraints.

Optimization levels and their impact

Qiskit provides four optimization levels, each balancing compilation time and circuit efficiency:

- **Level 0:** No optimization, only basic scheduling and mapping to hardware.
- **Level 1:** Light optimization, reducing gate count while preserving circuit structure.
- **Level 2:** More aggressive optimization, including gate cancellations and qubit reordering.
- **Level 3:** Maximum optimization, applying advanced techniques to minimize depth and noise effects, but may take longer to compile.

```
# Visualize the transformed circuit, hiding idle wires

isa_circuit.draw('mpl', idle_wires=False)
```

The following is the output:

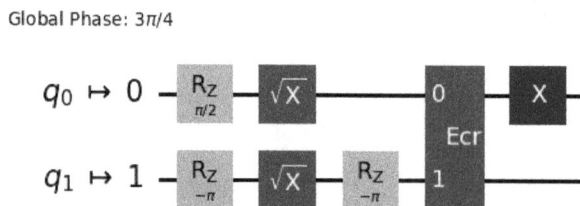

Figure 5.3: Optimized quantum circuit

After successfully running the Hello World example, you can proceed to explore more advanced operations using quantum primitives. These primitives allow you to execute quantum circuits multiple times and gather meaningful statistical data. The following explains how to use them:

- **Execute using the quantum primitives:** Quantum computers can produce random results, so it is typically necessary to run circuits multiple times to collect a sample of outputs. To estimate the value of an observable, you can use the estimator class. The estimator is one of two primary primitives in quantum computing, the other is sampler, which is used to gather data from a quantum computer. Both estimator and sampler objects have a **run()** method that executes a selection of circuits, observables, and parameters using a **Primitive Unified Block** (**PUB**).

- **Create an instance of the Estimator class:**

```
from qiskit_ibm_runtime import EstimatorV2 as Estimator


# Initialize the estimator with the selected backend
estimator = Estimator(backend=backend)
```

Note: **Use sampler if you need the probability distribution of measurement outcomes (e.g., simulating real quantum measurements). Use estimator if you need the expectation value of an observable (e.g., for variational algorithms in quantum chemistry or optimization).**

```
# Configure estimator options
estimator.options.resilience_level = 1
estimator.options.default_shots = 5000


# Adjust observables to align with the layout of the optimized circuit
aligned_observables = [
    observable.apply_layout(isa_circuit.layout) for observable in
    observables
]


# Submit a job with one circuit and multiple observables
job = estimator.run([(isa_circuit, aligned_observables)])


# Display the job ID for future reference
print(f">>> Job ID: {job.job_id()}")


# Example output:
```

```
# >>> Job ID: csbmgsbd3kwg008hdtp0

# The job ID can be used later to access the results
job_result = job.result()

# Retrieve the result for the single circuit and its corresponding
observables
circuit_result = job_result[0]
```

This example demonstrates how to use the estimator to calculate expectation values and the sampler to collect output data from a quantum circuit, illustrating how quantum computations can yield meaningful results through repeated sampling and estimation.

- **Analysis of results:** During the analysis phase, you typically refine your results using techniques such as measurement error mitigation or **Zero-noise extrapolation** (**ZNE**). These refined results can then be integrated into another workflow for deeper analysis or can be used to create visual representations of key data points. This phase is highly tailored to the specific challenges of your problem. For instance, in this case, you would create plots displaying each expectation value measured for our circuit:

```
# To retrieve the expectation values and standard deviations for the
observables defined in the estimator,
# access `circuit_result.data.evs` for expectation values and `circuit_
result.data.stds` for standard deviations.
# If using a sampler instead, you can use `circuit_result.data.meas.
get_counts()` to get a dictionary
# mapping bitstrings to their measurement counts.
# Refer to the "Get started with Sampler" documentation for additional
details.

# Importing Matplotlib for visualization
from matplotlib import pyplot as plt

# Extract the expectation values and standard deviations
values = circuit_result.data.evs
errors = circuit_result.data.stds

# Plotting the results
plt.plot(observable_labels, values, '-o')
```

```
plt.xlabel('Observables')
plt.ylabel('Expectation Values')
plt.title('Expectation Values of Observables')
plt.grid(True)
plt.show()
```

Notice that for qubits zero and one, the independent expectation values of both X and Z are zero, while the correlations (XX and ZZ) are one. This is a hallmark of quantum entanglement, as shown in *Figure 5.4*, which shows the measured expectation values for six different observables, and highlights the correlation between qubits in an entangled state.

The following is the output:

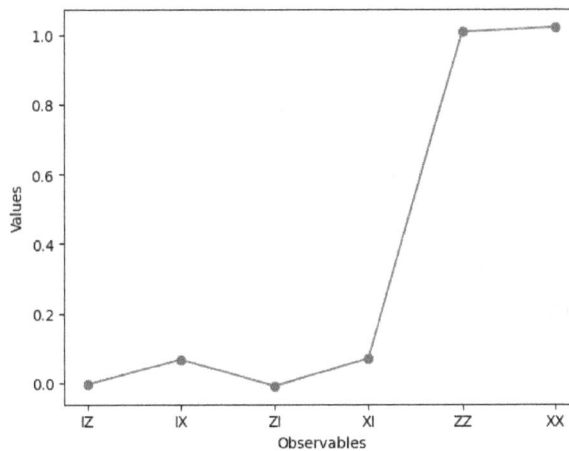

Figure 5.4: *Entanglement results*

Building quantum circuits

Quantum circuits are the foundational structures of quantum algorithms. They consist of qubits (quantum bits) and quantum gates that manipulate the qubits' states. In Qiskit, you can build circuits using the **QuantumCircuit** class, which provides methods to add various quantum gates and measurements.

Circuit design basics

Qiskit offers flexibility in managing circuits (and to some extent, operators) across different abstraction levels: abstract, virtual, physical, scheduled, and pulse programs. At the highest abstract level, circuits are task-focused within the circuit library. Operations can also be expressed abstractly using operators, isometries, and classical or Boolean functions. Virtual circuits translate these mathematical abstractions into a concrete representation using a specific gate set. At the physical level, these instructions are mapped onto physical qubits with instructions adapted to reflect the connectivity and native gates of the target hardware platform. Scheduled circuits incorporate timing details, while pulse programs represent signals on channels.

Let us see how to create a simple quantum circuit in Qiskit and visualize it:

```
From Qiskit, import QuantumCircuit:
circuit = QuantumCircuit(2)
circuit.qubits
circuit.draw('mpl')
```

The following is the output:

q_0 ──

q_1 ──

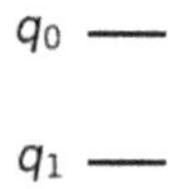

Figure 5.5: Quantum circuit initialization

```
circuit.x(0)   # Add X-gate to qubit 0
circuit.data
circuit.draw('mpl')
```

The following is the output:

q_0 ─ X ─

q_1 ───

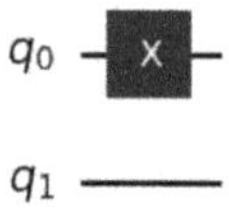

Figure 5.6: Single X-gate operation

```
circuit.x(0)   # Apply Pauli-X (NOT) gate to qubit 0
circuit.h(1)   # Apply Hadamard gate to qubit 1
circuit.cx(0, 1)  # Apply CNOT (Controlled-X) gate, using qubit 0 as control

circuit.draw('mpl')
```

Qiskit provides a wide range of quantum gates, including support for multi-controlled gates. The following demonstrates how to use some of these gates:

- **Gate functionality:**
    - **X-Gate (Pauli X):** Flips the qubit state ($|0\rangle$ ↔ $|1\rangle$)).
    - **H-Gate (Hadamard):** Creates superposition ($|0\rangle$ → $|+\rangle$, $|1\rangle$ → $|-\rangle$)).
    - **CNOT (CX-Gate):** Flips the target qubit **only if** the control qubit is in state $|1\rangle$.

- **Multi-controlled gates in Qiskit:** Qiskit supports **multi-controlled gates**, like the **multi-controlled X (MCXGate)** for larger circuits:

```
from qiskit.circuit.library import HGate, MCXGate

circuit = QuantumCircuit(4)


# Apply a Hadamard gate to qubit 0
circuit.append(HGate(), [0])


# Apply a Multi-Controlled X (MCX) gate
circuit.append(MCXGate(3), [0, 1, 2, 3])


circuit.draw('mpl')
```

- **Multi-controlled X-gate:** The X operation applies to the last qubit only when all control qubits are in state |1⟩.

```
from qiskit import QuantumCircuit

from qiskit.circuit.library import HGate, MCXGate

mcx = MCXGate(3)

hadamard = HGate()


circuit = QuantumCircuit(4)

circuit.append(hadamard, [0])

circuit.append(mcx, [0,1,2,3])

circuit.draw('mpl')
```

The following is the output:

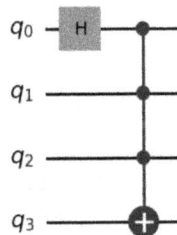

Figure 5.7: Multi-controlled gates

Classical feedforward and control flow

This guide outlines the capabilities in the Qiskit **software development kit (SDK)** for executing classical feedforward and control flow, often collectively known as dynamic circuits. Classical feedforward allows for the measurement of qubits during a circuit and subsequent quantum operations based on the measurement outcomes. Qiskit provides four control flow constructs for classical feedforward, each implemented as a method on quantum circuit:

- **If statement: `QuantumCircuit.if_test`**, use if when deciding between two possible operations based on a single classical result.

- **Switch statement: `QuantumCircuit.switch`**, use multiple if conditions to mimic a switch-case for handling multiple cases.

- **For loop: `QuantumCircuit.for_loop`**, use for to repeat a fixed number of quantum operations without relying on classical measurements.

- **While loop: `QuantumCircuit.while_loop`**, use while for iterative quantum operations based on classical feedback (e.g., error correction).

Let us look at each of them in detail:

- **If statement:** The if statement is used to conditionally execute operations based on the value of a classical bit or register.

  In the following example, a Hadamard gate is applied to a qubit, which is then measured. If the measurement result is one, an X gate is applied to the qubit, flipping it back to the zero state. The qubit is then measured again. The final measurement outcome should be 0 with 100% probability:

  ```
  # Importing necessary modules from Qiskit

  from   qiskit.circuit   import   QuantumCircuit,   QuantumRegister,
  ClassicalRegister

  from qiskit_aer.primitives import Sampler

  from qiskit.visualization import plot_histogram


  # Define a quantum register with one qubit and a classical register
  with one bit

  quantum_register = QuantumRegister(1)

  classical_register = ClassicalRegister(1)

  quantum_circuit = QuantumCircuit(quantum_register, classical_register)


  # Assign variables to the single qubit and classical bit for clarity

  qubit = quantum_register[0]

  classical_bit = classical_register[0]
  ```

```
# Add a Hadamard gate to the qubit
quantum_circuit.h(qubit)

# Perform a measurement from the qubit to the classical bit
quantum_circuit.measure(qubit, classical_bit)

# Add a conditional operation: apply an X gate to the qubit if the
classical bit equals 1
with quantum_circuit.if_test((classical_bit, 1)):
    quantum_circuit.x(qubit)

# Perform another measurement from the qubit to the classical bit
quantum_circuit.measure(qubit, classical_bit)

# Draw and display the circuit using Matplotlib
quantum_circuit.draw("mpl")
```

The following is the output:

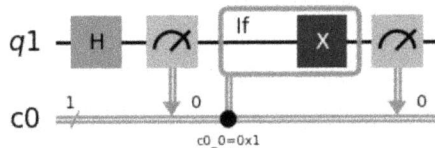

Figure 5.8: Conditional operation example

```
# Example output counts: {'0': 1000}

# Execute the circuit using the Sampler and obtain the quasi-probability
distributions
quasi_dists  =  Sampler().run(circuit,   shots=1000).result().quasi_
dists[0]

# Visualize the result using Matplotlib
plot_histogram(quasi_dists)

# The output will display the distribution as a histogram:
```

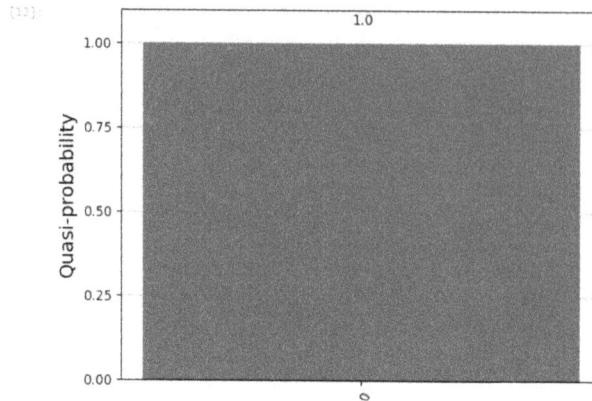

Figure 5.9: Measurement histogram

```
#Conditional if Statement with else
from qiskit import QuantumCircuit, ClassicalRegister

# Create a quantum circuit with 1 qubit and 1 classical bit
qc = QuantumCircuit(1, 1)

# Apply a Hadamard gate and measure
qc.h(0)
qc.measure(0, 0)

# Conditional statement: Apply X gate if measurement result is 1
with qc.if_test((0, 1)):  # Checks if classical bit 0 is 1
    qc.x(0)
with qc.else_():  # Else statement for completeness
    qc.h(0)
```

```
qc.draw('mpl')
```

#If the measurement result is 1, an X gate is applied. If the result is 0, an H gate is applied instead.

The **with** statement can accept an assignment target that acts as a context manager. This context manager can be stored and used later to create an **else** block, which is executed when the **if** block is not.

In the following example, we initialize registers with two qubits and two classical bits. A Hadamard gate is applied to the first qubit, which is then measured. If the measurement result is one, Hadamard gate is applied to the second qubit, otherwise, an X gate is applied to the second qubit. Finally, the second qubit is measured.

```python
# Define a quantum register with two qubits and a classical register
with two bits
qubits = QuantumRegister(2)
clbits = ClassicalRegister(2)
circuit = QuantumCircuit(qubits, clbits)

# Assign variables to the qubits and classical bits for clarity
(q0, q1) = qubits
(c0, c1) = clbits

# Apply a Hadamard gate to the first qubit
circuit.h(q0)

# Measure the first qubit and store the result in the first classical
bit
circuit.measure(q0, c0)

# Add a conditional block: if the first classical bit is 1, apply a
Hadamard gate to the second qubit
# Otherwise, apply an X gate to the second qubit
with circuit.if_test((c0, 1)) as else_:
    circuit.h(q1)
with else_:
    circuit.x(q1)

# Measure the second qubit and store the result in the second classical
bit
circuit.measure(q1, c1)

# Visualize the circuit using Matplotlib
circuit.draw("mpl")
```

The following is the output:

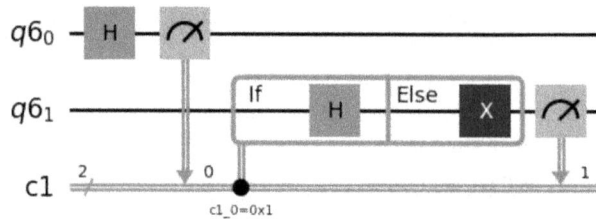

Figure 5.10: *Conditional Hadamard or X Operation*

```
# example output counts: {'01': 247, '11': 254, '10': 499}
```

The following is the output:

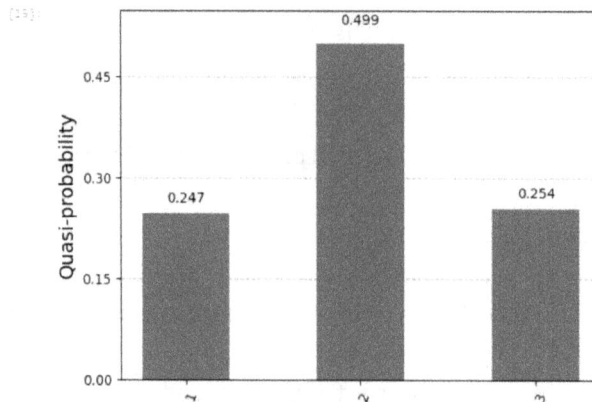

Figure 5.11: *Measurement probability of the Conditional Hadamard or X operation*

In addition to conditioning a single classical bit, you can also condition on the value of a classical register composed of multiple bits.

In the following example, Hadamard gates are applied to two qubits, which are then measured. If the result is 01 (meaning the first qubit is measured as one and the second qubit as zero), an X gate is applied to a third qubit. Finally, the third qubit is measured. For clarity, the condition is specified as the third classical bit being zero in the **if** statement. In the circuit diagram, the condition is shown with circles on the classical bits being conditioned on, a black circle indicates conditioning on one and a white circle indicates conditioning on zero.

```
# Create a quantum register with three qubits and a classical register
with three bits
qubits = QuantumRegister(3)
clbits = ClassicalRegister(3)
circuit = QuantumCircuit(qubits, clbits)
```

```
# Assign variables to the qubits and classical bits for clarity
(q0, q1, q2) = qubits
(c0, c1, c2) = clbits

# Apply Hadamard gates to the first two qubits
circuit.h([q0, q1])

# Measure the first and second qubits, storing results in the
corresponding classical bits
circuit.measure(q0, c0)
circuit.measure(q1, c1)

# Add a conditional operation: if the classical bits match the binary
value 0b001, apply an X gate to the third qubit
with circuit.if_test((clbits, 0b001)):
    circuit.x(q2)

# Measure the third qubit and store the result in the third classical
bit
circuit.measure(q2, c2)

# Visualize the circuit using Matplotlib
circuit.draw("mpl")
```

The following is the output:

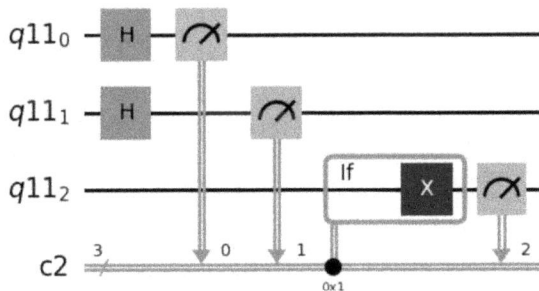

Figure 5.12: Multi-bit conditional operations

```
# example output counts: {'101': 258, '011': 258, '000': 252, '010':
232}
```

The following is the output:

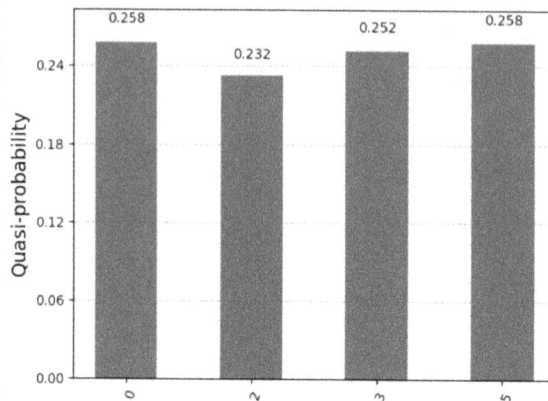

Figure 5.13 *Measurement probability of the multibit conditional operators*

Both Qiskit and OpenQASM support extended circuits, broadening the range of permissible operations to include real-time computations on classical values. Qiskit's tools for handling this expanded circuit family is given in detail in the classical feedforward and control flow section.

- **Switch statement:** The switch statement is used to select actions based on the value of a classical bit or register. Unlike an **if** statement, it allows for multiple cases in the branching logic. In the following example, Hadamard gate is applied to a qubit, which is then measured. If the result is zero, an X gate is applied to the qubit, if the result is one, a Z gate is applied. This ensures that the final measurement outcome is one with 100% probability, shown as follows:

```
# Create a quantum register with three qubits and a classical register
with three bits
qubits = QuantumRegister(3)
clbits = ClassicalRegister(3)
circuit = QuantumCircuit(qubits, clbits)

# Assign variables to the qubits and classical bits for clarity
(q0, q1, q2) = qubits
(c0, c1, c2) = clbits

# Apply Hadamard gates to the first two qubits
circuit.h([q0, q1])

# Measure the first and second qubits, storing results in the
corresponding classical bits
```

```
circuit.measure(q0, c0)
circuit.measure(q1, c1)


# Add a conditional operation: if the classical bits match the binary
value 0b001, apply an X gate to the third qubit
with circuit.if_test((clbits, 0b001)):
    circuit.x(q2)


# Measure the third qubit and store the result in the third classical
bit
circuit.measure(q2, c2)


# Visualize the circuit using Matplotlib
circuit.draw("mpl")
```

The following is the output:

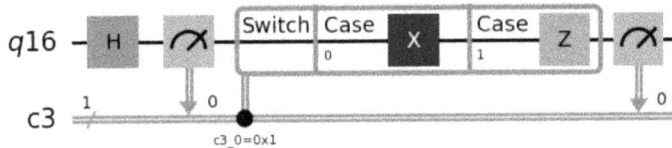

Figure 5.14: Switch statement

```
# example output counts: {'1': 1024}
```

Since the previous example used a single classical bit, there were only two possible cases, making it achievable with an if-else statement. The switch statement is particularly useful when branching on the value of a classical register composed of multiple bits. The example that we will see will demonstrate this, including how to construct a default case that is executed if none of the specified cases match. Note that in a switch statement, only one of the blocks is executed; there is no fallthrough.

In the following example, Hadamard gates are applied to two qubits, which are then measured. If the result is 00 or 11, a Z gate is applied to the third qubit. If the result is 01, a Y gate is applied. If none of these cases match, an X gate is applied. Finally, the third qubit is measured:

```
# Create a quantum register with three qubits and a classical register
with three bits
qubits = QuantumRegister(3)
clbits = ClassicalRegister(3)
```

```python
circuit = QuantumCircuit(qubits, clbits)

# Assign variables to the qubits and classical bits for clarity
(q0, q1, q2) = qubits
(c0, c1, c2) = clbits

# Apply Hadamard gates to the first two qubits
circuit.h([q0, q1])

# Measure the first and second qubits, storing the results in the
corresponding classical bits
circuit.measure(q0, c0)
circuit.measure(q1, c1)

# Implement a switch-case logic based on the classical register values
with circuit.switch(clbits) as case:
    with case(0b000, 0b011):  # If classical bits are 0b000 or 0b011,
apply a Z gate to the third qubit
        circuit.z(q2)
    with case(0b001):  # If classical bits are 0b001, apply a Y gate
to the third qubit
        circuit.y(q2)
    with case(case.DEFAULT):  # For all other cases, apply an X gate
to the third qubit
        circuit.x(q2)

# Measure the third qubit and store the result in the third classical
bit
circuit.measure(q2, c2)

# Visualize the circuit using Matplotlib
circuit.draw("mpl")
```

The following is the output:

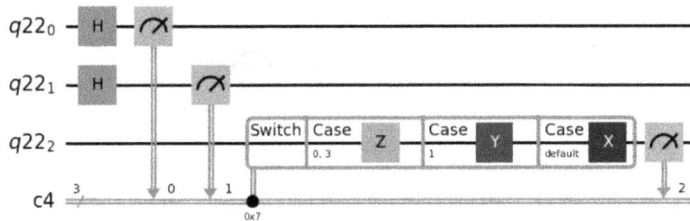

Figure 5.15: Extended switch conditional logic

```
# example output counts: {'101': 267, '110': 249, '011': 265, '000': 243}
```

The bitstrings with **higher counts** correspond to the states with **higher probability amplitudes** in the quantum superposition.

- **For loop:** A for loop is used to iterate over a sequence of classical values, performing specific operations during each iteration.

In the following example, a **for** loop is used to apply five X gates to a qubit, followed by a measurement. Since an odd number of X gates are applied, the qubit is flipped from the zero state to one state:

```
# Create a quantum register with one qubit and a classical register
with one bit
qubits = QuantumRegister(1)
clbits = ClassicalRegister(1)
circuit = QuantumCircuit(qubits, clbits)


# Assign variables to the single qubit and classical bit
(q0,) = qubits
(c0,) = clbits


# Apply a for-loop that repeats five iterations, applying an X gate to
the qubit in each iteration
with circuit.for_loop(range(5)) as _:
    circuit.x(q0)


# Measure the qubit and store the result in the classical bit
circuit.measure(q0, c0)


# Visualize the circuit using Matplotlib
circuit.draw("mpl")
```

The following is the output:

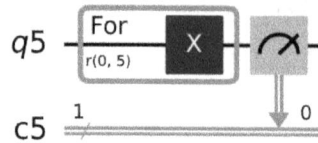

Figure 5.16: For loop operation

```
# example output counts: {'1': 1024}
```

- **While loop:** A **while** loop is used to repeat instructions as long as a specified condition is met. While loops do not run on quantum hardware—they are evaluated on classical control logic after measurement.

In the following example, Hadamard gates are applied to two qubits, followed by their measurement. A **while** loop is then used to repeat this procedure as long as the measurement outcome is 11. Consequently, the final measurement should never be 11, with the other outcomes appearing with approximately equal frequency:

```
# Create a quantum register with two qubits and a classical register
with two bits
qubits = QuantumRegister(2)
clbits = ClassicalRegister(2)
circuit = QuantumCircuit(qubits, clbits)


# Assign variables to the individual qubits and classical bits for
clarity
q0, q1 = qubits
c0, c1 = clbits


# Apply Hadamard gates to both qubits to create superposition
circuit.h([q0, q1])


# Measure the first qubit into the first classical bit and the second
qubit into the second classical bit
circuit.measure(q0, c0)
circuit.measure(q1, c1)


# Add a while loop that continues as long as the classical bits hold
the value 0b11
with circuit.while_loop((clbits, 0b11)):
```

```
# Inside the loop, reapply Hadamard gates to both qubits
circuit.h([q0, q1])
# Measure the qubits into their corresponding classical bits
circuit.measure(q0, c0)
circuit.measure(q1, c1)
```

```
# Visualize the circuit using Matplotlib
circuit.draw("mpl")
```

The following is the output:

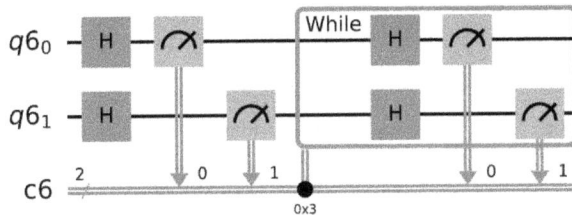

Figure 5.17: While loop operation

```
# example output counts: {'01': 334, '10': 368, '00': 322}
```

Qiskit's limitations on real quantum hardware

The following are some of Qiskit's limitations on real quantum hardware:

- **Control flow execution constraints:**
    - If and while are evaluated **on classical hardware** after measurement.
    - No **native quantum loops**; quantum circuits must be predefined before execution.
- **Noise and decoherence:** Real quantum devices suffer from **gate errors and qubit decoherence**, impacting execution reliability.
- **Limited qubit connectivity:** Some backends have restricted **qubit connectivity**, requiring additional **SWAP gates**, which increase circuit depth.

Grover's search using Qiskit

Amplitude amplification is a versatile quantum algorithm or subroutine that offers a quadratic speedup compared to several classical algorithms. Grover's algorithm was the first to showcase this advantage for unstructured search problems.

Practical applications of Grover's search

Grover's algorithm is a quantum search algorithm that provides a quadratic speedup for **unstructured search problems**. Some practical applications include:

- **Database search:** Finding a specific entry in an unsorted dataset faster than classical methods.

- **Cryptography:** Breaking symmetric encryption (e.g., cracking AES by searching for the correct key in fewer steps).

- **Pattern matching:** Speeding up search tasks in machine learning and optimization problems.

Understanding the Oracle with a real-world analogy

To formulate a Grover's search problem, an oracle function is needed to mark specific computational basis states as the ones we aim to find. Additionally, an amplification circuit enhances the amplitudes of these marked states while reducing the amplitudes of the others.

An **oracle** in Grover's algorithm is a **black box function** that identifies the correct solution by flipping its phase.

Imagine searching for a **marked card in a deck of playing cards**. Instead of flipping cards one by one (classical search), an oracle **magically highlights the correct card**, allowing Grover's algorithm to amplify its probability and find it faster.

The following example illustrates how to create Grover oracles and utilize the Grover operator from the Qiskit circuit library to set up a Grover's search instance efficiently. The runtime sampler primitive facilitates the seamless execution of Grover circuits:

```python
# Import standard Python libraries
import math


# Import necessary modules from Qiskit
from qiskit import QuantumCircuit
from qiskit.circuit.library import GroverOperator, MCMT, ZGate
from qiskit.visualization import plot_distribution


# Import required components from Qiskit Runtime
from qiskit_ibm_runtime import QiskitRuntimeService
from qiskit_ibm_runtime import SamplerV2 as Sampler
```

```
# Initialize the runtime service and select the backend with the shortest job
queue for hardware execution
service = QiskitRuntimeService(channel="ibm_quantum")
backend = service.least_busy(operational=True, simulator=False)
```

- o **operational=True** ensures only active quantum devices are considered.

- o **simulator=False** excludes simulators, selecting only real quantum processors.

- o **least_busy** sorts available devices by queue length and selects the one with the shortest wait time.

This method helps optimize execution time by avoiding heavily loaded backends.

```
# Display the name of the selected backend

print(backend.name)
```

Grover's algorithm leverages an oracle mechanism designed to identify specific target states to translate classical information into a quantum framework. Here is an overview of how this mapping process works:

- **Map classical inputs to a quantum problem:** Grover's algorithm utilizes an oracle that identifies specific computational basis states marked with a phase of -1. To mark the state corresponding to the binary representation **1 * N** (where all N bits are **1**), a controlled-Z gate or its multi-controlled counterpart over N qubits is employed. Marking basis states that include one or more **0's** in their binary representation involves applying X gates on the respective qubits before and after the controlled-Z gate, effectively creating an open-control condition on those qubits.

In the following code, we define an oracle that implements this marking process for one or more specified input basis states using their bit-string representation. The **multi-controlled multi-target** (**MCMT**) gate is utilized to realize the multi-controlled Z-gate operation:

```
def create_grover_oracle(marked_states):
    """

    Constructs a Grover oracle for identifying multiple marked states.

    Parameters:
        marked_states (str or list): Target states to be marked by the
    oracle.

    Returns:
        QuantumCircuit: A quantum circuit representing the Grover
    oracle.
    """
```

```
    # Ensure the input is treated as a list, even if a single string
is provided
    if not isinstance(marked_states, list):
        marked_states = [marked_states]

    # Determine the number of qubits required for the circuit
    num_qubits = len(marked_states[0])

    # Initialize a quantum circuit with the required number of qubits
    qc = QuantumCircuit(num_qubits)

    # Iterate through the marked states to encode them into the oracle
    for target_state in marked_states:
        # Reverse the target bit-string to align with Qiskit's bit-
ordering
        reversed_target = target_state[::-1]

        # Identify the positions of '0' bits in the reversed target
state
        zero_indices = [index for index in range(num_qubits) if
reversed_target[index] == "0"]

        # Apply X-gates to qubits corresponding to '0' bits, turning
them into open controls
        qc.x(zero_indices)

        # Add a multi-controlled Z gate to mark the state, using the
appropriate controls
        qc.compose(MCMT(ZGate(), num_qubits - 1, 1), inplace=True)
```

MCMT gates are multi-controlled multi-target gates, meaning they apply an operation to multiple target qubits based on the state of multiple control qubits. They are useful in Grover's algorithm, quantum arithmetic, and reversible computing.

```
        # Reapply X-gates to reset the qubits modified earlier
        qc.x(zero_indices)

    # Return the constructed quantum circuit
    return qc
```

- **Specific Grover's instance:** Now that we have the oracle function, we can define a specific instance of Grover search. In the following example, we will mark two computational states out of the eight available in a three qubit computational space:

```
# Define the list of marked states
target_states = ["011", "100"]
```

```
# Generate the Grover oracle for the specified states
grover_oracle_circuit = create_grover_oracle(target_states)
```

```
# Visualize the oracle circuit using Matplotlib with a specific style
grover_oracle_circuit.draw(output="mpl", style="iqp")
```

The following is the output:

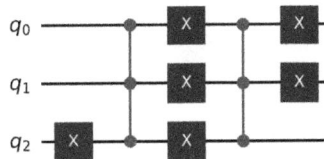

Figure 5.18: Grover Oracle

Grover operator

The built-in Qiskit Grover operator takes an oracle circuit and returns a circuit that is composed of the oracle circuit itself and a circuit that amplifies the states marked by the oracle. Here, we decompose the circuit to see the gates within the operator:

```
# Create the Grover operator using the constructed oracle
grover_operator = GroverOperator(grover_oracle_circuit)
```

```
# Decompose the Grover operator to display its internal structure and
visualize it
grover_operator.decompose().draw(output="mpl", style="iqp")
```

The following is the output:

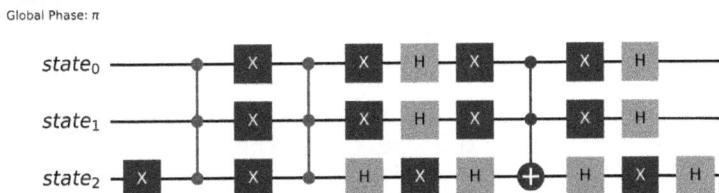

Figure 5.19: Grover operator

The provided visualization represents the quantum circuit for the **Diffusion operator** in Grover's algorithm:

- The **X gates** (blue) flip qubits to shift the amplitude distribution.
- The **Hadamard gates** (red) create and restore superpositions.
- The **controlled operations** (purple and blue) perform phase inversion.
- The **final Hadamard and X gates** return the marked state with higher probability.

Repeated applications of this `grover_op` circuit amplify the marked states, making them the most probable bit-strings in the output distribution from the circuit. There is an optimal number of such applications that is determined by the ratio of marked states to total number of possible computational states.

The following formula ensures that the algorithm achieves the highest probability of finding a marked state by balancing efficiency and accuracy:

```
optimal_num_iterations = math.floor(
    math.pi / (4 * math.asin(math.sqrt(len(marked_states) / 2**grover_op.num_
qubits)))
)
```

Full Grover circuit

A full Grover experiment begins by applying Hadamard gate to each qubit, creating an equal superposition of all possible computational basis states. This is followed by iteratively applying the Grover operator (**grover_op**) the optimal number of times. Here, we utilize the **QuantumCircuit.power (INT)**(integer value) method to efficiently repeat the application of the Grover operator:

```
# Initialize a quantum circuit with the same number of qubits as the Grover
operator
quantum_circuit = QuantumCircuit(grover_operator.num_qubits)

# Generate an equal superposition across all possible basis states
quantum_circuit.h(range(grover_operator.num_qubits))

# Apply the Grover operator for the calculated optimal number of iterations
quantum_circuit.compose(grover_operator.power(optimal_num_iterations),
inplace=True)

# Perform measurements on all the qubits in the circuit
quantum_circuit.measure_all()
```

```
# Visualize the complete quantum circuit using Matplotlib with the chosen
style
quantum_circuit.draw(output="mpl", style="iqp")
```

The following is the output:

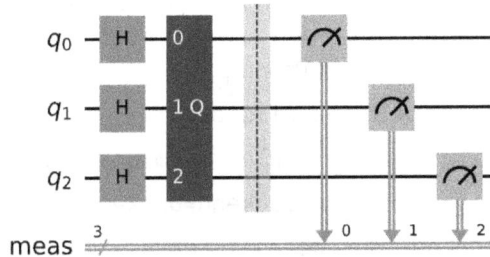

Figure 5.20: *Full Grover circuit*

- **Optimize problem for quantum execution using transpilers:** Transpiling is the process of converting a high-level quantum circuit into a form that can be executed on a specific quantum hardware backend. This involves optimizing the circuit to reduce the number of gates and adjusting the circuit layout to match the connectivity of the quantum device.

  Qiskit provides the transpile function, which takes a quantum circuit and a target backend as input and produces an optimized circuit. The process includes gate fusion, qubit reordering and other optimization techniques to enhance the circuit's performance.

  To execute quantum algorithms efficiently on actual quantum hardware, it is essential to adapt and optimize the quantum circuits for the specific constraints and capabilities of the target device. This step ensures that the circuits are both functional and optimized for performance. One key method to achieve this is through the process of transpilation:

  ```
  from qiskit.transpiler.preset_passmanagers import generate_preset_
  pass_manager

  # Extract the target configuration from the backend
  backend_target = backend.target

  # Create a preset pass manager with the specified target and optimization
  level
  pass_manager = generate_preset_pass_manager(target=backend_target,
  optimization_level=3)
  ```

```
# Apply the pass manager to optimize and transform the quantum circuit
optimized_circuit = pass_manager.run(quantum_circuit)
```

- **Execute using Qiskit primitives:** Amplitude amplification is a sampling task well-suited for execution using the runtime primitive called **Sampler**.

It is important to note that the **run()** method of the Qiskit Runtime's **SamplerV2** expects an iterable of PUBs. For a sampler, each PUB is an iterable formatted as (circuit, parameter_values). At its simplest, it requires a list of quantum circuits.

```
# For execution on a local simulator:
# Utilize the StatevectorSampler from qiskit.primitives instead
sampler_instance = Sampler(backend=backend)
sampler_instance.options.default_shots = 10_000

# Execute the sampler on the optimized circuit and retrieve the result
execution_result = sampler_instance.run([optimized_circuit]).result()

# Extract the measurement counts from the results
measurement_distribution = execution_result[0].data.meas.get_counts()

# Post-process and visualize the distribution in a classical format
plot_distribution(measurement_distribution)
```

The following is the output:

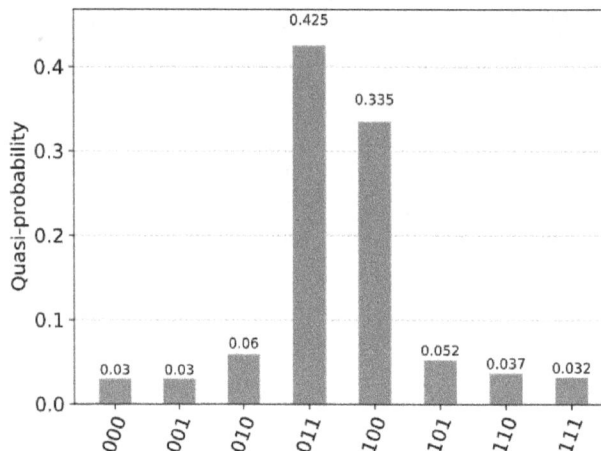

Figure 5.21: *Measurement from Grover's search with 3 Qubit operation*

Overview of Quantum Composer

The IBM Quantum Composer is an intuitive, user-friendly platform designed for both beginners and experts to experiment with quantum circuits. It provides a visual interface where users can easily design and simulate quantum algorithms without requiring in-depth programming knowledge. This makes it an ideal tool for exploring the principles of quantum computing and testing ideas in a hands-on manner.

Quantum Composer

IBM Quantum Composer is a graphical tool for quantum programming that enables users to construct quantum circuits by dragging and dropping operations. These circuits can then be executed on real quantum hardware or simulators.

Key features

The following are the key features of Quantum Composer:

- **Visualize qubit states:** Observes the state of qubits visually. Changes to your circuit are reflected in interactive q-sphere representations or histograms displaying measurement probabilities and state vector simulations.

- **Run on quantum hardware:** Executes your circuits on actual quantum hardware to experience the impact of device noise and other quantum effects.

- **Simulators versus real hardware:** Users can choose between:

  o **Single-shot statevector simulators** (for ideal, noise-free quantum state visualizations).

  o **Backend execution via "Setup and Run"** (for full, hardware-accurate quantum computations).

- **Inspect mode:** Step through the **evolution of qubit states** at each stage of computation, allowing for deeper analysis of how quantum gates affect state transformations.

- **Automated code generation:** Instead of manual coding, automatically generate equivalent OpenQASM or Python code based on the circuit designed using Quantum Composer as shown in *Figure 5.22*. This feature ensures that the generated code replicates the behavior of the graphical circuit seamlessly:

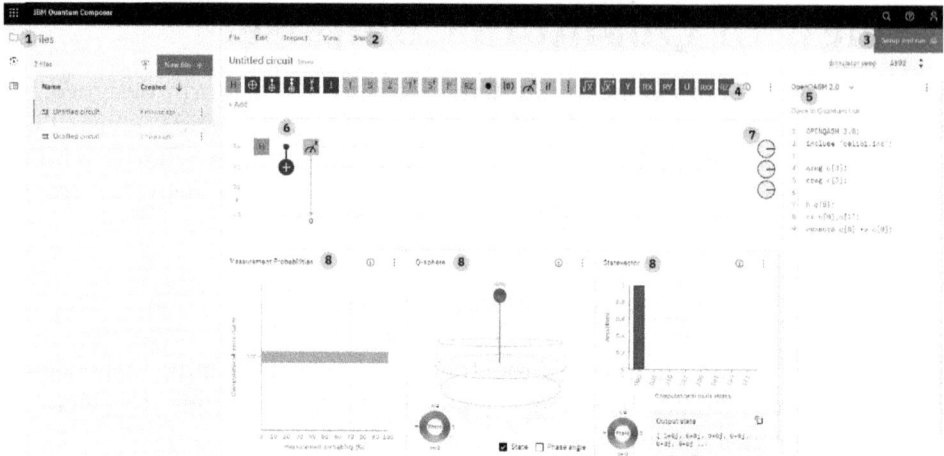

Figure 5.22: IBM Quantum Composer interface

- **Tools panel:** Utilize the side panel to access files, jobs, or documentation. Close the side panel by clicking the icon for the open tab.

- **Menu bar:** Access various menus to create new circuits, manage saved circuits and register, customize your workspace, and more.

- **Run area:** Adjust run settings and execute your circuit on a quantum system or simulator.

- **Composer files:** Automatically save and display the circuits you create in the composer files panel.

- **Circuit name:** Click here to assign a name to your circuit.

- **Operations catalog:** These are the fundamental elements used in quantum circuits. Drag and drop gates and operations onto the graphical circuit editor. Gates are color-coded for clarity, for instance, classical gates are dark blue, phase gates are light blue, and non-unitary operations are grey as shown in *Figure 5.23*. To explore available gates and operations, right-click on an operation and select **Info** to read its definition.

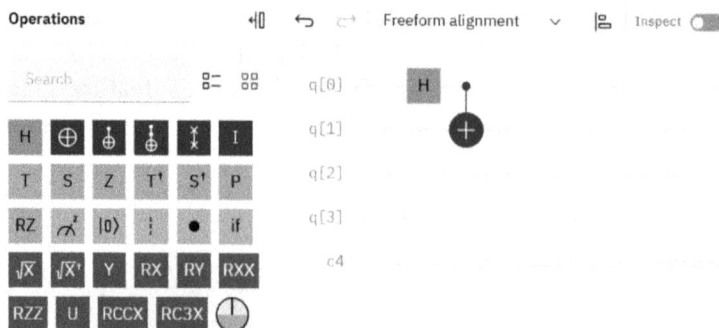

Figure 5.23: Quantum Composer operations

- **Code editor:** Open or close the code editor using the view menu. The code editor allows you to view and edit the OpenQASM or Qiskit code for the circuit.
- **Graphical circuit editor:** This is where you construct your quantum circuit. Drag gates and operations onto the horizontal qubit **wires** that form your quantum register. To delete a gate from a wire, select the gate and click the trash can icon. To adjust parameters and settings on gates that support editing, select the gate in the graphical editor and click **Edit**.
- **Toolbar:** Access commonly used tools such as undo and redo, gate alignment adjustments and switch to inspect mode. Inspect mode provides a step-by-step view of qubit states during circuit computation evolution. For more details, refer to **Inspect your circuit, step-by-step**.
- **Phase disks:** The phase of the qubit state vector in the complex plane is indicated by the line extending from the center of the diagram to the edge of the grey disk, rotating counterclockwise around the center point. Show or hide the phase disks using the view menu.
- **Visualizations:** Visualizations dynamically represent your circuit as you build it. They utilize a single-shot statevector simulator, distinct from the system specified in the setup and run settings. Note that visualizations do not account for any measurement operations you add. Sign in and click **Setup and run** to obtain results from the specified backend. To learn more about visualizations, refer to **visualizations**.

Potential of quantum computing

In the realm of quantum computing, building quantum circuits involves a variety of operations that manipulate qubits. These operations can be broadly categorized into several types, each serving a distinct purpose within a quantum algorithm.

Fundamentals of qubits and gates

Imagine a world where computers can solve problems millions of times faster than the ones we use today. Quantum computing operates on fundamental units called qubits, which adhere to the principles of quantum mechanics such as superposition and entanglement. Instead of just being a 0 or 1 like regular computer bits, qubits can be 0, 1, or even both at the same time. This strange behavior opens up incredible possibilities, but to harness this power, we need tools called quantum gates and operations. Let us explore them step by step.

Overview of quantum circuits

Think of a quantum circuit as a recipe. To bake a cake, you follow specific steps, adding ingredients and mixing them in a certain order. In a quantum computer, the *ingredients* are qubits, and the steps are the gates and operations we use to manipulate them. These gates allow us to:

- Flip a qubit from 0 to 1 or vice versa.
- Mix two qubits together to form connections.
- Adjust the **angle** of a qubit to make it behave in specific ways.
- Measure a qubit to see its final state.

Tools in our quantum toolbox

The quantum computing ecosystem offers a range of tools designed to help users build, simulate, and run quantum circuits efficiently. These tools provide seamless access to quantum hardware, powerful simulators, and comprehensive learning resources, enabling both beginners and experts to explore the potential of quantum computing.

Let us break down the key tools we use in quantum circuits.

Classical gates

Classical gates are the simplest tools, similar to what regular computers use. They are like switches that turn things on or off, or logic tools that say, *If this is true, then do that.*

- **NOT gate:** Like flipping a light switch, this gate changes a 0 to a 1 or a 1 to a 0. Refer to the following figure:

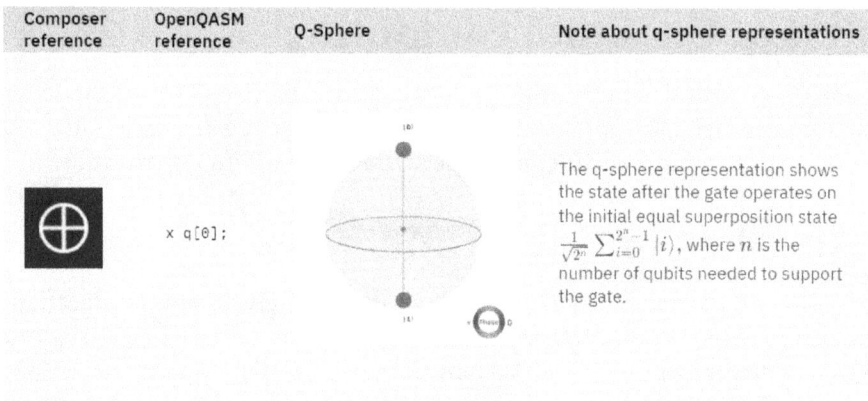

Composer reference	OpenQASM reference	Q-Sphere	Note about q-sphere representations
⊕	x q[0];		The q-sphere representation shows the state after the gate operates on the initial equal superposition state $\frac{1}{\sqrt{2^n}} \sum_{i=0}^{2^n-1} |i\rangle$, where n is the number of qubits needed to support the gate.

Figure 5.24: Classical NOT gate and composer reference in the interface

- **CNOT gate:** This one is a bit fancier. Imagine a light bulb that only turns on if one switch is already on and you flip another switch. It connects two qubits, creating a special link between them. Refer to the following figure:

Composer reference	OpenQASM reference	Q-Sphere	Note about q-sphere representations
	cx q[0], q[1];		The q-sphere representation shows the state after the gate operates on the initial equal superposition state $\frac{1}{\sqrt{2^n}} \sum_{i=0}^{2^n - 1} |i\rangle$, where n is the number of qubits needed to support the gate.

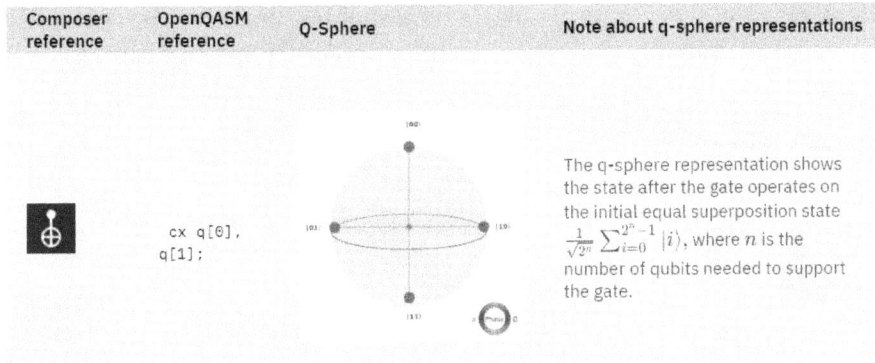

Figure 5.25: Visual representation of classical CNot gate

- **Toffoli gate:** Think of it as teamwork, two switches work together to decide whether a third one gets flipped. Refer to the following figure:

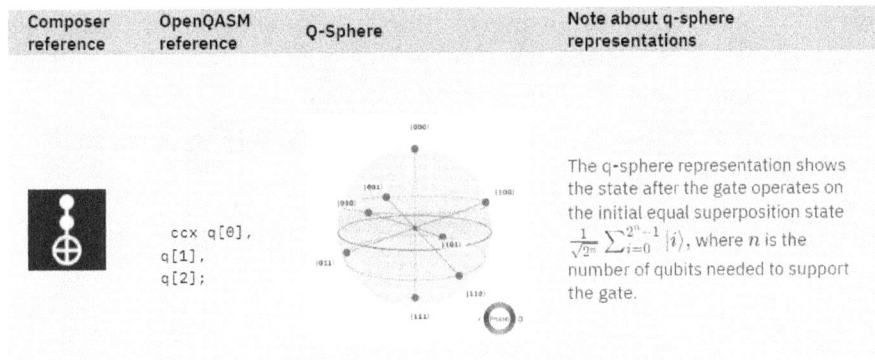

Composer reference	OpenQASM reference	Q-Sphere	Note about q-sphere representations
	ccx q[0], q[1], q[2];		The q-sphere representation shows the state after the gate operates on the initial equal superposition state $\frac{1}{\sqrt{2^n}} \sum_{i=0}^{2^n - 1} |i\rangle$, where n is the number of qubits needed to support the gate.

Figure 5.26: Visual representation of Toffoli gate

- **SWAP gate:** As the name suggests, this gate swaps the states of two qubits, like trading places in a game of musical chairs. The following figure is a representation of the SWAP gate as depicted in the Quantum Composer:

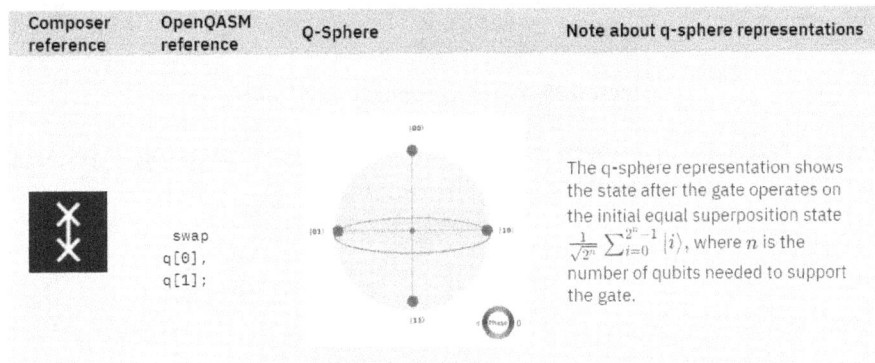

Composer reference	OpenQASM reference	Q-Sphere	Note about q-sphere representations
	swap q[0], q[1];		The q-sphere representation shows the state after the gate operates on the initial equal superposition state $\frac{1}{\sqrt{2^n}} \sum_{i=0}^{2^n - 1} |i\rangle$, where n is the number of qubits needed to support the gate.

Figure 5.27: Visual representation of swap gate

- **Identity gate:** This gate is like a placeholder, ensuring no changes happen momentarily. Identity gate representation in the Quantum Composer is given as follows:

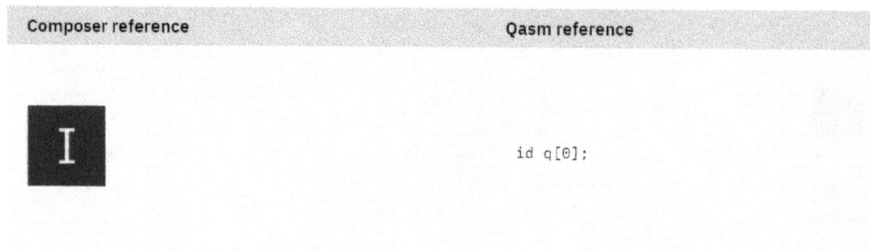

Composer reference	Qasm reference
I	`id q[0];`

Figure 5.28: Visual representation of the Identity gate

Phase gates

Phase gates are all about subtle adjustments. Imagine a DJ tweaking the balance of a song to make it sound just right. Phase gates change how qubits behave, but without altering their main state. Let us look at them in detail:

- **T gate:** A small adjustment that is crucial for fine-tuning quantum calculations. Refer to the following figure:

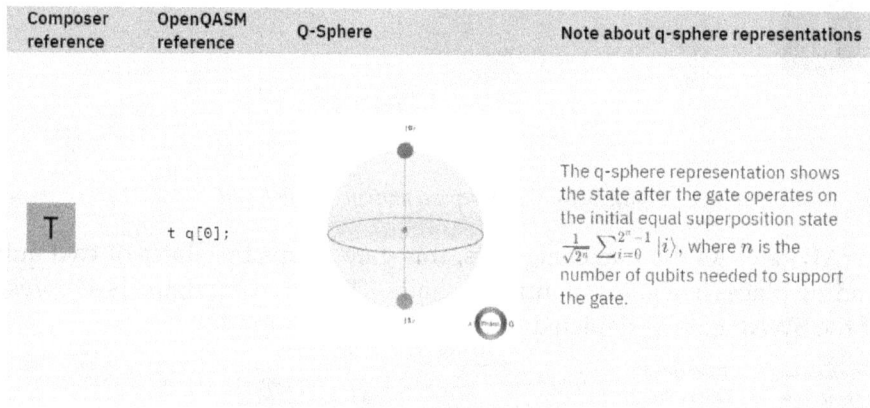

Composer reference	OpenQASM reference	Q-Sphere	Note about q-sphere representations
T	`t q[0];`		The q-sphere representation shows the state after the gate operates on the initial equal superposition state $\frac{1}{\sqrt{2^n}} \sum_{i=0}^{2^n-1} |i\rangle$, where n is the number of qubits needed to support the gate.

Figure 5.29: Visual representation of T gate

- **S gate:** Adds an imaginary twist to the qubit's state, making it ready for more complex operations. Refer to the following figure:

Composer reference	OpenQASM reference	Q-Sphere	Note about q-sphere representations
S	s q[0];	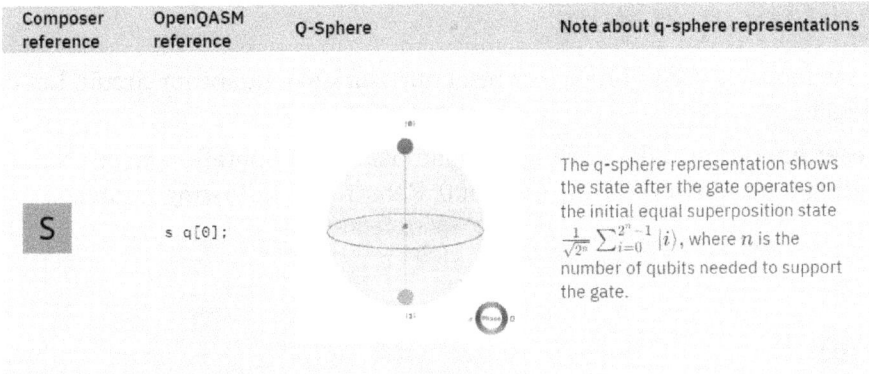	The q-sphere representation shows the state after the gate operates on the initial equal superposition state $\frac{1}{\sqrt{2^n}}\sum_{i=0}^{2^n-1}|i\rangle$, where n is the number of qubits needed to support the gate.

Figure 5.30: Visual representation of S gate

- **Z gate:** This gate flips part of the qubit's behavior, creating a sharper contrast, like adding bass to a song. Refer to the following figure:

Composer reference	OpenQASM reference	Q-Sphere	Note about q-sphere representations
Z	z q[0];	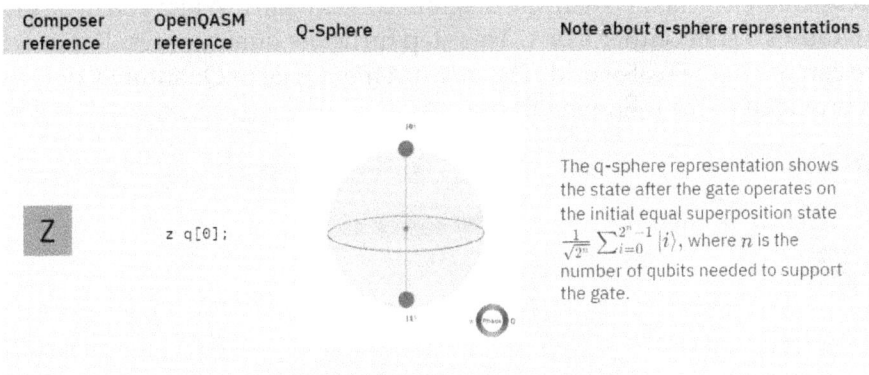	The q-sphere representation shows the state after the gate operates on the initial equal superposition state $\frac{1}{\sqrt{2^n}}\sum_{i=0}^{2^n-1}|i\rangle$, where n is the number of qubits needed to support the gate.

Figure 5.31: Visual representation of Z gate

- **RZ gate:** Rotates the qubit around an imaginary axis, adjusting it to the perfect angle for the task at hand. Refer to the following figure:

Composer reference	OpenQASM reference	Q-Sphere	Note about q-sphere representations
RZ	rz(angle) q[0];	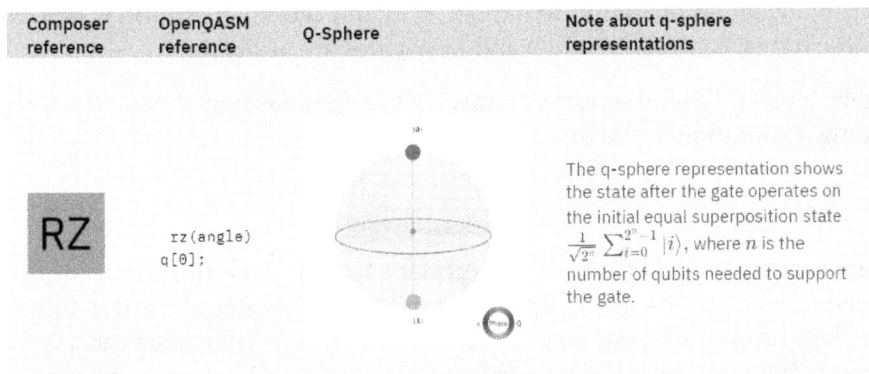	The q-sphere representation shows the state after the gate operates on the initial equal superposition state $\frac{1}{\sqrt{2^n}}\sum_{i=0}^{2^n-1}|i\rangle$, where n is the number of qubits needed to support the gate.

Figure 5.32: Visual representation of RZ gate

Non-unitary operators

These are the tools we use to finalize or reset our work in a quantum circuit. Let us look at them in detail:

- **Reset operation:** Like erasing a chalkboard, this operation wipes a qubit clean, setting it back to its starting state of 0. Refer to the following figure:

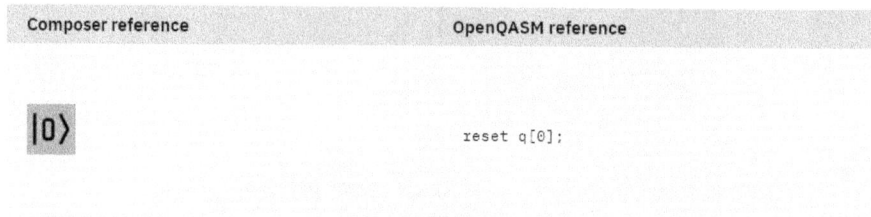

Composer reference	OpenQASM reference
$|0\rangle$	`reset q[0];`

Figure 5.33: Visual Representation of reset operator

- **Measurement:** This is where the magic becomes reality. When you measure a qubit, it **chooses** a state, either 0 or 1. This step turns the quantum result into something we can use in the real-world. The measurement gate in Quantum Composer looks as provided in the following figure:

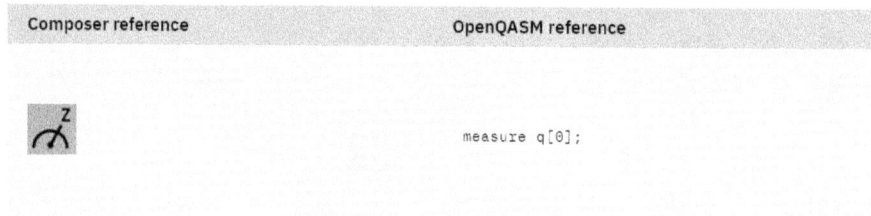

Composer reference	OpenQASM reference
	`measure q[0];`

Figure 5.34: Visual representation of measurement operator

Modifiers

Sometimes, we want an operation to happen only if a certain condition is met. Modifiers act like traffic lights, controlling when and how gates are applied.

For example, a control modifier lets you say, *Do this operation only if this qubit is in state 1* It is like adding a conditional rule to a game.

Hadamard gate

The Hadamard gate is one of the most important tools in quantum computing. It is like a magic wand that takes a qubit and makes it exist in two states at once, a superposition. This is the key to quantum parallelism, where a quantum computer can explore many possibilities at the same time. The Hadamard gate and its Q-sphere representation from Quantum Composer is provided in the following figure:

Composer reference	OpenQASM reference	Q-Sphere	Note about q-sphere representations
H	h q[0];	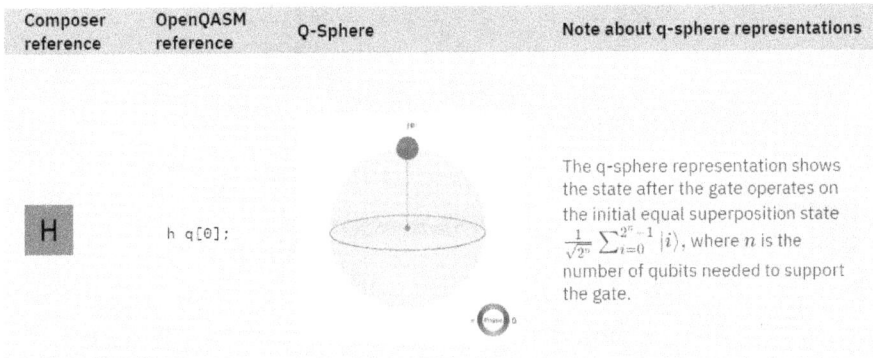	The q-sphere representation shows the state after the gate operates on the initial equal superposition state $\frac{1}{\sqrt{2^n}} \sum_{i=0}^{2^n-1} |i\rangle$, where n is the number of qubits needed to support the gate.

Figure 5.35: Visual representation of Hadamard gate

Quantum gates

Quantum gates are where things get really exciting. They can create amazing effects like entanglement, where two qubits become linked so that the state of one instantly affects the other, even if they are far apart. Some examples include:

- **√X Gate:** A softer version of the NOT gate, creating superposition with a twist. The following figure shows the representation of this gate in the Quantum Composer:

Composer reference	OpenQASM reference	Q-Sphere	Note about q-sphere representations
√X	sx q[0];	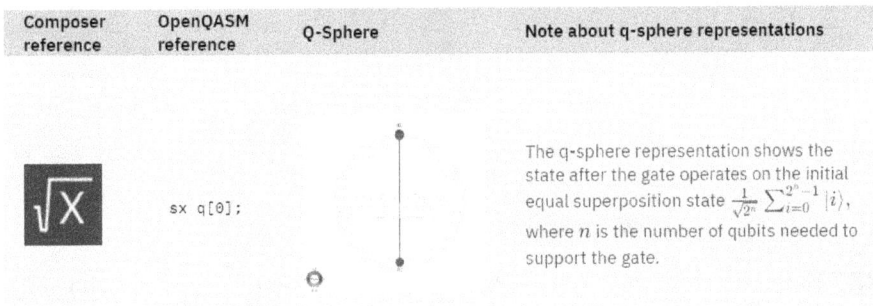	The q-sphere representation shows the state after the gate operates on the initial equal superposition state $\frac{1}{\sqrt{2^n}} \sum_{i=0}^{2^n-1} |i\rangle$, where n is the number of qubits needed to support the gate.

Figure 5.36: Visual representation of the quantum not gate

- **RX and RY gates:** These gates rotate the qubit around different axes, like spinning a globe to point to a specific location.
  - **RX gate:** The RX gate implements $exp(-i(\theta/2)X)$. On the Bloch sphere, this gate corresponds to rotating the qubit state around the x-axis by the given angle as depicted in the following figure:

Composer reference	OpenQASM reference	Q-Sphere	Note about q-sphere representations
RX	rx(angle) q[0];	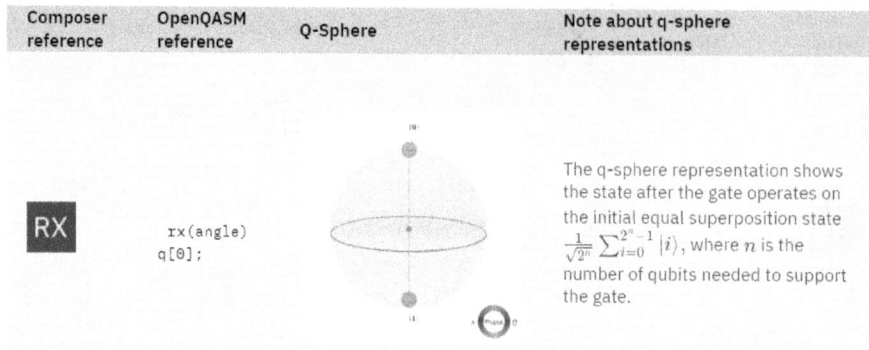	The q-sphere representation shows the state after the gate operates on the initial equal superposition state $\frac{1}{\sqrt{2^n}} \sum_{i=0}^{2^n-1} |i\rangle$, where n is the number of qubits needed to support the gate.

Figure 5.37: Visual representation of RX gate

o **RY gate:** The RY gate implements $exp(-i(\theta/2)Y)$. On the Bloch sphere, this gate corresponds to rotating the qubit state around the y axis by the given angle and does not introduce complex amplitudes as provided in the following figure:

Composer reference	OpenQASM reference	Q-Sphere	Note about q-sphere representations
RY	ry(angle) q[0];	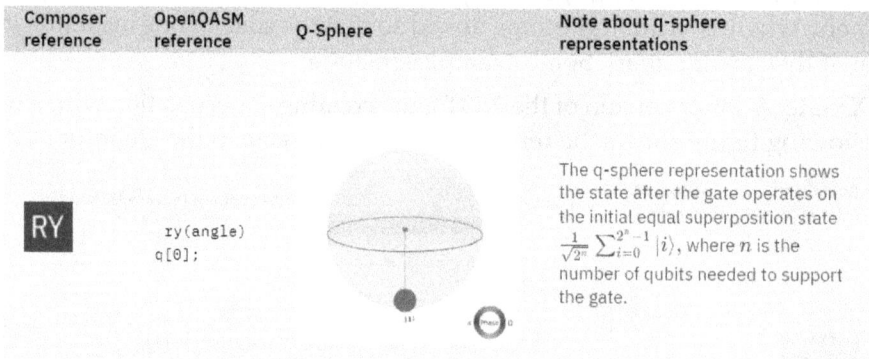	The q-sphere representation shows the state after the gate operates on the initial equal superposition state $\frac{1}{\sqrt{2^n}} \sum_{i=0}^{2^n-1} |i\rangle$, where n is the number of qubits needed to support the gate.

Figure 5.38: Visual representation of RY gate

• **RZZ gate:** A gate that connects two qubits and creates a special shared behavior. The following figure is a representation of the RZZ gate as depicted in the Quantum Composer:

Composer reference	OpenQASM reference	Q-Sphere	Note about q-sphere representations
RZZ	rzz(angle) q[0], q[1];	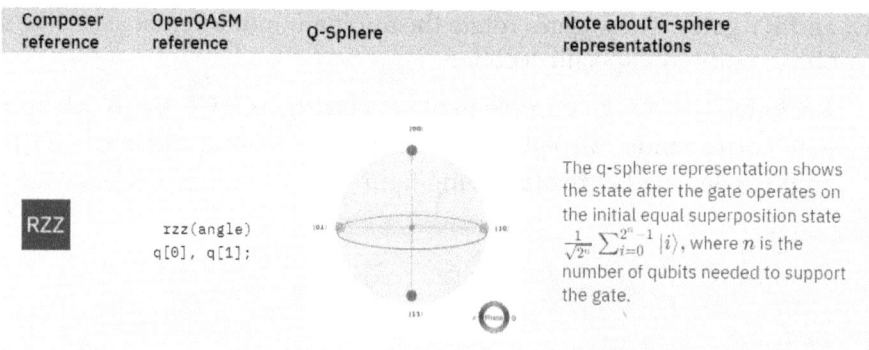	The q-sphere representation shows the state after the gate operates on the initial equal superposition state $\frac{1}{\sqrt{2^n}} \sum_{i=0}^{2^n-1} |i\rangle$, where n is the number of qubits needed to support the gate.

Figure 5.39: Visual representation of RZZ gate

- **U Gate:** The ultimate multitool, it can transform into any single-qubit gate and its circuit icon based pictorial representation in Quantum Composer is provided in the following figure:

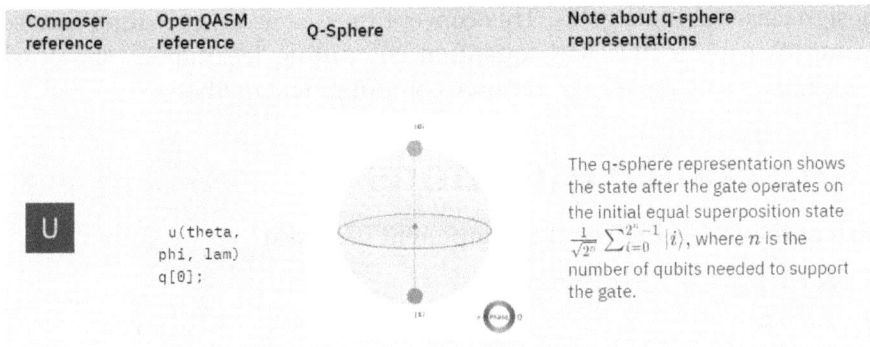

Composer reference	OpenQASM reference	Q-Sphere	Note about q-sphere representations
U	u(theta, phi, lam) q[0];		The q-sphere representation shows the state after the gate operates on the initial equal superposition state $\frac{1}{\sqrt{2^n}} \sum_{i=0}^{2^n-1} |i\rangle$, where n is the number of qubits needed to support the gate.

Figure 5.40: *Visual representation of U gate*

Quantum gates and operations are the building blocks of every quantum algorithm. They allow us to solve problems in ways classical computers never could, like simulating molecules to design new medicines or optimizing complex systems like global supply chains. Learning how these tools work is like learning to play an instrument, you start with simple notes, but soon you are composing symphonies.

Quantum computing may seem complex, but at its core, it elegantly balances multiple possibilities. By understanding the tools and how they interact, you are taking the first steps toward mastering this exciting new frontier. So, whether you are dreaming of building quantum circuits or just curious about the future, remember: the quantum world is yours to explore. The next chapter will explore about these gates and circuits in detail.

Conclusion

In conclusion, the integration of Python, Jupyter Notebook, Qiskit, and IBM Q forms a robust ecosystem that is propelling quantum computing into the future. Python's versatility and extensive library support provide a solid foundation for quantum algorithm development, while Jupyter Notebook enhances the interactive and collaborative aspects of quantum research and experimentation. Qiskit, as IBM's open-source framework, empowers researchers with tools ranging from circuit creation and simulation to advanced algorithm implementation across diverse domains. IBM Q complements this framework by offering cloud-based access to real quantum processors through intuitive tools such as Quantum Composer and Quantum Lab, making quantum computing accessible to both beginners and experts alike.

Together, these components not only facilitate the exploration and development of quantum applications but also pave the way for new discoveries and innovations in fields such as chemistry, optimization and machine learning. As quantum computing continues to evolve, understanding and leveraging these tools will be essential for anyone looking to harness the full potential of this groundbreaking technology.

In the upcoming chapter, we will discuss the innovative approach of leveraging quantum gates to design classical logic gates. This concept represents a fascinating intersection of classical computing principles with quantum computing techniques, showcasing how quantum mechanics can enhance traditional computational methods.

Multiple choice questions

1. **Which of the following is not a component of Qiskit?**

    a. Qiskit Terra

    b. Qiskit Air

    c. Qiskit Ignis

    d. Qiskit Aqua

2. **What is Jupyter Notebook primarily used for in the context of quantum computing?**

    a. Creating quantum hardware

    b. Writing and testing classical algorithms

    c. Experimenting with quantum circuits

    d. Managing cloud-based services

3. **IBM Q provides access to:**

    a. Only classical processors

    b. Real quantum processors via the cloud

    c. Quantum processors for purchase

    d. Quantum processors for academic use only

4. **Python is preferred in quantum computing mainly due to its:**

    a. Speed in executing quantum algorithms

    b. Ability to integrate with quantum hardware

    c. Native support for quantum circuit design

    d. Versatility and extensive library ecosystem

5. **Quantum Composer is best described as:**

    a. An open-source quantum computing framework

    b. An integrated development environment for quantum algorithms

    c. A graphical interface for designing and visualizing quantum circuits

    d. A simulator for testing quantum algorithms

Answer key

1. b
2. c
3. b
4. d
5. c

Questions

1. Name one advantage of using Python in quantum computing development.

   Answer: Python's extensive library ecosystem supports quantum algorithm implementation and integration with quantum frameworks.

2. How does Jupyter Notebook enhance the quantum computing experience?

   Answer: It provides an interactive environment for live code execution, documentation and visualization of quantum circuits.

3. List two key components of IBM Q's platform.

   Answer: Quantum Composer and Quantum Lab.

4. Briefly explain the role of Qiskit Terra in quantum computing.

   Answer: Qiskit Terra is used for creating and optimizing quantum circuits.

5. What is the primary function of Qiskit Aqua?

   Answer: Implementing quantum algorithms across various domains such as chemistry, optimization, and machine learning.

6. Compare and contrast the roles of Qiskit Terra and Qiskit Aqua in quantum computing.

   Answer: Qiskit Terra focuses on the creation and optimization of quantum circuits, the below optimizes a quantum circuit before execution on real hardware.

   ```
   from qiskit import QuantumCircuit, transpile

   qc = QuantumCircuit(2)
   qc.h(0)
   qc.cx(0,1)
   optimized_qc = transpile(qc, optimization_level=3)
   ```

print(optimized_qc), whereas Qiskit Aqua specializes in implementing quantum algorithms for specific applications such as chemistry simulations and optimization problems

from qiskit.algorithms import VQE

from qiskit.circuit.library import TwoLocal

ansatz = TwoLocal(rotation_blocks='ry', entanglement_blocks='cz')

vqe = VQE(ansatz)

This sets up a VQE for solving quantum chemistry problems.

7. Discuss the significance of Python in the context of quantum computing development, citing examples of its practical applications.

   Answer: Python's versatility makes it essential for quantum computing, enabling tasks like quantum circuit simulation, algorithm optimization, and hardware integration. Libraries such as Qiskit, Cirq, and PennyLane provide tools for designing, testing, and executing quantum algorithms efficiently. Its readability and extensive ecosystem simplify quantum research and development.

8. Describe the advantages of using IBM Q's Quantum Composer for beginners in quantum computing.

   Answer: IBM Q's Quantum Composer provides a drag-and-drop interface for designing and visualizing quantum circuits, making it ideal for beginners. It allows users to experiment with quantum gates and concepts without requiring programming skills. In contrast, Qiskit Terra offers a code-based approach, giving advanced users more flexibility and control over circuit optimization and execution on real quantum hardware.

9. In what ways do tools like Qiskit and IBM Q contribute to advancing the field of quantum computing? Provide examples to support your answer.

   Answer: Qiskit provides a comprehensive framework for quantum algorithm development and simulation, while IBM Q offers cloud-based access to real quantum processors. Together, they enable researchers to explore and implement quantum algorithms across various disciplines, paving the way for advancements in fields such as cryptography, materials science, and artificial intelligence.

## CHAPTER 6

Design of Classical Logic Gates Using Quantum Gates

Introduction

This chapter elucidates the principles of quantum gates and their efficacy in constructing classical logic gates, providing readers with a deep, practical understanding of quantum computation. It sets a strong foundation for exploring the intricate design, operation, and potential applications of classical logic gates built from quantum elements.

As essential building blocks of digital circuits, logic gates are experiencing a transformation through quantum computing. This chapter examines the theory and application of quantum gates in creating classical binary logic gates, along with their advantages and disadvantages.

Furthermore, readers will learn to apply these principles using IBM Q composer and IBM Qiskit SDK to design and analyze quantum circuits. By engaging with the various classical logic gates derived from quantum elements, readers will not only develop practical skills to design, execute, and optimize algorithms but also learn to apply this knowledge to solve real-world problems confidently.

Structure

The chapter will be structured in the following way:

- Classical gates using quantum gates
- Quantum circuit design
- Advantages of using quantum gates
- Disadvantages of using quantum gates

Objectives

By the end of this chapter, the reader will be able to comprehend the basics of quantum circuit design and gain the ability to construct simple quantum circuits. The chapter will familiarize you with IBM Q composer, demonstrating the capacity to utilize its tools and features for designing quantum circuits and executing quantum algorithms.

The reader will gain skills in utilizing IBM Qiskit SDK, showcasing the ability to execute quantum circuits, analyze results, and identify potential improvements or modifications. You will be able to identify the advantages of using quantum gates, such as superior speed, enhanced computational capabilities, and complex problem-solving.

You will be able to recognize the limitations of quantum gates, which can involve issues related to error rates and coherence. After reading this chapter, the reader will be able to apply the knowledge and skills acquired throughout the chapter to practical scenarios, gain confidence in working with quantum gates, and develop proficiency in quantum circuit design.

Classical gates using quantum gates

This section will explain the implementation of a few classical gates using quantum gates. All the circuits will begin with input qubits initialized to $|0\rangle$, unless stated otherwise. The purpose of this section is to demonstrate how quantum gates can be used to simulate the behavior of classical gates. The following classical gates will be covered:

- NOT
- AND
- NAND
- OR
- NOR
- XOR
- XNOR

NOT gate

The Pauli X gate is the equivalent of the classical NOT gate. Note that NOT gate operates on bits whereas Pauli X operates on quantum states. The Pauli X flips the state of the qubit, $|0\rangle$ is flipped to $|1\rangle$, and $|1\rangle$ is flipped to $|0\rangle$. *Figure 6.1(b)* gives the circuit for the Pauli X gate, which is denoted by the *plus* symbol. In *Figure 6.1(b)*, the gate to the right of Pauli X is the measurement gate. This gate measures the state of the qubit on the Z-axis. To recollect from previous chapters, this is the axis over which the state of the qubit is represented in the Bloch sphere. *Figure 6.1(a)* shows the classical NOT gate:

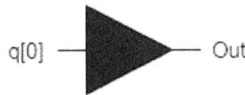

Figure 6.1(a): *Classical NOT*

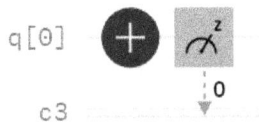

Figure 6.1(b): *NOT using quantum gate*

Table 6.1 gives the truth table for Pauli X gate. As can be seen, Pauli X flips the state of the qubit, which is a fundamental quantum operation and not just a simulation of the classical NOT gate. Pauli X is an essential gate in all quantum algorithms and implementations.

q[0]	Out (Classical)	Quantum Pauli X gate
0	1	Flips $|0\rangle$ to $|1\rangle$
1	0	Flips $|1\rangle$ to $|0\rangle$

Table 6.1: *Truth table for NOT*

AND gate

The AND gate is implemented using a CCNOT (Toffoli) gate. In *Figure 6.2(b)*, the target qubit q[2] is initialized to state $|0\rangle$, and CCNOT is applied with q[0] and q[1] as control qubits. The CCNOT gate implements the AND operation by flipping the target qubit only when both control qubits are $|1\rangle$. *Figure 6.2(a)* gives the classical AND gate:

Figure 6.2(a): *Classical AND*

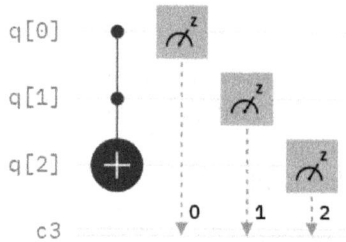

Figure 6.2(b): AND using quantum gates

Table 6.2 shows the truth table for the CCNOT gate. The first two columns are the inputs, and the fourth column is the output of the CCNOT gate. As can be seen, this is identical to the truth table of the AND gate.

q[0]	q[1]	Out (Classical)	q[2] (output), initial state is $|0\rangle$	Description
0	0	0	$|0\rangle$	The target qubit q[2] becomes 1 only when both the control qubits q[0] and q[1] are in the 1) state, effectively implementing the AND operation.
0	1	0	$|0\rangle$	
1	0	0	$|0\rangle$	
1	1	1	$|1\rangle$, since control qubits q[0] & q[1] are both 1	

Table 6.2: Truth table for AND

NAND gate

The NAND gate is an AND gate followed by a Pauli X gate, which flips the output state. This is represented in *Figure 6.3(b)*. The CCNOT gate changes the state of target qubit to $|1\rangle$ only when both the controls qubits are $|1\rangle$. The Pauli X unconditionally flips the target qubit's state after the CCNOT gate. This flip is crucial to convert the AND behavior into a NAND behavior. *Figure 6.3(a)* displays the classical NAND gate:

Figure 6.3(a): Classical NAND

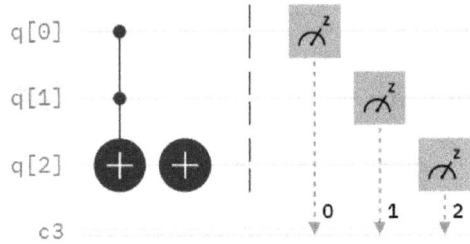

Figure 6.3(b): NAND using two quantum gates, CCNOT followed by Pauli X

Table 6.3 gives the truth table for the quantum NAND gate. This is identical to the classical NAND gate, wherein the output is 0 only when both the inputs are 1.

q[0]	q[1]	Out (Classical)	q[2] (output), initial state is $\lvert 0\rangle$	Description
0	0	1	$\lvert 1\rangle$	• The *CCNOT* flips the target qubit to 1 only when both the control qubits are 1. The Pauli X flips this 1 back to 0, as seen in row #4.
0	1	1	$\lvert 1\rangle$	
1	0	1	$\lvert 1\rangle$	
1	1	0	$\lvert 0\rangle$	• For the other three scenarios where at least one of the control qubits is 0, CCNOT will not flip the target qubit. The X gate, however, will flip it to 1. This is the NAND behavior.

Table 6.3: Truth table for NAND

OR gate

The OR gate is designed using one CCNOT and two CNOT gates. This is just one way to design and not the only way. The CNOT gate flips the target qubit only if the control qubit is in the state $\lvert 1\rangle$. There are two CNOTs in *Figure 6.4(b)*. Together, they ensure that the target qubit will be flipped from $\lvert 0\rangle$ to $\lvert 1\rangle$, or $\lvert 1\rangle$ to $\lvert 0\rangle$, only if both the control qubits are $\lvert 1\rangle$. The CCNOT, also known as the Toffoli gate, flips the target qubit only if both the control qubits are in the state $\lvert 1\rangle$. The circuit is represented in *Figure 6.4(b)*. *Figure 6.4(a)* shows the classical OR gate.

Figure 6.4(a): Classical OR

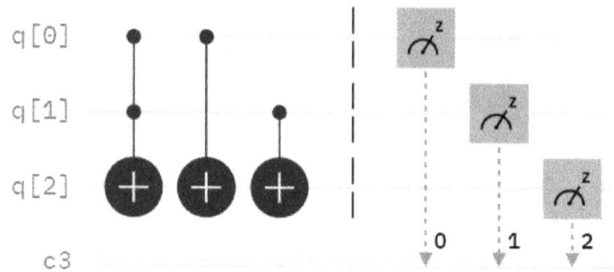

Figure 6.4(b): *OR using quantum gates*

Table 6.4 explains the truth table for the quantum OR gate:

q[0]	q[1]	Out (Classical)	q[2] (output), initial state is $\lvert 0 \rangle$	Description
0	0	0	$\lvert 0 \rangle$	• The first CCNOT will not flip q[2], as control qubits are NOT both 1. • The next two CNOTs will also not flip q[2] as q[0] and q[1] are 0. So, q[2] remains at 0.
0	1	1	$\lvert 1 \rangle$	• The first CCNOT will not flip q[2], as control qubits are NOT both 1. • The next CNOT will also not flip q[2]. However, the second CNOT will flip q[2] as q[1] is 1. So, q[2] becomes 1.
1	0	1	$\lvert 1 \rangle$	• The first CCNOT will not flip q[2], as control qubits are NOT both 1. • The next CNOT will flip q[2] as q[0] is 1. So, q[2] becomes 1. The second CNOT will have no effect as q[1] is 0.
1	1	1	$\lvert 1 \rangle$	• The first CCNOT will flip q[2] as both control qubits are 1. So, q[2] becomes 1. • The next CNOT will flip q[2] as q[0] is 1. So, q[2] becomes 0. The second CNOT will flip q[2] again as q[1] is 1. So, q[2] again becomes 1.

Table 6.4: *Truth table for OR*

NOR gate

The NOR gate is the inverse of the OR gate. Therefore, it has the same configuration as the OR gate, with a Pauli X gate at the end, as seen in *Figure 6.5(b)*. The purpose of Pauli X gate is to unconditionally flip the target qubit. This gate ensures that the output of OR gate is inverted to replicate the behavior of a NOR gate. *Figure 6.5(a)* gives the classical NOR gate:

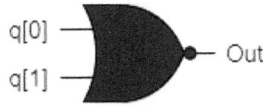

Figure 6.5(a): *Classical NOR*

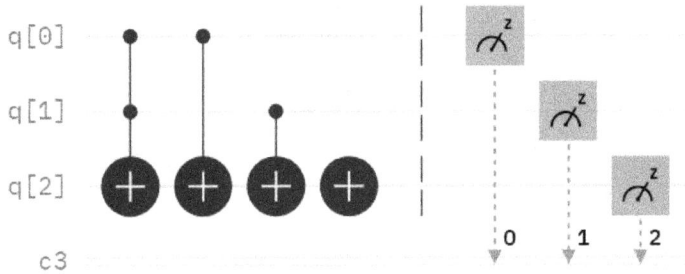

Figure 6.5(b): *NOR using quantum gates*

Table 6.5 contains the truth table for the quantum NOR gate:

q[0]	q[1]	Out (Classical)	q[2] (output), initial state is $|0\rangle$	Description
0	0	1	$|1\rangle$	• The first CCNOT will not flip q[2], as control qubits are NOT both 1. • The next two CNOTs will also not flip q[2] as q[0] and q[1] are 0. So, q[2] remains at 0. • However, the Pauli X flips q[2] unconditionally. So, q[2] becomes 1.
0	1	0	$|0\rangle$	• As control qubits are NOT both 1, the CCNOT will not flip q[2]. • The first CNOT will also not flip q[2]. However, the second CNOT will flip q[2] as q[1] is 1. So, q[2] becomes 1. • Finally, Pauli X flips it again to 0.
1	0	0	$|0\rangle$	• The *CCNOT* will not flip q[2], as control qubits are NOT both 1. • The first CNOT will flip q[2] as q[0] is 1. So, q[2] becomes 1. The second CNOT will have no effect as q[1] is 0. • However, Pauli X flips q[2] back to 0.

q[0]	q[1]	Out (Classical)	q[2] (output), initial state is $|0\rangle$	Description
1	1	0	$|0\rangle$	• In this case q[2] becomes 1, because the CCNOT will flip q[2] as both the control qubits are 1. • The first CNOT will flip q[2] as q[0] is 1. So, q[2] becomes 0. The second *CNOT* will flip q[2] as q[1] is 1. So, q[2] again becomes 1. • Finally, Pauli X flips it to 0.

Table 6.5: Truth table for NOR

XOR gate

The XOR gate performs an exclusive OR operation. It outputs a 1 when the inputs are different (one 0 and the other 1), and a 0 when the inputs are the same (both 0s or both 1s). The XOR gate can be implemented by adopting the quantum OR gate from the previous section and removing the CCNOT. *Figure 6.6(a)* and *Figure 6.6(b)* show the classical XOR gate and the quantum XOR gate, respectively. The CNOT in *Figure 6.6(a)* will flip the target qubit only when the control qubit is $|1\rangle$. If either one of the input qubits is $|1\rangle$, the output will be flipped to $|1\rangle$. In the inputs are same, the output will be zero.

Figure 6.6(a): Classical XOR

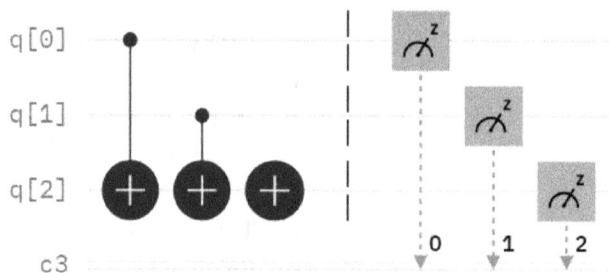

Figure 6.6(b): XOR using quantum gates

Table 6.6 contains the truth table for the quantum XOR gate:

q[0]	q[1]	Out (Classical)	q[2] (output), initial state is $|0\rangle$	Description
0	0	0	$|0\rangle$	Both the *CNOTs* will NOT flip q[2] as the respective control qubits are 0. So, q[2] remains at 0.
0	1	1	$|1\rangle$	The first *CNOT* will have no effect. However, the second *CNOT* will flip q[2] to 1 as q[1] is 1.
1	0	1	$|1\rangle$	The first *CNOT* will flip q[2] to 1 as q[0] is 1. The second *CNOT* will have no effect.
1	1	0	$|0\rangle$	The first *CNOT* will flip q[2] to 1. The second *CNOT* will again flip q[2] back to 0.

Table 6.6: Truth table for XOR

XNOR gate

The XNOR gate has the same configuration as the XOR gate, except that there is a Pauli X gate at the end to flip the state of the output. *Figure 6.7(a)* and *Figure 6.7(b)* displays the classical and quantum equivalent of the XNOR gate.

Figure 6.7(a): Classical XNOR

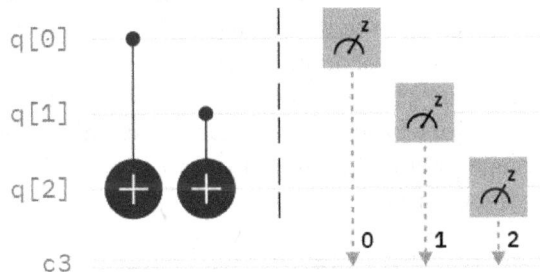

Figure 6.7(b): XNOR using quantum gates

Table 6.7 gives the truth table for the quantum XNOR gate:

q[0]	q[1]	Out (Classical)	q[2] (output), initial state is |0⟩	Description
0	0	1	|1⟩	Both the CNOTs will NOT flip q[2] as the respective control qubits are 0. So, q[2] remains at 0. However, Pauli X will flip it to 1.
0	1	0	|0⟩	The first CNOT will have no effect. However, the second CNOT will flip q[2] to 1 as q[1] is 1. Pauli X will flip it back to 0.
1	0	0	|0⟩	The first CNOT will flip q[2] to 1 as q[0] is 1. The second CNOT will have no effect. However, Pauli X will flip q[2] back to 0.
1	1	1	|1⟩	The first CNOT will flip q[2] to 1. The second CNOT will again flip q[2] back to 0. Pauli X will flip it once again to 1.

Table 6.7: Truth table for XNOR

Quantum circuit design

A quantum circuit is a sequence of quantum gates and measurements applied to a set of qubits and is used to perform quantum computation. Quantum circuits are built using different types of quantum gates, followed by a measurement gate to observe the outcome or result.

While the previous section focused on design of classical gates using quantum gates, the following section demonstrates actual implementation of quantum circuits that exhibit the behavior of classical gates. The examples given in the next section are run on IBM Quantum platform. Users can write quantum algorithms, submit them, and receive the results. IBM Q cloud provides both real quantum processors as well as simulators to execute quantum circuits. Real quantum processors are physical devices that utilize quantum bits (qubits) to perform computations based on quantum mechanics. They operate with actual quantum states and leverage phenomena like superposition and entanglement. Quantum simulators, on the other hand, are classical computers or software tools that emulate the behavior of quantum systems but do not execute genuine quantum computations. They help in studying quantum algorithms and behaviors without needing a physical quantum processor.

IBM Q offers quantum computers of different sizes to the public, researchers, and organizations, enabling them to experiment, learn, and create quantum algorithms and applications. A few of the key technical details of IBM Q are given as follows:

- **Architecture:** IBM Q uses the superconducting qubit architecture.

- **Qubit count:** Qubit count is similar to the transistor count in classical computers. However, in classical computers, the higher the transistor count, the greater is the processing power. In quantum computers, due to decoherence of the qubits, higher qubit count does not translate into greater processing power. IBM Q has a qubit count ranging from 5 qubits to 42 qubits.

- **Processor type:** Few of the main processor types are:
  - IBM canary with 5 to 16 qubits
  - IBM falcon with 27 qubits
  - IBM hummingbird with upto 65 qubits
  - IBM eagle with 127 qubits
  - IBM heron at 156 qubits
  - IBM osprey at 433 qubits

- **Fidelity:** A measure of how accurately quantum gates perform their intended operation. IBM Q provides a fidelity approaching 99.9% in two-qubit gates.

- **Coherence time:** The duration a qubit can remain in a superposition state without losing its quantum information due to interactions with the environment (decoherence). Coherence time for qubits range from about 20 to 400 microseconds, varying with design and conditions. High coherence times allow for longer computation durations and more complex algorithms, enhancing the reliability of quantum operations.

- **Quantum volume:** This is a quality metric used by IBM to measure the performance and capability of a quantum computer. It takes into account a few parameters such as number of qubits, how well qubits are interconnected, coherence and error rates. IBM Q processors demonstrate quantum volume up to 512.

The previous section represented circuits with both input and output states set to $|0\rangle$. In this section, we will harness the true potential of quantum computing by launching the input qubits into superposition using a Hadamard gate. Launching input qubits into superposition is essential in quantum computing because it allows qubits to exist in multiple states simultaneously, unlike classical bits, which can only be in one state at a time (0 or 1). This property enables quantum computers to perform many calculations at once, exponentially increasing their processing power for certain problems.

In the state of superposition, we will apply quantum gates and observe the results. All the following examples were executed on IBM Q cloud.

Two approaches will be covered here, one using IBM Q composer and the other using a Jupyter Notebook that runs the IBM Qiskit SDK.

IBM Q composer

IBM Q composer is a graphical interface tool available on IBM cloud for designing quantum computing circuits. It allows developers and researchers to build quantum algorithms and experiments without needing to know the underlying complex mathematics. Through point-and-click actions, users can add gates to their circuits, change their orders and run their experiments on a real quantum computer as well as a simulator on the IBM cloud. IBM Q composer provides an accessible way to understand and begin building quantum algorithms and experiments. This is done by creating, editing and visualizing quantum circuits, which are sequences of quantum gates that process quantum information.

Let us look at the updated circuit design where Hadamard gate is applied to all the input qubits in all the circuits. The Hadamard is applied to test the gate under all possible input conditions. The results are generated by executing on IBM Q simulator. The simulator used here is ibmq_qasm_simulator. It has 32 qubits capacity, that is, one can build circuits consisting of up to 32 qubits on this simulator. A total of 1024 iterations are run on the simulator to generate the output. The intent behind 1024 iterations is to provide a significant sample size for estimating probabilities and reducing statistical noise in the measurement results. This enhances the accuracy of the estimated outputs from the quantum system. While iteration count can also be 1000, but since computers operate in binary, using powers of two aligns well with digital computation. Hence, 1024 is usually preferred.

NOT gate

Circuit setup: The input qubit q[0] is launched into superposition using a Hadamard gate. *Figure 6.8* shows the corresponding circuit. Pauli X follows the Hadamard gate. The Hadamard gate creates a superposition, and the Pauli X gate flips the qubit within this superposition.

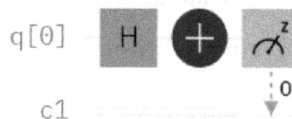

Figure 6.8: NOT gate

Simulation and results: The Hadamard gate spins the qubit into superposition with equal probabilities of $|0\rangle$ and $|1\rangle$. The Pauli X gate flips the qubit, and the output is still equiprobability states of $|1\rangle$ and $|0\rangle$. The measurement gate then collapses the qubit to either $|0\rangle$ or $|1\rangle$ with equal probabilities.

Figure 6.9 gives the quantum simulator output for the circuit in *Figure 6.8*:

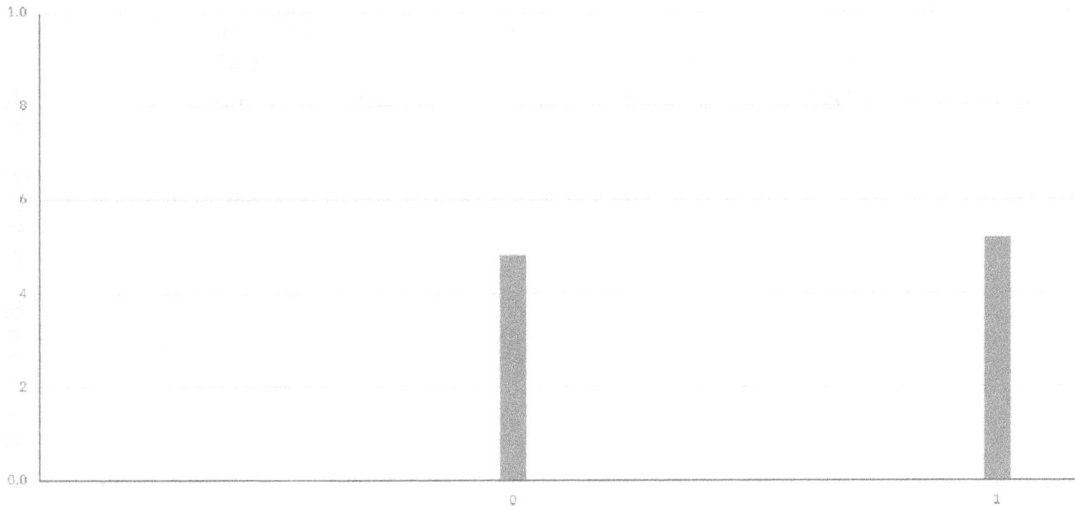

Figure 6.9: *Composer bar chart for NOT gate*

Interpretation of results: The NOT circuit is run on the simulator for 1024 iterations. The bar chart in *Figure 6.9* shows the spread of the outcome. However, the chart does not show perfectly equal probabilities. The results show a near 50:50 probability distribution due to the law of large numbers. However, minor deviations occur because 1024 iterations, though substantial, do not guarantee perfect convergence to the theoretical probabilities. This is the reason for the outcomes not being perfectly 50:50.

AND gate

Circuit setup: The input qubits q[0] and q[1] are launched into superposition using a Hadamard gate. *Figure 6.10* gives the circuit for this:

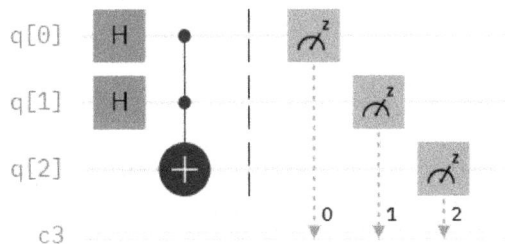

Figure 6.10: *AND gate*

Simulation and results: The output states of q[1] and q[0] after applying Hadamard gate will be a superposition state, as follows:

$$|\psi\rangle = \frac{1}{2}(|00\rangle + |01\rangle + |10\rangle + |11\rangle).$$

When these qubits act as control for the target q[2], the state of q[2] will be flipped only once, when |q[1] q[0] ⟩ is |11⟩. So, the output state |q[2] q[1] q[0] ⟩ will be a superposition of |000⟩, |001⟩, |010⟩ and |111⟩. All four states are equiprobable. This arises from the uniform superposition of q[0] and q[1] due to the Hadamard gate, and the deterministic control operation. *Figure 6.11* gives the output from quantum simulator for the circuit in *Figure 6.10*:

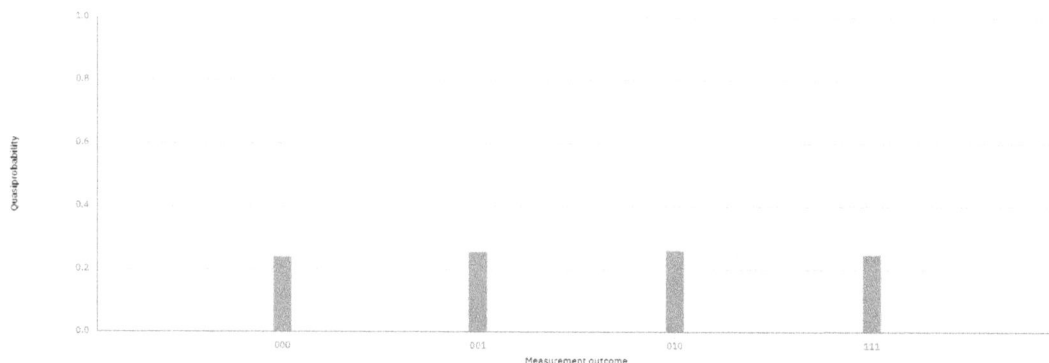

Figure 6.11: Composer bar chart for AND gate

Interpretation of results: *Figure 6.11* gives the various states of inputs and corresponding output. The first qubit under each bar is the output, and the remaining two qubits are the inputs. In the first bar, both the inputs are zero and output is zero. In the second and third bars, the inputs are a combination of 0 and 1, and output is 0. The last bar has both the inputs as 1, and the output is also 1. This aligns with the truth table of the AND gate.

Note that the probabilities of the four bars are not identical. The reason for this is the sampling error, while 1024 iterations is a sufficiently large number, but it is still not large enough that the results will converge to theoretical probabilities. However, from the perspective of demonstrating the AND behavior using quantum gates, these variations in probabilities do not matter. The key aspect is the state of the output qubit for different inputs.

NAND gate

Circuit setup: A Pauli X gate is applied to the output of AND gate in a quantum NAND circuit. *Figure 6.12* gives the corresponding circuit:

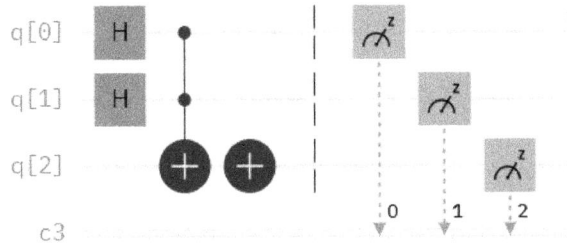

Figure 6.12: NAND gate

Simulation and results: Here too, just like the AND output, the output state |q[2] q[1] q[0] ⟩ will be a superposition of |000⟩, |001⟩, |010⟩ and |111⟩ before the Pauli X gate flips the output to make it a superposition of |100⟩, |101⟩, |110⟩ and |011⟩. *Figure 6.13* gives the quantum simulator output for the circuit in *Figure 6.12*:

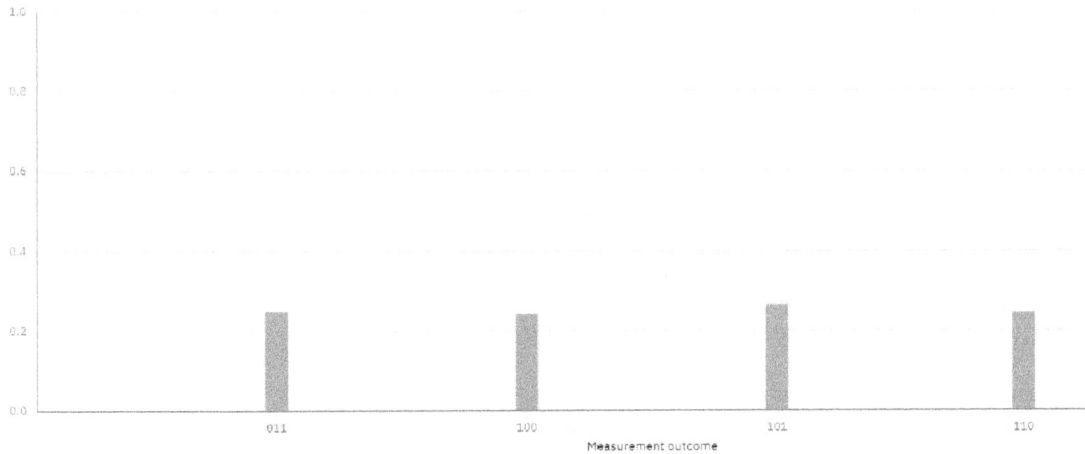

Figure 6.13: Composer bar chart for NAND gate

Interpretation of results: In *Figure 6.13*, the first qubit under each bar is the output and the remaining two qubits represent the inputs. In the first bar, both the inputs are 1, but the output is 0. In the second bar, the output is 1 when both inputs are 0. In the third and fourth bars, inputs are combination of 0 and 1, and the output is still 1. This depicts the NAND behavior.

OR gate

Circuit setup: The input qubits q[0] and q[1] are launched into superposition using a Hadamard gate. *Figure 6.14* gives the corresponding circuit:

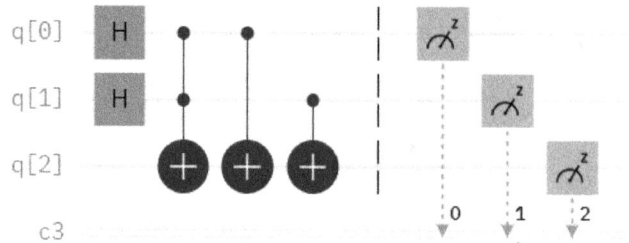

Figure 6.14: OR gate

Simulation and results: The output states of q[1] and q[0] after applying Hadamard gate will be a superposition state $|\psi\rangle = \frac{1}{2}(|00\rangle + |01\rangle + |10\rangle + |11\rangle)$.

The CCNOT will change the state of q[2] only when both q[1] and q[0] are 1. These qubits are 1 in the fourth state in the superposition. Therefore, q[2] becomes only in the fourth state. In the first three states, q[2] will remain 0. Therefore, the superposition state of |q[2] q[1] q[0] ⟩ post the application of CCNOT gate is|000⟩, |001⟩, |010⟩ and |111⟩. Note that q[2] is the leftmost qubit and q[0] is the rightmost.

The next CNOT will change the state of q[2] only when q[0] is 1. q[0] is 1 in the second and fourth states. Therefore, q[2] gets flipped in the second and fourth state. The new superposition state will be |000⟩, |101⟩, |010⟩ and |011⟩.

The last CNOT will change q[2] only when q[1] is 1. q[1] is 1 in third and fourth state. Therefore, q[2] gets flipped in the third and fourth state. The final state will be |000⟩, |101⟩, |110⟩ and |111⟩. That is, when one or more of q[0] and q[1] is 1, q[2] becomes 1, which is the OR behavior.

Figure 6.15 gives the output of quantum simulator for the circuit in *Figure 6.14:*

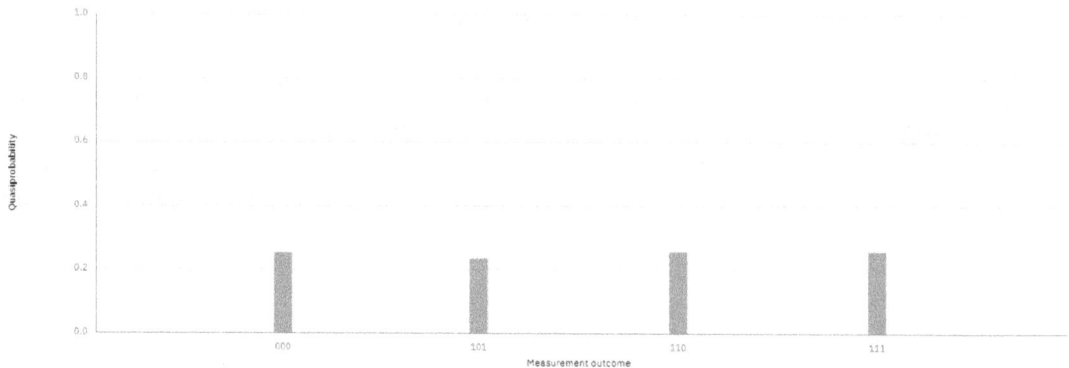

Figure 6.15: Composer bar chart for OR gate

Interpretation of results: In *Figure 6.15*, the first qubit is the output and the remaining two qubits are the inputs under each bar. Output is 0 in the first bar when both the inputs are

0. However, output is 1 in the remaining three bars where at least one input is 1. This acts as the OR gate.

NOR gate

Circuit setup: The input qubits q[0] and q[1] are launched into superposition using a Hadamard gate. *Figure 6.16* gives the corresponding circuit:

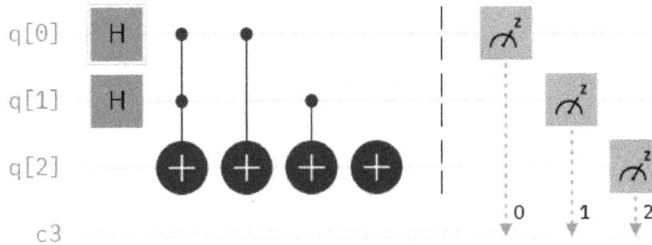

Figure 6.16: NOR gate

Simulation and results: The NOR gate is OR followed by the Pauli X gate. The output state | q[2] q[1] q[0] ⟩ of the OR gate, as seen in *Figure 6.16*, is |000⟩, |101⟩, |110⟩ and |111⟩.

Applying the Pauli X on q[2] will unconditionally flip its state. Hence, the new state will be - |100⟩, |001⟩, |010⟩ and |011⟩. This means that q[2] is 1 only when q[0] and q[1] are 1, otherwise it is 0. This is the NOR behavior.

Figure 6.17 gives the output from quantum simulator for the circuit in *Figure 6.16*:

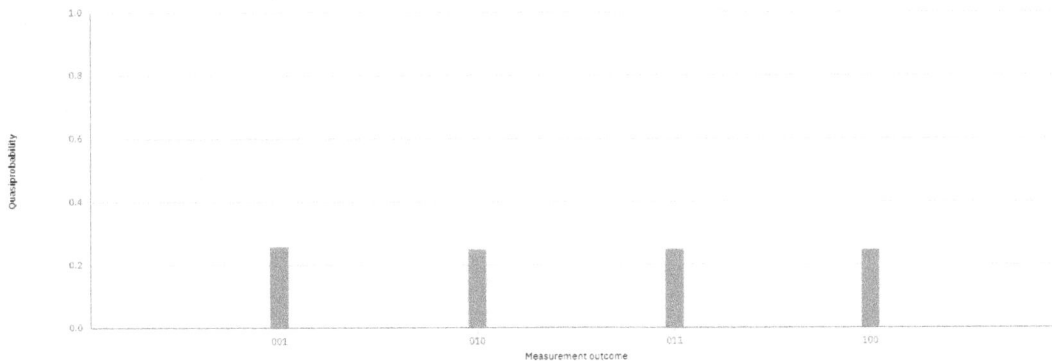

Figure 6.17: Composer bar chart for NOR gate

Interpretation of results: In *Figure 6.17*, the first qubit under each bar is the output and the remaining two qubits represent the inputs. The output is 0 in the first three bars, when either one or both the inputs are 1. However, output is 1 when both the inputs are 0. This represents the truth table of the NOR gate.

XOR gate

Circuit setup: The input qubits q[0] and q[1] are launched into superposition using a Hadamard gate. *Figure 6.18* gives the corresponding circuit:

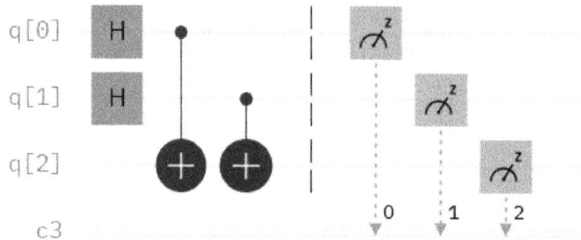

Figure 6.18: XOR gate

Simulation and results: The output states of q[1] and q[0] after applying Hadamard gate will be a superposition state $|\psi\rangle = \frac{1}{2}(|00\rangle + |01\rangle + |10\rangle + |11\rangle)$.

With q[2] in the initial state of 0, the state $|q[2]\,q[1]\,q[0]\,\rangle$ will be $|000\rangle$, $|001\rangle$, $|010\rangle$ and $|011\rangle$. The first CNOT will change the state of q[2] if q[0] is 1. Therefore, the state $|q[2]\,q[1]\,q[0]\,\rangle$ becomes $|000\rangle$, $|101\rangle$, $|010\rangle$ and $|111\rangle$.

The next CNOT will change the state of q[2] when q[1] is 1. Therefore, the state $|q[2]\,q[1]\,q[0]\,\rangle$ will change to $|000\rangle$, $|101\rangle$, $|110\rangle$ and $|011\rangle$. q[2] is 1 only when q[0] and q[1] are different. This is the expected output of the XOR gate.

Figure 6.19 gives the quantum simulator output for the circuit in *Figure 6.18*:

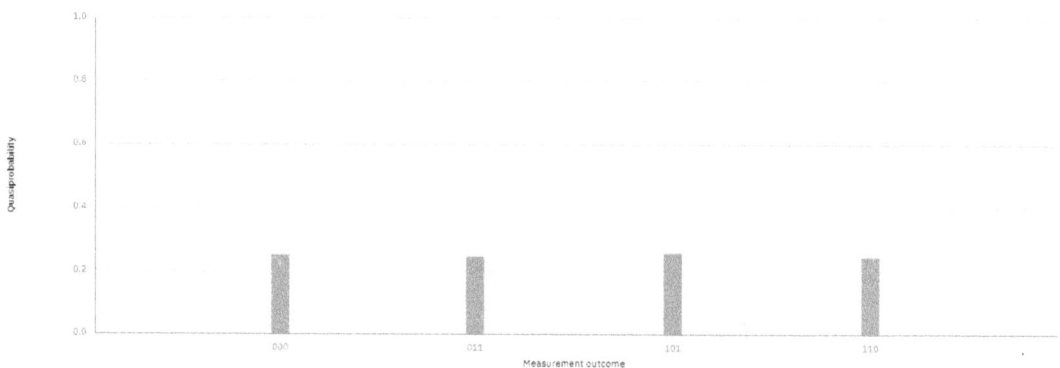

Figure 6.19: Composer bar chart for XOR gate

Interpretation of results: In *Figure 6.19*, the first qubit under each bar is the output and the remaining two qubits are the inputs. As can be seen in the first two bars, output is 0 when both the inputs are same, either both 0 or both 1. Output is 1 when the inputs are different in third and fourth bars. This is akin to a XOR gate truth table, wherein the output is 1 when one of the inputs is 1, and output is 0 when both the inputs are same.

XNOR gate

Circuit setup: The input qubits q[0] and q[1] are launched into superposition using a Hadamard gate. *Figure 6.20* gives the corresponding circuit:

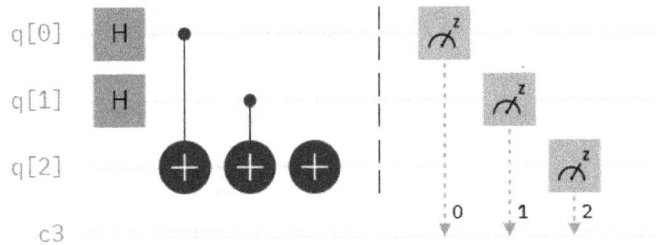

Figure 6.20: XNOR gate

Simulation and results: XNOR is XOR followed by a NOT gate. In quantum circuit, this is XOR followed by the Pauli X gate. As we have seen in the previous section, XOR superposition state |q[2] q[1] q[0]) is |000), |101), |110) and |011). The Pauli X will unconditionally flip q[2]. Therefore, the final state will be |100), |001), |010) and |111). Here, q[2] is 1 when both the inputs are identical, which is the XNOR behavior.

Figure 6.21 gives the quantum simulator output for the circuit in *Figure 6.20*:

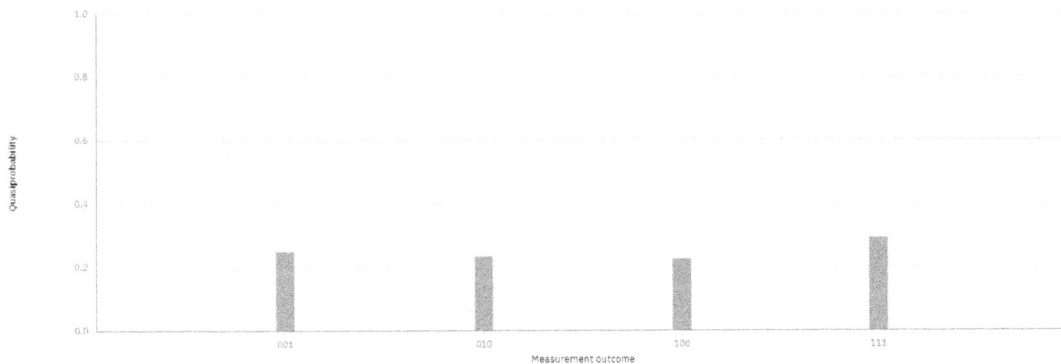

Figure 6.21: Composer bar chart for XNOR gate

Interpretation of results: Just like the previous figures, *Figure 6.21* has the first qubit as output and the remaining two qubits as the inputs. Here, the behavior is exactly opposite to the XOR gate. When both the inputs are same in third and the fourth bar, output is 1. When the inputs are different, as seen in the first and second bars, output is 0. This is the XNOR gate behavior.

IBM Qiskit SDK

Quantum Information Software Kit (Qiskit) is an open-source framework developed by IBM for programming and running quantum computers. It allows users to design, simulate, and execute quantum circuits on IBM's quantum hardware and simulators. With Qiskit, one can run code in Jupyter Notebook or on an IDE for Python. Qiskit provides quantum simulators for running circuits on classical hardware, tools for quantum hardware verification, noise characterization, and error correction, and a library of quantum algorithms and components to build quantum applications.

Key features of Qiskit are as follows:

- **Quantum circuit programming:** Allows users to create and manipulate quantum circuits using Python.

- **Simulation and execution:** Run quantum programs on IBM's real quantum processors or classical simulators.

- **Quantum algorithms and applications:** Supports machine learning, chemistry, optimization, and finance applications.

- **Modular design:** Divided into different components for flexibility and usability.

In this sub-section, we will implement the same circuits from the previous section (*IBM Q composer*), but on a Jupyter Notebook. These programs will be executed on both IBM Q simulators as well as real quantum processors. We will look at the updated circuit design where Hadamard gate is applied to all the input qubits. The results are generated by executing it on IBM Q simulator as well as IBM Q processor. The simulator used is ibmq_qasm_simulator. The IBM Q processor used here depends on the least busy processor. A block of code will check for the least busy processor and execute the program there. The available processors are ibm_brisbane, ibm_osaka, and ibm_kyoto, which are all 127-qubits processors.

A few of the key differences between a simulator and a real processor are:

- Simulator does not suffer from noise or decoherence since it is a simulated environment. Qubits experience noise, decoherence, and gate errors in real processors, leading to inaccuracies in results.

- Simulator can handle quantum circuits efficiently without the latency of real hardware. In a real processor, jobs are queued based on the availability of the processor. This can cause a long waiting time.

- In a simulator, the response is consistent across runs, which is deterministic. In a real processor, response can sometimes change depending on the noise and gate errors.

- Simulator cannot scale beyond a point because the backend is still a classical computer. Quantum processors, on the other hand, have the potential to scale exponentially for certain use cases.

- Real-world experimentation and prototyping must be run on a real quantum processor to understand the true behavior of qubits and explore error correction techniques. There is no value in running such use cases on a simulator.

Before we get into individual gates, let us look at boilerplate code that will be common for all the gates.

The following are the libraries that are required to run the quantum circuit on a simulator and a real processor:

Boilerplate code:

Import libraries at the start to avoid runtime errors:

```
#initialization
from qiskit import Aer, assemble, transpile
from qiskit import QuantumCircuit, ClassicalRegister, QuantumRegister
from qiskit.providers.ibmq import least_busy
from qiskit.providers.ibmq.job import job_monitor
import enum
# import basic plot tools
from qiskit.visualization import plot_histogram
```

The following Enum represents various logic gates. Each gate is assigned a unique integer value. Enumerations help in making code more readable and prevent the use of arbitrary numbers.

```
#Define enum for different gates.
class gateEnum(enum.Enum):
    NOT = 1
    AND = 2
    NAND = 3
    OR = 4
    NOR = 5
    XOR = 6
    XNOR = 7
```

Note: **For NOT gate, change the quantum register count from three to one in the first line as there is only one input qubit, and change the classical register count to 1 as only one qubit has to be measured.**

```
#Initialize quantum circuit
Qreg = QuantumRegister(3)
```

```
Creg = ClassicalRegister(3)
qc = QuantumCircuit(Qreg, Creg)
```

Simulator execution:

```
#Set the backend simulator, assemble the quantum circuit and submit it.
def output(qc):
    # Get the quantum simulator backend
    aer_sim = Aer.get_backend('qasm_simulator')
    # Assemble the quantum circuit into an object (Quantum Object)
    qobj = assemble(qc)
    # Run the circuit on the simulator and get the result
    res = aer_sim.run(qobj).result()
    # Extract the measurement counts (frequency of results)
    count = res.get_counts()
    return count


count = output(qc)
#Plot the output.
plot_histogram(count)
```

Processor execution:

The following block of code is to execute the quantum circuit on a real quantum processor:

```
#Below block of code will check for the least busy quantum processor.
# Load the IBMQ account (this must be done before accessing IBM Quantum
devices)
provider = IBMQ.load_account()


# Get the specific IBMQ provider (IBM provides different hubs, groups, and
projects)
provider = IBMQ.get_provider("ibm-q")


# Find the least busy quantum processor that meets the following conditions:
# - Has at least 3 qubits
# - Is not a simulator (must be a real quantum device)
# - Is currently operational (available for running jobs)
device = least_busy(provider.backends(filters=lambda x: x.configuration().n_
qubits >= 3 and
```

```
not x.configuration().simulator and x.status().operational==True))
```

```
print("Find the least busy processor: ", device)
```

The following code will transpile the quantum circuit on the least busy processor and run it there. Monitor the execution of the job in the queue.

```
# Import job_monitor to track the execution status of a quantum job
from qiskit.tools.monitor import job_monitor
# Transpile (optimize) the quantum circuit for the selected quantum device
# - `qc`: The quantum circuit to be transpiled
# - `device`: The selected IBM Quantum device to run the circuit on
# - `optimization_level=3`: Maximum optimization level to increase accuracy
and reduce execution time, at the expense of longer transpilation time.
transpiled_circuit = transpile(qc, device, optimization_level=3)
```

The following job takes anywhere from few minutes to few hours to run, depending on the time of the day and the number of users concurrently executing their jobs. The status of jobs can also be seen on IBM Q cloud under the Workloads tab. In case the job fails, rerun the following two lines of code.

```
# Submit the transpiled circuit for execution on the selected quantum device
job = device.run(transpiled_circuit)
# Monitor the status of the job, updating every 2 seconds
job_monitor(job, interval=2)
# Retrieve the results of the executed quantum job
results = job.result()
# Extract the measurement counts from the results
# - This returns a dictionary where keys are measured bitstrings (e.g., '00',
'01', '10', '11')
# - Values are the number of times each bitstring was observed
answer = results.get_counts(qc)
# Plot a histogram of the measurement results to visualize the output
distribution
plot_histogram(answer)
```

Setup of superposition:

Launch the qubits into superposition by applying Hadamard. For NOT gate, comment out the second line as there will be only one input qubit.

```
qc.h(0)
```

```
qc.h(1)
qc.barrier()
```

NOT gate

The following code is used to build a quantum NOT gate. *Figure 6.22* gives the circuit generated by the code:

```
#Define the gate.
def NOT(qc):
    qc.x(0)
    return qc


#Apply the NOT gate and measure
qc = NOT(qc)
qc.measure(0, 0)

#Plot the circuit.
style = {'fontsize':10}
qc.draw(output='mpl', style=style)
```

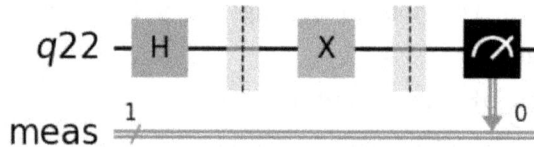

Figure 6.22: IBM lab circuit for NOT gate

Let us look at the results when run on a quantum simulator and a real quantum device.

Quantum simulator

Refer to the explanation for NOT gate results under the IBM Q composer section. The simulator (ibmq_qasm_simulator) gives an almost equal probability for the two states after 1024 iterations. The reason the outcomes are not perfectly equal is that this is like tossing an unbiased coin 1024 times. While the theoretical probabilities of getting heads and tails are equal, in reality, however, they will be close to 50:50 but not perfectly 50:50. That is the reason why the outcomes in *Figure 6.23* are not perfectly 50:50:

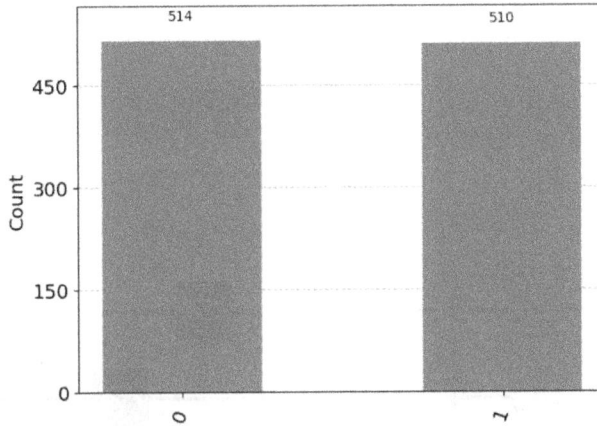

Figure 6.23: IBM lab bar chart for NOT gate on simulator

Quantum hardware

The results in *Figure 6.24* are from an actual quantum processor, ibm_kyoto. Just like the simulator, the output probabilities are close to 50:50 after 4000 iterations.

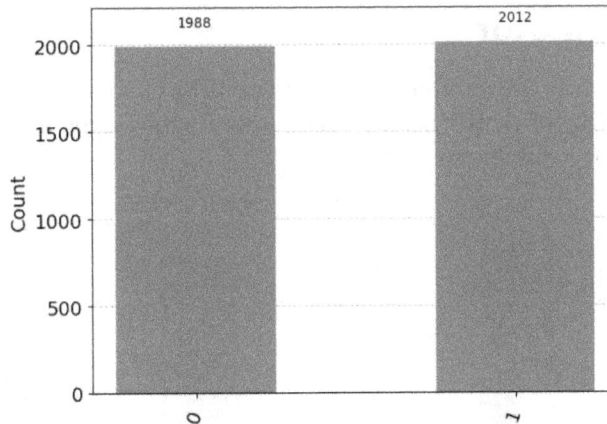

Figure 6.24: IBM lab bar chart for NOT gate on quantum processor

AND gate

The following is the code for the quantum AND gate. *Figure 6.25* gives the circuit generated by the code:

```
#Define the gate.
def AND(qc):
    qc.ccx(0,1,2)
    return qc
```

```
#Plot the circuit.
qc = AND(qc)
qc.measure(0, 0)
style = {'fontsize':10}
qc.draw(output='mpl', style=style)
```

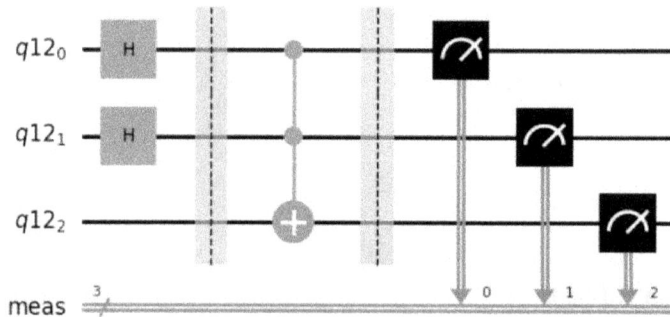

Figure 6.25: *IBM lab circuit for AND gate*

Quantum simulator

The results in *Figure 6.26* are similar to those from IBM Q composer. The qubits are in a superposition of $|000\rangle$, $|001\rangle$, $|010\rangle$, and $|111\rangle$, wherein the target or output is the leftmost qubit and the other two qubits are inputs.

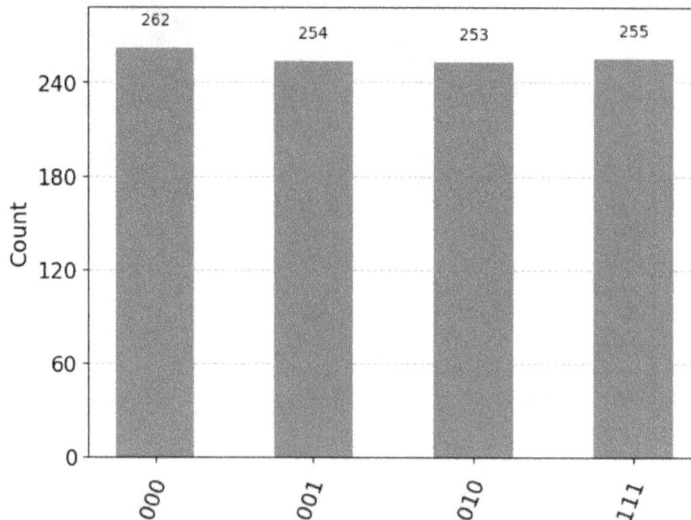

Figure 6.26: *IBM lab bar chart for AND gate on A simulator*

Quantum hardware

The results in *Figure 6.27* are from an actual quantum processor, ibm_brisbane, after 4000 iterations. Unlike the simulator, the output probabilities are varying. This is because of decoherence and other interferences that real qubits are susceptible to. That is the reason for the small probabilities of the states that are not part of the expected results. However, the superposition states 000, 001, 010, and 111 still stand out, which reflects the AND behavior.

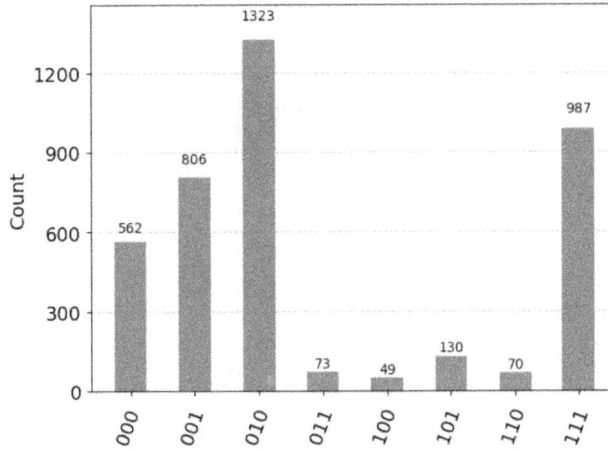

Figure 6.27: *IBM lab bar chart for AND gate on quantum processor*

NAND gate

Following is the code for the quantum NAND gate. *Figure 6.28* gives the circuit generated by the code:

```
#Define the gate.
def NAND(qc):
    qc = AND(qc)
    qc.x(2)
    return qc


#Plot the circuit.
qc = NAND(qc)
qc.measure(0, 0)
style = {'fontsize':10}
qc.draw(output='mpl', style=style)
```

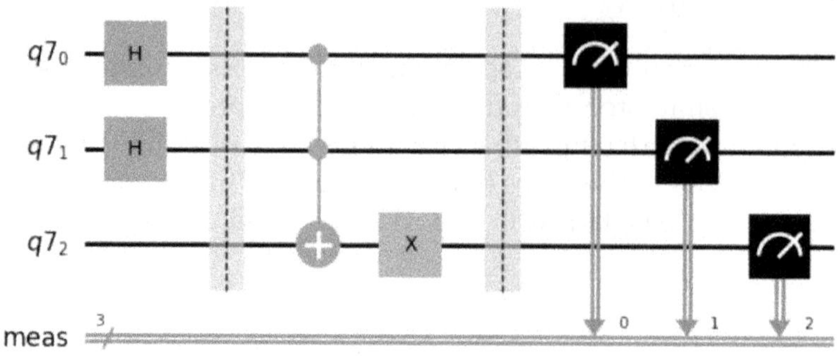

Figure 6.28: IBM lab circuit for NAND gate

Quantum simulator

The results in *Figure 6.29* are similar to the results from IBM Q composer. The qubits are in a superposition of $|100\rangle$, $|101\rangle$, $|110\rangle$ and $|011\rangle$, wherein the target is the leftmost qubit and the other two qubits are inputs.

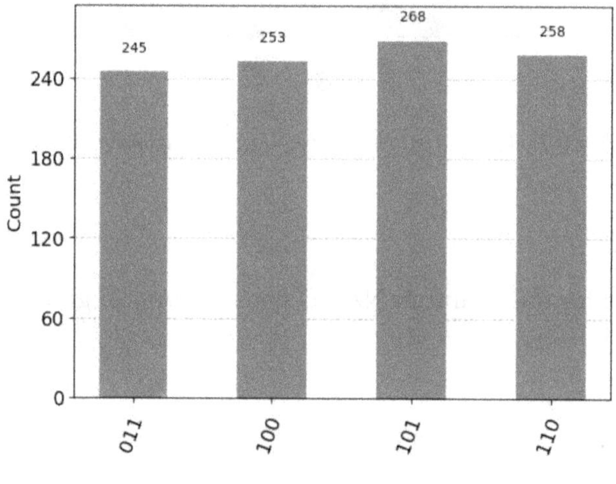

Figure 6.29: IBM lab bar chart for NAND gate ona simulator

Quantum hardware

The results in *Figure 6.30* are from an actual quantum processor, ibm_brisbane, after 4000 iterations. Unlike the simulator, the output probabilities are varying, this is because of decoherence and other interferences that real qubits are susceptible to. That is the reason for small probabilities of the states that are not part of the expected results. However, the superposition states 011, 100, 101 and 110 still stand out, which reflects the NAND behavior.

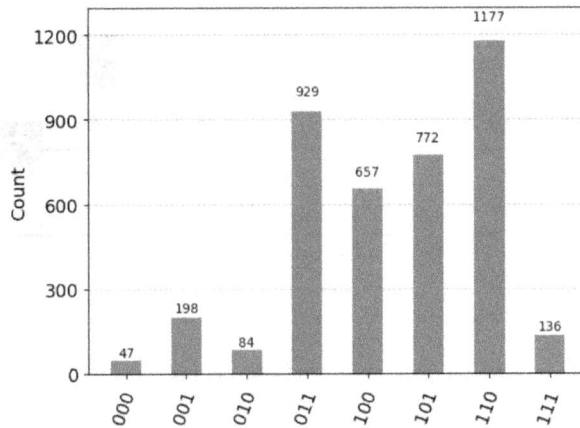

Figure 6.30: *IBM lab bar chart for NAND gate on quantum processor*

OR gate

The following is the code for the quantum OR gate. *Figure 6.31* gives the circuit generated by the code:

```
#Define the gate.
def OR(qc):
    qc = AND(qc)
    qc.cx(0,2)
    qc.cx(1,2)
    return qc

#Plot the circuit.
qc = OR(qc)
qc.measure(0, 0)
style = {'fontsize':10}
qc.draw(output='mpl', style=style)
```

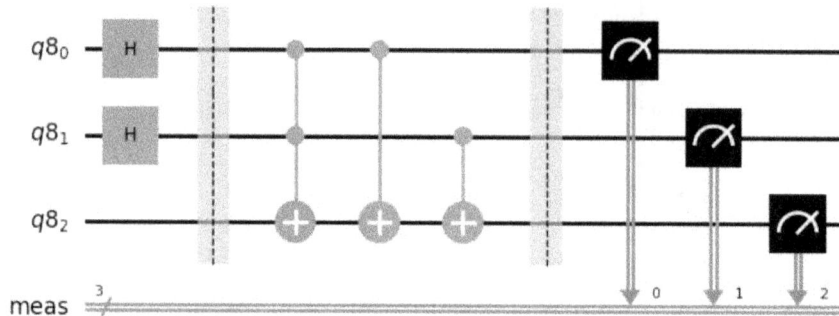

Figure 6.31: IBM lab circuit for OR gate

Quantum simulator

The results in *Figure 6.32* are similar to the results from IBM Q composer. The qubits are in a superposition of $|000\rangle$, $|101\rangle$, $|110\rangle$, and $|111\rangle$, wherein the target is the leftmost qubit and the other two qubits are inputs.

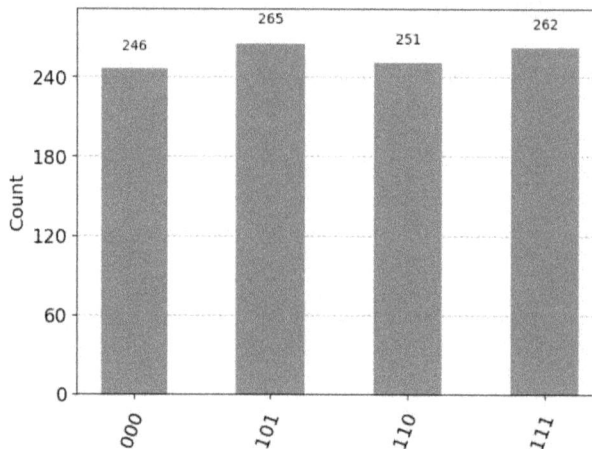

Figure 6.32: IBM lab bar chart for OR gate on simulator

Quantum hardware

The results in *Figure 6.33* are from an actual quantum processor, ibm_brisbane, after 4000 iterations. Unlike the simulator, the output probabilities are varying, this is because of decoherence and other interferences that real qubits are susceptible to. That is the reason for the small probabilities of the states that are not part of the expected results. However, the superposition states 000, 101, 110, and 111 still stand out, which reflects the OR behavior.

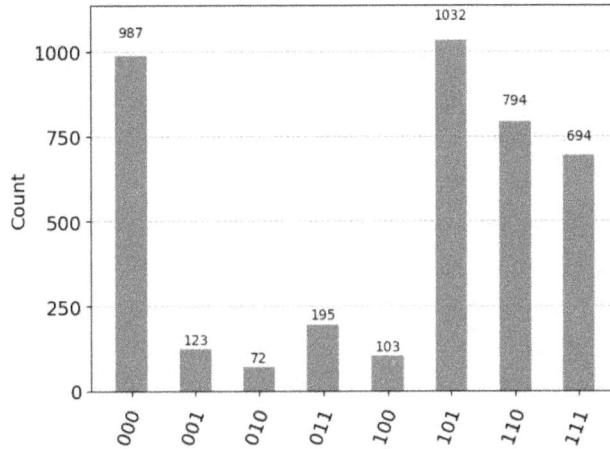

Figure 6.33: *IBM lab bar chart for OR gate on quantum processor*

NOR gate

The following is the code for the quantum NOR gate. *Figure 6.34* gives the circuit generated by the code:

```
#Define the gate.
def NOR(qc):
    qc = OR(qc)
    qc.x(2)
    return qc


#Plot the circuit.
qc = NOR(qc)
qc.measure(0, 0)
style = {'fontsize':10}
qc.draw(output='mpl', style=style)
```

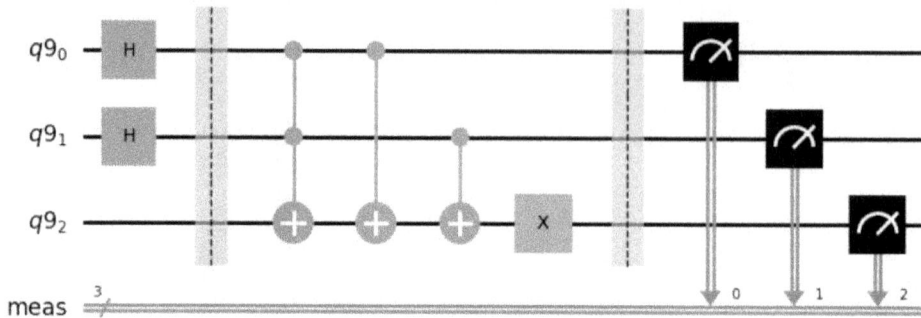

Figure 6.34: *IBM lab circuit for NOR gate*

Quantum simulator

The results in *Figure 6.35* are similar to those from IBM Q composer. The qubits are in a superposition of $|001\rangle$, $|010\rangle$, $|011\rangle$, and $|100\rangle$, wherein the target is the leftmost qubit and the other two qubits are inputs.

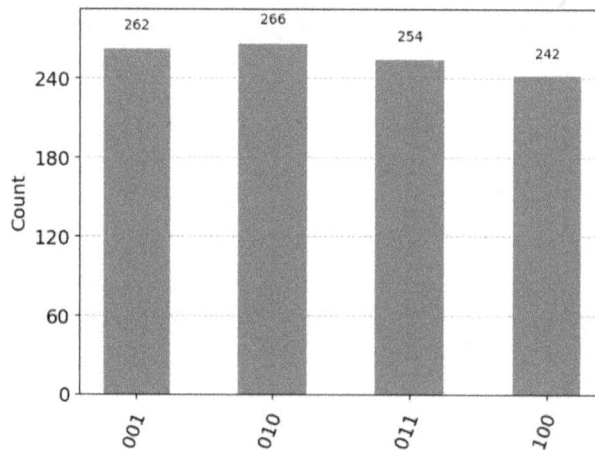

Figure 6.35: *IBM lab bar chart for NOR gate on simulator*

Quantum hardware

The results from *Figure 6.36* are from an actual quantum processor, ibm_osaka, after 4000 iterations. Here, the superpositions 001, 010, 011, and 100 stand out, which reflects the NOR behavior.

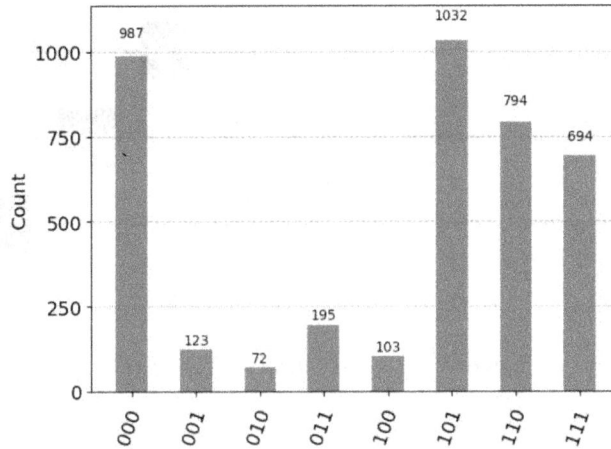

Figure 6.36: *IBM lab bar chart for NOR gate on quantum processor*

XOR gate

The following is the code for the quantum XOR gate. *Figure 6.37* gives the circuit generated by the code:

```
#Define the gate.
def XOR(qc):
    qc.cx(0,2)
    qc.cx(1,2)
    return qc

#Plot the circuit.
qc = XOR(qc)
qc.measure(0, 0)
style = {'fontsize':10}
qc.draw(output='mpl', style=style)
```

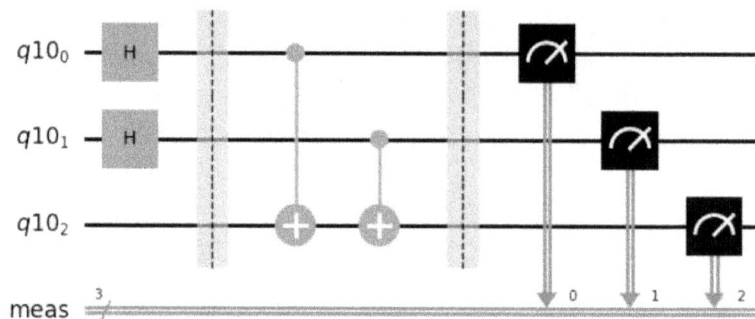

Figure 6.37: IBM lab circuit for XOR gate

Quantum simulator

The results in *Figure 6.38* are similar to the results from the IBM Q composer. The qubits are in a superposition of $|000\rangle$, $|011\rangle$, $|101\rangle$, and $|110\rangle$, wherein the target is the leftmost qubit and the other two qubits are inputs.

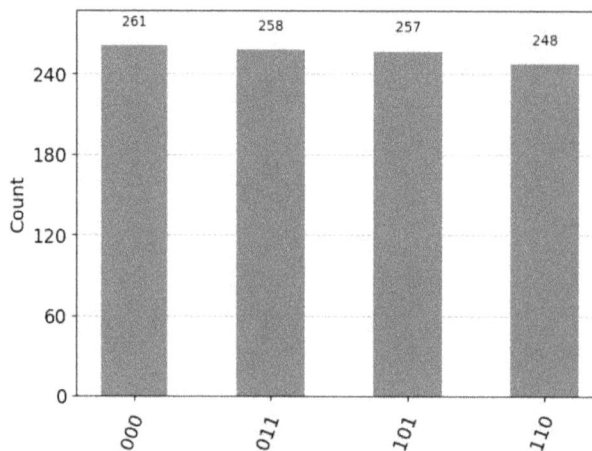

Figure 6.38: IBM lab bar chart for XOR gate on simulator

Quantum hardware

The results in *Figure 6.39* are from an actual quantum processor – ibm_kyoto, after 4000 iterations. Here, the superposition states 000, 011, 101 and 110 stand out, which reflects the XOR behavior.

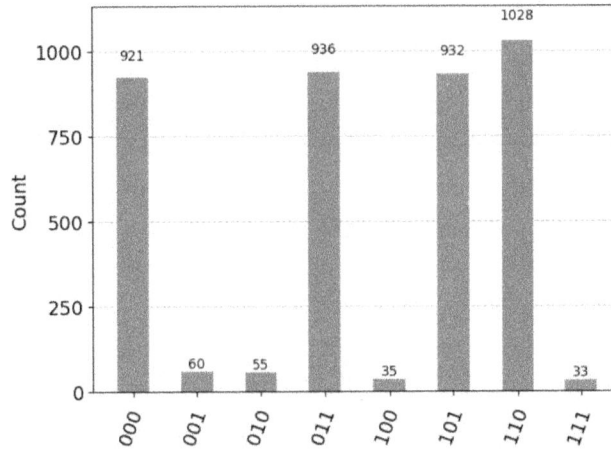

Figure 6.39: *IBM lab bar chart for XOR gate on quantum processor*

XNOR gate

Following is the code for the quantum XNOR gate. *Figure 6.40* gives the circuit generated by the code.

```
#Define the gate.
def XNOR(qc):
    qc.cx(0,2)
    qc.cx(1,2)
    qc.x(2)
    return qc


#Plot the circuit.
qc = XNOR(qc)
qc.measure(0, 0)
style = {'fontsize':10}
qc.draw(output='mpl', style=style)
```

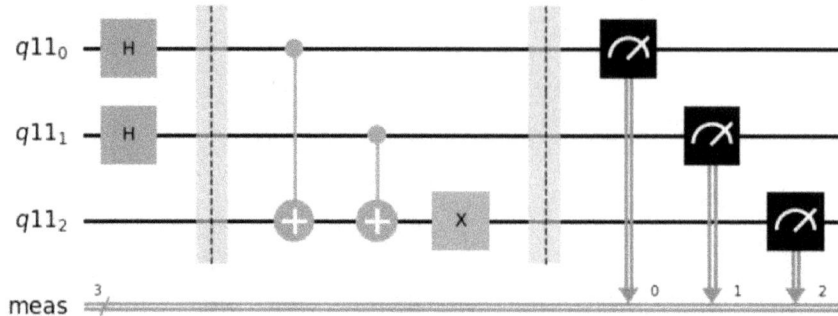

Figure 6.40: IBM lab circuit for XNOR gate

Quantum simulator

The results in *Figure 6.41* are similar to those from IBM Q composer. The qubits are in a superposition of $|001\rangle$, $|010\rangle$, $|100\rangle$, and $|111\rangle$, wherein the target is the leftmost qubit and the other two qubits are inputs.

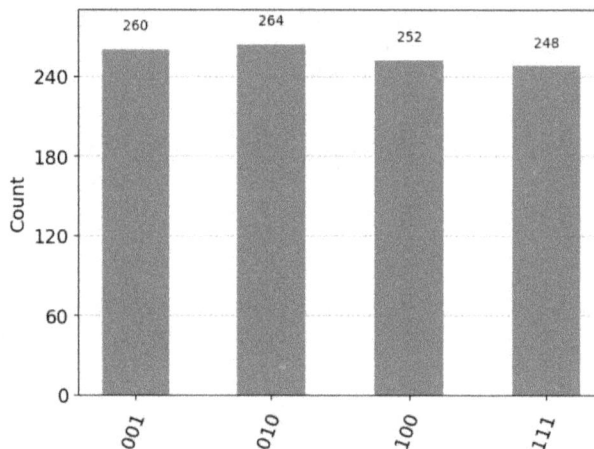

Figure 6.41: IBM lab bar chart for XNOR gate on simulator

Quantum hardware

The results in *Figure 6.42* are from an actual quantum processor, ibm_kyoto, after 4000 iterations. Here, the superposition states 001, 010, 100 and 111 stand out, which reflects the XNOR behavior.

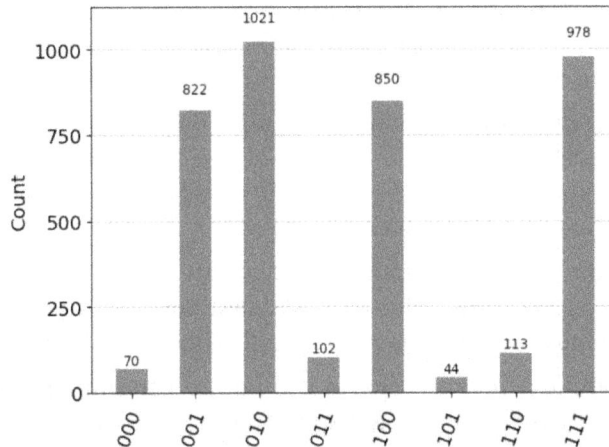

Figure 6.42: IBM lab bar chart for XNOR gate, quantum processor

Advantages of using quantum gates

Quantum gates offer several advantages, such as drastically improved computational speed and power, which enables them to tackle complex algorithms that are infeasible for classical computers to compute. Quantum gates can also execute multiple calculations simultaneously due to the property of superposition, thus providing parallelism, which is unattainable in classical computing

The following are the advantages of using quantum gates:

- **Quantum parallelism:** Quantum gates use the principle of superposition, where qubits can exist in multiple states at once, as opposed to classical bits that can only exist in one of two states. Due to this feature, a quantum computer can process a large number of possibilities at once. This allows for parallel computation, thereby improving the efficiency and speed of complex computational tasks exponentially. Tasks such as factoring large numbers, simulating quantum systems or optimizing complex systems can be performed much more efficiently with quantum computers. Algorithms such as Shor's factorization, Grover's search, etc., exploit the inherent parallelism in quantum processing. This property is useful in quantum cryptography, search and optimization, drug discovery and many other use cases.

- **Quantum entanglement:** Another important feature offered by quantum gates is entanglement, which allows two qubits to become linked such that the state of one immediately influences the state of the other no matter the distance between them. This feature is key to quantum communication and information processing. Entanglement is used in quantum teleportation, superdense coding, and quantum key distribution. The real-world applications of entanglement are in quantum cryptography, quantum networking, and quantum communication.

- **Superior problem-solving capability:** Some types of calculations, which are extremely time-consuming or even impossible for classical computers, can be performed efficiently by a quantum computer.

- **Optimization problems:** Quantum gates enable the resolution of complex optimization problems more efficiently because of the property of superposition. This feature can be useful in business logistics, scenario simulation, and risk management, among other areas.

- **Advanced data analysis:** Quantum gates, due to the capabilities of quantum computers, allow for the analysis of vast quantities of data in less time. This ability can revolutionize fields such as medicine, finance, and big data.

- **Quantum searches:** Quantum gates can be used to implement quantum search algorithms (such as Grover's algorithm) that can perform more efficient searches on unsorted data than any classical algorithm.

- **Quantum cryptography and security:** By utilizing quantum gates, we can create cryptographic keys and codes that cannot be easily deciphered except by the intended recipient using the correct quantum key. This can revolutionize cybersecurity.

Disadvantages of using quantum gates

A major disadvantage is using quantum gates is their susceptibility to error, as quantum states can easily be affected by external environmental conditions leading to high error rates. Additionally, making and maintaining the state of quantum entanglement necessary for quantum gates is immensely challenging, limiting the practical implementation of quantum computing.

The following are the disadvantages of using quantum gates:

- **Quantum decoherence:** Quantum computers require maintaining coherence of qubits to perform computations. Decoherence happens because of interference from the outside environment, leading to loss of quantum properties and causing errors in computation. Hence, maintaining coherence over a sufficient period to complete computation tasks is a significant challenge. There are few methods to mitigate this error, such as dynamic decoupling, fault tolerant **quantum error correction (QEC)**, etc. In dynamic decoupling, the qubits are maintained in superposition state by applying quick, precisely timed pulses. These pulses average out the effect of the external noise, thus improving stability of the qubit. In fault tolerant QEC, redundancy is added to detect and correct errors. In this, logical qubits are encoded using multiple physical qubits.

- **High error rates:** Quantum computations at the moment are prone to errors due to physical operations not being perfect. Errors in a quantum computer can propagate and create further errors. Classical error correction methods do not work here due to the **No-cloning** theorem of quantum mechanics. Also, quantum logic gates do not function deterministically as classical gates do. The fidelity of a quantum gate operation is not perfect; hence, increasing the number of gates would also increase the probability of errors. One of the key measures to enhance the fidelity at the qubit level is hardware improvements such as cryogenic cooling of the quantum processor, better qubit isolation so that they don't interfere with each other, etc.

- **Complex control mechanism:** Quantum gates require highly precise control mechanisms to ensure the accurate manipulation of qubits. Any small inaccuracies can lead to drastic computation errors.

- **Expensive:** The building and maintenance of a large-scale quantum computer presents a huge engineering challenge. Quantum computers are highly sensitive to environmental noise, require cooling to near absolute zero temperatures, and need isolation from all vibrations, making the technology quite expensive and less accessible than classical computers.

- **Limited algorithms:** While there are particular problems that quantum computers could theoretically solve more quickly than classical computers, as of now, the number of these algorithms is quite limited. This limits the practical applications of quantum computers.

- **Scaling:** Quantum volume, a measure of the complexity of problems solvable by a quantum computer, is limited in the current state of technology. While the number of qubits can be increased, the precision and coherence of quantum gates are usually compromised when scaling up, which limits potential applications. Scaling requires a mix of solutions such as hybrid processing wherein classical processors handle certain computations thus reducing quantum hardware demands, error correction wherein focus is on logical qubits rather than adding more physical qubits, and a modular design that connects multiple smaller quantum processors to operate as a larger system.

- **Compatibility:** Quantum computers use a totally different computational approach compared to classical computers. Many classical algorithms will not work on quantum computers or need to be significantly adapted.

To summarize, while quantum gates present exciting possibilities to enhance the power, capacity and speed of computing, overcoming their current challenges requires considerable scientific and technological advancements.

Conclusion

The chapter provided an in-depth exploration of quantum gates and their application in constructing classical logic gates. Through a detailed examination of implementing various classical gates such as NOT, AND, NAND, OR, NOR, XOR and XNOR using quantum equivalents, readers were equipped with a fundamental understanding of the intersection between classical digital logic and quantum computing paradigms. Furthermore, the use of tools like IBM Q composer and IBM Qiskit SDK illustrated the practical aspects of designing quantum circuits, highlighting both the potential and the challenges of leveraging quantum hardware and simulators for these purposes. The next chapter will present different approaches in quantum communication.

Multiple choice questions

1. **If a classical gate, say an OR gate, is to be simulated using quantum gates as described in this section, what is the assumed initial state for its input qubits, unless explicitly stated otherwise?**

    a. A superposition of $|0\rangle$ and $|1\rangle$

    b. $|1\rangle$

    c. $|0\rangle$

    d. An uninitialized, random state

2. **Which of the following statements is TRUE regarding the implementation of quantum AND and NAND gates in this chapter?**

    a. The AND gate is implemented using a single Pauli X gate.

    b. The NAND gate is realized by applying a CCNOT gate followed by a Pauli X gate to the target qubit.

    c. The output of the CCNOT gate is always $|1\rangle$ regardless of the control qubits' states.

    d. The NAND gate does not require any quantum gates for its implementation.

3. **Why do classical error correction methods NOT work for quantum computers?**

    a. Because quantum logic gates function deterministically

    b. Due to the No-cloning theorem of quantum mechanics

    c. Because quantum computations are not prone to errors

    d. Due to the high fidelity of quantum gate operations

4. **Which of the following is a key difference between a real quantum processor and a quantum simulator?**

    a. Real quantum processors use classical bits, while simulators use qubits.

    b. Quantum simulators perform computations based on quantum mechanics, while real processors only emulate behavior.

    c. Quantum simulators can achieve higher qubit counts than real quantum processors.

    d. Real quantum processors leverage phenomena like superposition and entanglement, whereas quantum simulators do not execute genuine quantum computations.

5. **What is the primary function of res.get_counts() in the output(qc) function within the "Simulator execution" section?**

   a. To obtain the frequency of measurement results (counts) from the simulation.

   b. To retrieve the raw measurement data from the simulator.

   c. To extract the number of qubits used in the simulation.

   d. To plot a histogram of the simulation outcomes.

Answer key

1. c
2. b
3. b
4. d
5. a

Questions

1. From a conceptual standpoint, what does the endeavor to simulate common classical gates (like NOT, AND, XOR) using quantum gates signify about the relationship between classical and quantum computing?

   Answer: This endeavor signifies that quantum computing is not an entirely separate paradigm but rather a more generalized framework that can encompass and reproduce classical computation as a specific instance. It demonstrates a foundational link where classical logic can be viewed through a quantum lens, suggesting quantum computation can perform at least what classical computers can, potentially with additional capabilities.

2. What is a quantum circuit, and what are its primary components?

   Answer: A quantum circuit is a model for quantum computation in which a sequence of quantum gates is applied to a set of qubits to manipulate their states. Its primary components include qubits (quantum bits), quantum gates (the operations that change qubit states), and measurement operations (used to observe or read out the final state of the qubits).

3. What are two key technical details used to measure the performance and capability of an IBM Q quantum computer?

   Answer: Two key technical details are **fidelity**, which measures how accurately quantum gates perform their intended operation, and **quantum volume**, a quality metric that considers factors like the number of qubits, their interconnectivity, coherence, and error rates to assess the overall computational ability of a quantum processor.

4. What is the role of transpile in the "Processor execution" section, and what does optimization_level=3 signify?

   Answer: The transpile function optimizes a quantum circuit (qc) for the specific quantum device (device) by adapting the circuit to the hardware's constraints and layout, helping it run more efficiently and accurately. The parameter optimization_level=3 specifies the highest level of optimization, which applies the most advanced techniques to minimize gate errors and circuit depth. This can lead to longer transpilation time but often results in higher overall execution accuracy and performance on the real device.

5. Give examples of few types of problems that quantum gates can solve more efficiently than classical computers.

   Answer: Factoring large numbers, simulating quantum systems, optimizing complex systems, and quantum search problems are some examples.

Join our Discord space

Join our Discord workspace for latest updates, offers, tech happenings around the world, new releases, and sessions with the authors:

https://discord.bpbonline.com

CHAPTER 7

Quantum Communication

Introduction

This chapter aims to elucidate four avenues of quantum communication, which are, superdense coding, quantum teleportation, quantum key distribution and post quantum cryptography. Each of these explores quantum mechanics from different perspectives, laying the foundations for future technologies, altering how we think about information, and perfecting secure communication. Superdense coding allows transmission of vast amounts of information with minimal particles without the trade-off of functionality or accuracy. Quantum teleportation, where quantum states, instead of physical entities, travel instantaneously, redefining our understanding of distance and connectivity. Quantum key distribution secures communication channels using the principles of quantum mechanics. Finally, we will delve into **post-quantum cryptography (PQC)**, which lays the groundwork for the security of conventional cryptosystems in the era of quantum computers. This chapter will help grasp a deeper understanding of these realms that merges advanced theoretical concepts with practical applications.

Structure

The chapter will cover the following topics:
- Introduction to quantum communication
- Quantum superdense coding

- Quantum teleportation
- Quantum key distribution
- Post-quantum cryptography

Objectives

This chapter aims to discuss several key aspects of quantum communication and cryptography by exploring principles of quantum mechanics. It explores the principles and practical implementations of **quantum key distribution** (**QKD**), illustrating how it leverages quantum mechanics to establish secure communication channels resistant to eavesdropping. The chapter also analyzes the process and advantages of quantum teleportation, highlighting its role in transferring quantum information with high fidelity over long distances, which is essential for the future of quantum networks. Additionally, it investigates the concept and applications of superdense coding, showcasing its ability to enhance data transmission efficiency by encoding two classical bits of information within a single quantum bit (qubit). Furthermore, the chapter examines the necessity and development of post-quantum cryptographic algorithms designed to protect information systems from the potential risks posed by quantum computing, thereby ensuring the long-term security and integrity of data.

Introduction to quantum communication

Quantum communication represents an advanced technological paradigm exploiting the principles of quantum physics to transmit information. It provides a new approach to processing, storing, and transmitting information in ways that offer capabilities, including security, compute power, and information density, beyond what current technology can practically achieve. It involves the use of quantum mechanical effects to perform communication tasks that may be impossible or infeasibly complex using classical communication. These tasks range from QKD to quantum teleportation to quantum superdense coding.

The core principles of quantum communication include quantum entanglement and quantum superposition. Quantum superposition allows an entity, like a quantum bit (or qubit), to exist simultaneously in multiple states, each with a certain probability, which only resolves into a specific state when measured. It is akin to flipping a coin but allowing it to be heads and tails simultaneously until observed. Quantum entanglement links two qubits in such a way that the measurement of one instantaneously affects the state of the other, regardless of the distance between them.

The following list gives a brief overview of the different forms of quantum communication:

- **Quantum superdense coding:** Superdense coding is a technique used in quantum information theory to send two classical bits of information using only one qubit, exploiting the phenomenon of quantum entanglement. It indicates that far more information can be contained within the same amount of quantum information than classically possible. One of its significant applications lies in optimizing bandwidth in modern networks, as it allows for the efficient use of communication channels, thereby increasing data transmission rates without requiring additional physical resources.

- **Quantum teleportation:** Another profound feature of quantum communication is quantum teleportation. This involves the transfer of quantum information from one point to another, without the physical transportation of the actual particle carrying the information. This is achieved using quantum entanglement, where the states of two or more particles can become linked so that a change to one will instantly affect the others, no matter how far apart they are. Though it is not teleportation in the science-fiction sense, this is an essential aspect of quantum communication as it allows for the secure and instantaneous transmission of information. Bell states play a crucial role in enabling quantum teleportation. They are specific types of entangled quantum states that form a shared quantum link between two qubits. This entanglement provided by Bell states allows the sender and receiver to correlate their measurements in a way that makes the accurate reconstruction of the original quantum state at the destination possible.

- **Quantum key distribution (QKD):** One key application in quantum communication is QKD. It establishes secure communication by using quantum physics to randomly generate and share a secret key between two users. This key is later used for encrypting and decrypting information. Any third-party eavesdropping on the communication is detectable because of a fundamental property of quantum physics that the act of measuring a quantum system in general disturbs the system. This feature ensures the security of the communication. However, one of the limitations of QKD is a dependency on quantum repeaters for long distances.

- **Quantum satellite communication:** Recent advancements in quantum communication have seen the successful deployment of quantum satellites, such as the Micius satellite launched by China in 2016. Quantum satellites can beam pairs of entangled photons to ground stations on Earth, enabling secure quantum communication over great distances, ideally even on a global scale. Micius successfully performed QKD between ground stations separated by up to 1,200 kilometres (approximately 746 miles). Government and military can employ satellite-based QKD for ultra-secure communication channels. The ability to detect any eavesdropping attempts makes it ideal for transmitting sensitive information and ensure confidentiality and integrity of classified information, which is critical for national security.

- **Post-quantum cryptography:** It refers to cryptographic algorithms designed to remain secure against the potential threats posed by quantum computers. Unlike classical cryptographic methods, which could be compromised by quantum algorithms like Shor's algorithm, post-quantum cryptographic techniques, such as lattice-based, hash-based, code-based, and multivariate polynomial cryptography, aim to safeguard data and communications in a quantum era. Current cryptographic practices rely on mathematical problems like factoring large integers (RSA) and discrete logarithms (DSA/ECC) that are considered hard for classical computers but are vulnerable to future quantum attacks. Quantum-resistant cryptography employs new algorithms based on hard problems that remain difficult for quantum computers. These approaches are vital for ensuring the confidentiality and integrity of information as quantum computing capabilities continue to advance. Ongoing research focuses on developing, standardizing, and implementing these algorithms to transition seamlessly from current cryptographic systems. The challenge remains in integrating these protocols with existing systems.

Quantum communication presents revolutionary opportunities in secure communication, giving us essentially un-hackable modes of transmitting information. However, the technology is in its infancy and challenges in practical implementation, such as maintaining quantum coherence over long distances and creating robust quantum repeaters, remain to be overcome. Moreover, as a future-oriented discipline, there is a vast scope for discovery and many of its potentials remain to be unearthed by more research and experimentation.

Quantum superdense coding

Superdense coding is a quantum communication protocol that allows for the transmission of two classical bits of information by sending just one qubit, given that the two parties share an entangled pair of qubits in advance. Essentially, two bits of classical information can be transferred by physically transmitting just one qubit. The process begins with the preparation of an entangled pair of qubits, also known as Bell states. One qubit from this pair is sent to each communicator, say Alice and Bob. To send her two-bit message, Alice performs a certain unitary operation on her qubit, which depends on the message she wants to send. There are four possible operations she can perform, corresponding to the four states of classical information: 00, 01, 10, 11, that she might want to send. Once this operation is performed, Alice sends the qubit over to Bob. Upon receiving Alice's qubit, Bob now holds both the qubits of the entangled pair and performs a measurement on them. This measurement allows Bob to distinguish which of the four operations Alice performed, thereby allowing him to determine which state of classical information Alice was trying to send. Note that it is important to maintain the entanglement and protect the qubits from decoherence throughout the process.

Superdense coding showcases the power of quantum entanglement and quantum superposition in achieving communication efficiencies far beyond the capabilities of classical systems. It also proves to be extremely secure, as the information cannot be decoded unless the recipient has the correct entangled qubit. This security is because of the property of entanglement. Entangled particles create a strong correlation between their states, allowing for the transmission of information between parties without the risk of eavesdropping. Any attempt to intercept the quantum states will inevitably disturb the system, thus alerting any security breaches. Also, intrinsic properties of quantum mechanics, such as the No-cloning theorem, prevent unauthorized duplication of the quantum states, further safeguarding the information from interception.

Figure 7.1 shows the high-level flow diagram for superdense coding. An entangled pair of qubits are generated, of which one each is sent to Alice and Bob. Alice encodes a 2-bit message that she wants to send into her qubit, which is then sent to Bob. Bob receives the qubit, and successfully decodes the message using his own qubit. We will look at the details as follows:

First, entangled pair of qubits are generated by a third-party. This is done with the help of a Hadamard gate and a CNOT gate, as shown in *Figure 7.1*. This results in one of the Bell states, $\frac{1}{\sqrt{2}}$ ($|00\rangle + |11\rangle$)):

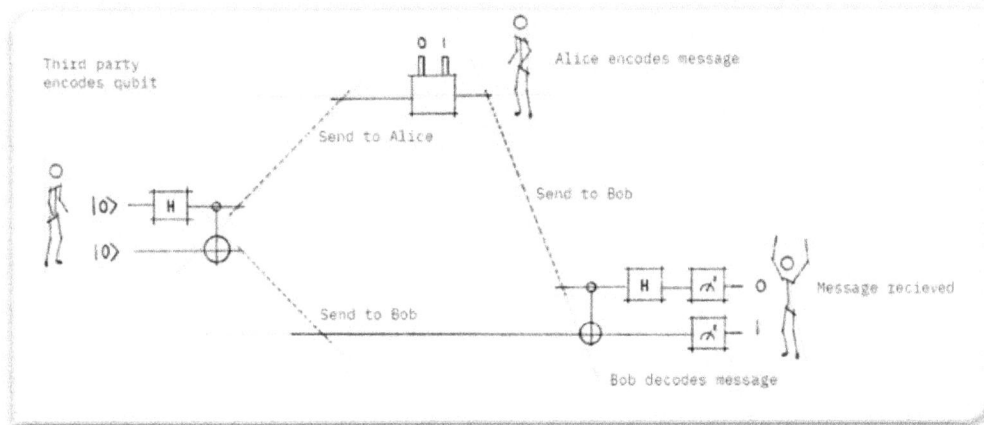

Figure 7.1: *Flow diagram for Superdense Coding (Source: QISKIT Textbook)*

The first qubit, q0 is sent to Alice, who will encode the message and send to Bob. The second qubit q1 is sent to Bob by some means. Alice wants to send information encoded in two classical bits, which means she can send at the most four messages, that is, – 00, 01, 10, 11. The communication channel between Alice and Bob is a quantum channel, such as optical fiber. So, Alice has to send classical information encoded in the form of qubits. In superdense coding, the 2-bit classical information is condensed into one qubit. Depending on what information Alice wants to send, she will encode it accordingly with quantum gates.

Table 7.1 gives the various gates that Alice will apply to encode the four different classical information into a single qubit:

Intended message (m0, m1)	Applied gate	Resulting state (1/√2) that Alice sends
00	Identity	$\lvert 00\rangle + \lvert 11\rangle$
01	X	$\lvert 10\rangle + \lvert 01\rangle$
10	Z	$\lvert 00\rangle - \lvert 11\rangle$
11	XZ	$-\lvert 10\rangle + \lvert 01\rangle$

Table 7.1: Encoding of classical information using quantum gates

Note: The qubits under the column 'Resulting State' in the previous table displays both Alice's as well as Bob's qubits. The first qubit is Alice's and second qubit is Bob's.

If Alice wants to send 00, she will apply identity gate, which does nothing. The state of qubit with Alice remains unchanged. In the previous table, Alice's qubits are in a quantum superposition of states $\lvert 0\rangle$ and $\lvert 1\rangle$. Bob applies two gates on the incoming qubit from Alice, a CNOT gate followed by a Hadamard gate.

So, after CNOT, $\frac{1}{\sqrt{2}}$ ($\lvert 00\rangle + \lvert 11\rangle$) becomes $\frac{1}{\sqrt{2}}$ ($\lvert 00\rangle + \lvert 10\rangle$)

After Hadamard, it becomes $\frac{1}{2}$ ($\lvert (0+1)0\rangle + \lvert (0-1)0\rangle$) ➔ $\frac{1}{2}$ ($\lvert 00\rangle + \lvert 10\rangle + \lvert 00\rangle - \lvert 10\rangle$) ➔ $\lvert 00\rangle$

This is the original message that Alice had sent. Following is an example:

- Let us say that Alice wants to send 01 now. She will apply Pauli X gate to her qubit. So, as given in *Table 7.1*, the state of qubits (Alice + Bob) would be $\frac{1}{\sqrt{2}}$ ($\lvert 10\rangle + \lvert 01\rangle$) Bob, on receiving this qubit, will apply CNOT first.

  So, $\frac{1}{\sqrt{2}}$ ($\lvert 10\rangle + \lvert 01\rangle$) becomes $\frac{1}{\sqrt{2}}$ ($\lvert 11\rangle + \lvert 01\rangle$)

  The Hadamard will make it $\frac{1}{\sqrt{2}}$ ($\lvert (0-1)1\rangle + \lvert (0+1)1\rangle$) ➔ $\lvert 01\rangle$, which is the original message that Alice sent.

- Let us say Alice wants to send 10. She will apply Paul-Z gate to her qubit, which will change the state to $\frac{1}{\sqrt{2}}$ ($\lvert 00\rangle - \lvert 11\rangle$)

  At Bob's end, the CNOT will change the state from $\frac{1}{\sqrt{2}}$ ($\lvert 00\rangle - \lvert 11\rangle$) to $\frac{1}{\sqrt{2}}$ ($\lvert 00\rangle - \lvert 10\rangle$)

  Hadamard will make it $\frac{1}{\sqrt{2}}$ ($\lvert (0+1)0\rangle - \lvert (0-1)0\rangle$) ➔ $\lvert 10\rangle$, which is the original message.

- Let us say Alice wants to send 11. She will apply both Pauli X gate and Pauli Z gate. This will change $\frac{1}{\sqrt{2}}$ (|00⟩ + |11⟩) to $\frac{1}{\sqrt{2}}$ (−|10⟩ + |01⟩)

At Bob's end, CNOT will make it $\frac{1}{\sqrt{2}}$ (−|11⟩ + |01⟩)

Hadamard will make it $\frac{1}{\sqrt{2}}$ (−|(0 − 1)1⟩ + |(0 + 1)1⟩) ➜ |11⟩, which is the original message.

Table 7.2 gives a summary of the exercise:

Bob receives (1/√2)	After CNOT gate (1/√2)	After H gate... same as Alice's original message
|00⟩ + |11⟩	|00⟩ + |10⟩	|00⟩
|10⟩ + |01⟩	|11⟩ + |01⟩	|01⟩
|00⟩ - |11⟩	|00⟩ - |10⟩	|10⟩
-|10⟩ + |01⟩	-|11⟩ + |01⟩	|11⟩

Table 7.2: *Decoding of information at receiver end*

Let us look at the implementation of the superdense coding circuit. Here, IBM Composer has been used to design the circuit with the aid of the GUI, and the results are obtained from a real quantum computer, ibm_osaka.

Message 00

Figure 7.2(a) shows the circuit to encode classical information *00* at Alice's end, and decode it at Bob's end. Here, identity gate is used to encode the message. The bar chart in *Figure 7.2(b)* shows that *00* has been correctly decoded at Bob's end:

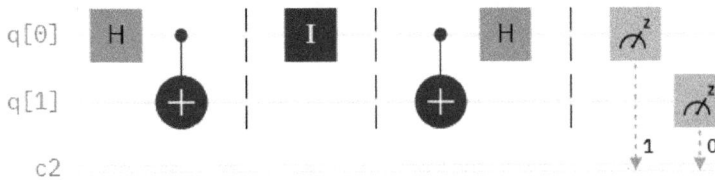

Figure 7.2(a): *Circuit to encode message 00 and decode it at the receiver end*

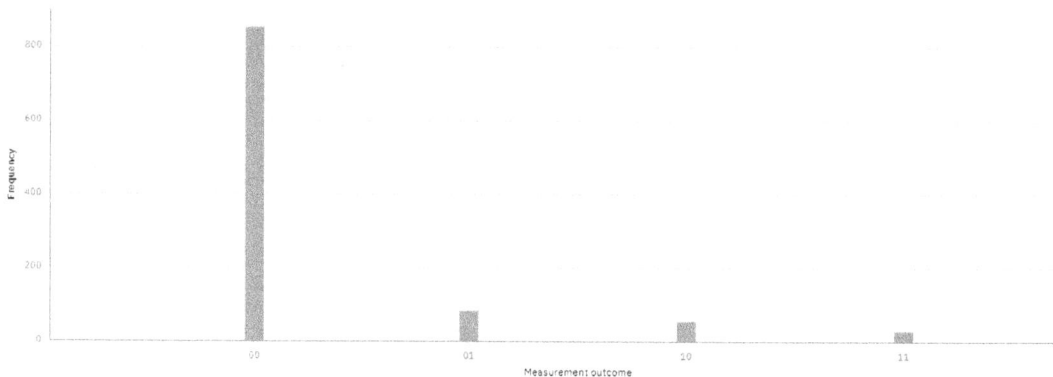

Figure 7.2(b): Results of message 00

Message 01

Figure 7.3(a) shows the circuit to encode classical information *01* at Alice's end, and decode it at Bob's end. Pauli X gate is used to encode the message. The bar chart in *Figure 7.3(b)* shows that *01* has been correctly decoded at Bob's end:

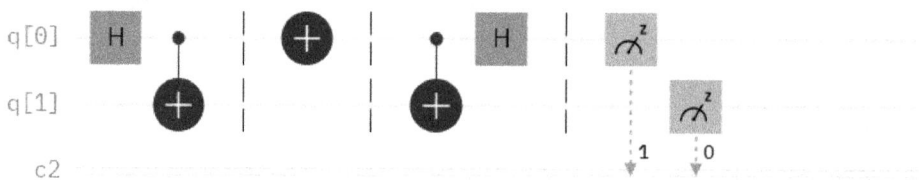

Figure 7.3(a): Circuit to encode message 01 and decode it at the receiver end

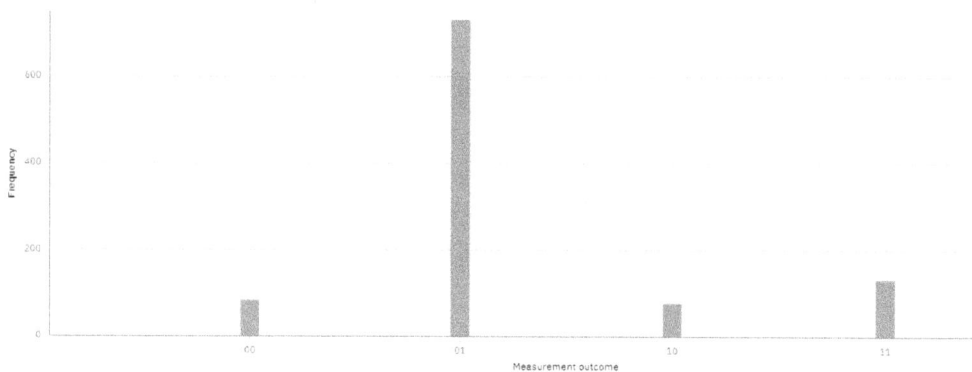

Figure 7.3(b): Results of message 01

Message 10

Figure 7.4(a) shows the circuit to encode classical information *10* at Alice's end, and decode it at Bob's end. Pauli Z gate is used to encode the message. The bar chart in *Figure 7.4(b)* shows that *10* has been correctly decoded at Bob's end:

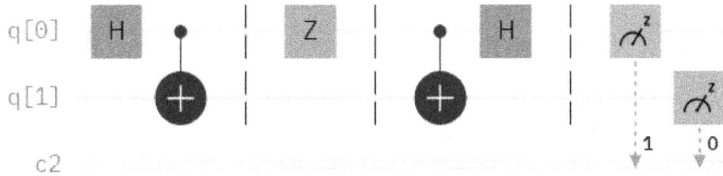

Figure 7.4(a): *Circuit to encode message 10 and decode it at the receiver end*

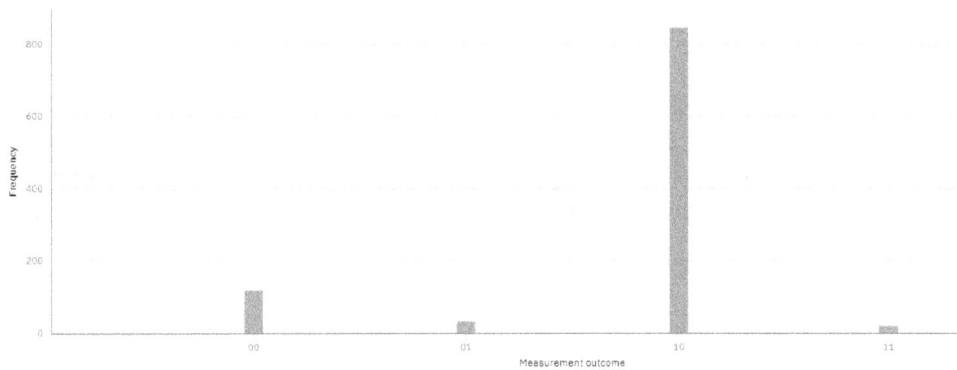

Figure 7.4(b): *Results of message 10*

Message 11

Figure 7.5(a) shows the circuit to encode classical information *11* at Alice's end, and decode it at Bob's end. The message is encoded using a combination of Pauli X and Pauli Z gates. The bar chart in *Figure 7.5(b)* shows that *11* has been correctly decoded at Bob's end:

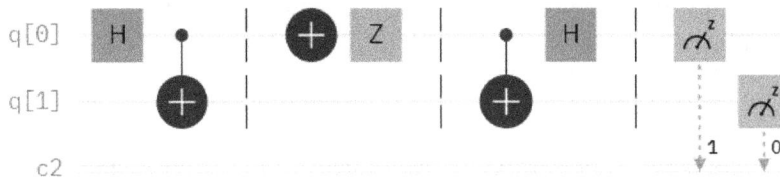

Figure 7.5(a): *Circuit to encode message 11 and decode it at receiver end*

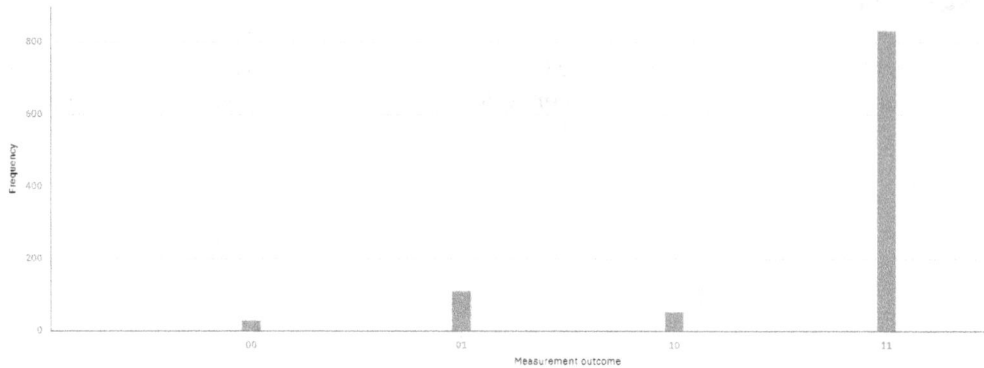

Figure 7.5(b): Results of message 11

Quantum teleportation

Quantum teleportation is a fascinating concept in the realm of quantum mechanics that deals with transmission of quantum state from one place to another. Unlike science-fiction movies where teleportation means transmitting physical objects instantly across space, quantum teleportation is about sending the state of a quantum system from one location to another, not the physical particle itself.

At the heart of quantum teleportation lies entanglement. When two quantum particles are entangled, their properties become irrevocably linked, no matter how far apart they are. If one is measured, the other instantly assumes the corresponding state.

In a quantum teleportation process, a pair of entangled particles is first created. One is sent to the receiver while the sender retains the other. The sender then preps a third particle, the one to be teleported, in the desired quantum state. This third particle interacts with the sender's half of the entangled pair, and through a careful measurement process, the sender can then obtain information to send to the receiver via a classical communication channel. With this information, the receiver can manipulate their own entangled particle to replicate the quantum state of the third particle. Thus, the quantum state of the third particle has effectively been **teleported** to the distant entangled particle at the receiver's end. Note that the physical particle is not teleported, only the quantum state is. *Figure 7.6* gives the high-level flow.

It is noteworthy that quantum teleportation not only hinges on entanglement, but also on classical communication, which is restricted to the speed of light. Thus, it is not exactly instantaneous teleportation. Furthermore, in the process, the original state of the third particle at the sender's end is destroyed, due to the properties of quantum measurement, thereby complying with the **No-cloning** theorem in quantum mechanics.

Quantum teleportation opens new avenues for quantum communication and quantum computing, potentially revolutionizing the way we secure, transmit, and process information. Recent experiments have demonstrated quantum teleportation between different locations on Earth and even across space to a satellite, albeit with single-photon qubits. However, there is still some way to go to make teleportation practically applicable and research is ongoing to explore its full potential.

Figure 7.6 shows the high-level flow diagram for quantum teleportation:

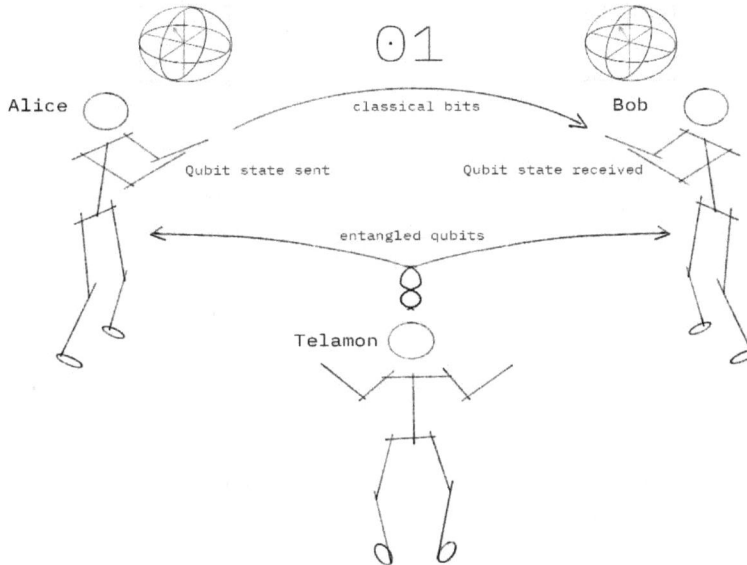

Figure 7.6: *Flow diagram for quantum teleportation (Source: QISKIT Textbook)*

Figure 7.9 shows the circuit for teleportation. As you can see, the first combination of Hadamard and CNOT is to entangle the qubits. The first qubit q1 is kept with Alice (source system), and the second qubit q2 is sent to the destination, Bob, by some means. The function of next set of CNOT and Hadamard gates is to manipulate the states of q0 and q1. The qubits are measured and the information is sent to Bob as two classical bits over the classical channel. Depending on the measure of the bits, Bob applies different gates on his qubit q2. *Table 7.3* gives this mapping:

Bits received	State of Bob's qubit q2	Gate applied
00	$\alpha 0 + \beta 1$	I
01	$\alpha 1 + \beta 0$	X
10	$\alpha 0 - \beta 1$	Z
11	$\alpha 1 - \beta 0$	XZ

Table 7.3: *Mapping between bits received and quantum gate applied*

We will do the math for one of the states of qubit that has to be teleported, before diving into the code, as follows:

- Let us say q0 is in a superposition of $\alpha|0\rangle - \beta|1\rangle$.

  q1 and q2 are in a Bell state $| \rightarrow \frac{1}{\sqrt{2}} (|00\rangle + |11\rangle)$

  Combined state of q0, q1 & q2 is $\frac{1}{\sqrt{2}} (\alpha|000\rangle + \alpha|011\rangle - \beta|100\rangle - \beta|111\rangle)$

  CNOT is applied on q0 and q1. The new state is as follows:

  $\frac{1}{\sqrt{2}} (\alpha|000\rangle + \alpha|011\rangle - \beta|110\rangle - \beta|101\rangle)$

- **Hadamard is applied on q0 as follows:**

  $\frac{1}{2} (\alpha|(0+1)00\rangle + \alpha|(0+1)11\rangle - \beta|(0-1)10\rangle - \beta|(0-1)01\rangle)$

  $\frac{1}{2} (\alpha(|000\rangle + |100\rangle + |011\rangle + |111\rangle) - \beta(|010\rangle - |110\rangle + |001\rangle - |101\rangle))$

  $\frac{1}{2} (|00(\alpha 0 - \beta 1)\rangle + |01(\alpha 1 - \beta 0)\rangle + |10(\alpha 0 + \beta 1)\rangle + |11(\alpha 1 + \beta 0)\rangle)$

This state is in superposition. Let us measure q0 and q1. The superposition will collapse into one of four eigenstates: 00, 01, 10, 11. Let us take any one state, say, it collapses into 11. The state 11 will be sent using classical bits to Bob. Looking at *Table 7.3*, Bob will apply Pauli X and Pauli Z gates to q2.

The state of q2 corresponding to 11 is $(\alpha 1 + \beta 0)$. After application of X and Z gates, it will become $(\alpha 0 - \beta 1)$, which is the original state of q0. Hence, the state of q0 has been successfully teleported to q2.

You can start with any state of q0, and the end result will be that q2 will possess the same state as q0.

Let us look at the Python code for teleportation. This code has been run on a local Jupyter Notebook using Aer simulator of Qiskit:

Import all the libraries:

```
from qiskit import QuantumCircuit, QuantumRegister, ClassicalRegister
from qiskit import transpile, assemble, Aer
from qiskit.visualization import plot_histogram, plot_bloch_multivector, array_to_latex
from qiskit.extensions import Initialize
from qiskit.quantum_info import random_statevector
```

Create entangled qubits:

```
def create_bell_pair(qc, a, b):
    """The below gates are used to entangle the qubits a & b"""
    qc.h(a) # Put qubit a into state |+>
    qc.cx(a,b) # CNOT with a as control and b as target
```

Apply CNOT and Hadamard gates to q0 and q1 at Alice's end:

```
def alice_gates(qc, psi, a):
    qc.cx(psi, a)
    qc.h(psi)
```

Measure q0 and q1 onto classical bits, which will be sent to Bob:

```
def measure_qubits(qc, a, b, crz, crx):
    qc.barrier()
    qc.measure(a,crz)
    qc.measure(b,crx)
```

This function reads the classical bits to decide which quantum gates to apply:

```
def bob_gates(qc, qubit, crz, crx):
    # Here, c_if is used to control quantum gates with a classical bit instead
    of a qubit
    qc.x(qubit).c_if(crx, 1) # Apply X if crx is 1
    qc.z(qubit).c_if(crz, 1) # Apply Z if crz is 1
```

```
Create random 1-qubit state for q0
psi = random_statevector(2)
# Display the vector
display(array_to_latex(psi, prefix="|\\psi\\rangle ="))
```

$$|\psi\rangle = \begin{bmatrix} 0.38364 - 0.01542i & -0.90789 + 0.1683i \end{bmatrix}$$

Figure 7.7: *Superposition state*

Show it on a Bloch sphere, which helps provide an intuitive understanding of the quantum state. Refer to the following figure:

```
plot_bloch_multivector(psi)
```

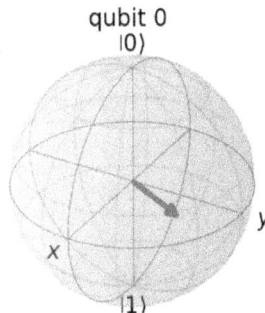

Figure 7.8: *Bloch sphere representing superposition state*

Create initialization gate, which will represent the superposition state:

```
init_gate = Initialize(psi)
init_gate.label = "init"
```

Build a circuit to teleport and view Bloch sphere for destination qubit:

```
# Define registers - quantum register for 3 qubits, and 2 classical bits in
2 different registers
qr = QuantumRegister(3, name="q")
crz, crx = ClassicalRegister(1, name="crz"), ClassicalRegister(1, name="crx")

# Declare quantum circuit
teleportation_circuit = QuantumCircuit(qr, crz, crx)

## STEP 0
# Apply init_gate to q0 to assign it a state of superposition
teleportation_circuit.append(init_gate, [0])

teleportation_circuit.barrier()

## STEP 1
# Entangle qubits q1 and q2
create_bell_pair(teleportation_circuit, 1, 2)

# Use barrier to separate stepsteleportation_circuit.barrier()

## STEP 2
# Apply gates on Alice's qubits - q0 and q1
alice_gates(teleportation_circuit, 0, 1)

## STEP 3
# Measure q0 and q1 onto classical bits, which will be sent to Bob.
measure_qubits(teleportation_circuit, 0, 1 ,crz ,crx)

teleportation_circuit.barrier()

## STEP 4
# Apply gates on Bob's qubit depending on message in classical bits
```

```
bob_gates(teleportation_circuit, 2, crz, crx)
```

Figure 7.9 is the circuit diagram representation of *Figure 7.6*. The **init** circuit block launches qubit q0 into superposition. The state of this qubit is being teleported. The next pair of Hadamard and CNOT gates entangles two qubits q1 and q2. The next pair of CNOT and Hadamard are the gates that Alice applies on q0 and q1. The measurement gates measure qubits q0 and q1 that gets stored in classical registers. These bits are sent over classical network to Bob. The last two gates are applied by Bob to manipulate the state of q2 based on the classical bits. Thus, q2 will inherit the state of qubit q0.

```
# Draw the circuit:

teleportation_circuit.draw(output='mpl')
```

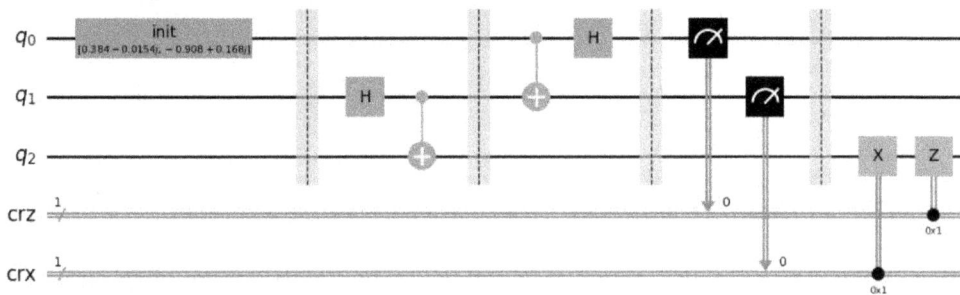

Figure 7.9: *Teleportation circuit*

Run the circuit on a simulator:

```
# Define the simulator

sim = Aer.get_backend('aer_simulator')

# Save the statevector of the quantum circuit for later viewing on the Bloch sphere

teleportation_circuit.save_statevector()

# Assemble the circuit

qobj = assemble(teleportation_circuit)

# Execute

job = sim.run(qobj)
```

Display the state of the quantum circuit. Note that there are three qubits, so the vectors of all the different combinations formed by the three qubits will be displayed.

```
out_vector = job.result().get_statevector()

display(array_to_latex(out_vector, prefix="|\\psi\\rangle ="))
```

$$|\psi\rangle = \begin{bmatrix} 0 & 0.38364 - 0.01542i & 0 & 0 & 0 & -0.90789 + 0.1683i & 0 & 0 \end{bmatrix}$$

Figure 7.10: *Statevector of q2, q1, q0*

As can be seen in the figure, there are 8 states formed by the three qubits (q2, q1, q0) – 000, 001, 010, 011, 100, 101, 110, 111. However, only states 001 and 101 have non-zero vector values. This means that q1 and q0 have collapsed to states 0 and 1 respectively due to measurement, while q2 is in a superposition of 0 and 1 whose amplitudes are identical to the original amplitudes of q0 as shown in *Figure 7.7*.

Let us look at the Bloch sphere. The Bloch sphere will represent the state vectors of the three qubits that were derived in the previous step. Refer to the following figure:

```
plot_bloch_multivector(out_vector)
```

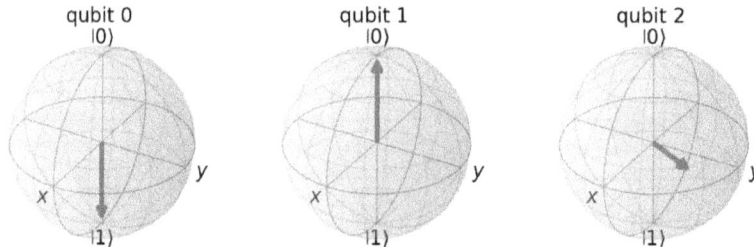

Figure 7.11: Bloch sphere representing the states of the three qubits

The Bloch sphere of q2 in this figure is identical to the Bloch sphere of q0 in *Figure 7.8*. Identical Bloch spheres highlight the No-cloning theorem, as the state is transferred, not duplicated. It signifies the successful transfer of the quantum state from q0 to q2. All properties of the original qubit, such as its amplitude and phase, have been transferred without any loss or alteration. The quantum state of input qubit q0 is exactly reconstructed on the output qubit q2, even though the qubits themselves are physically separate.

Quantum key distribution

QKD is a standout technology in the field of quantum information science, designed to tackle the issues of data security in data encryption. It leverages the principles of quantum mechanics, especially quantum superposition and quantum entanglement, to enable two communicating parties to share cryptographic keys securely. Even the most secure encryption algorithm relies heavily on how securely cryptographic keys are distributed and stored. Intercepting this key during transmission is one of the common ways to breach conventional encryption systems. In contrast to classical key distribution methods, where the security comes from the computational hardness of certain mathematical problems, QKD's security is based on the laws of quantum mechanics, particularly the Heisenberg uncertainty principle and the No-cloning theorem. According to the Heisenberg uncertainty principle, it is impossible to measure certain properties (e.g., position and momentum, or the polarization states of a photon) of a quantum system simultaneously with perfect accuracy. In the context of QKD, if an eavesdropper tries to measure the quantum key information (e.g., photon polarization or phase), the act of measuring inevitably disturbs the system by altering the quantum state of the photon. This disturbance leads to detectable errors when the qubit states are later analyzed by the sending and receiving parties, say Alice and Bob. By publicly comparing some portions of the received keys, Alice and Bob can detect discrepancies introduced by potential eavesdropping. This means that even with unlimited computational power, an eavesdropper cannot determine the key without disturbing the quantum system and revealing its presence.

QKD fundamentally changes the mechanism of key distribution by utilizing properties unique to quantum mechanics. For instance, the principle of quantum superposition allows a quantum system to be in multiple states simultaneously, thus quantum bits (qubits) can be in more than one state at a time, making interception significantly more complex. Moreover, quantum entanglement is used in QKD to generate correlation between pairs of qubits such that their states are instantaneously linked, irrespective of the distance between them. The cornerstone of QKD's impenetrability lies in Heisenberg's uncertainty principle, stating that the act of measuring a quantum system, such as a photon, inevitably disturbs the system. Thus, an eavesdropper trying to intercept the quantum keys will inadvertently change the keys and reveal their presence.

In QKD, the sender and receiver will exchange information over quantum channel using qubits to determine the secret key. Once that is established, the actual messages will be encrypted using that key and transmitted over classical channel.

The following are the different steps in QKD:

(Note that Alice is initiating communication with Bob and Eve is the eavesdropper.)

1. Alice and Bob need a common key for symmetric encryption. So, Alice decides on a random set of qubits. She encodes this data using a random combination of X-basis and Z-basis.

2. Alice transmits the data.

3. Bob receives the data, and uses his own random set of X & Z bases to measure the data.

4. Alice and Bob share with each other their own set of bases. For common basis, they preserve the qubits in data.

5. Alice and Bob select a random sample of qubits from the previously mentioned preserved set and share with each other.

6. If there is no interference (measurement) by Eve, Alice's and Bob's sample qubits will match. The preserved qubits from *Step 4* are retained for key generation and will form the secret key for encryption.

7. If there is interference from Eve, the sample qubits in *Step 5* will not match at both Alice's and Bob's end. According to the Heisenberg uncertainty principle, it is impossible to simultaneously know both the position and momentum of a particle with perfect accuracy; the act of measuring one property inevitably affects the other, altering the particle's state. Therefore, any measurement by Eve will disturb the state of the transmitted qubits, such as collapsing the superposition,

or breaking the entanglement between qubit pairs. In this scenario, the whole sequence will restart from *Step 1*.

The following is an example that will help explain this:

Let us look at *Table 7.4* as we walk through the example. Consider that Alice generated 5 random qubits: 1, 0, 1, 0, 0, as can be seen in *row #1*. *Row #2* gives the random bases that Alice generated. What are bases? Each of the qubits are measured on a certain axis, or basis. The first qubit is measured on Z-axis. So, randomly generate qubit-1 '1', is measured on randomly generated basis Z. A value of 1 on Z-axis on Bloch sphere corresponds to |1⟩. Therefore *row #3* shows |1⟩ corresponding to qubit-1. Similarly, qubit-2 '0' measured on 'X' axis is |+⟩. Why? A qubit lying on the positive X-axis is in a state of superposition of $\frac{1}{\sqrt{2}}$ (|0⟩ + |1⟩)), which is represented as |+⟩. Just like states 0 and 1 lie on the top and bottom of the Z-axis on Bloch sphere, a 0 and 1 on X-axis will lie on the positive and negative ends of X-axis. Qubit-3 '1' on X-axis lies on negative X-axis and corresponds to a superposition of $\frac{1}{\sqrt{2}}$ (|0⟩ - |1⟩)), which is represented as |-⟩. On Similar lines, qubit-4 '0' on Z-axis is |0⟩, and qubit-5 '0' on X-axis is |+⟩. All these states are represented in *row #3*.

Row #4 shows five qubits in initial state, on which gates in *row #5* are applied in order to generate the states in *row #3*. These qubits are then transmitted over a quantum channel, as shown in *row #6*. Bob also randomly generates bases at his end in order to measure the qubits transmitted by Alice. These bases are depicted in *row #7*. Bob uses quantum gates to decode the message. *Row #8* gives the gates. If Bob's randomly generated measurement basis is Z-axis, then Identify gate is applied. If Bob's measurement basis is X-axis, then Hadamard gate is applied. By applying the gates in *row #8* to the transmitted qubits in *row #6*, *row #9* is generated. These are keys as decoded by Bob.

Both Alice and Bob will send their bases to each other. If Bob measures a qubit in the same basis that Alice encoded it with, then the result must match. If Alice and Bob used a different basis for a qubit, then the result will not match, and hence, that basis and qubit will be discarded. This comparison is done by both Alice and Bob. As can be seen in the table, Alice and Bob chose same bases for qubits 1, 3, 4, and 5. These are highlighted in bold. Therefore, they will compare only these qubits. For these four qubits, Alice's keys (*row #1*) and Bob's keys (*row #9*) are identical, again highlighted in bold. This means that the information was not tampered with. For Alice and Bob to know this, they will share a random subset of these qubits and compare. If they are identical, which is true in this case, it means that Alice and Bob can use the state of these four qubits (1100) as the key for encryption. In reality, the sample qubits are discarded from the overall keyset since it is no longer secret, because it is sent over a network accessible to public.

What happens if Eve tries to hack the information? Refer to the following table:

Rows	Category	Qubit-1	Qubit-2	Qubit-3	Qubit-4	Qubit-5
#1	Alice Key	**1**	**0**	**1**	**0**	**0**
#2	Alice Bases	**Z**	X	X	Z	X
#3	Alice State	$|1\rangle$	$|+\rangle$	$|-\rangle$	$|0\rangle$	$|+\rangle$
#4	Qubit initial state	$|0\rangle$	$|0\rangle$	$|0\rangle$	$|0\rangle$	$|0\rangle$
#5	Gate	Pauli X	Hadamard	P-X + H	I	Hadamard
#6	Transmitted Qubits	$|1\rangle$	$\frac{1}{\sqrt{2}}(|0\rangle + |1\rangle)$	$\frac{1}{\sqrt{2}}(|0\rangle - |1\rangle)$	$|0\rangle$	$\frac{1}{\sqrt{2}}(|0\rangle + |1\rangle)$
#7	Bob Bases	Z	Z	X	Z	X
#8	Message Decoder	I	I	H	I	H
#9	Bob Key (decoded data)	$|1\rangle$	$\frac{1}{\sqrt{2}}(|0\rangle + |1\rangle)$	$|1\rangle$	$|0\rangle$	$|0\rangle$

Table 7.4: *Exchange of qubits between Alice and Bob*

Table 7.5 shows the state of information when Eve tries to intercept data sent by Alice to Bob. Information sent by Alice is same as that given in *Table 7.4*. Until row #6, data in *Table 7.5* is same that in *Table 7.4*. Eve, in order to intercept and measure the data, generates her own random set of bases. Let us assume she selects X-axis as the measurement basis for all the qubits (*row #7*). *Row #8* gives the decoder gate - Hadamard for X-basis. *Row #9* gives the decoded information after applying gates in *row #8* to qubits in *row #6*. This is what Eve sees. Eve's interception has changed the state of the qubits. Let us see how Bob views the tampered data. Refer to the following table:

Rows	Category	Qubit-1	Qubit-2	Qubit-3	Qubit-4	Qubit-5
#1	Alice Key	1	0	1	0	0
#2	Alice Bases	Z	X	X	Z	X
#3	Alice State	$|1\rangle$	$|+\rangle$	$|-\rangle$	$|0\rangle$	$|+\rangle$
#4	Qubit initial state	$|0\rangle$	$|0\rangle$	$|0\rangle$	$|0\rangle$	$|0\rangle$
#5	Gate	Pauli-X	Hadamard	P-X + H	I	Hadamard
#6	Transmitted Qubits	$|1\rangle$	$\frac{1}{\sqrt{2}}(|0\rangle + |1\rangle)$	$\frac{1}{\sqrt{2}}(|0\rangle - |1\rangle)$	$|0\rangle$	$\frac{1}{\sqrt{2}}(|0\rangle + |1\rangle)$
#7	Eve Bases	X	X	X	X	X
#8	Eve Message Decoder	Hadamard	H	H	H	H
#9	Eve Key (decoded data)	$\frac{1}{\sqrt{2}}(|0\rangle - |1\rangle)$	$|0\rangle$	$|1\rangle$	$\frac{1}{\sqrt{2}}(|0\rangle + |1\rangle)$	$|0\rangle$

Table 7.5: *Eve tries to read information sent by Alice to Bob*

Rows #1 to #3 in *Table 7.6* contain the same data as rows #7 to #9 from *Table 7.5*. *Row #3* shows the tampered qubits. Bob will apply his randomly chosen bases in *row #4* on these qubits (*row #3*) to measure their state. The decoded information is in *row #6*. Both Alice and Bob will send their bases to each other. If Bob measures a qubit in the same basis that Alice encoded it with, then the result must match. If Alice and Bob used a different basis for a qubit, then the result will not match, and hence, that basis and qubit will be discarded. This comparison is done by both Alice and Bob. As can be seen in the table, Alice and Bob chose same bases for qubits 1, 3, 4 and 5. These are highlighted in bold. Therefore, they will keep only these qubits and discard the others. Again, Alice and Bob will share a subset of these qubits over public network to check whether they are matching.

As can be seen in the highlighted text in *Table 7.7* and *row #6* in *Table 7.6*, all four qubits are mismatching. This means that someone has tried to intercept the data. So, Alice starts all over again with a new set of random qubits and random bases. The process repeats until the selected qubits match between Alice and Bob.

In reality, a large number of qubits are involved in this transaction. Alice and Bob will share a large sample size with each other over public network to verify whether the protocol worked correctly. Higher the sample size, smaller is the error rate. These randomly selected samples are removed from the final keyset, which is then used to encrypt actual data between Alice and Bob over a classical channel.

Rows	Category	Qubit-1	Qubit-2	Qubit-3	Qubit-4	Qubit-5
#1	Eve Bases	X	X	X	X	X
#2	Eve Message Decoder	Hadamard	H	H	H	H
#3	Eve Key	$\frac{1}{\sqrt{2}}(\lvert 0\rangle - \lvert 1\rangle)$	$\lvert 0\rangle$	$\lvert 1\rangle$	$\frac{1}{\sqrt{2}}(\lvert 0\rangle + \lvert 1\rangle)$	$\lvert 0\rangle$
#4	Bob Bases	Z	Z	X	Z	X
#5	Message Decoder	I	I	H	I	H
#6	Bob Key (decoded data)	$\frac{1}{\sqrt{2}}(\lvert 0\rangle - \lvert 1\rangle)$	$\lvert 0\rangle$	$\frac{1}{\sqrt{2}}(\lvert 0\rangle - \lvert 1\rangle)$	$\frac{1}{\sqrt{2}}(\lvert 0\rangle + \lvert 1\rangle)$	$\frac{1}{\sqrt{2}}(\lvert 0\rangle + \lvert 1\rangle)$

Table 7.6: Information as viewed by Bob after interception by Eve

Category	Qubit-1	Qubit-2	Qubit-3	Qubit-4	Qubit-5
Alice Key	1	0	1	0	0

Table 7.7: Alice's original key

Let us now look at the code to implement this circuit. This code is run on a local Jupyter Notebook using Aer simulator of Qiskit.

Import the libraries.

```
from qiskit import QuantumCircuit, Aer, assemble
from numpy.random import randint
import numpy as np
```

Encode qubits into respective states using the bases. That is, it takes qubits in *row #4* and transforms it to *row #6* in *Table 7.4*.

```
def encode_message(bits, bases):
    message = []
    # Iterate through each bit to encode
    for i in range(n):
        qc = QuantumCircuit(1,1)          # Apply gates as given in row #5 in
                                          table 7.4.
        if bases[i] == 0: # Prepare qubit in Z-basis
            if bits[i] == 0:
                # Do nothing for the bit value 0 in Z-basis (|0⟩ state)
                pass
            else:
                # Apply X gate to flip the qubit if bit value is 1
                qc.x(0)
        else: # Prepare qubit in X-basis
            if bits[i] == 0:
                # Apply Hadamard gate to prepare |+⟩ state for bit value 0
                qc.h(0)
            else:
                # Apply X gate to prepare |1⟩ state first
                qc.x(0)
                # Then apply Hadamard gate to get |1⟩ in X-basis as |-⟩
                # state
                qc.h(0)
        qc.barrier()
        message.append(qc)
    return message
```

Following function will measure the qubits after applying a particular gate depending on the basis. That is, it will take qubits from *row #6* in *Table 7.4*, decode it, and generate key in *row #9*.

```
def measure_message(message, bases):
    backend = Aer.get_backend('aer_simulator')
    measurements = []
    # Iterate through all the qubits
    for q in range(n):
    # If basis is Z, then apply Identity gate, or do nothing, just
        # measure
        if bases[q] == 0: # measuring in Z-basis
            message[q].measure(0,0)
    # If basis is X, apply Hadamard gate and then measure
        if bases[q] == 1: # measuring in X-basis
            message[q].h(0)
            message[q].measure(0,0)
        # Get the Aer simulator backend for running quantum circuits
        aer_sim = Aer.get_backend('aer_simulator')
        # Assemble the quantum object (qobj) from the encoded message
        qobj = assemble(message[q], shots=1, memory=True)
        # Run the quantum object on the simulator and obtain the result
        result = aer_sim.run(qobj).result()
        # Retrieve the measured bit from the result's memory
        # The first element in the memory is converted to an integer
        measured_bit = int(result.get_memory()[0])
        # Append the measured bit to the measurements list for further use
        measurements.append(measured_bit)
    return measurements, message
```

Alice and Bob will discard qubits where their bases do not match.

```
def remove_garbage(a_bases, b_bases, bits):
    good_bits = []
    for q in range(n):
        if a_bases[q] == b_bases[q]:
            # If both used the same basis, add
            # this to the list of 'good' bits
            good_bits.append(bits[q])
    return good_bits
```

Alice and Bob will select sample qubits from the overall set, which they will send to each other to verify whether the protocol worked and there was no eavesdropping.

```python
def sample_bits(bits, selection):
    sample = []
    for i in selection:
        # use np.mod to make sure the bit we sample is always in the list
        # range
        i = np.mod(i, len(bits))
        # pop(i) removes the element of the
        # list at index 'i'
        sample.append(bits.pop(i))
    return sample
```

The following function prints the results:

```python
def print_results(alice_key, bob_key, bob_sample, alice_sample):
    #print('Alice sample ', alice_sample)
    #print('Bob sample ', bob_sample)
    print('Alice key ', alice_key)
    print('Bob key ', bob_key)
    print('Key matches? ', alice_key == bob_key)
    print('Sample matches? ',alice_sample == bob_sample)
```

The following function will verify whether Eve's interception was detected or not:

```python
def validate(alice_key, bob_key, bob_sample, alice_sample ):
    global detected, undetected
    print_results(alice_key, bob_key, bob_sample, alice_sample)
    # No eavesdropping
    if alice_key == bob_key:
        if bob_sample == alice_sample:
            print('There was no eavesdropper')
        else:
            print("Strange error!")
    else:
        # Eve eavesdropped
        if bob_sample == alice_sample:
            print("Eve went undetected!")
```

```
        undetected += 1
    else:
        print("Eve's interference was detected.")
        detected += 1
```

The following function orchestrates the whole flow:

```
def main(n, sample_size, interception=True):
    # Step 1
    # Generate 'n' random bits (0s and 1s) for Alice's message
    alice_bits = randint(2, size=n)
    # Generate 'n' random bases (0s and 1s) to determine measurement basis
    alice_bases = randint(2, size=n)    # Step 2
    # Encode Alice's bits into quantum messages based on her chosen bases
    message = encode_message(alice_bits, alice_bases)

    if interception:
        # Interception!
        # Generate 'n' random bases for Eve's measurements
        eve_bases = randint(2, size=n)
        intercepted_message, eve_mesg = measure_message(message, eve_bases)
    else:
        eve_mesg = None

    # Step 3
    # Generate 'n' random bases to measure the incoming message by Bob
    bob_bases = randint(2, size=n)
    # Alternative option where Bob can use Alice's bases (commented out)
    #bob_bases = alice_bases
    # Measure the quantum message using Bob's bases and retrieve results
    bob_results, bob_mesg = measure_message(message, bob_bases)

    # Step 4
        # Alice and Bob will discard qubits where their bases do not match
    bob_key = remove_garbage(alice_bases, bob_bases, bob_results)
    alice_key = remove_garbage(alice_bases, bob_bases, alice_bits)
```

```
# Step 5
# Select bit positions to determine sample bits
bit_selection = randint(n, size=sample_size)
# Bob will select sample bits to send to Alice
bob_sample = sample_bits(bob_key, bit_selection)
# Alice will select sample bits to send to Bob
alice_sample = sample_bits(alice_key, bit_selection)

    # Verify whether Eve's interception was detected or not

validate(alice_key, bob_key, bob_sample, alice_sample )

# Returns eve's and bob's messages
return eve_mesg, bob_mesg
```

Run the program:

```
# 100 qubits will be randomly generated along with the bases.
n = 100
# Sample size of qubits that will be shared by Alice and Bob
sample_size = 5
# Initialize counts.
detected, undetected = 0, 0
# Run the main function 10 times.
for i in range(10):
    print(f'Result {i+1} ')
    eve_mesg , bob_mesg = main(n, sample_size)
    print('\n')
print(f'Interference detected {detected} times. It went undetected {undetected}
times.')
```

The result from the execution is:

```
Interference detected 6 times. It went undetected 4 times.
```

While each run will give different results due to the randomness of sample selection, the result alludes to the fact that if the sample size is small then there is a high chance that the sample might match, but there could be mismatch in rest of the qubits. Therefore, sample size should be large enough to reduce the probability of error.

If we increase the **sample_size** to 20 in the code and run it 200 times, this is the result:

```
Interference detected 200 times. It went undetected 0 times.
```

Even if we run the code 200 times, we are able to detect Eve's interference every single time.

In order to test for the scenario where there was no interference from Eve, pass a 3rd parameter to **main** function:

```
eve_mesg , bob_mesg = main(n, sample_size, False)
```

The result will display a message:

```
There was no eavesdropper
```

Post-quantum cryptography

Quantum computers hold great promise to solve complex problems exponentially faster than classical computers. However, this formidable power also brings potential threats to current cryptographic systems, which secure the internet and vital data. PQC, also known as quantum-resistant cryptography, focuses on developing algorithms that cannot be broken by quantum computers. This field is about developing cryptographic systems that are secure against both quantum and classical computers, ensuring our digital security future. Although quantum computers currently do not have enough processing power to break encryption keys, future versions might.

To understand PQC, one must first comprehend quantum computing's impact on conventional cryptographic systems. Let us look at the two types of cryptography: symmetric and asymmetric. In symmetric cryptography, both parties share a key that is private to them, which is used to encrypt the data. In Asymmetric, the client encrypts the data with a public key and the server decrypts it with a private key. The risk of future quantum systems breaking both types of cryptography is real. For example, Grover's algorithm can be used to decipher keys in symmetric cryptography, whereas Shor's algorithm can break asymmetric cryptography. However, the approach to both problems in a post-quantum world is different.

The most commonly used symmetric algorithm is the **Advanced Encryption Standard** (**AES**). The strength of the algorithm lies in the number of bits used to define the key. With 128 bits, there are 2^{128} possible combinations, which is 300 undecillion, 3 followed by 38 zeros. To guess the key, even the most advanced supercomputer would take trillions of years. While quantum algorithms such as Grover's can reduce the order of time by a quadratic factor, that is, 128 bits will seem like 64 bits. This can be circumvented by increasing the bits to 256.

Public-key cryptography, however, is vulnerable because of how the math works. Current cryptographic systems, including RSA, Diffie-Hellman, and elliptic curves, rely heavily on the difficulty of factoring in large numbers or solving discrete logarithm problems. It is possible to find the private key without trying all combinations if there is a way to factor a semi-prime number, which is a product of two prime numbers. Public key encryption provides security by using very long key pairs, for example, 2048 bits, which is a number with 617 decimal digits. Quantum computers, using a method called Shor's algorithm, can theoretically break even 4096-bit key pairs in just a few hours. This will render current cryptographic systems vulnerable and ineffective.

Present quantum computers have a high error rate and do not have the processing power to crack cryptography codes. However, **Cryptographically Relevant Quantum Computer (CRQC)** can change the picture when it becomes a reality. A CRQC is a quantum computer powerful enough, has an advanced error correction circuit, and is equipped with the software necessary to break the cipher keys used in encryption. With CRQC, cryptographic methods, especially the algorithms for asymmetric cryptography, will become vulnerable to hacking. If these encryption algorithms are broken, we will not be able to trust the data that is transmitted or received over the internet, even if it is encrypted, be it banking transactions, emails etc. Even if CRQC is not available today, hackers can intercept and archive encrypted communications, which can then be decrypted with a quantum computer at a later time. This poses an additional risk to present-day communication. This is explained by the Mosca model. It states that organizations have to worry if the threat of CRQC arrives sooner than the sum of the years it takes to implement the quantum-safe solution and the duration for which information has to be protected.

That is, if $X + Y > Z$, where:

- **X:** The number of years the information has to be secured due to data protection laws, compliance requirements, or company policies.
- **Y:** The number of years it will take to upgrade the present infrastructure to a quantum-safe setup.
- **Z:** The years it will take for CRQC to become a reality.

If this equation becomes true, then organizations may not be able to protect its data for the duration $Z - (X + Y)$ from the *harvest and decrypt later* attack. Large organizations will be at risk of litigation and extortion. Nation states and military, however, would be the primary targets of this kind of impending attack at a future date.

Consider an example where a financial organization is required to retain customer data for five years ($X = 5$) as part of its compliance requirement. The organization also estimates that it will take an additional three years ($Y = 3$) to upgrade its systems to become quantum-safe and comply with new security regulations. However, the government has set a compliance deadline of 7 years (CRQC timeline) for all financial institutions to meet the new regulations. So, $Z = 7$.

In this case, $X + Y = 5 + 3 = 8$, which exceeds Z by one year ($Z < X + Y$). Consequently, one year's worth of sensitive customer data would be exposed to the "harvest now, decrypt later" threat, underscoring the urgency for the organization to accelerate its transition to quantum-safe systems to mitigate this risk.

Figure 7.12 gives the timeframe of when CRQC will become a reality. There are optimistic and pessimistic probabilities. There is a 4-11% possibility that CRQC will come into existence within the next 5 years. Note that this report was generated in December 2023. There is a 17-31% chance that CRQC will disrupt modern-day communication within the next 10 years. While these may not sound like high probabilities, the pace at which technology has been advancing and the fact that breakthroughs by nature are unpredictable, this risk can materialize much sooner. Major breakthroughs in **quantum error correction (QEC)** and physical architecture can catapult the realization of CRQC. Given the catastrophe that this can unleash, there is a pressing need to expedite the process of designing and implementing quantum-safe hardware and software solutions.

2023 OPINION-BASED ESTIMATES OF THE CUMULATIVE PROBABILITY OF A DIGITAL QUANTUM COMPUTER ABLE TO BREAK RSA-2048 IN 24 HOURS, AS FUNCTION OF TIMEFRAME

Estimates of the cumulative probability of a cryptographically-relevant quantum computer in time: range between average of an optimistic (top value) or pessimistic (bottom value) interpretation of the estimates indicated by the respondents, and mid-point. [*Shaded grey area corresponds to the 25-year period, not considered in the questionnaire.]

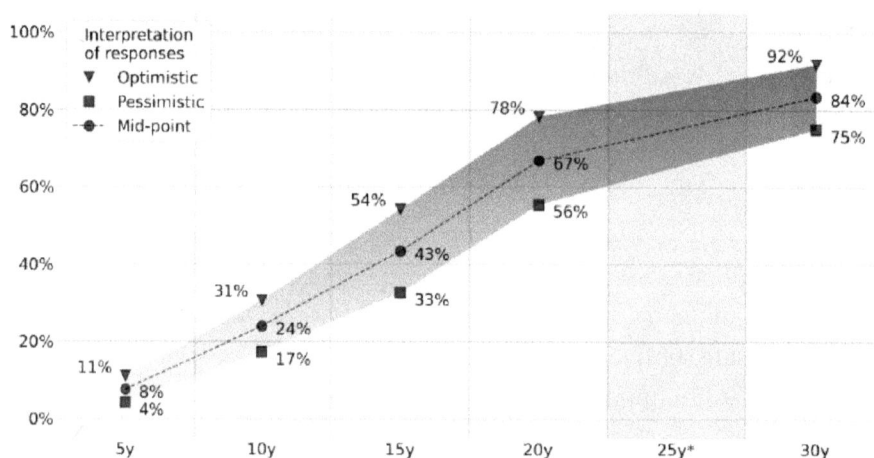

Figure 7.12: [1]*Timeframe when CRQC will become a reality*

There are two kinds of solutions to circumvent the impending risks that CRQC carries: Quantum-based solutions, and classical solutions replying on cryptographic algorithms QKD, from the previous section, is an example of a quantum-based solution. However, the challenge with QKD is that it requires special hardware. While this, too, will form one of the facets of quantum cryptography, for the foreseeable future, finding algorithms that can withstand the force of quantum computers becomes imperative. This is the field of PQC.

PQC involves creating security mechanisms that can withstand the assault of both classical and quantum computers, preserving the security and integrity of data. The implementation of PQC is not about displacing classical cryptography but enhancing it to stand the power of quantum computing.

---

1   *Source: Global Risk Institute*

Institutes, organizations, and quantum computing experts around the globe are experimenting to develop and standardize cryptographic techniques, understanding well the risk that quantum computing would eventually pose to the current cryptographic infrastructure. Several techniques have emerged to build quantum-safe algorithms and resist attacks from quantum computers. Let us briefly examine some of the leading contenders:

- **Lattice-based cryptography:** This method relies on the difficulty of specific mathematical problems in lattice theory. A lattice is a set of vectors in a multi-dimensional geometric plane that creates an equally spaced grid of points. This form of cryptography is considered as one of the promising alternatives to traditional factoring and discrete logarithm-based cryptographic algorithms that will be vulnerable to attacks by quantum computers. Lattice-based cryptography has several significant advantages, including being resistant to quantum computer attacks, high performance in key generation, encryption, and decryption, and providing solutions for many advanced cryptographic tasks. Two common computational problems used in lattice-based cryptography are the **Shortest Vector Problem (SVP)** and the **Closest Vector Problem (CVP)**. The hard-to-solve nature of these problems lies at the core of the security of lattice-based cryptography. Examples of lattice-based cryptography include CRYSTALS-Kyber, designed for public key encryption and key establishment, and CRYSTALS-Dilithium, developed for secure digital signatures. Both are recognized for their strong resistance to quantum computer attacks and have been selected by NIST as PQC standards. Another notable example is NTRUEncrypt, which leverages lattice structures to facilitate encryption, making it a pioneering approach in lattice-based cryptographic systems.

- **Hash-based cryptography:** An area of cryptography that primarily uses cryptographic hash functions. These hash functions take input message data (which may be of any size) and output a fixed-size string of bytes, which is unique to each unique input. Hash-based cryptographic techniques are widely used in a variety of applications, such as digital signatures and message integrity checks. The primary features of hash-based digital signatures, such as the Merkle and Lamport signature schemes, are their simplicity and extremely high-security level. They utilize one-way hash functions, which are easy to compute in one direction but very hard to reverse engineer without the original input, creating a sort of digital fingerprint. One downside to hash-based cryptography is that it typically requires larger key sizes and more computational resources than many other forms of cryptography.

- **Code-based cryptography:** This is a class of post-quantum cryptographic algorithms that are based on the mathematical properties of error-correcting codes. Error-correcting codes are usually used to detect and correct errors in data transmission, but in code-based cryptography, they are used as a computational problem to secure data. The security of code-based cryptographic systems resides in the difficulty of decoding randomly chosen linear codes. This problem is believed to be NP-hard, even for a quantum computer, making code-based cryptosystems secure against quantum attacks. One of the early and well-known examples of a code-based cryptosystem is the McEliece cryptosystem. These systems offer a number of advantages, including fast decryption and immunity to attacks from both classical and quantum computers. However, they also tend to require much larger keys than other cryptosystems, which can be a disadvantage in some applications.

- **Multivariate polynomial cryptography:** A branch of PQC that focuses on crypto systems whose security is based on the mathematical difficulty of solving systems of multivariate polynomials. These cryptographic schemes provide encryption, digital signatures, pseudorandom generators, and more. The security of multivariate cryptosystems is based on the complexity of solving general systems of multivariate polynomials, an NP-hard problem. In this technique, the public and private keys are multivariate polynomials. The public key is a set of multivariate polynomial equations, which is easy to compute for encryption or signing. However, solving the equations which is required for decryption or verification is broadly believed to be difficult and computationally intensive, equivalent to NP-hard problems. A well-known example of this kind of system is the **Unbalanced Oil and Vinegar (UOV)** scheme, which is a digital signature whose security relies on the hardness of solving a particular type of multivariate polynomial equation. In UOV, the signatures are very short as compared to lattice-based or code-based methods, and the computation is also fast, however, size of the public key is an issue. Also, a poorly chosen system of polynomials can lead to a broken cryptosystem.

Table 7.8 gives the comparison among the aforementioned cryptographic techniques based on different parameters:

Cryptogra-phy type	Advantages	Disadvantages	Key sizes	Performance metrics	Use cases
Lattice-based	Strong resistance to quantum attacks, versatile, supports encryption and signatures, good performance	Computation-ally intensive for certain operations	Moderate to large (few kilobytes to several kilobytes)	Fast encryption/decryption, moderate signature generation time	Secure key exchange, digital signatures, homomorphic encryption

Cryptography type	Advantages	Disadvantages	Key sizes	Performance metrics	Use cases
Hash-based	Simple to implement, highly secure against quantum attacks	Large signature size	Key size is typically larger than traditional cryptography	Good signature generation speed and verification speed	Digital signatures
Code-base	Good for encryption and key exchange, relatively mature area	Larger key sizes compared to other schemes	Very large	Moderate speed for encryption and decryption	Secure messaging, encryption, digital signatures
Multivariate polynomial	Relatively compact key sizes, highly resistant to quantum attacks	Complexity of implementation	Moderate	Fast encryption and decryption	Secure key exchange and communication

Table 7.8: Comparison of different PQC cryptography types

Migration to PQC does, however, present significant challenges. Notably, these include efficiency, most PQC algorithms require more computational resources and generate larger keys, interoperability, seamlessly integrating PQC into existing systems and the assurance of long-term security against future advances in quantum computing. These challenges necessitate intensive research and development efforts. Undeniably, there is an urgent need to transition to quantum-resistant cryptographic systems.

There are open-source projects to help build quantum-resistant cryptography. One such project is **Open Quantum Safe (OQS)**. This project enables the development and prototyping of quantum-resistant cryptography. OQS is part of the Linux Foundation's *Post-Quantum Cryptography Alliance*. It provides an open-source C library named liboqs for prototyping and experimenting with quantum-resistant cryptography. This is available on GitHub.

In summary, PQC represents a critical frontier in the realm of cybersecurity. It is a complex yet fascinating field that combines elements of theoretical computer science, abstract algebra, and quantum mechanics. So, while we look forward to the quantum leap in computing, there is also the undeniable urgency to gear up and fortify the cryptographic defenses to protect the digital world against potential threats.

Conclusion

Quantum communication, leveraging the principles of quantum mechanics, is revolutionizing communication systems by providing unprecedented security and speed benchmarks. These advances have sparked a global race in the research and development of quantum technologies. It presents significant opportunities for secure communication, scalable quantum computing, and precise long-range measurement. However, it also introduces significant practical and theoretical challenges such as noise handling, error correction, and device connectivity.

Advancements in quantum communication can penetrate several sectors, including cybersecurity, defense, telecommunications, finance, and fundamental sciences, contributing significantly to a nation's strategic advancement in the ongoing technology race. This rapidly evolving field is a harbinger of a future where quantum computers, quantum networks, and quantum information shape the basis of our technological world. Even though the full realization of quantum communication technology might take a few more years of dedicated research and problem-solving, the promise held by this technology makes all the effort worthwhile.

In this ever-evolving field, we are on the cusp of a new era of communication. Undoubtedly, the exploration and development of quantum communication technology will open numerous research avenues, and the discoveries made will continue to mold the landscape for future communication capabilities.

In the next chapter, we will explore quantum error management, including the classification of quantum errors, techniques for error mitigation and correction, the design of quantum error correcting circuits, and the implementation of advanced codes like Shor's code to enhance the reliability of quantum computations.

Multiple choice questions

1. **Which quantum communication technique allows the transmission of two classical bits using only one qubit, leveraging quantum entanglement?**

    a. Quantum key distribution (QKD)

    b. Quantum Teleportation

    c. Quantum superdense coding

    d. Quantum Satellite Communication

2. **Which of the following statements about quantum teleportation is true?**

    a. It involves the instantaneous transfer of physical objects across space.

    b. It relies solely on classical communication channels for transmitting quantum states.

    c. It allows for the perfect cloning of quantum states.

    d. It destroys the original quantum state of the particle being teleported.

3. **Which principle of quantum mechanics is most directly responsible for QKD's ability to detect eavesdropping?**

    a. Quantum superposition

b. Quantum entanglement

c. Heisenberg uncertainty principle

d. No-cloning theorem

4. **Which of the following algorithms pose a significant threat to currently used asymmetric cryptographic systems?**

   a. Shor's algorithm.

   b. Advanced Encryption Standard (AES).

   c. Grover's algorithm.

   d. Mosca model.

5. **Which of the following is NOT presented as a leading contender in post-quantum cryptography (PQC)?**

   a. Lattice-based cryptography

   b. Symmetric-key cryptography

   c. Hash-based cryptography

   d. Code-based cryptography

Answer key

1. c
2. d
3. c
4. a
5. b

Questions

1. What is quantum superdense coding and what key advantage does it offer?

   Answer: Quantum superdense coding is a quantum communication protocol that allows a sender to transmit two classical bits of information by sending only a single qubit, provided the sender and receiver share a pair of entangled qubits in advance. The key advantage of this technique is that it enables the transmission of more classical information per qubit than is possible using classical communication alone, effectively doubling the channel's classical capacity and optimizing bandwidth.

2. What is quantum teleportation, and what happens to the original quantum state during this process?

   Answer: Quantum teleportation is a process in quantum mechanics that transmits the quantum state of a particle from one location to another, without physically moving the particle itself. During this process, the original quantum state at the sender's location is destroyed due to the principles of quantum measurement, in accordance with the No-cloning theorem. This ensures that the quantum information is not duplicated during teleportation.

3. Is quantum teleportation instantaneous?

   Answer: No, quantum teleportation is not instantaneous. While the entangled particles' states correlate instantly, the process also requires classical communication to transmit measurement information, and this communication is limited by the speed of light.

4. What type of channel is used to transmit the actual encrypted message after a secret key is established in QKD?

   Answer: A classical channel.

5. What is the primary focus of post-quantum cryptography (PQC)?

   Answer: The primary focus of **post-quantum cryptography** (**PQC**) is developing cryptographic algorithms that remain secure against attacks from both quantum computers and classical computers.

Join our Discord space

Join our Discord workspace for latest updates, offers, tech happenings around the world, new releases, and sessions with the authors:

https://discord.bpbonline.com

CHAPTER 8

Quantum Error Correction

Introduction

Quantum error correction (**QEC**) is a foundational aspect of quantum computing that addresses one of the most significant challenges in the field: the susceptibility of quantum information to errors due to decoherence that results from a variety of factors such as thermal fluctuations, electromagnetic interference, defects and impurities in materials used for qubits, interactions with the environment, and imperfections in gate operations. Unlike classical bits, which store information as either a 0 or a 1, quantum bits (qubits) can exist in any superposition of these states, making the information they carry incredibly potent for computational processes yet exceedingly fragile. Qubits are extremely sensitive to their environments, leading to computational errors that can easily disrupt their delicate quantum states. This fragility necessitates the development of sophisticated error correction techniques to identify and correct errors without collapsing the qubits' delicate quantum states. At its core, this involves encoding a logical qubit into a system of several physical qubits. If an error affects one or more of the physical qubits, the overall state can be analyzed and corrected without directly measuring the quantum information. This process relies on intricate algorithms and quantum principles, such as entanglement and superposition, to ensure the robustness of quantum computations against errors. As the field of quantum computing advances, the refinement of QEC methods remains a crucial endeavor, leading to the realization of reliable and scalable quantum computers capable of tackling problems far beyond the realm of classical systems.

Structure

The chapter will be structured in the following way:

- Overview of quantum error correction
- Types of quantum errors
- Techniques for quantum error mitigation
- Techniques for quantum error correction
- Quantum circuit design for QEC

Objectives

This chapter discusses QEC by first exploring the concept of decoherence and its impact on qubit states, followed by fault tolerance and the advent of the NISQ era. It categorizes different types of quantum errors and examines error mitigation techniques. The chapter also describes various types of QEC codes and demonstrates the design of quantum circuits for correcting specific errors. By the end of this chapter, readers will understand the mechanisms of various quantum errors, the strategies to mitigate and correct them, and the practical skills to design quantum circuits that enhance the reliability and scalability of quantum computations.

Overview of quantum error correction

QEC remains one of the most vibrant areas of quantum computing research, driven by the ongoing quest to build a fault-tolerant quantum computer. The strategies mentioned previously have been pivotal in demonstrating that quantum computing can, in principle, be made as reliable as classical computing despite the fundamental challenges posed by quantum mechanics. As physical qubit technologies mature and quantum operations' fidelity improves, QEC codes' development and refinement continue to adapt to emerging needs and insights. This ongoing innovation cycle is crucial for the transition from experimental quantum computing setups to practical, scalable quantum computers that can solve real-world problems beyond the reach of classical machines.

Furthermore, advancements in fault-tolerant protocols, which incorporate QEC techniques to ensure that errors corrected during quantum computations do not propagate and multiply, are essential. This involves not only the choice of the QEC code but also the architecture of the quantum circuit, including the layout of physical qubits, the scheduling of quantum gates, and the implementation of logical qubits and logical operations that are resilient to errors.

The interplay between theory and experiment in QEC is particularly pronounced. As theoretical models predict the feasibility and efficacy of certain QEC approaches under idealized conditions, experimental implementations provide feedback that refines these models, leading to new generations of codes and error correction techniques.

Each type of QEC technique offers unique advantages and poses specific challenges. The choice of QEC code in a quantum computing architecture depends on several factors, including the physical implementation of qubits (for example, superconducting circuits, trapped-ions, quantum dots, etc.), the primary types of errors to which the system is susceptible, and the operational requirements of the quantum algorithms to be executed. QEC is highly pivotal in enabling the development of robust and reliable quantum computers. Its multidisciplinary nature, intersecting quantum mechanics, information theory, and computer science, makes it a rich field of study that continuously evolves in response to theoretical advancements and experimental discoveries. As we edge closer to realizing the full potential of quantum computing, the importance of QEC will only grow, ensuring that future quantum computers can operate effectively in the face of inevitable quantum noise and errors. The progress in QEC techniques not only promises to unlock the practical applications of quantum computing, ranging from cryptography and optimization to simulation of quantum systems and beyond, but also deepens our understanding of quantum mechanics itself, shedding light on the fundamental properties of quantum states and their resilience to interactions with the environment.

While the availability of large quantum computers for industrial and commercial use may still be a few years away, NISQ, or Noisy Intermediate-Scale Quantum computing, refers to a current era of quantum computing hardware that is not yet fault-tolerant, meaning errors in qubits are common and need to be corrected. These devices are considered **intermediate-scale** because they have around 50-100 qubits, which is not yet enough for solving real-world problems efficiently. Despite their noise and error-prone nature, NISQ computers hold promise for early applications like quantum simulation and optimization. The challenge lies in developing effective QEC codes to mitigate noise and increase the reliability of computations on NISQ devices. As quantum technology advances, researchers are working towards achieving scalable, fault-tolerant quantum computers that can outperform classical systems in several use cases. Until then, commercial NISQ devices will likely rule the roost as they become more accessible in the near future.

Types of quantum errors

There are three main types of quantum errors:

- **Bit flip error:** When the state of a qubit in superposition gets flipped due to the environment, it is called a bit flip error. This leads to the loss of information or fidelity in a quantum system. Factors in the environment, such as thermal vibrations, can cause qubits to flip states, which can lead to inaccuracies in quantum computations.
- **Phase flip error:** When the phase of a qubit in superposition gets disturbed due to the environment, it is called a phase flip error. This can occur due to various

factors such as environmental noise, imperfections in the quantum hardware, or interactions with surrounding particles. Phase flip errors are also associated with **dephasing**, which can result in the loss of coherence in quantum systems, making it difficult to perform quantum computations accurately and leading to errors in the final results. To mitigate dephasing errors, techniques such as error correction codes and error mitigation methods are employed in quantum computing.

- **Gate operation error:** In quantum computing, gate operation errors refer to the mistakes or inaccuracies that can occur when applying quantum gates to a quantum circuit. Quantum gates are fundamental building blocks for performing operations on qubits. Various factors can lead to gate operation errors in quantum computing. One of the main sources of errors is the noise and imperfections present in the physical qubits and quantum hardware used to implement the quantum gates. These imperfections can lead to deviations from the intended gate operations, resulting in errors in the final output of the quantum circuit. Another factor contributing to gate operation errors is decoherence, which is the loss of coherence of qubits due to interactions with their surrounding environment. Decoherence can cause qubits to lose their quantum properties and result in errors in the gate operations. Additionally, errors in gate operations can also arise from issues related to the control and calibration of the quantum gates, such as inaccurate timing or voltage levels. These technical challenges can lead to errors in the application of quantum gates and impact the overall performance of a quantum algorithm. Techniques such as QEC codes and fault-tolerant quantum computing methods are employed to mitigate gate operation errors in quantum computing. These approaches aim to reduce the impact of errors and improve the reliability of quantum computations. However, there are some trade-offs in implementing QEC techniques such as resource overhead due to multiple physical qubits encoding a single logical qubit, increased latency due to additional instructions for error correction, and complexity in scaling. Additionally, advancements in quantum hardware technology and the development of more precise control techniques can help minimize gate operation errors in quantum computing systems.

Techniques for quantum error mitigation

To reduce the impact of errors, even before implementing error correction, several vendors are working on *error mitigation* techniques. **Quantum error mitigation (QEM)** offers lower resource overhead because it does not require full redundancy of error correction. It also involves less complexity than error correction. QEM is more practical for NISQ devices.

Error mitigation techniques often involve identifying and minimizing the effect of errors on the results of quantum computations by using statistical methods. For instance, techniques like **error averaging** perform quantum computations multiple times and then average the results. There are two limitations to this approach. One is that it increases computational cost due to multiple circuit executions to average out the error in order to obtain reliable results. The other is sensitivity to systematic errors, as the premise for error averaging is that errors are random. **Post-processing** aims to improve the results of a quantum computation after it has been performed to reduce the impact of errors through statistical bootstrapping and resampling. **Noise extrapolation** involves running the same quantum computation multiple times with varying levels of artificially added noise and then comparing the results to extrapolate a **noise-free** result. However, some issues could hinder the effectiveness of this approach, such as inaccurate noise modeling, limited operational ranges, statistical uncertainties, and error accumulation. Let us look at the techniques:

- **Post-processing error mitigation:** Post-processing techniques involve analyzing the outcomes of quantum computations to infer and correct errors that may have occurred during the computation. For post-processing error mitigation, methods such as Bayesian inference or **maximum likelihood estimation** (MLE) can be used. For example, in a quantum algorithm, after taking several measurements, Bayesian inference can help refine the probabilities of possible outcomes by considering known errors or biases. For example, if there is a prior belief that a particular qubit is more likely to result in 0, Bayesian inference can adjust the results accordingly, leading to more accurate overall probabilities. Both Bayesian inference and MLE help enhance the fidelity of quantum computation. These methods have been effective in real-world use cases such as improving accuracy in molecular simulations, boosting fidelity of NISQ devices, error correction in quantum communication to enhance reliability of quantum key distribution protocols, etc.

- **Error detection and correction:** In this technique, errors are detected and corrected as they occur. This can be achieved using various error detection and correction algorithms, such as majority voting or syndrome extraction techniques:

  o **Majority voting technique:** In the majority voting technique, multiple measurements are taken on each qubit to detect errors. By performing repeated measurements on the same qubit and comparing the results, a voting scheme can be used to determine the correct state of the qubit. This technique is based on the principle that errors are more likely to cause a deviation from the correct state, and by taking a majority vote of the measurements, one can correct errors and mitigate their impact on the quantum computation. Implementing this method generally involves a greater number of physical qubits. Majority voting can require further gates for preparation and measurement, thus increasing the execution time and potentially exceeding the coherence time of the qubits and leading to additional errors. Also, high noise level makes the results unreliable.

  o **Syndrome extraction technique:** The syndrome extraction technique is an essential part of QEC codes, such as the popular quantum error correcting codes like the surface code. In this technique, ancillary qubits, called **syndrome**

qubits, are used to extract information about errors that may have occurred in the quantum computation. By measuring the syndrome qubits and analyzing the results, one can deduce the presence and location of errors in the encoded quantum information. This information is then used to apply corrective operations to the qubits and restore the original state of the quantum system. An example of the syndrome extraction technique is the 3-qubit circuit for detecting bit-flip errors, which is discussed in a later section of this chapter. However, there is overhead and complexity associated with implementing this method. Additional ancilla qubits complicate the architecture. Also, the syndrome extraction process is iterative and involves multiple steps, and at the end requires classical logic for error correction. All of these factors contribute to increased computational complexity and latency, which can potentially affect the overall performance of quantum algorithms.

- **Error mitigation:** Randomized compiling, measurement-error mitigation, zero-noise extrapolation, probabilistic error cancellation, symmetry constraints, purity constraints, subspace expansions, N-representability, learning-based

- **Error mitigation algorithms:** Various algorithms and techniques have been developed to mitigate errors in quantum computations, such as **error mitigation via noise-agnostic quantum error suppression** (**EMNQS**) and **error mitigation via randomized compiling** (**EMRC**). These algorithms aim to estimate and correct errors in quantum computations without requiring detailed knowledge of the noise model.

- **Error suppression:** Quantum error suppression techniques aim to reduce the occurrence of errors by implementing error suppression mechanisms in the quantum system. This can include techniques such as dynamical decoupling or error-avoiding codes.

- **Error-resilient quantum gates:** Error-resilient quantum gates are gates designed to be less sensitive to errors, making them more robust against noise and errors in the quantum hardware. Techniques such as randomized compiling or gate set tomography can be used to optimize quantum gates for error resilience.

- **Machine learning-based error mitigation:** Machine learning techniques can be used to learn patterns in the errors occurring in a quantum system and develop error mitigation strategies based on this learning. Machine learning algorithms can help predict and correct errors in real-time, improving the overall performance of quantum computations.

Techniques for quantum error correction

Quantum data is inherently vulnerable to disruption from noise, decoherence, or errors during quantum gate operations. These errors can lead to the loss of quantum information and disrupt quantum computations. QEC techniques allow for the detection and correction of these errors, unlike error mitigation, which aims to prevent the error from occurring, thereby preserving the integrity of quantum states and ensuring the reliable execution of quantum algorithms. Without QEC, the practical realization of fault-tolerant quantum systems would be impossible.

Error correction demands higher resource overhead, as a single logical qubit may require entangling of several physical qubits. It is also inherently complex due to its reliance on sophisticated mathematical frameworks and algorithms. However, compared to error mitigation techniques, QEC is more robust and is crucial for building scalable, fault-tolerant systems.

One of the key aspects of QEC is the concept of logical qubits. These are quantum bits of information protected from errors by encoding them across multiple physical qubits. For example, in classical computing, a bit of value 0 will be encoded as 000, and one with value 1 will be encoded as 111. If an error causes the bits to change from 000 to 100, it can still be inferred correctly by looking at the majority of the bits. However, the main difference in quantum computing is that the state of a qubit cannot be cloned due to the No-cloning theorem in quantum mechanics. Therefore, the encoding scheme for error correction is more complex than in classical computing.

This section will give an overview of a few of the techniques for error correction:

- **Shor's code:** This technique is named after *Peter Shor*, who is also the inventor of a quantum factoring algorithm named Shor's algorithm. Shor's code encodes information in a single logical qubit into nine physical qubits. It can correct both bit-flip and phase-flip errors on a single qubit. A detailed circuit diagram and code will be explained in the next section.

- **Steane's code:** Steane's code, named after physicist *Andrew Steane*, is a specific quantum error correcting code that encodes information in a single logical qubit into seven physical qubits. It can rectify any single-qubit error, be it a bit-flip or phase-flip error. Steane's code can identify single-qubit errors without directly measuring the logical qubit. By gauging specific error syndromes, the code can pinpoint whether a bit-flip or phase-flip error has occurred and on which qubit. The error correction method in Steane's code entails utilizing ancillary qubits and a sequence of controlled operations. It encompasses both bit-flip and phase error detection, with subsequent corrective actions as necessary. What sets Steane's code apart is its ability to correct errors without directly measuring the logical qubit, thereby preserving the quantum information. This code is well-suited for applications in quantum communication, fault-tolerant computing, and quantum memory.

- **Toric code:** Toric code belongs to a class of QEC codes called surface codes. Toric code is a powerful quantum error correcting code that leverages the topological properties of the lattice to provide robust protection against errors. It encodes a logical qubit in a two-dimensional lattice of physical qubits. It can detect and correct both bit-flip and phase-flip errors. Errors in the physical qubits are detected and corrected by measuring the syndromes of chains of stabilizer operators corresponding to plaquettes and vertices on the lattice. The Toric code has a high threshold for error correction, making it a robust method for fault-tolerant quantum computing.

- **Quantum Convolutional code:** At the core, QEC codes are of three broad categories:

  o Stabilizer codes such as Shor's code and Steane's code

  o Topological codes such as the Toric code

  o Convolutional codes

  These codes are used primarily in quantum communication. Their differentiating attribute is their memory structure. This leads to the reuse of qubits during the encoding process, which requires fewer qubits. Therefore, large numbers of qubits can be transmitted, as fewer qubits are required to correct the errors.

- **Cat qubits:** Cat qubits are superconducting qubits that are in a superposition of two quantum states instead of being in a superposition of 0 and 1 in a single quantum state. Cat qubits require fewer physical qubits to encode a logical qubit as compared to other superconducting qubits. Also, in contrast to other qubits, Cat qubits significantly decrease bit-flip error at the cost of slightly higher phase-flip error.

- **GKP Code:** GKP code is an error correction code named after its inventors, *Gottesman*, *Kitaev*, and *Preskill*. This is applied to a GKP qubit, which is a bosonic qubit. A bosonic qubit is a qubit encoded in an oscillator mode, such as a microwave resonator. The GKP code is created to be resilient against small shift errors present in momentum and position quadrature. This approach gives good fault tolerance with fewer qubits.

There are many other techniques for QEC, and it is a field of continuous research. In the next section, we will examine Shor's code in more detail.

Quantum circuit design for QEC

This section will cover the design and implementation of QEC circuits. The first two circuits will correct bit-flip and phase-flip errors in a 1-qubit system. The third circuit will correct both bit-flip and phase-flip errors in a 1-qubit system using Shor's code. To recap from an earlier chapter, we can use either IBM Q Lab or Composer to design and execute the circuit. We can run the code on a simulator as well as the real quantum device. The Python-Jupyter code in IBM Q Lab can be run from local machine as well. That is, we can invoke a simulator or real quantum processor from IBM Q Lab as well as from a local Jupyter Notebook. For a demonstration of QEC in this section, Python code was executed on a Jupyter Notebook running locally, which uses ibmq_qasm_simulator.

3-qubit circuit for bit flip error

Figure 8.1 depicts a circuit to correct bit flip error on a single qubit. The main qubit, which is the first qubit, is in a state of superposition, and two redundant, ancillary qubits are introduced to correct the error. The rectangular block named E-bit represents the error and intentionally flips the state of the first qubit. The CNOT and CCNOT gates comprise the error correction circuit. Let us look at the steps:

1. The qubit is in a state of superposition $|\psi> = \alpha|0) + \beta|1)$, where α and β are probabilities of states 0 and 1. The state of the circuit with the two ancillary qubits is $\alpha|000) + \beta|100)$. The most significant qubit is the topmost qubit in the circuit, and the least significant qubit is the one at the bottom.

2. The first CNOT will not change the 2nd qubit's state when the first qubit is 0, but it will flip the 2nd qubit to 1 when the first qubit is 1. So, the state of the circuit becomes:

$$\alpha|000) + \beta|110)$$

3. The second CNOT will impact the 3rd qubit when the first qubit is 1. Therefore, the new state will be:

$$\alpha|000) + \beta|111)$$

4. The error block will flip the state of the first qubit. So, the new state of the circuit is:

$$\alpha|100) + \beta|011)$$

5. The first CNOT after the error block will flip the 2nd qubit when the first qubit is 1. The state of the circuit becomes:

$$\alpha|110) + \beta|011)$$

6. The second CNOT will flip the 3rd qubit when the first qubit is 1, and so the new state is:

$$\alpha|111) + \beta|011)$$

7. The CCNOT flips the first qubit when both the 2nd and 3rd qubits are 1. So, the final state of the circuit is:

$$\alpha|011) + \beta|111)$$

If you look at the state of just the first qubit, it is $\alpha|0) + \beta|1)$, which is the original or the starting state. Even with a bit flip error on the first qubit introduced by the error block, the two redundant qubits could correct it.

Take a scenario where there was no error:

1. Let us take the state of the circuit just before the error block:

$$\alpha|000) + \beta|111)$$

2. Since there is no error, that is, no error block, the state remains the same.

3. The first CNOT after the error block will flip the 2nd qubit when the first qubit is 1:

$$\alpha|000\rangle + \beta|101\rangle$$

4. The second CNOT will flip the 3rd qubit when the first qubit is 1:

$$\alpha|000\rangle + \beta|100\rangle$$

5. The CCNOT flips the first qubit when both 2nd and 3rd qubits are 1. However, the 2nd and 3rd qubits are both 0, so nothing happens. The final state of the circuit is:

$$\alpha|000\rangle + \beta|100\rangle$$

The first qubit is $\alpha|0\rangle + \beta|1\rangle$, which is the starting state. Therefore, this circuit returns the original state of the main qubit whether there is an error.

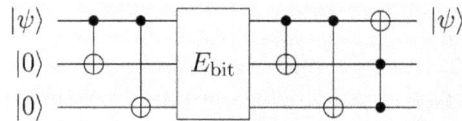

Figure 8.1: QEC for bit flip[1]

Let us look at the Python-Jupyter code and the results generated by the simulator. This code can be run on IBM Q Lab or a local machine.

First, import the libraries:

```
from qiskit import QuantumRegister, QuantumCircuit, assemble, ClassicalRegister
from qiskit import Aer
from qiskit.visualization import plot_histogram, plot_bloch_multivector, array_to_latex
from qiskit.extensions import Initialize
from qiskit.quantum_info import random_statevector
from qiskit_textbook.tools import vector2latex
```

The main qubit has to be in a state of superposition. While Hadamard gate is usually used to launch a qubit into superposition, but it creates two states of equal probability of . To view the bit flip error, the probabilities or amplitudes have to be different so that we can see the flip in amplitudes. Please note that the amplitude is the square root of probability. The following function will help create a superposition of different amplitudes. This function will generate two random state vectors representing the amplitudes, given as follows:

```
# This function generates a random quantum state for a single qubit and creates an # initialization gate that can be used to prepare that state in a quantum circuit.
```

---

1   (Source: Wikipedia)

```
def superposition_gate():
    # Create random 1-qubit state
    psi = random_statevector(2)
    # Create a gate that will assign random amplitudes
    init_gate = Initialize(psi)
    init_gate.label = "init"
    # Display the vector
    display(array_to_latex(psi, prefix="|\\psi\\rangle ="))
    return init_gate
```

The following function will print the states of the qubits and display them on the Bloch sphere:

```
def plot_bloch_sphere(qc):
    # Get the backend for the quantum simulator
    simulator = Aer.get_backend('qasm_simulator')
    # Save the current statevector of the quantum circuit
    qc.save_statevector()
    # Assemble the quantum circuit into a quantum object (qobj) for execution
    qobj = assemble(qc)
    # Run the quantum circuit on the simulator and obtain the results
    res = simulator.run(qobj).result()
    # Extract the statevector from the results of the simulation
    statevec = res.get_statevector()
    # Display the vector
    vector2latex(statevec, pretext="|\\psi\\rangle =")
    # Display it horizontally
    display(array_to_latex(statevec, prefix="|\\psi\\rangle ="))
    return statevec
```

Define the bit-flip function. Apply Pauli X gate to the qubit, as follows:

```
# Function to introduce bit-flip error
def bit_error(qc):
    # Apply the Pauli X gate (bit-flip) to the first qubit
    qc.x(0)
    return qc
```

The following is the error correction function. It also introduces a bit-flip error depending on a flag-named error. Whether there is an error or not, this circuit will retain the original state of the main qubit, which is qubit [0]. This is demonstrated by the following code:

```
# This function implements error correction for bit-flip error in a quantum
# circuit. It utilizes CNOT gates to add redundancy to the qubit q[0] that is
# being transmitted. If the 'error' flag is set to True, it introduces a simulated
# bit-flip error to test the correction process. The final portion of
# the function containing CNOT and Toffoli gates after the error block is
# the error correction circuit.

def bit_error_correction(qc, error):
    # Apply a CNOT gate from qubit 0 to qubit 1
    qc.cx(0,1)
    # Apply a CNOT gate from qubit 0 to qubit 2
    qc.cx(0,2)    # Introduce error if the 'error' flag is set to True

    if error:
        qc.barrier() # Add a barrier for clarity in visualization
        # Call the bit_error function to introduce a bit-flip error
        qc = bit_error(qc)
        qc.barrier()  # Add another barrier after introducing the error
    # Apply CNOT gate from qubit 0 to qubit 1
    qc.cx(0,1)
    # Apply CNOT gate from qubit 0 to qubit 2
    qc.cx(0,2)
    # Apply a Toffoli gate (CCX) with qubits 1 & 2 as control and 0 as target
    qc.ccx(2,1,0)
    return qc
```

Declare the quantum registers. The classical registers are for measurement.

```
qreg = QuantumRegister(3, 'q')
creg = ClassicalRegister(3, 'c')
```

Define three quantum circuits. The first one will display the original state of the qubits on the Bloch sphere. The second circuit **qc_error** will show the state of the main qubit after the bit-flip error. As we will see, the Bloch sphere will show the amplitudes of the two states in a reversed manner. The third circuit **qc_correction** will display the state of the main qubit after error correction. This state will be identical to the state displayed by the first circuit qc, whether or not there is an error:

```
# Create a quantum circuit for the main operation
qc = QuantumCircuit(qreg, creg)
# Create a separate quantum circuit to model the error
qc_error = QuantumCircuit(qreg, creg)
# Create a quantum circuit dedicated to the error correction process
qc_correction = QuantumCircuit(qreg, creg)
```

Create the gate:

```
# initialize psi
init_gate = superposition_gate()
```

Since the function generates the state vectors randomly, so each execution will give different values. It does not matter though as the end objective is to see the same values post error correction. The state vectors created in the aforementioned step are shown as follows:

```
|ψ⟩ = [0.1054504084 + 0.0809746684i       0.6662656455 - 0.7337665869i]
```

Append the gate to the three quantum circuits:

```
# Append the initialization gate to qubit 0 in the main circuit
qc.append(init_gate, [0])
# Append the same initialization gate to the error circuit
qc_error.append(init_gate, [0])
# Append the same initialization gate to the error correction circuit
qc_correction.append(init_gate, [0])
```

Display the state vector of the 3-qubit qc circuit:

```
st1 = plot_bloch_sphere(qc)
```

The output is as follows:

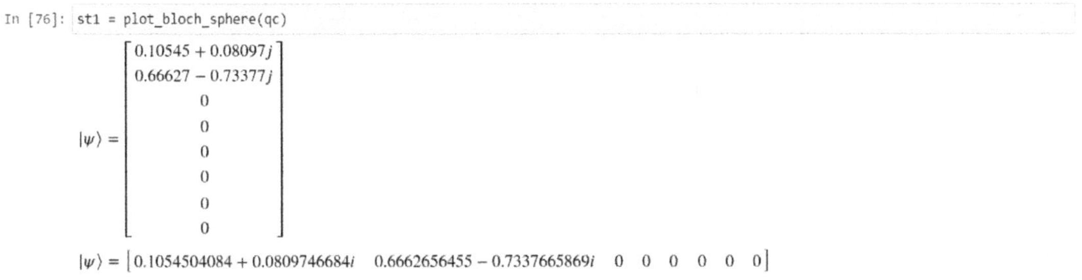

$$|\psi\rangle = \begin{bmatrix} 0.10545 + 0.08097j \\ 0.66627 - 0.73377j \\ 0 \\ 0 \\ 0 \\ 0 \\ 0 \\ 0 \end{bmatrix}$$

$$|\psi\rangle = \begin{bmatrix} 0.1054504084 + 0.0809746684i & 0.6662656455 - 0.7337665869i & 0 & 0 & 0 & 0 & 0 & 0 \end{bmatrix}$$

Figure 8.2: State vector of original circuit qc

Display it on the Bloch sphere:

```
plot_bloch_multivector(st1)
```

The output is shown as follows. Qubit 0 is the main qubit, so observe its output. The probability of $|1\rangle$ is much higher than $|0\rangle$; hence, the arrow is towards $|1\rangle$ in the Bloch sphere. The probability can be derived by squaring the amplitude, that is, summing the squares of real and imaginary values. The probability of $|0\rangle$ is $(0.1054504084)^2 + (0.0809746684)^2 = 0.01768 \sim 1.77\%$. The probability of $|1\rangle$ is $(0.6662656455)^2 + (0.7337665869)^2 = 0.98232 \sim 98.23\%$. Hence, the vector that represents qubit 0 is closer to $|1\rangle$. Note that the sum of the two probabilities is 1, as expected.

The state of qubit 1 and qubit 2 is $|0\rangle$, which is the initial state. These are ancillary qubits. Refer to the following figure:

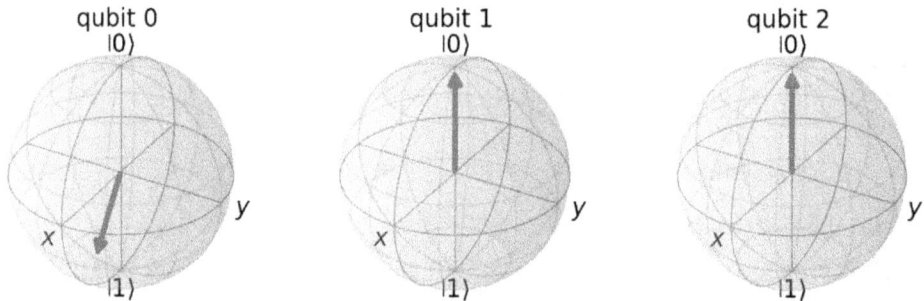

Figure 8.3: *Bloch sphere of original circuit qc*

Let us apply the error to **qc_error** and draw the circuit. The ensuing circuit is shown in *Figure 8.4*. The code is given as follows:

```
# Apply bit-flip error to qc_error circuit
qc_error.barrier()    # Apply a barrier for clarity in visualization
# Introduce a bit-flip error to the qc_error circuit by calling the function
qc_error = bit_error(qc_error)
qc_error.barrier() # Add another barrier to separate operations
# Draw and display the qc_error circuit
qc_error.draw(output='mpl')
```

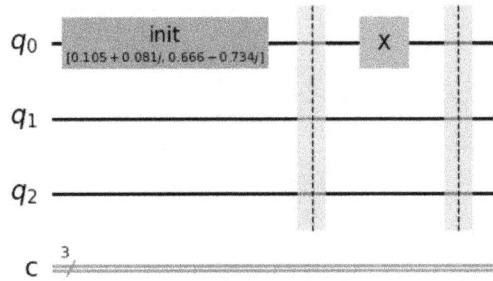

Figure 8.4: Error circuit design

Let us look at the state vectors of the circuit after the bit-flip error:

st2 = plot_bloch_sphere(qc_error)

As you can see, the states of |0⟩ and |1⟩ have been flipped in the following figure:

In [79]: st2 = plot_bloch_sphere(qc_error)

$$|\psi\rangle = \begin{bmatrix} 0.66627 - 0.73377j \\ 0.10545 + 0.08097j \\ 0 \\ 0 \\ 0 \\ 0 \\ 0 \\ 0 \end{bmatrix}$$

$$|\psi\rangle = \begin{bmatrix} 0.6662656455 - 0.7337665869i & 0.1054504084 + 0.0809746684i & 0 & 0 & 0 & 0 & 0 & 0 \end{bmatrix}$$

Figure 8.5: State vector of error circuit

Now, let us look at the Bloch sphere in *Figure 8.6*. The vector representing the main qubit q[0] is at a diametrically opposite end along the Z-axis. This is because the amplitudes of |0⟩ and |1⟩ have been flipped by the error. The vector is closer to |0⟩ instead of |1⟩, and the probability of |0⟩ is higher than |1⟩.

```
In [87]: plot_bloch_multivector(st2)
```
Out[87]:

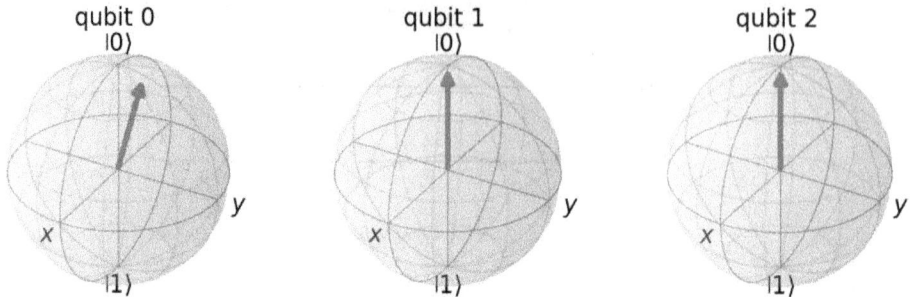

Figure 8.6: Bloch sphere of error circuit

Call the error correction circuit:

```
error = True
qc_correction = bit_error_correction(qc_correction, error)
```

Display the state vectors of the circuit after the error correction. If you look at *Figure 8.7*, the amplitudes of |0⟩ and |1⟩ have been restored to their original values. The amplitudes, however, may seem out of place. Here is the explanation. The non-zero amplitudes are against states |110⟩ and |111⟩. Just note that the most significant bit represents q[2], and the least significant bit q[0]. After the error correction function is run, qubits [1] and [2] become |1⟩. Hence, the amplitudes that stood originally at |000⟩ and |001⟩ are now assigned to |110⟩ and |111⟩ because q[1] and q[2] have become |1⟩. If you ignore the ancillary qubits q[1] and q[2] and focus just on the main qubit q[0], you will see that |0⟩ has amplitude 0.10545+0.08097j and |1⟩ has amplitude 0.66627−0.73377j, which is the same as the state vector of the original circuit qc.

```
In [85]: st3 = plot_bloch_sphere(qc_correction)
```

$$|\psi\rangle = \begin{bmatrix} 0 \\ 0 \\ 0 \\ 0 \\ 0 \\ 0 \\ 0.10545 + 0.08097j \\ 0.66627 - 0.73377j \end{bmatrix}$$

$$|\psi\rangle = \begin{bmatrix} 0 & 0 & 0 & 0 & 0 & 0 & 0.1054504084 + 0.0809746684i & 0.6662656455 - 0.7337665869i \end{bmatrix}$$

Figure 8.7: State vector of error correction circuit

Display the **qc_correction** qubits on the Bloch sphere, as shown in *Figure 8.8*. The representation of the main qubit q[0] on the Bloch sphere for **qc_correction** circuit is identical to that of the main circuit **qc**. This shows that bit-flip error introduced in the circuit has been rectified.

In [86]: plot_bloch_multivector(st3)

Out[86]:

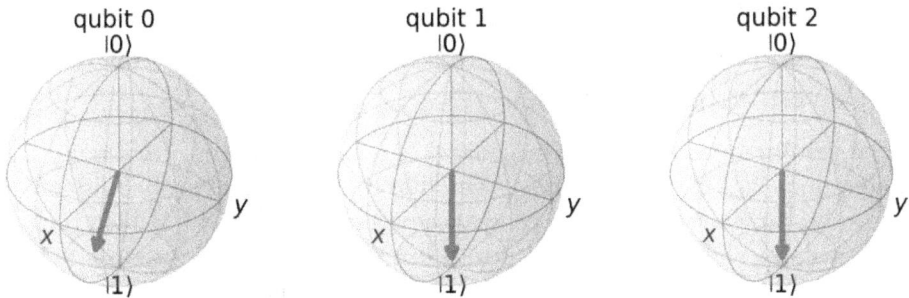

Figure 8.8: Bloch sphere of error correction circuit

We will now measure the qubits in all three circuits to observe their state. As |1⟩ has a higher probability than |0⟩ in the original circuit qc, we will see a greater number of |1⟩ s as compared to |0⟩s across multiple executions. Since the error circuit qc_error has the amplitudes flipped for the main qubit, the occurrence of |0⟩ will be more than |1⟩ after multiple runs. The circuit post-correction, **qc_correction**, will have more occurrences of |1⟩ than |0⟩, just like qc, after multiple executions. Let us look at the results.

Draw the circuit **qc** and measure the qubits, as given in the following code. *Figure 8.9* shows the results:

```
qc.measure([0],[0])
qc.draw(output='mpl')
```

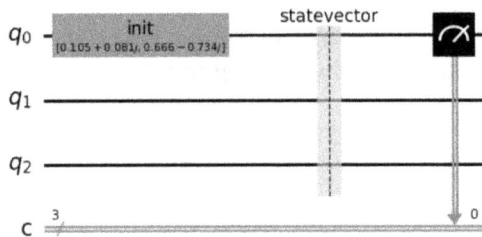

Figure 8.9: Design of original circuit qc

Assemble and run the circuit on the simulator over 1000 iterations:

```
# Get the backend for the quantum simulator
simulator = Aer.get_backend('qasm_simulator')
# Assemble the circuit
qobj = assemble(qc)
```

```
# Run the quantum circuit on the simulator  over 1000 iterations
results = simulator.run(qobj, shots=1000).result()
# Get count of occurrences of |0⟩ and |1⟩ over 1000 iterations.
answer = results.get_counts()
```

Plot the result. As can be seen in *Figure 8.10*, |1⟩ occurs more frequently than |0⟩ over 1000 iterations, as expected. We have seen that the theoretical probability of |1⟩ is 98.23%, whereas the bar chart shows the occurrence percentage as 97.4%, which is close. Each run of the simulator will give different counts, but they will always be close to the theoretical probability. The following code plots the histogram, which is shown in *Figure 8.10*:

```
plot_histogram(answer)
```

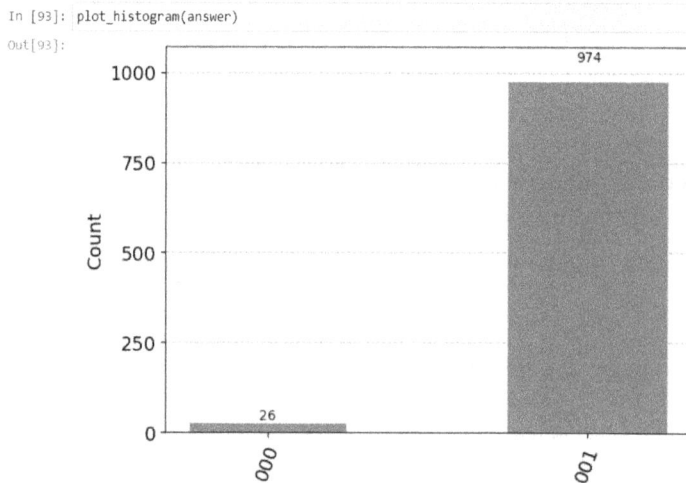

Figure 8.10: Result from original circuit qc

We will now look at the error circuit and its results. Run the code to measure and draw the error circuit - **qc_error**, which is shown in *Figure 8.11*:

```
qc_error.measure([0],[0])
qc_error.draw(output='mpl')
```

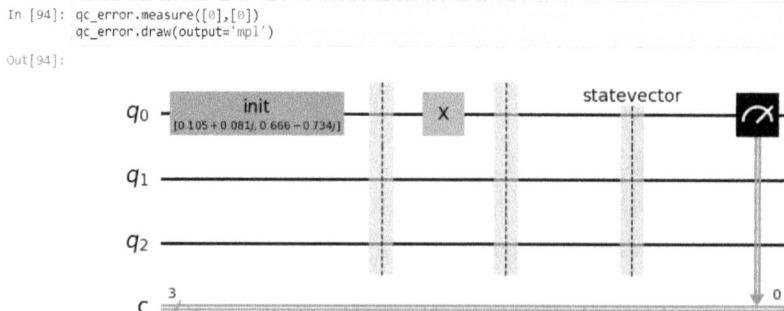

Figure 8.11: Design of error circuit

Submit the circuit on the simulator and plot the result. As can be seen in *Figure 8.12*, the count of $|0\rangle$ is more than $|1\rangle$ because of the bit flip. $|0\rangle$ was flipped to $|1\rangle$, and $|1\rangle$ got flipped to $|0\rangle$, hence the probability also got flipped. The code to run the simulator is given as follows:

```
# Get the backend for the quantum simulator
simulator = Aer.get_backend('qasm_simulator')
# Assemble the circuit
qobj = assemble(qc_error)
# Run the quantum circuit on the simulator over 1000 iterations
results = simulator.run(qobj, shots=1000).result()
# Get count of occurrences of |0) and |1) over 1000 iterations.
answer = results.get_counts()
plot_histogram(answer)
```

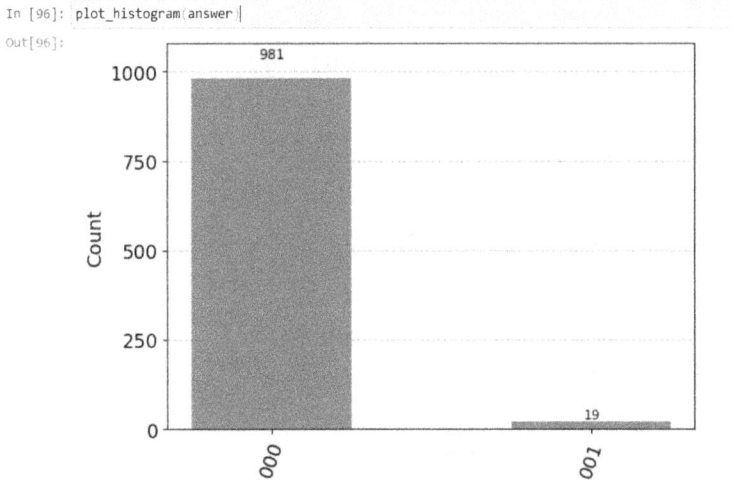

Figure 8.12: Result from error circuit

Finally, let us look at the design of the complete circuit, **qc_correction**, with the bit-flip error and the error correction gates, as given in the following code. *Figure 8.13* gives the complete circuit.

```
qc_correction.measure([0,1,2], [0,1,2])
qc_correction.draw(output='mpl')
```

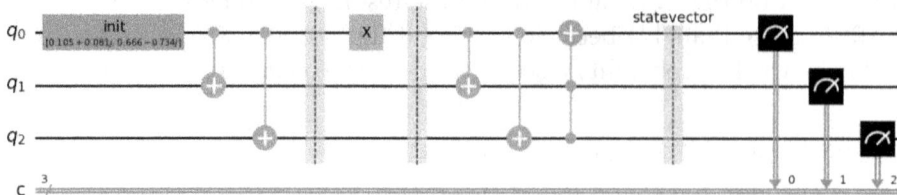

Figure 8.13: *Design of overall circuit, with error and error correction gates*

Submit the circuit on the simulator and plot the result. The bar chart (*Figure 8.14*) shows that the majority of the time, |1⟩ is observed just like the original circuit, as the bit flip error was corrected. In this run, the observed occurrence percentage is 98.3%, which is close to the theoretical probability. Also, note that the ancillary qubits q[1] and q[2] have become |1⟩. This is the same as what is shown on the Bloch sphere in *Figure 8.8*. The final state of ancillary qubits is not important as its purpose is to aid in correcting error introduced in q[0]. The code to run on the simulator is given as follows:

```
# Get the backend for the quantum simulator
simulator = Aer.get_backend('qasm_simulator')
# Assemble the circuit
qobj = assemble(qc_correction)
# Run the quantum circuit on the simulator over 1000 iterations
results = simulator.run(qobj, shots=1000).result()
# Get count of occurrences of |0⟩ and |1⟩ over 1000 iterations.
answer = results.get_counts()
plot_histogram(answer)
```

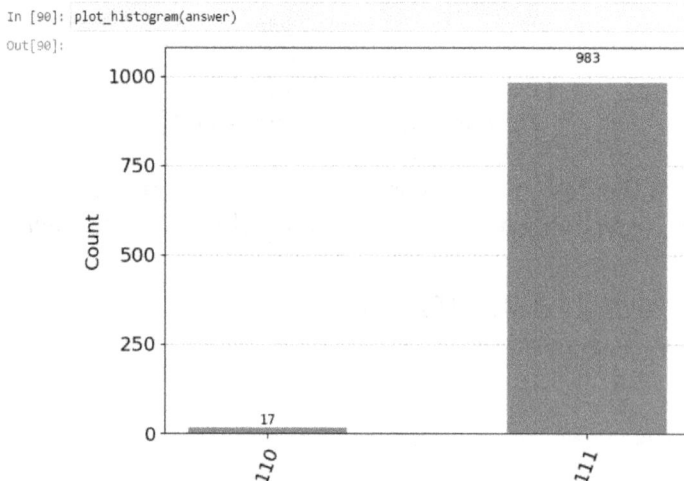

Figure 8.14: *Result from error correction circuit*

3-qubit circuit for phase error

Figure 8.15 represents a circuit to correct phase error on a single qubit. The main qubit, which is the first qubit, is in a state of superposition, and two redundant, ancillary qubits are introduced to correct the error. The rectangular block named E-phase introduces a phase shift on the first qubit. The Hadamard, CNOT, and CCNOT gates comprise the error correction circuit.

The qubit is in a state of superposition $|\psi> = \alpha|0\rangle + \beta|1\rangle$, where α and β are probabilities of states 0 and 1.

The state of the circuit with the two ancillary qubits is $\alpha|000\rangle + \beta|100\rangle$. The most significant qubit is the topmost qubit in the circuit, and the least significant qubit is the one at the bottom.

The first CNOT will not change the 2nd qubit's state when the first qubit is 0, but it will flip the 2nd qubit to 1 when the first qubit is 1. So, the state of the circuit becomes:

$$\alpha|000\rangle + \beta|110\rangle$$

The second CNOT will impact the 3rd qubit when the first qubit is 1. Therefore, the new state will be –

$$\alpha|000\rangle + \beta|111\rangle$$

Hadamard gates are applied to all three qubits. This will change the state to:

$$\frac{1}{2\sqrt{2}}\,\alpha|(0+1)^3\rangle + \beta|(0-1)^3\rangle \quad \rightarrow$$

$$\frac{1}{2\sqrt{2}}\,\alpha|(0+1)(0+1)^2\rangle + \beta|(0-1)(0-1)^2\rangle$$

The error block will flip the phase of the first qubit. This means state 0 will remain 0, but state 1 will become -1:

$$\frac{1}{2\sqrt{2}}\,\alpha|(0-1)(0+1)^2\rangle + \beta|(0+1)(0-1)^2\rangle$$

Post the error block, Hadamard gates are again applied to all the three qubits. This will change the state to:

$$\frac{1}{8}\,\alpha|(\,(0+1)-(0-1)\,)\,(\,(0+1)+(0-1))^2\,) + \beta|(\,(0+1)+(0-1)\,)\,(\,(0+1)-(0-1)\,)^2\,) \quad \rightarrow$$

$$\frac{1}{8}\,\alpha|(\,2.1\,)\,(\,2.0\,)^2\rangle + \beta|(\,2.0\,)\,(\,2.1\,)^2\rangle \quad \rightarrow$$

$$\frac{1}{8}\,\alpha|\,8(100)\rangle + \beta|\,8(011)\rangle \quad \rightarrow$$

$$\alpha|100\rangle + \beta|011\rangle$$

The first CNOT after the error block will flip the 2nd qubit when the first qubit is 1. The state of the circuit becomes:

$$\alpha|110\rangle + \beta|011\rangle$$

The second CNOT will flip the 3rd qubit when the first qubit is 1, and so the new state is:

$$\alpha|111\rangle + \beta|011\rangle$$

The CCNOT flips the first qubit when both 2nd and 3rd qubits are 1. So, the final state of the circuit is:

$$\alpha|011\rangle + \beta|111\rangle$$

If you look at the state of just the first qubit, it is $\alpha|0\rangle + \beta|1\rangle$, which is the original or the starting state. Even with a phase error on the first qubit introduced by the error block, the two redundant qubits were able to correct it.

Just like the bit flip error correction circuit, the following circuit will return the original state of the first qubit even when there is no phase error. You can work these equations and try it out for yourself.

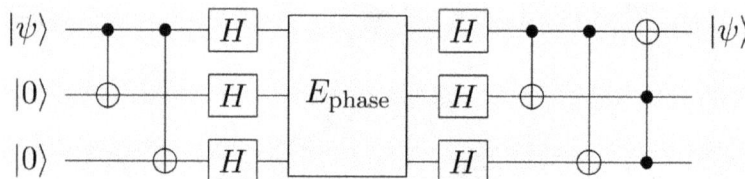

Figure 8.15: QEC for phase error [2]

Let us look at the Python-Jupyter code and the results generated by the simulator. This code can be run on IBM Q Lab or a local machine.

Import the libraries:

```
from qiskit import QuantumRegister, QuantumCircuit, assemble, ClassicalRegister
from qiskit import Aer
from qiskit.visualization import plot_histogram, plot_bloch_multivector, array_to_latex
from qiskit.extensions import Initialize
from qiskit.quantum_info import random_statevector
from qiskit_textbook.tools import vector2latex
```

In the bit flip error circuit, it was important to have different amplitudes for the two superposition states to visualize the flipping of the qubit states. In the phase error circuit we are going to apply a Pauli Z gate to change the phase of the qubit, which will flip the sign of $|1\rangle$ to $-|1\rangle$ while having no impact on $|0\rangle$. However, for the sake of consistency, we

2   (Source: Wikipedia)

will still use the same **superposition_gate** function from the previous section to define the amplitudes of the superposition states:

This function generates a random quantum state for a single qubit and creates an initialization gate that can be used to prepare that state in a quantum circuit.

```
def superposition_gate():
    # Create random 1-qubit state
    psi = random_statevector(2)
    # Create a gate that will assign random amplitudes
    init_gate = Initialize(psi)
    init_gate.label = "init"
    # Display the vector
    display(array_to_latex(psi, prefix="|\\psi\\rangle ="))
    return init_gate
```

The following function will print the states of the qubits and display them on the Bloch sphere:

```
def plot_bloch_sphere(qc):
    # Get the backend for the quantum simulator
    simulator = Aer.get_backend('qasm_simulator')
    # Save the current statevector of the quantum circuit
    qc.save_statevector()
    # Assemble the quantum circuit into a quantum object (qobj) for execution
    qobj = assemble(qc)
    # Run the quantum circuit on the simulator and obtain the results
    res = simulator.run(qobj).result()
    # Extract the statevector from the results of the simulation
    statevec = res.get_statevector()
    # Display the vector
    vector2latex(statevec, pretext="|\\psi\\rangle =")
    # Display it horizontally
    display(array_to_latex(statevec, prefix="|\\psi\\rangle ="))
    return statevec
```

Define the function that will introduce phase error. Apply Pauli Z gate to the qubit:

```
# This function applies a phase error to the first qubit of the given quantum
# circuit by utilizing the Pauli Z gate, which flips the phase of the qubit's
```

```
# state.
def phase_error(qc):
    # Apply the Pauli Z gate to flip the phase of the first qubit
    qc.z(0)
    return qc
```

The following is the error correction function. It also introduces a phase error depending on a flag-named error. Whether there is an error or not, this circuit will retain the original state of the main qubit, which is qubit [0].

```
# This function implements phase error correction for a given quantum
# circuit. It uses CNOT and Hadamard gates to add redundancy to the qubit q[0]
# that is being transmitted. If the 'error' flag is set to True, it introduces a
# simulated phase error to test the correction process. The final portion of
# the function containing CNOT, Hadamard and Toffoli gates after the error block
# is the error correction circuit.
def phase_error_correction(qc, error):
    # Apply a CNOT gate from qubit 0 to qubit 1
    qc.cx(0,1)
    # Apply a CNOT gate from qubit 0 to qubit 2
    qc.cx(0,2)
    # Launch qubits 0, 1 & 2 into superposition using Hadamard gate
    qc.h(0)
    qc.h(1)
    qc.h(2)
    # Error block - introduce error if the 'error' flag is set to True
    if error:
        qc.barrier()
        qc = phase_error(qc)
        qc.barrier()
    # Apply Hadamard gate again to the three qubits
    qc.h(0)
    qc.h(1)
    qc.h(2)
    # Apply CNOT gate from qubit 0 to qubit 1
```

```
qc.cx(0,1)
# Apply CNOT gate from qubit 0 to qubit 2
qc.cx(0,2)
# Apply a Toffoli gate (CCX) with qubits 1 & 2 as control and 0 as target
qc.ccx(2,1,0)
return qc
```

Declare the quantum registers. The classical registers are for measurement:

```
qreg = QuantumRegister(3, 'q')
creg = ClassicalRegister(3, 'c')
```

Define three quantum circuits. The first one will display the original state of the qubits on the Bloch sphere. The second circuit **qc_error** will show the state of the main qubit after the phase error. As we will see, the Bloch sphere will show the phase of the qubit rotated around the Z-axis by 180 degrees. Just to recap from a previous chapter, the phase angle φ is the angle made by qubit with respect to the X-axis. So, the phase changes when the qubit is rotated around the Z-axis. The third circuit, **qc_correction**, will display the state of the main qubit after error correction. This state will be identical to the state displayed by the first circuit qc, whether or not there is an error.

```
# Create a quantum circuit for the main operation
qc = QuantumCircuit(qreg, creg)
# Create a separate quantum circuit to model the error
qc_error = QuantumCircuit(qreg, creg)
# Create a quantum circuit dedicated to the error correction process
qc_correction = QuantumCircuit(qreg, creg)
```

Create the gate:

```
# initialize psi
init_gate = superposition_gate()
```

The state vectors created in the step is shown as follows. Since the function generates the state vectors randomly, so each execution will give different values. It does not matter, though, as the end objective is to see the same values post error correction.

$$|\psi\rangle = [0.1539194941 - 0.9789010184i \quad -0.1211170762 - 0.0582429344i]$$

Append the init_gate to the three quantum circuits:

```
# Append the initialization gate to qubit 0 in the main circuit
qc.append(init_gate, [0])
# Append the same initialization gate to the error circuit
```

```
qc_error.append(init_gate, [0])
# Append the same initialization gate to the error correction circuit
qc_correction.append(init_gate, [0])
```

Display the state vector of the 3-qubit qc circuit.

```
st1 = plot_bloch_sphere(qc)
```

The output is as follows:

In [60]: st1 = plot_bloch_sphere(qc)

$$|\psi\rangle = \begin{bmatrix} 0.15392 - 0.97890j \\ -0.12112 - 0.05824j \\ 0 \\ 0 \\ 0 \\ 0 \\ 0 \\ 0 \end{bmatrix}$$

$$|\psi\rangle = \begin{bmatrix} 0.1539194941 - 0.9789010184i & -0.1211170762 - 0.0582429344i & 0 & 0 & 0 & 0 & 0 & 0 \end{bmatrix}$$

Figure 8.16: State vector of original circuit

Display the state vector of the circuit on the Bloch sphere:

```
plot_bloch_multivector(st1)
```

The output is *Figure 8.17*. Qubit 0 is the main qubit, so just observe its output. Note the direction of the vector, as the phase error will change the phase or the direction of this vector. The state of qubit 1 and qubit 2 is |0⟩, which is the initial state. These are ancillary qubits.

In [61]: plot_bloch_multivector(st1)
Out[61]:

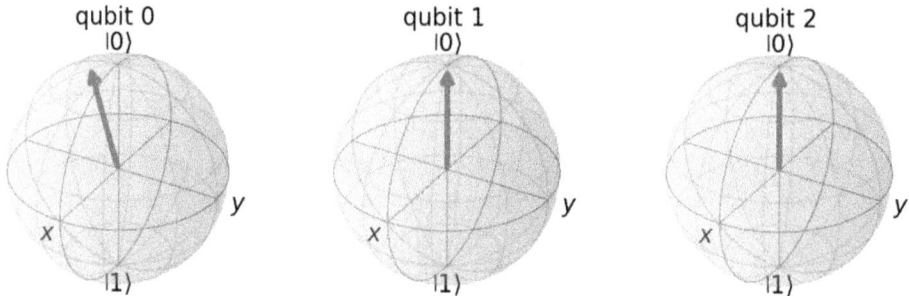

Figure 8.17: Bloch sphere of original circuit qc

Let us apply the error to qc_error and draw the circuit, as given in the following code. *Figure 8.18* gives the circuit:

```
# Apply phase error to qc_error circuit
qc_error.barrier() # Apply a barrier for clarity in visualization
# Introduce a phase-flip error to the qc_error circuit by calling the function
qc_error = phase_error(qc_error)
qc_error.barrier() # Add another barrier to separate operations
# Draw and display the qc_error
qc_error.draw(output='mpl')
```

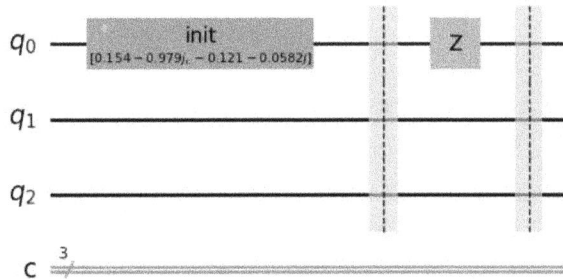

Figure 8.18: Error circuit design

We will look at the state vectors of the circuit after the phase error. This is shown in *Figure 8.19*.

```
st2 = plot_bloch_sphere(qc_error)
```

Note that the sign of the amplitude for |1⟩ has reversed. From a negative value, it has become positive. This is because the Pauli Z gate reversed the sign of the amplitude of |1⟩.

$$|\psi\rangle = \begin{bmatrix} 0.15392 - 0.97890j \\ 0.12112 + 0.05824j \\ 0 \\ 0 \\ 0 \\ 0 \\ 0 \\ 0 \end{bmatrix}$$

$$|\psi\rangle = \begin{bmatrix} 0.1539194941 - 0.9789010184i & 0.1211170762 + 0.0582429344i & 0 & 0 & 0 & 0 & 0 & 0 \end{bmatrix}$$

Figure 8.19: State vector of error circuit

Now, let us look at the Bloch sphere in *Figure 8.20*. The vector representing the main qubit q[0] is at a diametrically opposite end around the Z-axis. This is because Pauli Z has rotated the qubit around the Z-axis by 180 degrees.

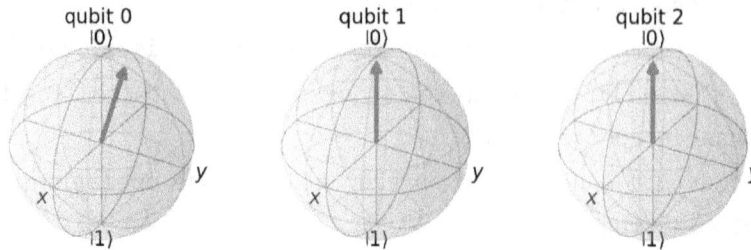

Figure 8.20: Bloch sphere of error circuit

Call the error correction circuit:

```
error = True

qc_correction = phase_error_correction(qc_correction, error)
```

Display the state vectors of the circuit after the error correction. If you look at *Figure 8.21*, the sign of the amplitude of |1⟩ has been restored to its original value. The amplitudes, however, may seem out of place. Here is the explanation. The non-zero amplitudes are against states |110⟩ and |111⟩. Just note that the most significant bit represents q[2] and least significant bit q[0]. After the error correction function is run, qubits [1] and [2] become |1⟩. Hence the amplitudes that stood originally at |000⟩ and |001⟩ are now assigned to |110⟩ and |111⟩ because q[1] and q[2] have become |1⟩. If you ignore the ancillary qubits q[1] and q[2] and focus just on the main qubit q[0], you will see that |0⟩ has amplitude 0. 0.15392−0.97890j and |1⟩ has amplitude −0.12112−0.05824j, as can be seen in *Figure 8.21*, which is the same as the state vector of the original circuit qc:

```
st3 = plot_bloch_sphere(qc_correction)
```

$$|\psi\rangle = \begin{bmatrix} 0 \\ 0 \\ 0 \\ 0 \\ 0 \\ 0 \\ 0.15392 - 0.97890j \\ -0.12112 - 0.05824j \end{bmatrix}$$

$$|\psi\rangle = \begin{bmatrix} 0 & 0 & 0 & 0 & 0 & 0 & 0.1539194941 - 0.9789010184i & -0.1211170762 - 0.0582429344i \end{bmatrix}$$

Figure 8.21: State vector of error correction circuit

Display the **qc_correction** qubits on the Bloch sphere. The representation of the main qubit q[0] on the Bloch sphere for **qc_correction** circuit is identical to that of the main circuit qc, as demonstrated in *Figure 8.22*. This shows that the phase error introduced in the circuit has been rectified.

```
plot_bloch_multivector(st3)
```

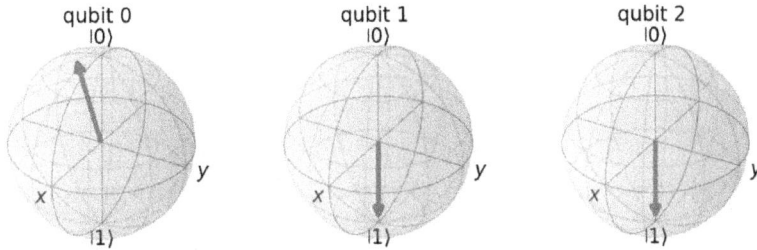

Figure 8.22: *Bloch sphere of error correction circuit*

In case of phase error, the absolute value of the amplitude remains the same; the sign gets reversed. However, we cannot measure the sign on a bar plot. That is why we use the Bloch sphere to observe the phase error because the bar plot just displays the absolute value of the amplitude. Hence, we will see that in all three circuits, the bar chart will show a high probability for $|0\rangle$ as compared to $|1\rangle$. This is because the probability of $|0\rangle$ is $(0.1539194941)^2 + (-0.9789010184)^2 = 98.19\%$, and probability of $|1\rangle$ is $(-0.1211170762)^2 + (-0.0582429344)^2 = 1.81\%$. We will see the actual results. First, let us look at the overall error correction circuit as given in *Figure 8.23*:

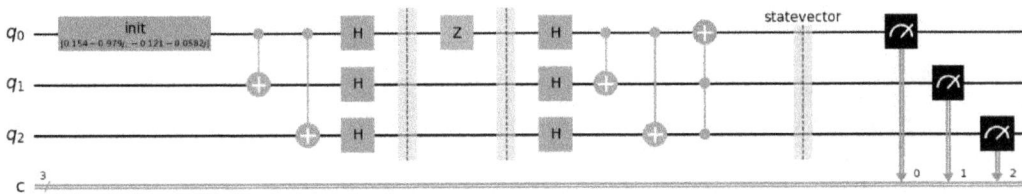

Figure 8.23: *Design of the overall circuit, with error and error correction gates*

Figure 8.24 shows the results from the three quantum circuits. As expected, across 1000 iterations, all the three circuits have high occurrence of $|0\rangle$ as per their amplitudes. The reason is that introducing a phase error changes the relative phases of the states without affecting the magnitudes of the amplitudes. This means that, although the signs of the amplitudes can change (indicating a relative phase shift), the probabilities associated with measuring once the system collapses to either $|0\rangle$ or $|1\rangle$ remain unchanged. This is because probabilities depend solely on the squared magnitudes of the complex amplitudes.

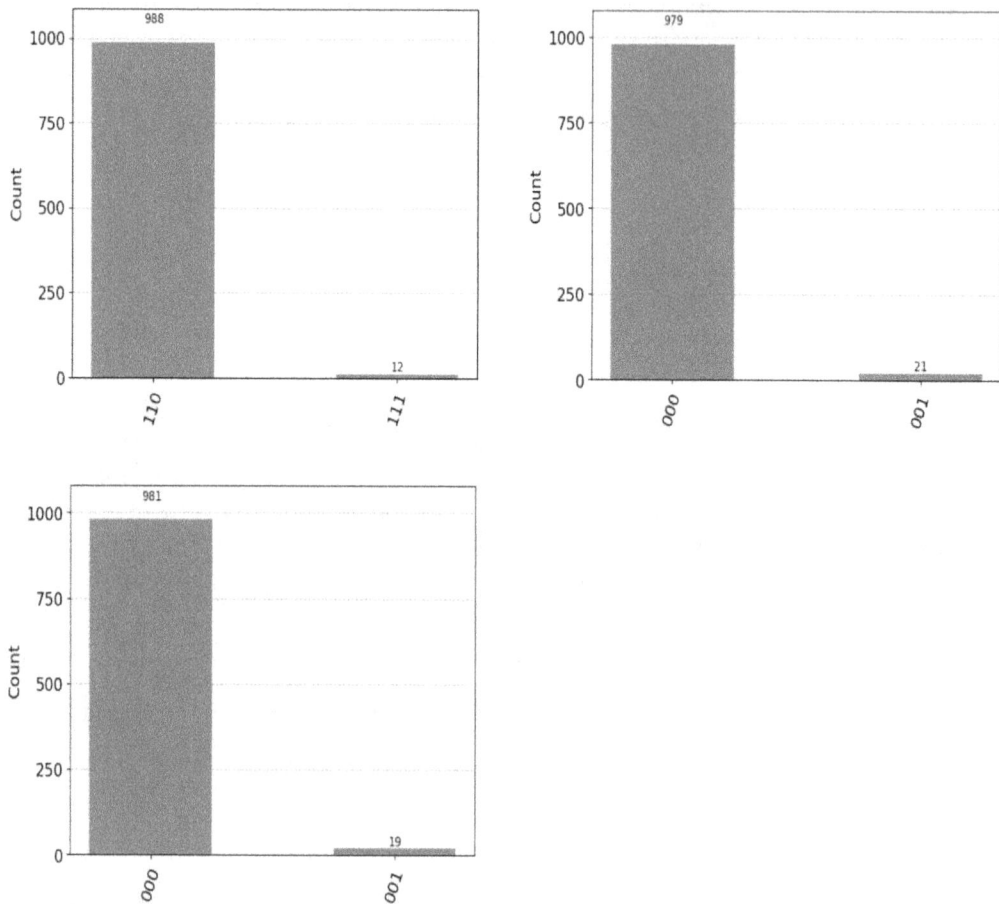

Figure 8.24: Results from error correction circuit, the original circuit, and error circuit

Shor's code for QEC

Figure 8.25 represents a circuit that corrects both bit-flip error and phase error (sign-flip) for a single qubit. This error correction code is called Shor's code. It encodes information contained in a single logical (main) qubit onto nine physical qubits that are entangled. Qubits 1, 4 and 7 handle sign flip error, while the three groups of qubits: (1,2,3), (4,5,6) and (7,8,9), are for bit-flip errors. The Shor's code can correct a single bit-flip error in each of the aforementioned groups. If the three groups are considered as three inputs, then the circuit is reduced to a 3-qubit circuit and the implementation of the gates between those three inputs represents the phase error circuit from the previous section.

The main qubit is in a state of superposition $|\psi\rangle = \alpha|0\rangle + \beta|1\rangle$, where α and β are probabilities of states 0 and 1. The Shor's code will transform this state into a product of nine qubits as follows:

$$|\psi'\rangle = \alpha |0_s\rangle + \beta |1_s\rangle, \text{ where}$$

$$|0_s\rangle = \frac{1}{2\sqrt{2}} (|000\rangle + |111\rangle) \otimes (|000\rangle + |111\rangle) \otimes (|000\rangle + |111\rangle)$$

Qubits 1, 2, 3   Qubits 4, 5, 6   Qubits 7, 8, 9

$$|1_s\rangle = \frac{1}{2\sqrt{2}} (|000\rangle - |111\rangle) \otimes (|000\rangle - |111\rangle) \otimes (|000\rangle - |111\rangle)$$

Qubits 1, 2, 3   Qubits 4, 5, 6   Qubits 7, 8, 9

The state is generated by the gates just before the error block, which is illustrated in *Figure 8.29(a)*.

Let us consider that the main qubit (first qubit) got its state flipped.

$$|0_s\rangle = \frac{1}{2\sqrt{2}} (|100\rangle + |011\rangle) \otimes (|000\rangle + |111\rangle) \otimes (|000\rangle + |111\rangle)$$

$$|1_s\rangle = \frac{1}{2\sqrt{2}} (|100\rangle - |011\rangle) \otimes (|000\rangle - |111\rangle) \otimes (|000\rangle - |111\rangle)$$

The combination of the two CNOTs and the Toffoli after the error block (*Figure 8.25*) will lead to this:

$$|0_s\rangle = \frac{1}{2\sqrt{2}} (|011\rangle + |111\rangle) \otimes (|011\rangle + |111\rangle) \otimes (|011\rangle + |111\rangle)$$

$$|1_s\rangle = \frac{1}{2\sqrt{2}} (|011\rangle - |111\rangle) \otimes (|011\rangle - |111\rangle) \otimes (|011\rangle - |111\rangle)$$

Apply the Hadamard on qubits 1, 4, and 7:

$$|0_s\rangle = \frac{1}{8} (|(0+1)11\rangle + |(0-1)11\rangle) \otimes (|(0+1)00\rangle + |(0-1)11\rangle) \otimes (|(0+1)00\rangle +$$
$$|(0-1)11\rangle) \rightarrow |0_s\rangle = \frac{1}{8} (8(|011\rangle \otimes |011\rangle \otimes |011\rangle)) \rightarrow |011\rangle \otimes |011\rangle \otimes |011\rangle$$

$$|1_s\rangle = \frac{1}{8} (|(0+1)11\rangle - |(0-1)11\rangle) \otimes (|(0+1)00\rangle - |(0-1)11\rangle) \otimes (|(0+1)00\rangle -$$
$$|(0-1)11\rangle) \rightarrow |1_s\rangle = \frac{1}{8} (8(|111\rangle \otimes |111\rangle \otimes |111\rangle)) \rightarrow |111\rangle \otimes |111\rangle \otimes |111\rangle$$

Therefore, the state for $|\psi'\rangle$ can be written as:

$$|\psi'\rangle = \alpha (|011\rangle \otimes |011\rangle \otimes |011\rangle) + \beta (|111\rangle \otimes |111\rangle \otimes |111\rangle)$$

Apply the last two CNOTs and Toffoli. The state of the circuit becomes:

$$|\psi'\rangle = \alpha (|011\rangle \otimes |011\rangle \otimes |011\rangle) + \beta (|111\rangle \otimes |011\rangle \otimes |011\rangle)$$

The bit flip error has been corrected, and the original amplitudes α and β are restored for states $|0\rangle$ and $|1\rangle$.

Let us now assume that the main qubit (first qubit) got its phase/sign flipped in the error block. The state of the circuit would be:

$$|0_s\rangle = \frac{1}{2\sqrt{2}} (|000\rangle - |111\rangle) \otimes (|000\rangle + |111\rangle) \otimes (|000\rangle + |111\rangle)$$

$$|1_s\rangle = \frac{1}{2\sqrt{2}} (|000\rangle + |111\rangle) \otimes (|000\rangle - |111\rangle) \otimes (|000\rangle - |111\rangle)$$

The combination of the two CNOTs and the Toffoli after the error block (*Figure 8.25*) will lead to this:

$$|0_s\rangle = \frac{1}{2\sqrt{2}} (|000\rangle - |100\rangle) \otimes (|000\rangle + |100\rangle) \otimes (|000\rangle + |100\rangle)$$

$$|1_s\rangle = \frac{1}{2\sqrt{2}} (|000\rangle + |100\rangle) \otimes (|000\rangle - |100\rangle) \otimes (|000\rangle - |100\rangle)$$

Apply the Hadamard on qubits 1, 4, and 7:

$$|0_s\rangle = \frac{1}{2\sqrt{2}} (|(0 + 1)00\rangle - |(0 - 1)00\rangle) \otimes (|(0 + 1)00\rangle + |(0 - 1)00\rangle) \otimes (|(0 + 1)00\rangle +$$
$$|(0 - 1)00\rangle) \;\; \rightarrow \;\; |0_s\rangle = \frac{1}{8} (8(|100\rangle \otimes |000\rangle \otimes |000\rangle)) \;\; \rightarrow \;\; |100\rangle \otimes |000\rangle \otimes |000\rangle$$

$$|1_s\rangle = \frac{1}{2\sqrt{2}} (|(0 + 1)00\rangle + |(0 - 1)00\rangle) \otimes (|(0 + 1)00\rangle - |(0 - 1)00\rangle) \otimes (|(0 + 1)00\rangle -$$
$$|(0 - 1)00\rangle) \;\; \rightarrow \;\; |1_s\rangle = \frac{1}{8} (8(|000\rangle \otimes |100\rangle \otimes |100\rangle)) \;\; \rightarrow \;\; |000\rangle \otimes |100\rangle \otimes |100\rangle$$

Therefore, state for $|\psi'\rangle$ can be written as:

$$|\psi'\rangle = \alpha (|100\rangle \otimes |000\rangle \otimes |000\rangle) + \beta (|000\rangle \otimes |100\rangle \otimes |100\rangle)$$

Apply the last two CNOTs and Toffoli. The state of the circuit becomes:

$$|\psi'\rangle = \alpha (|000\rangle \otimes |100\rangle \otimes |100\rangle) + \beta (|100\rangle \otimes |100\rangle \otimes |100\rangle)$$

As you can see, the sign flip error has been corrected, and the original state and sign of the main qubit have been restored, which is $\alpha |0\rangle + \beta |1\rangle$.

Now, let us induce both the errors, phase error followed by the bit-flip error, to the main qubit (first qubit) in the error block. *Figure 8.31* demonstrates this. The state of the circuit would be:

$$|0_s\rangle = \frac{1}{2\sqrt{2}} (|000\rangle - |111\rangle) \otimes (|000\rangle + |111\rangle) \otimes (|000\rangle + |111\rangle)$$

$$|1_s\rangle = \frac{1}{2\sqrt{2}} (|000\rangle + |111\rangle) \otimes (|000\rangle - |111\rangle) \otimes (|000\rangle - |111\rangle)$$

The following set of gates apply error correction logic, which is shown in *Figure 8.32*.

The combination of the two CNOTs and the Toffoli to the circuit after the error block (*Figure 8.25*) will lead to this:

$$|0_s\rangle = \frac{1}{2\sqrt{2}} \left(|000\rangle - |100\rangle\right) \otimes \left(|000\rangle + |100\rangle\right) \otimes \left(|000\rangle + |100\rangle\right)$$

$$|1_s\rangle = \frac{1}{2\sqrt{2}} \left(|000\rangle + |100\rangle\right) \otimes \left(|000\rangle - |100\rangle\right) \otimes \left(|000\rangle - |100\rangle\right)$$

Apply the Hadamard on qubits 1, 4, and 7:

$$|0_s\rangle = \frac{1}{2\sqrt{2}} \left(|(0+1)11\rangle - |(0-1)11\rangle\right) \otimes \left(|(0+1)00\rangle + |(0-1)00\rangle\right) \otimes \left(|(0+1)00\rangle + \right.$$
$$\left.|(0-1)00\rangle\right) \;\blacktriangleright\; |0_s\rangle = \frac{1}{8} \left(8(|111\rangle \otimes |000\rangle \otimes |000\rangle)\right) \quad\blacktriangleright\quad |111\rangle \otimes |000\rangle \otimes |000\rangle$$

$$|1_s\rangle = \frac{1}{2\sqrt{2}} \left(|(0+1)11\rangle + |(0-1)11\rangle\right) \otimes \left(|(0+1)00\rangle - |(0-1)00\rangle\right) \otimes \left(|(0+1)00\rangle - \right.$$
$$\left.|(0-1)00\rangle\right) \;\blacktriangleright\; |1_s\rangle = \frac{1}{8} \left(8(|011\rangle \otimes |100\rangle \otimes |100\rangle)\right) \quad\blacktriangleright\quad |011\rangle \otimes |100\rangle \otimes |100\rangle$$

Therefore, state for $|\psi'\rangle$ can be written as:

$$|\psi'\rangle = \alpha \left(|111\rangle \otimes |000\rangle \otimes |000\rangle\right) + \beta \left(|011\rangle \otimes |100\rangle \otimes |100\rangle\right)$$

Apply the last two CNOTs and Toffoli. The state of the circuit becomes:

$$|\psi'\rangle = \alpha \left(|000\rangle \otimes |100\rangle \otimes |100\rangle\right) + \beta \left(|111\rangle \otimes |111\rangle \otimes |111\rangle\right)$$

Thus, the original state and sign of the main qubit has been restored, which is $\alpha|0\rangle + \beta|1\rangle$.

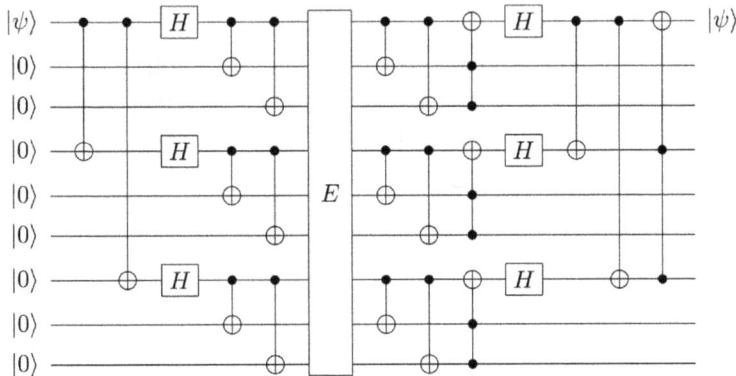

Figure 8.25: QEC with Shor's code [3]

Let us look at the Python-Jupyter code and the results generated by the simulator. This code can be run on IBM Q Lab or local machine. For brevity, we will exclude all boilerplate code that includes importing of libraries, initialization of quantum registers and circuits, defining functions for superposition, bit and phase errors, plotting etc., and only look at essential code.

Create the gate:

```
# initialize psi
init_gate = superposition_gate()
```

3   (Source: Wikipedia)

$|\psi\rangle$ = [-0.7895414668 + 0.3259130441i -0.1722658576 - 0.4906418594i]

The following figures show the state vectors and Bloch spheres for the original circuit, error circuit, and the error correction circuit respectively:

$$
\begin{bmatrix}
-0.78954 + 0.32591j \\
-0.17227 - 0.49064j \\
0 \\
0 \\
0
\end{bmatrix}
\quad
\begin{bmatrix}
0.17227 + 0.49064j \\
-0.78954 + 0.32591j \\
0 \\
0 \\
0
\end{bmatrix}
\quad
\begin{bmatrix}
-0.78954 + 0.32591j \\
-0.17227 - 0.49064j \\
0 \\
0 \\
0
\end{bmatrix}
$$

Figure 8.26(a): *State vectors for the original circuit, error circuit and error correction circuit*

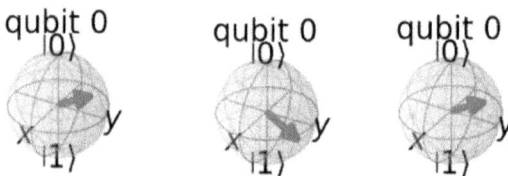

Figure 8.26(b): *Bloch sphere for the original circuit, error circuit, and error correction circuit*

As you can see, the error circuit introduced a phase error and then a bit-flip error, which first flipped the sign of [-0.17227 -0.49064j] and then swapped position with [-0.78954 + 0.32591j]. The Bloch sphere of the error circuit shows the change in direction of the vector representing the main qubit after it has been subjected to Pauli Z and Pauli X gates. The error correction circuit corrects both the errors, as can be seen by its state vector and Bloch sphere, which are identical to the original circuit.

Figure 8.27 shows the design of the error correction circuit:

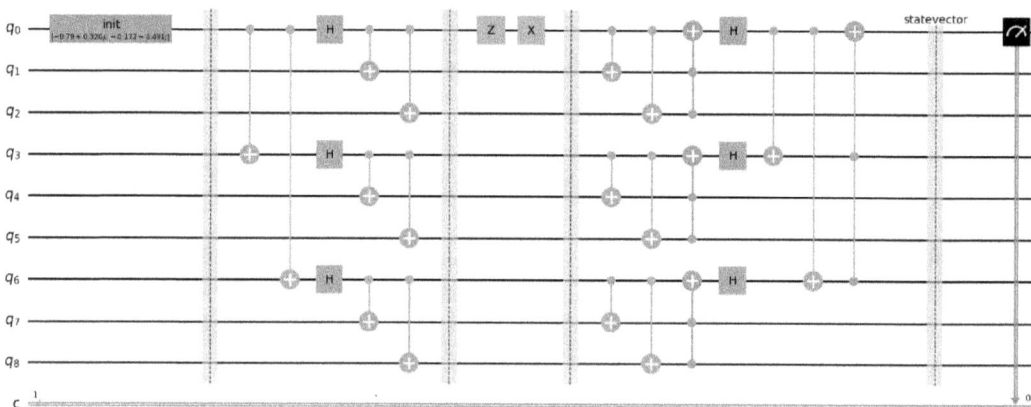

Figure 8.27: *Error correction circuit*

We will also measure the three circuits and observe their results:

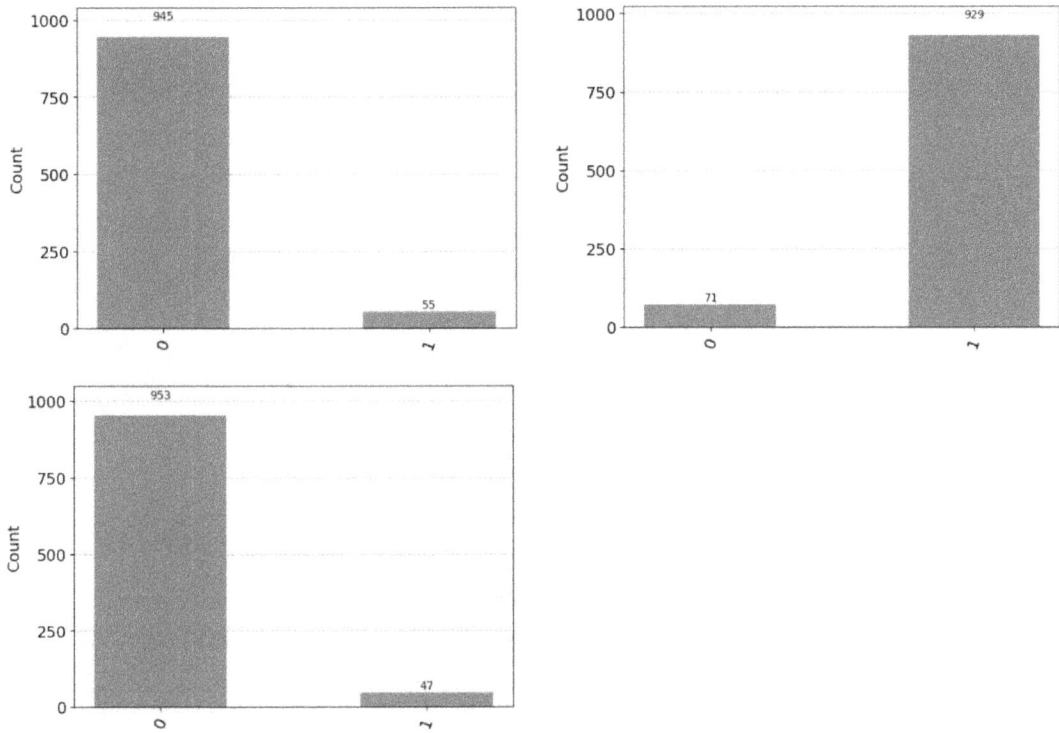

Figure 8.28: Results from the original circuit, error circuit, and error correction circuit

The bit-flip error can be observed in the error circuit where the occurrence of $|1\rangle$ is higher than $|0\rangle$ across 1000 iterations. As mentioned earlier, the phase error can only be observed in the Bloch sphere. Refer to the following figures:

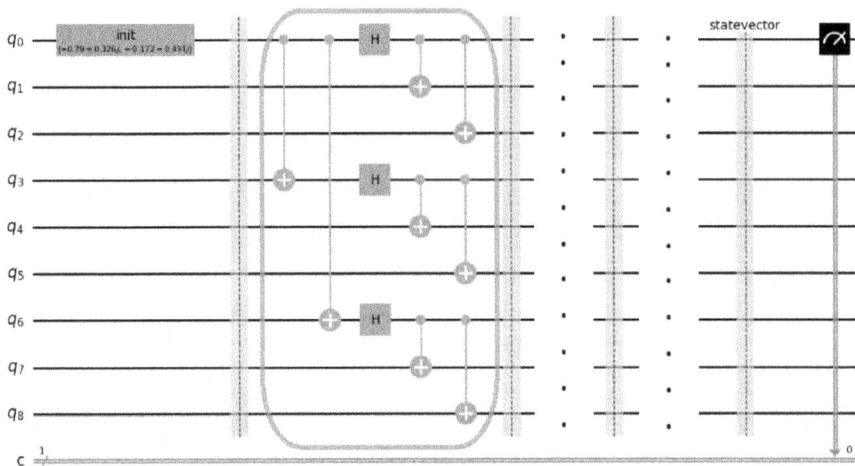

Figure 8.29(a): Section of circuit that adds redundancy

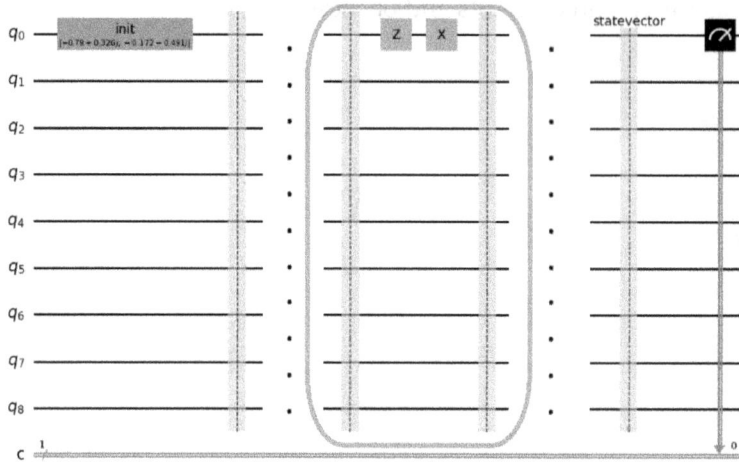

Figure 8.29(b): Section of circuit that induces bit and phase flip errors

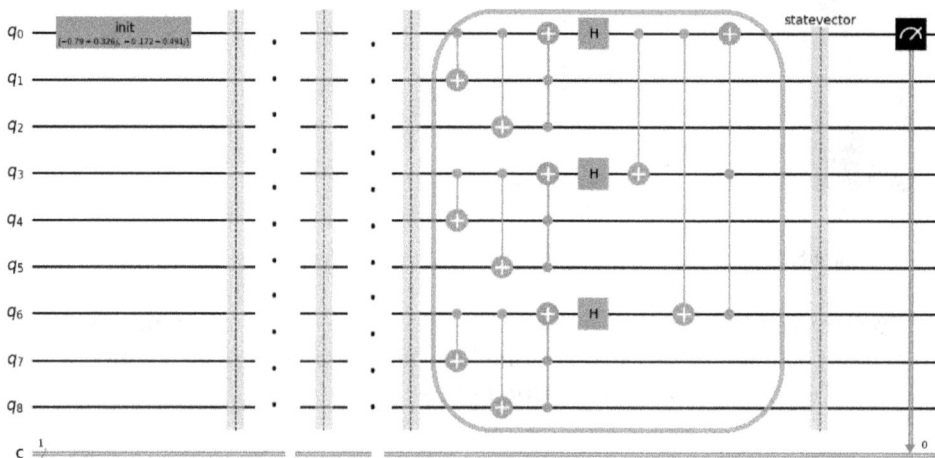

Figure 8.29(c): Section of circuit that corrects error

There are few limitations of Shor's code, given as follows:

- **Overhead:** Shor's code requires a significant number of physical qubits (nine) to encode a single logical qubit, which increases the resource demands.

- **Complexity:** The implementation of Shor's code involves multiple rounds of syndrome measurements and error corrections. This adds to the circuit depth and complexity, leading to longer execution times.

- **Error threshold:** Shor's code is effective only when the physical error rate is below a certain threshold. If the rate of errors in the individual qubits is too high, the logical qubit will experience significant errors.

While Shor's code was foundational in the development of QEC, there are other codes such as surface codes and topological codes that provide more efficient error correction. Surface codes require fewer physical qubits per logical qubit and has less overhead than Shor's code. It can easily scale and have higher threshold for physical error rates. Similarly, topological codes involve lesser overhead than Shor's codes and therefore, scale better. It can tolerate higher rates of noise and are more robust for large scale, fault tolerant systems.

Conclusion

In the fast-paced realm of quantum computing, QEC is vital to effectively combat the inherent fragility and susceptibility to noise that quantum systems exhibit. Sophisticated encoding techniques and fault-tolerant strategies are required to make significant strides toward building scalable and reliable quantum computers. As quantum computing progresses, the importance of QEC will undoubtedly grow, serving as a crucial element in maintaining the stability and dependability of quantum circuits. While QEC provides a promising path forward, implementing practical, efficient error correction in large-scale quantum systems remains challenging. Continued research and development in QEC are crucial for advancing the capabilities and reliability of quantum computers. The next chapter will focus on few of the most popular quantum algorithms such as Shor's algorithm, Grover's algorithm, Phase kickback and few others.

Multiple choice questions

1. **A phase flip error in a qubit primarily affects its:**
   a. Probability of being measured in the $|0\rangle$ or $|1\rangle$ state.
   b. Superposition of $|0\rangle$ and $|1\rangle$.
   c. Physical location within the quantum computer.
   d. Relative phase between the $|0\rangle$ and $|1\rangle$ components of its superposition.

2. **Which of the following is a characteristic of quantum error mitigation (QEM)?**
   a. It is generally more practical for NISQ devices.
   b. It requires full redundancy like error correction.
   c. It has higher resource overhead compared to error correction.
   d. It always eliminates errors completely.

3. **Which of the following statements is true regarding the resource overhead of quantum error correction (QEC)?**
   a. QEC generally requires fewer physical qubits than error mitigation.
   b. Implementing QEC has minimal impact on the number of qubits needed.

c. QEC and error mitigation have similar resource requirements.

d. QEC demands higher resource overhead, often requiring multiple physical qubits to encode a single logical qubit.

4. **What is the primary purpose of the two ancillary qubits in the described 3-qubit circuit?**

a. To perform quantum computations.

b. To introduce superposition.

c. To detect and correct bit flip errors on the main qubit.

d. To entangle with the main qubit for faster processing.

5. **Which type of error(s) can Shor's code correct for a single qubit, according to the provided text?**

a. Only bit-flip errors.

b. Only phase-flip errors.

c. Both bit-flip and phase-flip errors.

d. Neither bit-flip nor phase-flip errors.

Answer key

1. d
2. a
3. d
4. c
5. c

Questions

1. What are some causes of gate operation errors in quantum computing?

    Answer: Some causes of gate operation errors include environmental noise, imperfections in quantum hardware, decoherence, crosstalk between nearby qubits and issues related to the control and calibration of quantum gates.

2. Briefly describe the main idea behind noise extrapolation.

    Answer: Noise extrapolation involves running the same quantum computation multiple times with varying levels of artificially added noise and then comparing the results to extrapolate a noise-free result.

3. What is a logical qubit, and why is it important in the context of QEC?

   Answer: A logical qubit is a quantum bit of information that is protected from errors by encoding it across multiple physical qubits. This encoding allows for the detection and correction of errors that might occur in the individual physical qubits, thus preserving the integrity of the quantum information.

4. How many physical qubits are used to encode one logical qubit in Shor's code, and what is the purpose of the three groups of qubits (1,2,3), (4,5,6), and (7,8,9)?

   Answer: Shor's code uses nine physical qubits to encode one logical qubit. The three groups of qubits, (1,2,3), (4,5,6), and (7,8,9), are for correcting bit-flip errors. Each group can correct a single bit-flip error within that group. Qubits 1, 4, and 7 together handle the sign (phase) flip error.

5. What are some of the factors that influence the choice of a specific QEC code in a quantum computing architecture?

   Answer: The choice of QEC code depends on several factors, including the physical implementation of qubits (e.g., superconducting circuits, trapped-ions), the primary types of errors the system is susceptible to, and the operational requirements of the quantum algorithms to be executed.

Join our Discord space

Join our Discord workspace for latest updates, offers, tech happenings around the world, new releases, and sessions with the authors:

https://discord.bpbonline.com

CHAPTER 9
Quantum Algorithms

Introduction

The realm of classical computing has revolutionized our world, but for certain problems, its capabilities reach a limit. Quantum algorithms provide a revolutionary approach, harnessing the principles of quantum mechanics to tackle problems intractable for classical computers. Quantum algorithms take advantage of quantum superposition and entanglement to outperform classical algorithms, potentially sparking a revolution in various fields ranging from cryptography, optimization, machine learning to simulation of molecules and material science. This chapter discusses few such algorithms, each offering a unique solution and showcasing the immense potential of quantum computation.

We will explore how these algorithms leverage quantum principles to achieve exponential speedups or tackle problems deemed impossible classically. These algorithms demonstrate a paradigm shift in the way problems are solved. It is not just about superfast calculations or unimaginable data storage, it is about re-envisioning the way we perceive, approach, and solve computational problems. Algorithms such as **Grover's search** would offer significant speedups for searching through vast datasets as compared to classical counterparts. Others, such as **Shor's algorithm** would tackle problems previously deemed mathematically impossible to solve efficiently. Through these specific examples, we will witness the transformative potential of quantum computing. They will uncover numerous research possibilities and areas of further study in the fields of computer science, physics, mathematics, and, more importantly, the interdisciplinary field of quantum computing.

This chapter serves as a roadmap to the exciting world of quantum algorithms that hold the potential to revolutionize computing as we know it.

Structure

The chapter will cover the following topics in detail:

- Phase kickback
- Grover's algorithm
- Shor's algorithm
- Deutsch-Jozsa algorithm
- Bernstein–Vazirani algorithm

Objectives

By the end of this chapter, you will be able to understand the concept of phase kickback and explain how phase kickback is utilized within quantum algorithms to transfer phase information between qubits. Additionally, we will analyze Grover's algorithm for a quadratic speedup in unsorted database search problems, and interpret the results. We will also describe how Shor's algorithm efficiently factorizes large numbers and its impact on cryptography. You will also be able to execute the Deutsch-Jozsa algorithm on sample functions to determine their constant or balanced nature. We will also understand the Bernstein–Vazirani algorithm in finding hidden binary strings.

By achieving these objectives, you will gain a comprehensive understanding of key quantum algorithms and their applications, equipping you with the knowledge to explore the field of quantum computing and its potential to revolutionize various industries.

Phase kickback

Quantum phase kickback is a fundamental concept in quantum computing that refers to the transfer or **kickback** of a phase change from one qubit to another. This phenomenon is an inherent feature in quantum entanglement and is exploited in various quantum computing algorithms.

In a typical quantum phase kickback scenario, two qubits are in an entangled state. The phase change in target qubit due to a quantum operation causes a mirrored or **kicked back** phase change in the control qubit. Importantly, this phase change occurs even if there is no direct operation applied to the control qubit. This is because of the way entanglement and quantum interference work. When two qubits are in an entangled state, their quantum states are correlated such that the state of one qubit cannot be described independently of the state of the other qubit. When a phase change occurs in the target qubit due to a quantum operation (like applying a phase gate such as CZ, Controlled-S, etc.), it alters the overall phase of the entangled state. Because the states are intertwined, this change is reflected in the control qubit's state. The phase change affects how the amplitudes of the entangled state combine when measured. Depending on the relative phases of the states, the resulting probabilities can constructively or destructively interfere. This means that while measuring the control qubit, the phase shift from the target qubit can lead to a redistribution of probabilities among the possible measurement outcomes for the control qubit, effectively *kicking back* the phase information.

Phase kickback is used in numerous quantum computing applications, including quantum teleportation and quantum algorithms such as Shor's algorithm, Deutsch-Josza algorithm, Grover's algorithm, etc. Understanding this property of quantum systems is crucial for designing and implementing advanced quantum circuits and computations.

Let us look at an example to understand this concept. At a high level, when there are two qubits in superposition: one control and the other target in a CNOT relation, the change that the control qubit applies on the target is **kicked back** to the control qubit as a phase shift.

There are two qubits in superposition: q0 and q1. The state of q0 is $|+\rangle$, which represents a point on positive X-axis on the surface of the Bloch sphere, and q1 is $|-\rangle$. Refer to the following figure:

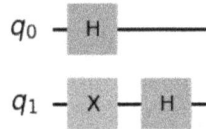

Figure 9.1: Circuit for qubits in superposition

q0 is in state $|+\rangle$ which is equal to $\frac{1}{\sqrt{2}}(|0\rangle + |1\rangle)$

q1 is in state $|-\rangle$ which is equal to $\frac{1}{\sqrt{2}}(|0\rangle - |1\rangle)$

The state of this quantum system is,

$$|\psi\rangle = \underbrace{\frac{1}{\sqrt{2}}(|0\rangle + |1\rangle)}_{--q0--} \otimes \underbrace{\frac{1}{\sqrt{2}}(|0\rangle - |1\rangle)}_{--q1--}$$

$$= \frac{1}{2}(|00\rangle - |01\rangle + |10\rangle) - |11\rangle\,)$$

We will measure the same on Bloch sphere, as shown in *Figure 9.2*:

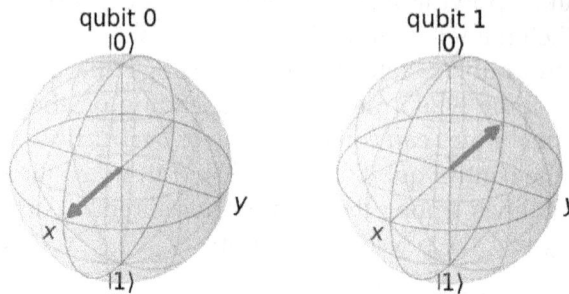

Figure 9.2: *Bloch sphere of qubits in superposition*

Let us apply CNOT such that q0 is control and q1 is target qubit, as shown in *Figure 9.3*:

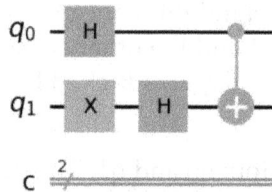

Figure 9.3: *Circuit for CNOT between the qubits*

Therefore, $|\psi\rangle = \frac{1}{2} (|00\rangle - |01\rangle + |11\rangle) - |10\rangle)$

What has happened is that CNOT swapped the amplitudes of 10 and 11. Rearranging the state, we get

$$|\psi\rangle = \frac{1}{\sqrt{2}} (|0\rangle - |1\rangle) \otimes \frac{1}{\sqrt{2}} (|0\rangle - |1\rangle)$$

$$\text{--}q0\text{--} \qquad\qquad \text{--}q1\text{--}$$

It can be observed from the preceding equation that q0 has undergone a phase shift. It was originally $\frac{1}{\sqrt{2}} (|0\rangle + |1\rangle)$, but now it is $\frac{1}{\sqrt{2}} (|0\rangle - |1\rangle)$. Even though q0 controls q1 via the CNOT, q0 has undergone a phase shift, as can be viewed in the Bloch sphere in *Figure 9.4*. This is the phase kickback. It does not matter whether it is a CNOT or any other control gates such as CZ or a controlled-S gate, the effect on q0 is still the same: it undergoes a phase shift. Note that a rotation around the Z axis of the Bloch sphere is a phase shift.

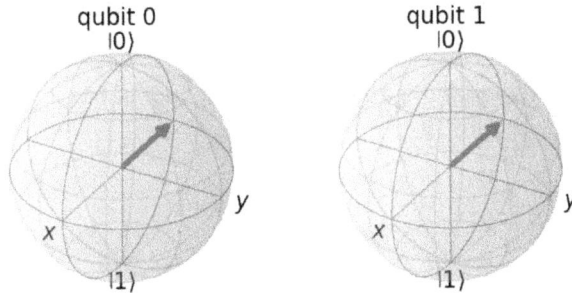

Figure 9.4: Bloch sphere of qubits after phase kickback

Let us now look at the code:

1. Import the libraries.

```
import numpy as np

from qiskit import QuantumRegister, QuantumCircuit, assemble,
ClassicalRegister

from qiskit.quantum_info import Statevector

from qiskit import IBMQ, Aer

from qiskit.visualization import plot_bloch_multivector, plot_
histogram, array_to_latex
```

2. Define function to launch the qubits into superposition.

```
# This function constructs a quantum circuit that demonstrates
# phase kickback. It initializes two qubits in a quantum register,
# applies quantum gates to create superposition, and then
# prepares the circuit for further operations.
def phase_kickback():
    # Create a quantum register with 2 qubits named 'q'
    qreg = QuantumRegister(2, 'q')
    # Create a classical register with 2 bits named 'c'
    creg = ClassicalRegister(2, 'c')
    # Initialize a quantum circuit using the defined quantum and
    classical
    # registers
    qc   = QuantumCircuit(qreg, creg)

    # Apply a Hadamard gate to the first qubit to create superposition
    qc.h(qreg[0])
```

```
# Apply an X gate (bit-flip) to the second qubit
qc.x(qreg[1])
# Apply a Hadamard gate to the second qubit
qc.h(qreg[1])

# Return circuit
return qc
```

3. Create the circuit. The circuit design of the following code can be seen in *Figure 9.1*.

```
circ = phase_kickback()
circ.draw('mpl')
```

4. Plot the Bloch sphere. Output is presented in *Figure 9.2*. It shows q0 to be in state $|+\rangle$ (positive X-axis) and q1 to be in $|-\rangle$ (negative X-axis).

```
statevector = Statevector(circ)
plot_bloch_multivector(statevector)
```

5. Display circuit after CNOT. This is shown in *Figure 9.3*.

```
# Apply CNOT, or controlled X - qubit 0 (q0) is control and qubit 1
(q1) is target.
circ.cx(0,1)
circ.draw('mpl')
```

6. Plot the Bloch sphere to observe the effect of applying CNOT on q0 and q1. This can be viewed in *Figure 9.4*. q0 has undergone a phase shift of π radians and is now in state $|-\rangle$.

```
statevector = Statevector(circ)
plot_bloch_multivector(statevector)
```

Let us see another example where q0 applies a controlled S gate on q1. To recollect from *Chapter 4, Quantum Gates and Circuits,* S gate introduces a phase shift of $\frac{\pi}{2}$ radians. Even though q0 applies a controlled phase shift of $\frac{\pi}{2}$ radians on q1, due to phase kickback, the expected result is that q0 will undergo that phase shift. The before and after Bloch sphere can be viewed in *Figure 9.6(a), Figure 9.6(b)*. The before and after circuits are shown in *Figure 9.5*.

To demonstrate this clearly, we will launch q0 in superposition and flip q1 to $|1\rangle$.

```
def phase_kickback():
    qreg = QuantumRegister(2, 'q')
    creg = ClassicalRegister(2, 'c')
```

```
qc   = QuantumCircuit(qreg, creg)

# Apply Hadamard gate to create superposition
qc.h(qreg[0])
# Apply X gate for bit-flip
qc.x(qreg[1])
# Return circuit
return qc
```

Apply controlled S gate.

```
circ.cp(np.pi/2, 0, 1)      # where circ.cp is controlled phase shift,
# np.pi/2 is the angle in radians, 0 and 1 are q0 and q1
# respectively.
circ.draw('mpl')
```

The circuit is displayed in *Figure 9.5*:

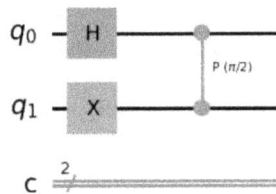

Figure 9.5: *Circuit for Controlled S gate between the qubits*

Plot the Bloch sphere before and after applying the controlled S gate. As expected, due to phase kickback, q0 has undergone a phase shift of $\frac{\pi}{2}$ radians.

```
statevector = Statevector(circ)
plot_bloch_multivector(statevector)
```

The Bloch sphere is shown in *Figure 9.6(a)* (before) and *Figure 9.6(b)* (after):

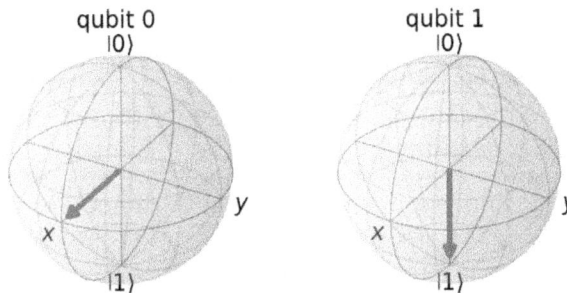

Figure 9.6(a): *Before Controlled S gate is applied*

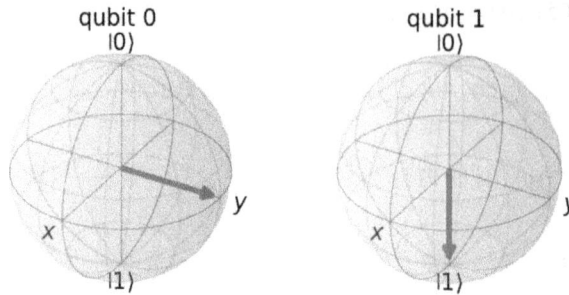

Figure 9.6(b): Phase kickback after Controlled S gate is applied

Grover's algorithm

Grover's search algorithm is one of the well-known algorithms, enabling quantum computers to perform search of unsorted data array and quadratically outperform their classical counterparts in terms of time. Unlike classical algorithms which require linear time to search for an element, Grover's algorithm can do it in a square root of that time, which is a quadratic speedup. That is, if a classical algorithm needs N steps to do a job, Grover's algorithm can do it in about $\sqrt{N}$ steps.

This algorithm is based on the principles of quantum mechanics. It uses the property of quantum superposition (the ability of a quantum system to be in multiple states at the same time), quantum entanglement (a phenomenon where quantum particles become interconnected and the state of one can directly influence the other, no matter the distance), and quantum interference (where probability amplitudes interfere with each other like waves) to perform the search faster. However, Grover's algorithm is not suitable for all types of search problems. While it guarantees to find the correct answer with high probability, it is just probabilistic: likely but not certain. For smaller databases or problems, classical algorithms can sometimes perform more efficiently. Grover's algorithm shines in situations where the problem or dataset is large and unsorted.

Grover's algorithm has many potential applications. It is commonly used in searching databases, hash function inversion, and solving NP-complete problems faster than any known classical algorithm. The potential of Grover's algorithm has proved particularly appealing in the fields of cryptography. Grover's algorithm is highly significant as it was one of the earliest demonstrations of the theoretical power of quantum computing. It remains a cornerstone of quantum computing research and provides a fundamental subroutine for many other quantum algorithms.

There are two parts to the implementation of this algorithm: Oracle and Diffusion. Oracle is responsible for flipping the phase of the amplitude of the entity or the state that is being searched. *Figure 9.7(a)* gives the initial amplitudes of all the states. The phase shift in Oracle inverts the amplitude of the search state over the zero-plane as shown in *Figure 9.7(b)*. The other states retain their original amplitude. The Diffusion layer amplifies the amplitude of the search state. It does so by inverting the state over the new mean, as shown in *Figure 9.7(c)*. The effect of this is that the amplitude of the search state increases significantly, while the amplitudes of other states fall. Together, in tandem, the Oracle and Diffusion increase the amplitude of the search state, and thus its probability. In $\sqrt{N}$ iterations, where N is the total number of states, the Grover's algorithm finds the entity with a probability greater than $\frac{2}{3}$. The search problem in this instance becomes a **bounded-error quantum polynomial time (BQP)** problem. A BQP is a type of problem that a quantum computer can solve with an error probability of at most $\frac{1}{3}$.

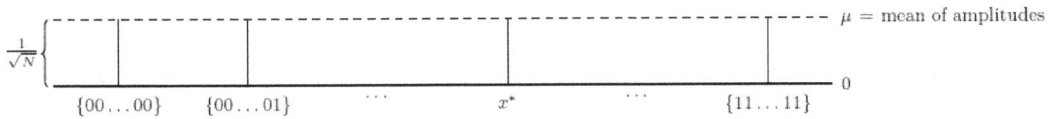

Figure 9.7(a): Initial amplitude of the states in superposition (source: CMU university)

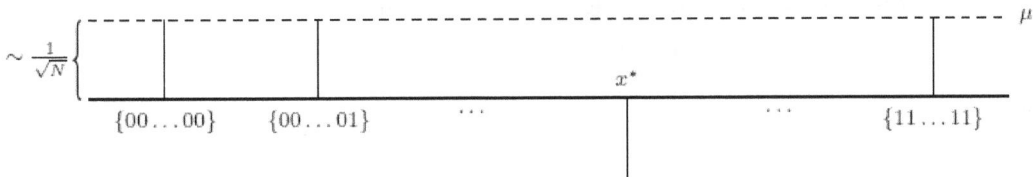

Figure 9.7(b): Oracle flips the amplitude over zero-line (source: CMU university)

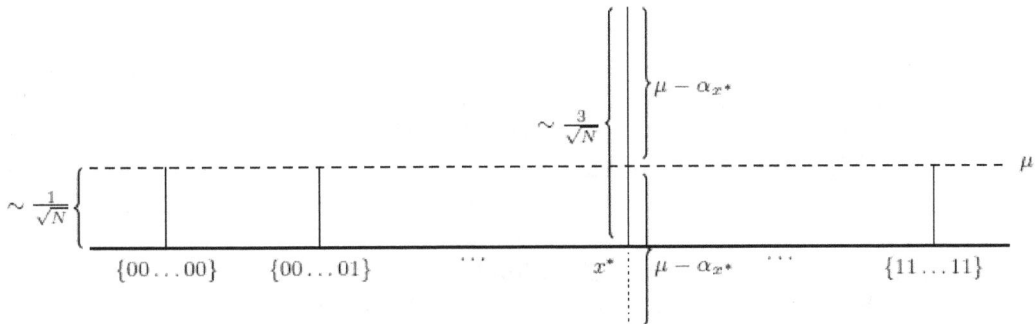

Figure 9.7(c): Diffusion flips the amplitude over mean (source: CMU university)

Let us look at the steps in detail.

For a n-qubit data structure, there will be $2^n = N$ entities in the search space. The probability of each state will be $\frac{1}{N}$, which means the amplitude is $\frac{1}{\sqrt{N}}$.

The Oracle will flip the amplitude of the entity to be searched, making it $\frac{-1}{\sqrt{N}}$.

The other states are at amplitude $\frac{+1}{\sqrt{N}}$, therefore, the mean is:

$$\mu^{(0)} = \frac{((N-1) * a^{(0)} + \alpha^{(0)})}{N}$$

Where the superscript (0) indicates the first iteration of Oracle, α is the amplitude of the state to be searched, and 'a' is the amplitude of rest of the states.

Here, is $\alpha^{(0)}$ is $\frac{-1}{\sqrt{N}}$ and a is $\frac{+1}{\sqrt{N}}$.

Therefore,

$$\mu^{(0)} = \frac{((N-1) * \frac{+1}{\sqrt{N}} + \frac{-1}{\sqrt{N}})}{N} = \frac{(N-2)}{N\sqrt{N}}$$

The Diffusion inverts the search state again, but over the mean. The equation for amplitude after Diffusion layer is as follows:

$\alpha^{(1)} = 2 * \mu^{(0)} - \alpha^{(0)}$, where $\alpha^{(1)}$ is amplitude of search state at the start of second iteration (after first iteration of Diffusion), $\mu^{(0)}$ is mean of all amplitudes after Oracle in the first iteration, and $\alpha^{(0)}$ is amplitude of search state after Oracle in the first iteration.

Therefore,

$$\alpha^{(1)} = 2 * \frac{(N-2)}{N\sqrt{N}} - \frac{-1}{\sqrt{N}}$$

$$= \frac{3}{\sqrt{N}} - \frac{4}{N\sqrt{N}}$$

For n = 3, the search space is $2^3 = N = 8$ states. Substitute this value in the preceding equation. We get mean 0.265. The output of Diffusion at the end of first iteration after substituting values in the preceding equation is 0.884. This is same as that generated by the code in *Figure 9.10*, which shows the state vector that contains the amplitudes of all the 8 states. The search state 010 has amplitude -0.88388. Ignore the sign, the main point is that all the states are in the same phase. Remember that Oracle flips the phase of search state with respect to other states, whereas Diffusion keeps the search state in the same phase as other states. Essentially, the probability of finding 010 after one iteration of Grover's is $0.884^2 = 78\%$.

Let us find the probability after second iteration of Grover's.

The second Oracle will flip the sign of the search state, so the amplitude becomes -0.884. To find the mean amplitude, we need the sum of amplitudes of rest of the states.

First, let us find the sum of probabilities of the remaining states. Amplitude will be square root of that.

The sum of probabilities of rest of the states

$$= 1 - (\frac{3}{\sqrt{N}} - \frac{4}{N\sqrt{N}})^2$$

The probability of each such state $= \dfrac{1-(\frac{3}{\sqrt{N}} - \frac{4}{N\sqrt{N}})^2}{N-1}$

The amplitude of each of the rest of the states is square root of this value. Therefore, after solving for it we get:

$$\frac{(N-4)}{N\sqrt{N}}$$

Substituting the values from the example in the preceding equation, we get amplitude as 0.1768.

The new mean is $\dfrac{(7*0.1768-0.884)}{8} = 0.0442$

As we saw earlier, the output of Diffusion will be $\alpha^{(2)} = 2 * \mu^{(1)} - \alpha^{(1)}$

$$= 2 * 0.0442 - (\text{-}0.884) = 0.9724$$

This value is almost same as the amplitude derived by code in *Figure 9.11*.

We will now look at how to implement Oracle. For the search state, Oracle reverses the sign of the state. So, we need a function f(x) that gives either $+|1\rangle$ or $-|1\rangle$, as shown in *Figure 9.8*, where f(x) will return $-|1\rangle$ for the search state, and $+|1\rangle$ for the rest. However, this is not a unitary gate, i.e., the gate is not reversible. We cannot regenerate the input by passing the output back into the gate, as input is n-qubit string and output is 1-qubit.

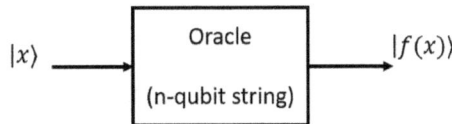

Figure 9.8: *Oracle where f(x) is either $+|1\rangle$ or $-|1\rangle$*

The input and output should have same number of qubits. We can have a function f(x) such that it flips the sign of only the search state while it maintains the sign of rest of the states. This way the input and output will have same number of qubits. The following function satisfies this condition:

$$(-1)^{f(x)}|x\rangle = \begin{cases} |x\rangle, & if\ f(x) = 0 \\ -|x\rangle, & if\ f(x) = 1 \end{cases}$$

When n qubits are passed through the Oracle, the sign of only the search state will become negative. If we pass the output back into the gate, the sign of search state will get flipped back to positive while the rest remains unchanged. This means that the gate is reversible, which is a requirement for quantum gates. *Figure 9.9* shows the circuit:

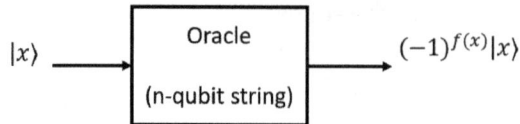

Figure 9.9: Oracle for Grover's algorithm

Note that in the preceding explanation we are assuming the search list to be unique and of size 2^n, and the values in the list are represented as n-qubit Boolean strings.

Let us now look at the code to search 010 using Grover's algorithm. The results are run on a simulator.

1. Import the libraries:

```
#initialization
import matplotlib.pyplot as plt
import numpy as np

# importing Qiskit
from qiskit import IBMQ, Aer, assemble, transpile
from qiskit import QuantumCircuit, ClassicalRegister, QuantumRegister

# import basic plot tools
from qiskit.visualization import plot_histogram
```

2. Define the Oracle:

```
def oracle(circuit, state):
    for ii, qubit in enumerate(state):
        if qubit == 0:
            circuit.x(qreg_q[len(state) - 1 - ii])
    circuit.h(qreg_q[2])
    circuit.ccx(qreg_q[0], qreg_q[1], qreg_q[2])
    circuit.h(qreg_q[2])
    for ii, qubit in enumerate(state):
        if qubit == 0:
            circuit.x(qreg_q[len(state) - 1 - ii])

    #circuit.x(qreg_q[0])
    #circuit.x(qreg_q[1])
    circuit.barrier
```

3. Define the Diffusion function:

```
def diffusion(circuit):
    qbit_list = [qreg_q[0], qreg_q[1], qreg_q[2]]
    # Apply Hadamard and X gates to the three qubits
    for qbit in qbit_list:
        circuit.h(qbit)
        circuit.x(qbit)
    circuit.barrier(qreg_q[0], qreg_q[1], qreg_q[2])
    circuit.h(qreg_q[2])
    circuit.ccx(qreg_q[0], qreg_q[1], qreg_q[2])
    circuit.h(qreg_q[2])
    circuit.barrier(qreg_q[0], qreg_q[1], qreg_q[2])
    # Apply X and Hadamard gates to the three qubits
    for qbit in qbit_list:
        circuit.x(qbit)
        circuit.h(qbit)
    return circuit
```

4. Initialize the registers:

```
qreg_q = QuantumRegister(3, 'q')
creg_c = ClassicalRegister(3, 'c')
grover_circuit = QuantumCircuit(qreg_q, creg_c)
# Apply Hadamard to all the three qubits to
# create superposition
grover_circuit.h(qreg_q[0])
grover_circuit.h(qreg_q[1])
grover_circuit.h(qreg_q[2])
```

5. Select the search string:

```
SEARCH = [0,1,0]
```

6. Build the circuit with one iteration of Oracle + Diffusion, as shown in *Figure 9.10*, and display it:

```
# Call the Oracle function with search state in variable
# SEARCH
grover_circuit = oracle(grover_circuit, SEARCH)
```

```
# Apply diffusion function
grover_circuit = diffusion(grover_circuit)
# Add barriers for clarity
grover_circuit.barrier(qreg_q[0], qreg_q[1], qreg_q[2])
grover_circuit.draw('mpl')
```

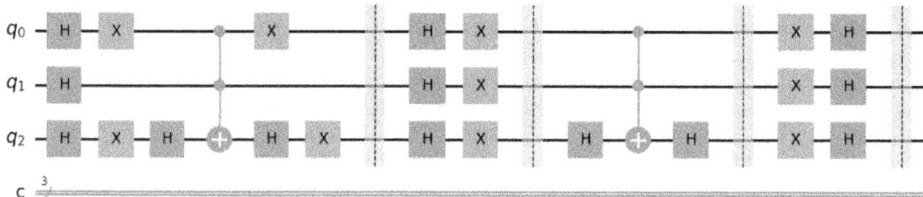

Figure 9.10: Circuit for 010 with one iteration of Oracle + Diffusion

7. Assemble the circuit using a simulator:

```
sim = Aer.get_backend('aer_simulator')
# Make a copy of the circuit with the 'save_statevector'
# instruction to run on the Aer simulator
grover_circuit_sim = grover_circuit.copy()
grover_circuit_sim.save_statevector()
qobj = assemble(grover_circuit_sim)
```

8. View the state vector, as shown in *Figure 9.11*, which gives the amplitudes of the states:

```
result = sim.run(qobj).result()
statevec = result.get_statevector()
from qiskit_textbook.tools import vector2latex
# Display the state vector
vector2latex(statevec, pretext="|\\psi\\rangle =")
```

$$|\psi\rangle = \begin{bmatrix} -0.17678 \\ -0.17678 \\ -0.88388 \\ -0.17678 \\ -0.17678 \\ -0.17678 \\ -0.17678 \\ -0.17678 \end{bmatrix}$$

Figure 9.11: State vector for 010 with one Oracle + Diffusion

Let us look at the state vector after second iteration of Oracle and Diffusion. *Figure 9.12* shows the amplitudes:

$$|\psi\rangle = \begin{bmatrix} -0.08839 \\ -0.08839 \\ 0.97227 \\ -0.08839 \\ -0.08839 \\ -0.08839 \\ -0.08839 \\ -0.08839 \end{bmatrix}$$

Figure 9.12: State vector for 010 with two iterations of Oracle + Diffusion

9. Run the circuit:

```
# Measure the states of qubits 0, 1, and 2 in
# the Grover circuit and store the results in
# classical bits 0, 1, and 2
grover_circuit.measure([0,1,2],[0,1,2])
aer_sim = Aer.get_backend('aer_simulator')
qobj = assemble(grover_circuit)
result = aer_sim.run(qobj, shots=1000).result()
```

10. Display the results. As can be seen in *Figure 9.13*, out of 1000 shots, 010, which is the search entity, has been generated 953 times:

```
counts = result.get_counts()
plot_histogram(counts)
```

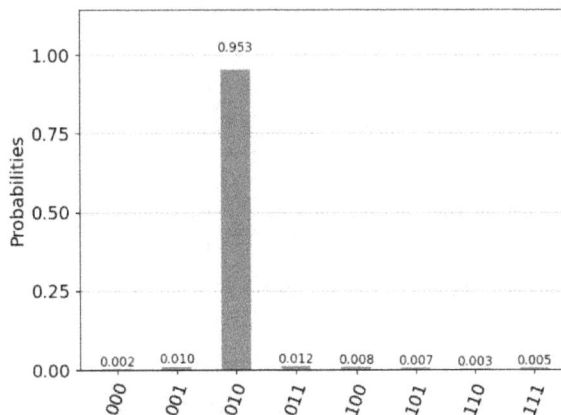

Figure 9.13: Result of search (010) with two iterations of Oracle + Diffusion

Let us run the Grover's method for another search state: 100. *Figure 9.14(a)*, *Figure 9.14(b)* show the circuit and the result. Notice that the Oracle is different, but Diffusion remains the same. The Python function named *oracle* gives different configurations for various search states. This is shown in the following figures:

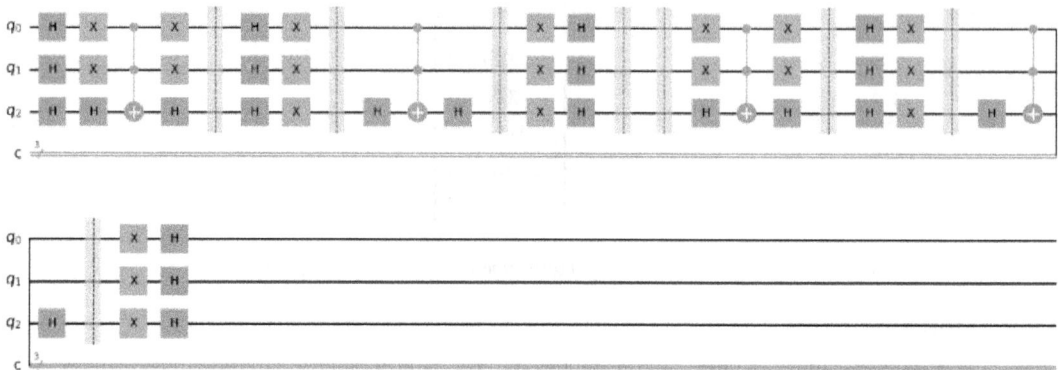

Figure 9.14(a): *Circuit for 100 with two iterations of Oracle + Diffusion*

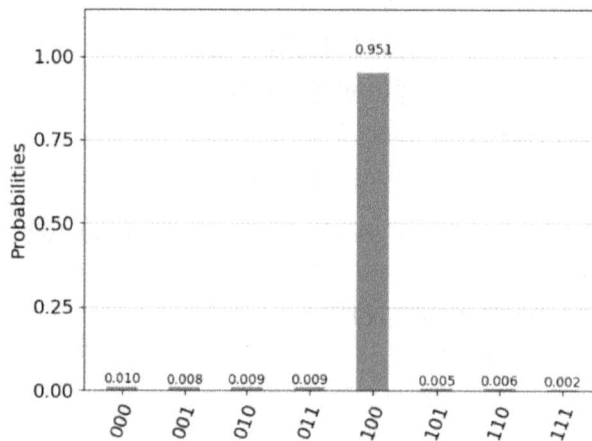

Figure 9.14(b): *Result of search (100) with two iterations of Oracle + Diffusion*

We will now look at the Oracle and Diffusion for N=4 (2 qubits). Define the Oracle and Diffusion for N=4.

This function applies the S gate (phase shift gate) to qubits in a quantum circuit depending on the provided binary **state** string. It modifies the first or second qubit based on the specific input state:

```
def s_gate(qc, state):
    # For '01', it applies the S gate to the first qubit
    # and the identity gate to the second.
```

```
    if state == '01':
        qc.s(qreg_q[0])
        qc.i(qreg_q[1])
    # For '10', it applies the S gate to the second qubit
    # and the identity gate to the first.
    elif state == '10':
        qc.s(qreg_q[1])
        qc.i(qreg_q[0])
    # For '00', it applies the S gate to both qubits
    # simultaneously.
    elif state == '00':
        qc.s([qreg_q[0], qreg_q[1]])
    # If the state is not recognized, no operations are
    # performed, and the circuit is returned unchanged.
    else:
        #qc.cz(0,1)
        pass
    return qc


# Define the Oracle function
def oracle(qc, state):
    # Call s_gate function with the state passed to this function
    qc = s_gate(qc, state)
    # Apply controlled Z from qubit 0 to qubit 1
    qc.cz(0,1)
    qc = s_gate(qc, state)
    return qc


# Define the diffusion function
def diffusion(qc):
    # Apply Hadamard gate to create superposition on both qubits
    qc.h([0,1])
    # Apply Z gate to both qubits
```

```
qc.z([0,1])
# Apply controlled Z from qubit 0 to qubit 1
qc.cz(0,1)
# Apply Hadamard on both qubits
qc.h([0,1])
return qc
```

1. Build the circuit with one iteration.

```
# Apply Oracle with the state to be searched - '10'.
# Change the state value for different search states.
grover_circuit = oracle(grover_circuit, state='10')
# Apply diffusion logic
grover_circuit = diffusion(grover_circuit)
# Draw the circuit
grover_circuit.draw(output='mpl')
```

Figure 9.15(a) illustrates the Grover's circuit (one iteration) for all the four search states: 00, 01, 10 and 11. *Figure 9.15(b)* gives the corresponding results. As can be seen, the search states are identified with 100% probability after just one iteration. This is shown in the following figures:

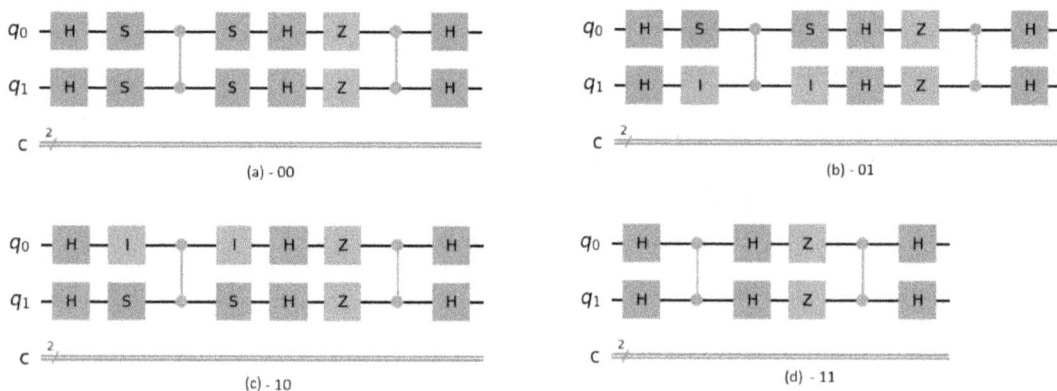

(a) - 00

(b) - 01

(c) - 10

(d) - 11

Figure 9.15(a): *Circuit for 00, 01, 10 and 11 with one iteration of Oracle + Diffusion*

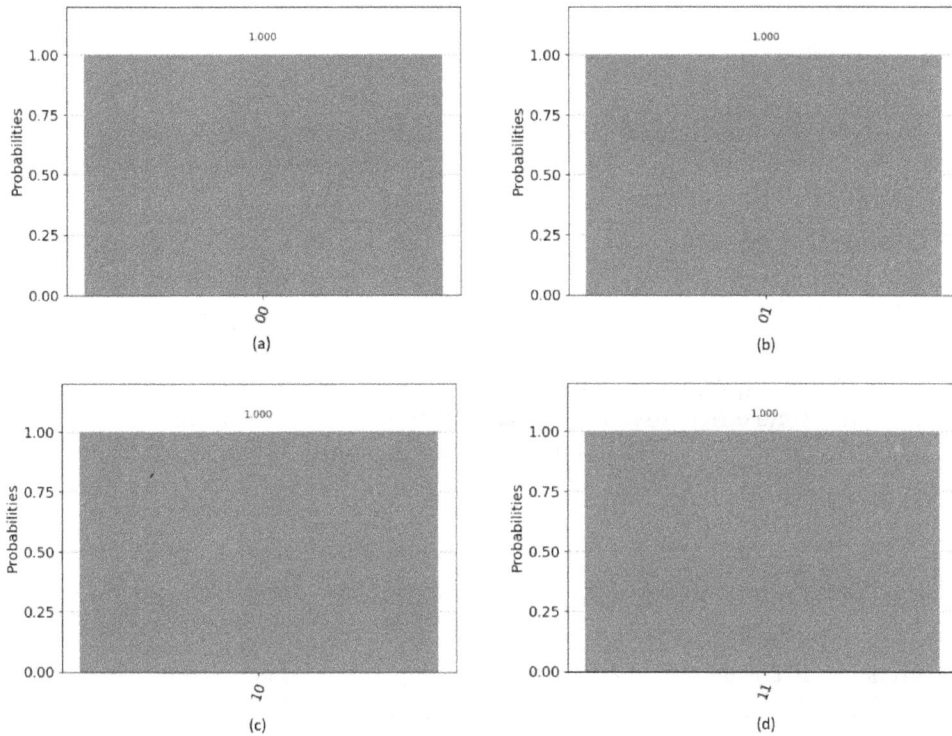

Figure 9.15(b): Result for 00, 01, 10 and 11 with one iteration of Oracle + Diffusion

Shor's algorithm

Shor's algorithm is a quantum algorithm developed by mathematician *Peter Shor* in 1994. It is designed to solve the problem of integer factorization exponentially faster than classical algorithms, which has implications for cryptography, particularly the widely used RSA encryption system. RSA involves encryption using a large integer, which is a product of two large prime numbers. The RSA system is considered secure because no efficient classical algorithm can factor large integers. However, running on a sufficiently powerful quantum computer, Shor's algorithm could factor large numbers efficiently, breaking the RSA encryption. Currently, Shor's algorithm cannot be practically implemented due to the lack of sufficiently powerful quantum computers.

Shor's algorithm can find prime factors of a large number N in the order of $O((logN)^3)$ time. Classical algorithms and classical computers will take exponential time to solve the same problem. This algorithm is a significant milestone in the realm of quantum computing, demonstrating the immense capabilities of quantum algorithms to tackle issues previously regarded as insurmountable. Its discovery was a landmark on both theoretical and practical aspects of quantum computing and its application in cryptography.

Shor's algorithm is a combination of classical and quantum computing. Let N be an odd semiprime integer. A semiprime number is a product of two prime numbers. The algorithm has three parts:

- **Classical computing:** Reduce factorization problem to a problem of finding period of the function $f(k) = x^k \bmod N$, where N is the integer to be factored, and x is a random number such that $x < N$.

- **Quantum computing:** To find period using **quantum fourier transform (QFT)**. QFT is a quantum analogue of the classical **discrete fourier transform (DFT)**, which transforms a sequence of complex numbers into another sequence of complex numbers, highlighting their frequency components. QFT utilizes the principles of quantum superposition and interference to perform the transformation of a quantum state efficiently. It is utilized primarily in quantum computing due to its ability to operate exponentially faster than its classical counterpart.

- **Classical:** Using the period, calculate the factors

Let us look at the solution of factoring a large number N without quantum computing.

1. Randomly choose a number x such that $x < N$.

2. Check whether x and N have a common divisor by finding the **greatest common divisor (GCD)** using **Euclid's algorithm**. If gcd $!= 1$, then that is it, we have found the factor. Basically, x and N should be coprime.

3. Or else, carry out the following steps:

    a. Consider this equation: $x^p = m.N + 1$. This means that there is some number 'p' such that x^p when divided by a multiple 'm' of N gives a remainder 1.

    b. $x^p - 1 = m.N$

    c. $(x^{p/2} + 1) * (x^{p/2} - 1) = m.N$ → So, this is basically like factor1 * factor2 = m.N, and if we solve for p, we will get the factors for N. There are two caveats to this, however, and they are as follows:

        i. If one of the factors in the previous step is a factor of m, and the other factor is a multiple of N, then this fails, and we have to repeat the steps by choosing a new random x.

        ii. p cannot be odd, or else p/2 will give an irrational number. Again, we need to repeat from start with a new random x.

How to find p in the classical way? Using trial and error. For large numbers, this iteration will take ages even with supercomputers.

Let us take an example, say $N = 15$ and x is randomly chosen to be 11. GCD is 1, so, execute *step 3*:

$$11^p = m.15 + 1$$

$$11^p - 1 = m.15$$

$$(11^{p/2} + 1) * (11^{p/2} - 1) = m.15$$

Start with p = 1. However, it is an odd number, and we cannot proceed as per caveat *step 3.c.ii* mentioned previously. So, let us move on to p = 2:

$$(11^{2/2} + 1) * (11^{2/2} - 1) = m.15$$

$$12 * 10 = m .15 \qquad \rightarrow (2*2*3) * (2*5) = m.15 \qquad \rightarrow (2*2*2) * (3*5) = m.15.$$

Note the following:

- The first part of **left-hand side** (**LHS**) is m, which is 2*2*2, and the second part of LHS – 3 and 5, are the factors of 15.
- Alternatively, check whether *step 3a.* is true:

  x^p is $11^2 = 121$. Calculate 121 mod 15, which is 1, so *step 3a.* is true. Therefore, the period is 2.
- Find the GCD of $(x^{p/2} \pm 1)$ and N using Euclid's algorithm. GCD of $(11^{2/2} + 1)$ and 15 yields 3. GCD of $(11^{2/2} - 1)$ and 15 is 5. Therefore, both the factors are derived.

If let us say x was chosen to be 7. By iteration, we will find that for p = 4, the equation gets satisfied.

$7^{4/2} + 1 = 50$, and $7^{4/2} - 1 = 48$. GCD of 50 and 15 is 5, and GCD of 48 and 15 is 3. Therefore, the factors are 5 and 3.

In Shor's approach, QFT is used to harness the power of superposition to find the period p in the preceding equation in just one step. This is where an exponential leap is achieved in quantum computing vis-à-vis classical computing.

Let us go through an example to find a period using quantum algorithm. The inputs are two coprime numbers: N and x, where N is the number to be factored, and x is a random number such that $1 < x < N$, and the output r is the period of the function $f(a)= x^a \bmod N$. We will consider N=15, and x=7. Let us look at the steps:

1. Choose a number T such that $N^2 \le T \le 2N^2$. The number of qubits to denote T would be t, where $T = 2^t$. For N=15, the smallest value of t for T to be $\ge N^2$ is 8, and T is $2^t = 256$. Initialize two quantum registers, the first will have t = 8 qubits, and the second will have $n = \log_2 N = 4$ qubits.

$$|\psi 0\rangle = |0\rangle|0\rangle$$

2. Apply Hadamard gate on the first register to launch these qubits into superposition of integers from 0 to T.

$$|\psi 1\rangle = \frac{1}{\sqrt{T}} \sum_{a=0}^{T-1} |a\rangle|0\rangle$$

3. Apply modular exponential function x^a on second register.

$$|\psi2\rangle = \frac{1}{\sqrt{T}} \sum_{a=0}^{T-1} |a\rangle|x^a \bmod N\rangle$$

Let us substitute x = 7, N = 15 and T = 256.

$$|\psi2\rangle = \frac{1}{\sqrt{256}} \sum_{a=0}^{255} |a\rangle|7^a \bmod 15\rangle$$

$$= \frac{1}{\sqrt{256}} \ (|0\rangle|1\rangle + |1\rangle|7\rangle + |2\rangle|4\rangle + |3\rangle|13\rangle +$$

$$|4\rangle|1\rangle + |5\rangle|7\rangle + |6\rangle|4\rangle + |7\rangle|13\rangle +$$

$$|8\rangle|1\rangle + |9\rangle|7\rangle + |10\rangle|4\rangle + |11\rangle|13\rangle + \ ... \ )$$

$$= \frac{1}{\sqrt{256}} \ [\ (|0\rangle + |4\rangle + |8\rangle + .. + |252\rangle) \ |1\rangle +$$

$$(|1\rangle + |5\rangle + |9\rangle + ... + |253\rangle) \ |7\rangle +$$

$$(|2\rangle + |6\rangle + |10\rangle + ... + |254\rangle) \ |4\rangle +$$

$$(|3\rangle + |7\rangle + |11\rangle + ... + |255\rangle) \ |13\rangle \ ]$$

4. Measure the second register. This will yield one of the four states: 1, 7, 4, or 13. It does not matter what the result is, the focus is on the period of repetition in the first register, which is 4 for all the results. Let us say the measurement collapsed the superposition to state $|7\rangle$.

$$|\psi3\rangle = \tfrac{1}{\sqrt{64}} \ (|1\rangle + |5\rangle + |9\rangle + \ ... \ + |253\rangle) \ |7\rangle \ ➜ \ = \tfrac{1}{\sqrt{64}}\sum_{a=0}^{63} |4a + 1\rangle |7\rangle$$

5. Perform QFT on the first register.

$$|\psi4\rangle = \frac{1}{\sqrt{T}} \sum_{a=0}^{T-1} \sum_{z=0}^{T-1} e^{(2\pi i)\left(\frac{az}{T}\right)}|z\rangle \ |7\rangle$$

With a combination of destructive interference and constructive interference, only states with z = qT/r will have a significant amplitude. Here, q ranges from 0 to r-1. The states 0, 64, 128 and 192 will have a significant amplitude.

6. Measure the first register. The superposition will collapse to one of the four states mentioned in the previous step. Using Euclidean algorithm, find the GCD between the measured value and T. Assuming 192 was measured in the previous step, the GCD of 192 and 256 will be 64. With continued fraction of $\frac{T}{GCD}$, which is $\frac{256}{64}$, we will get the value 4, which is the period.

Now, find the GCD of $(x^{p/2} \pm 1)$ and N using Euclid's algorithm. Given that N = 15, x = 7, and p is derived as 4, GCD of $(x^{p/2} \pm 1)$ and N is GCD of (49 ± 1) and 15, which is 5 and 3 respectively: these are the desired factors.

Let us look at the code. The following is a python code running on a Jupyter Notebook locally. It executes Shor's algorithm on an IBM Quantum device: **ibm_osaka**:

1. Import the libraries. 5

   ```
   from qiskit import IBMQ, Aer, assemble, execute

   from qiskit.utils import QuantumInstance

   from qiskit.algorithms import Shor

   from time import time
   ```

2. Assign the backend to **ibm_osaka** device:

   > Note: **Enable your IBM Quantum account using your unique API key. This can be obtained by signing up in IBM Q cloud. IBM key is sensitive information and should not be shared.**

   ```
   IBMQ.enable_account('# Enter your IBM API key here')

   # Retrieve the IBM Quantum provider associated with the specified hub

   provider = IBMQ.get_provider(hub='ibm-q')

   # Specify the quantum backend (device) to be used from the provider

   backend = provider.get_backend('ibm_osaka')
   ```

3. Create an instance of the Shor's algorithm with the backend:

   ```
   # Note that qiskit has a readymade library for Shor factorization

   # that creates a Shor's algorithm instance using the specified

   # quantum backend. The algorithm will execute 10 times.

   factors  =  Shor(QuantumInstance(backend,  shots=10,  skip_qobj_
   validation=False))
   ```

4. The number to be factorized:

   ```
   number = 15
   ```

5. Run the algorithm. N is the integer to be factored, random number chosen is 11:

   ```
   # Factor the number using Shor's algorithm with a

   # specified value of 'a'

   result_dict = factors.factor(N=number, a=11)

   # Extract the factors from the result dictionary

   result = result_dict.factors
   ```

6. Print the result:

```
print(result)
```

The result is [[3, 5]].

Deutsch-Jozsa algorithm

The Deutsch-Jozsa algorithm is a deterministic quantum algorithm, proposed by *David Deutsch* and *Richard Jozsa* in 1992. It was one of the earliest examples of a quantum algorithm that performs better than the best classical algorithm.

This algorithm makes it possible to determine with 100% confidence whether an unknown Boolean function f(x) is either balanced or constant, with only a single call to the function.

There is a black box Boolean function f(x) that takes a string of n bits as input and produces either a 0 or a 1 as output. With all combinations of the input bits, if the function returns 1 and 0 equal number of times, then the function is balanced. However, if the output is either 1 or 0 for all combinations of inputs, then the function is constant.

Classically, the best-case scenario of determining the type of function is by executing the function just two times. If the first output is 1, and the second output is 0, then we know the function is balanced. In the worst case, $2^{n-1} + 1$ iterations are required. That is, we have to check more than half of the inputs to be absolutely sure whether the function is balanced or constant. For n bits, there are 2^n combination of inputs. It may so happen that the output is constant, say 0, for half of the input scenarios (2^{n-1}), and yet we will not know whether the function is constant or balanced. However, the subsequent output will tell us the type of function. If the output is still 0, then it means the function is constant. If not, it is balanced. Therefore, $2^{n-1} + 1$ iterations are required in a worst-case scenario.

Deutsch-Jozsa algorithm will solve the same problem in exactly one iteration on a quantum computer. The key to this is the ability of a quantum computer to hold a superposition of states and to manipulate those states in parallel. The algorithm uses a quantum system to calculate the function f(x) simultaneously for a superposition of all possible inputs, and the result obtained through interference of the quantum states gives the answer. At the center of Deutsch-Jozsa algorithm is the quantum Oracle. The Oracle is a black box function that performs a specific operation that modifies the phase of the qubits based on the function's value for each state. This phase change is crucial as it encodes the information about the function's behaviour without directly revealing it. If the function is balanced, the Oracle introduces a phase shift that flips the ancilla qubit. If the function is constant, the Oracles does not change any phase. After the Oracle call, Hadamard gate is applied to the qubits. The phase changes introduced by the Oracle create constructive and destructive interference patterns among all the states. Through this interference of the qubits' amplitudes, the system evolves to a state which encodes the answer to the problem. When measured, if all qubits are observed to be in state 0, the function f(x) is constant. If not, the function is balanced.

Implement a quantum oracle U_f that maps the state $|x\rangle|y\rangle$ to $|x\rangle|y \oplus f(x)\rangle$. $\oplus$ is addition modulo 2, and $f(x)$ is the Boolean function. $|x\rangle$ is the state of the n qubits, and $|y\rangle$ is the ancilla qubit. *Figure 9.16* shows the circuit diagram to implement the *Deutsch-Jozsa* algorithm:

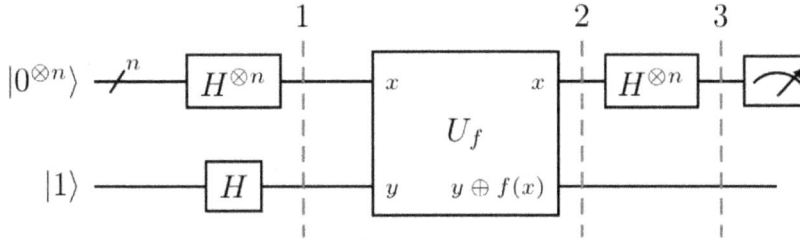

Figure 9.16: *Circuit for Deutsch-Jozsa algorithm (Source: QISKIT Textbook)*

The initial state of n qubits is all zeros. The ancilla qubit is initialized to $|1\rangle$.

$$|\Psi_0\rangle = |0^{\otimes N}\rangle \otimes |1\rangle$$

Let us look at the steps:

1. Apply Hadamard on all the inputs: n qubits which is the main input, and one ancilla qubit. The new state will be:

$$|\Psi_1\rangle = H^{\otimes n}|0^{\otimes n}\rangle \otimes H|1\rangle$$

Let us look at two input qubits, then extrapolate for n qubits.

$$H^{\otimes 2}|0^{\otimes 2}\rangle = H|0\rangle \otimes H|1\rangle$$

$$= \frac{1}{\sqrt{2}}(|0\rangle + |1\rangle) \otimes \frac{1}{\sqrt{2}}(|0\rangle + |1\rangle)$$

$$= \frac{1}{(\sqrt{2})^2}(|00\rangle + |01\rangle + |10\rangle + |11\rangle)$$

$$= \frac{1}{(\sqrt{2})^2}(|0\rangle + |1\rangle + |2\rangle + |3\rangle)$$

$$= \frac{1}{(\sqrt{2})^2}\sum_{x=0}^{2^2-1}|x\rangle$$

Therefore, to get $H^{\otimes n}|0^{\otimes n}\rangle$, just replace the power of 2 in previous equation with the power of n. The resultant equation will be:

$$\frac{1}{(\sqrt{2})^n}\sum_{x=0}^{2^n-1}|x\rangle$$

Hadamard is also applied to the ancilla qubit. Combining the two registers,

$$|\Psi_1\rangle = H^{\otimes n}|0^{\otimes n}\rangle \otimes H|1\rangle =$$

$$\frac{1}{(\sqrt{2})^n} \sum_{x=0}^{2^n-1} |x\rangle \otimes \frac{1}{\sqrt{2}} (|0\rangle - |1\rangle)$$

2. Apply the quantum oracle U_f, which only acts on the second register (ancilla qubit), as stated previously. Therefore, the new state is:

$$|\Psi_2\rangle = \frac{1}{\sqrt{2}} \frac{1}{(\sqrt{2})^n} \sum_{x=0}^{2^n-1} |x\rangle \otimes [(|0\rangle \oplus f(x)) - (|1\rangle \oplus f(x))]$$

If we look just at the second register, $(|0 \oplus f(x)\rangle) - (|1 \oplus f(x)\rangle)$

$f(x)$ is a Boolean function, so it can be either 0 or 1. Hence, $|0\rangle \oplus f(x)$ will be the same as $f(x)$.

So, the second register is $(|f(x)\rangle) - (|1 \oplus f(x)\rangle)$

If $f(x)$ is 0, then $|f(x)\rangle - (|1\rangle \oplus f(x)) = |0\rangle - |1\rangle$

If $f(x)$ is 1, then $|f(x)\rangle - (|1\rangle \oplus f(x)) = |1\rangle - |0\rangle = -(|0\rangle - |1\rangle)$

Therefore $|1\rangle \oplus f(x)$ can be denoted as $(-1)^{f(x)}(|0\rangle - |1\rangle)$

So, $|\Psi_2\rangle$ would be:

$$|\Psi_2\rangle = \frac{1}{\sqrt{2}} \frac{1}{(\sqrt{2})^n} \sum_{x=0}^{2^n-1} |x\rangle \otimes (-1)^{f(x)}(|0\rangle - |1\rangle) \;\rightarrow$$

$$\frac{1}{2^{n/2}} \sum_{x=0}^{2^n-1} (-1)^{f(x)} |x\rangle \otimes \frac{1}{\sqrt{2}}(|0\rangle - |1\rangle)$$

3. Apply Hadamard to just the first register. So, let us only look at the first register.

Following is the equation for the output when Hadamard gates are applied to state $|x\rangle$:

$$H^{\otimes n} |x\rangle = \frac{1}{(\sqrt{2})^n} \sum_{y=0}^{2^n-1} (-1)^{x.y} |y\rangle,$$

where $x.y = x_0 y_0 \oplus x_1 y_1 \oplus \dots x_{n-1} y_{n-1}$ modulo 2.

Replace $|x\rangle$ on the LHS of the previous equation with the first register's equation from *step 2*.

Therefore, $H^{\otimes n} [\frac{1}{2^{n/2}} \sum_{x=0}^{2^n-1} (-1)^{f(x)} |x\rangle]$ will become

$$\frac{1}{2^{n/2}} \sum_{x=0}^{2^n-1} (-1)^{f(x)} [\frac{1}{(2^{n/2}} \sum_{y=0}^{2^n-1} (-1)^{x.y} |y\rangle]$$

Combining the two registers,

$$|\Psi_3\rangle = \frac{1}{2^{n/2}} \sum_{x=0}^{2^n-1} (-1)^{f(x)} [\frac{1}{(2^{n/2}} \sum_{y=0}^{2^n-1} (-1)^{x.y} |y\rangle] \otimes \frac{1}{\sqrt{2}}(|0\rangle - |1\rangle)$$

Rearranging:

$$|\Psi_3\rangle = \frac{1}{2^n} \sum_{y=0}^{2^n-1} \left[\sum_{x=0}^{2^n-1} (-1)^{f(x)} (-1)^{x.y} \right] |y\rangle \otimes \frac{1}{\sqrt{2}}(|0\rangle - |1\rangle)$$

4. Measure the first register. Probability is the square of amplitude, which is within square brackets. Therefore, the probability of getting $|y\rangle = 0$ is:

$$\left| \frac{1}{2^n} \sum_{x=0}^{2^n-1} (-1)^{f(x)} (-1)^{x.0} \right|^2 \quad = \quad \left| \frac{1}{2^n} \sum_{x=0}^{2^n-1} (-1)^{f(x)} \right|^2$$

If f(x) is constant, the probability is:

$$\left| \frac{1}{2^n} (-1)^{f(x)} \sum_{x=0}^{2^n-1} \right|^2 \quad = \quad \left| \frac{2^n}{2^n} (-1)^{f(x)} \right|^2 \quad = \quad 1$$

If f(x) is balanced, it will yield equal number of 0s and 1s. So, $(-1)^{f(x)}$ will result in equal number of +1 and -1, which will cancel out each other. So, the probability is:

$$\left| \frac{1}{2^n} (1 + 1 + 1 \dots - 1 - 1 - 1 \dots) \right|^2 = 0$$

Therefore, if we measure $|y\rangle$ as 0, then f(x) is constant. For any other value of $|y\rangle$, f(x) is balanced. Hence, with one call to the Oracle we can determine whether the function is constant or balanced. *Figure 9.17* gives the circuit when the Boolean function is balanced.

Let us look at code that is run on a real quantum device: **ibm_osaka**.

1. Import the libraries:

```
# initialization
import numpy as np
# importing Qiskit
from qiskit import IBMQ, Aer
from qiskit.providers.ibmq import least_busy
from qiskit import QuantumCircuit, transpile
# import basic plot tools
from qiskit.visualization import plot_histogram
```

2. Define a Boolean function that can be either constant or balanced depending on the argument passed to it:

```
from enum import Enum
# Define an enumeration for the function types
class FunctionType(Enum):
    CONSTANT = "constant"
    BALANCED = "balanced"
```

```
def boolean_function(qc, n, type):
    for qubit in range(n):
        # 'type' indicates whether the function is 'constant' or
        # 'balanced'
        if type == FunctionType.CONSTANT :
            # Apply the identity operation to the qubit (no change)
            # for constant functions
            qc.id(qubit)
        elif func_type == FunctionType.BALANCED:
                # Apply a Controlled-NOT (CNOT) gate for balanced
                # functions
            qc.cx(qubit, n)
        else:                       raise  ValueError("Invalid   function
                                    type. Choose
                    'CONSTANT' or 'BALANCED'.")

    return qc
```

3. Initialize number of qubits in the input and the Boolean function:

```
n = 2
f_x = "balanced" # or "constant"
```

4. Define the quantum Oracle:

```
# Create an oracle quantum circuit with n+1 qubits
oracle = QuantumCircuit(n+1)\
# Define the binary string that represents the function values
b_str = "000"
# Place X-gates on qubits corresponding to '1' in b_str
for qubit in range(len(b_str)):
    if b_str[qubit] == '1':
        # Apply an X gate (bit-flip) to the qubit if the
        # corresponding bit is '1'
        oracle.x(qubit)
# Use a barrier to visually separate sections of the circuitoracle.
barrier()
```

```
# Apply the boolean function f_x to the oracle circuit
oracle = boolean_function(oracle, n, f_x)
# Use another barrier for clarity before the next section
oracle.barrier()
# Place X-gates on qubits corresponding to '1' in b_str after applying
# the boolean function
for qubit in range(len(b_str)):
    if b_str[qubit] == '1':
        # Apply an X gate (bit-flip) to the qubit again if the
        # corresponding bit is '1'
        oracle.x(qubit)
```

5. Design the overall circuit, by applying Hadamard on the qubits and calling oracle function, as given in the preceding theory section:

```
# Create a quantum circuit with n+1 qubits and n classical bits
dj_circuit = QuantumCircuit(n+1, n)
# Apply Hadamard gates to the first n qubits to create superposition

for qubit in range(n):
    dj_circuit.h(qubit)
# Prepare the last qubit in the |-⟩ state

dj_circuit.x(n) # Apply an X gate to flip the state to |1⟩
dj_circuit.h(n) # Apply a Hadamard gate to transform |1⟩ to |-⟩
# Add the oracle to the quantum circuit
dj_circuit = dj_circuit.compose(oracle)
# Repeat Hadamard gates on the first n qubits after the oracle

for qubit in range(n):
    dj_circuit.h(qubit)
# Add a barrier for better visualization of the circuit structure
dj_circuit.barrier()
# Measure the first n qubits and store the results in corresponding
# classical bits
for i in range(n):
    dj_circuit.measure(i, i)
```

```
# Display the quantum circuit
dj_circuit.draw('mpl')
```

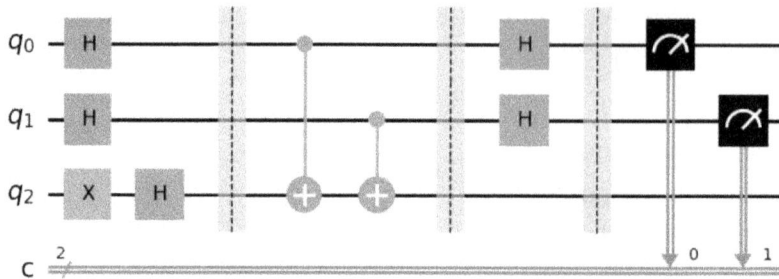

Figure 9.17: Circuit when Boolean function is balanced

6. Identify the least busy IBM Quantum device and execute the circuit:

```
# Load the IBM Quantum account for access to the available resources
IBMQ.load_account()
# Retrieve the IBM Quantum provider for the specified hub
provider = IBMQ.get_provider(hub='ibm-q')
# Find the least busy backend that can accommodate the required
# number of qubits (n+1)
backend = least_busy(provider.backends(filters=lambda x:
    x.configuration().n_qubits >= (n+1) and
    not x.configuration().simulator and x.status().operational==True))
print("least busy backend: ", backend)
# Run our circuit on the least busy backend. Monitor the execution of
the job in the queue
from qiskit.tools.monitor import job_monitor
# Transpile the circuit for the specified backend with the highest
# optimization level
transpiled_dj_circuit = transpile(dj_circuit, backend, optimization_
level=3)
# Execute the transpiled circuit on the backend
job = backend.run(transpiled_dj_circuit)
# Monitor the job status at 2-second intervals
job_monitor(job, interval=2)
```

7. Get the result. *Figure 9.18* displays the result.

```
# Get the results of the computation
```

```
results = job.result()
# Retrieve the counts of measurement outcomes
answer = results.get_counts()
# Plot a histogram of the measurement results
plot_histogram(answer)
```

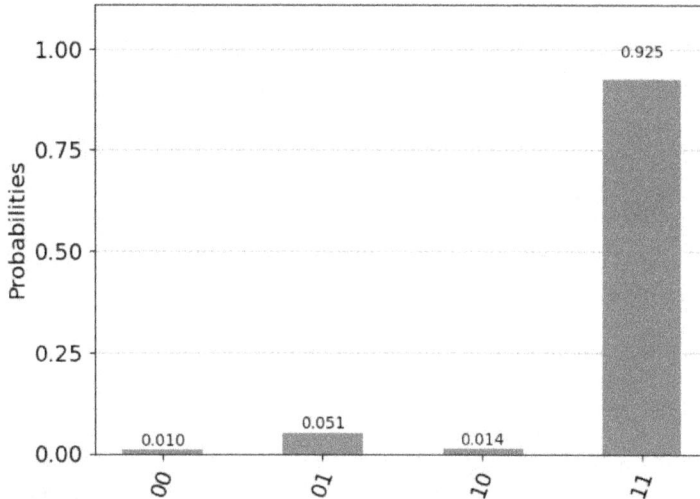

Figure 9.18: Result of algorithm when Boolean function is balanced

As can be seen in the preceding figure, probability of *11* is highest. Since this is run on a real quantum device, few other occurrences are also seen due to noise. On a simulator, *11* will be observed 100% of the time. If the output is not *00*, then the Boolean function is balanced, which is the case here.

Let us run the same circuit for a constant Boolean function. Just change f_x = constant in the preceding code and run. The following figures show the circuit diagram and corresponding results. An output of *00* means the Boolean function is constant, which is the correct result. *Figure 9.19(a)* gives the circuit when the Boolean function is constant. *Figure 9.19(b)* displays the corresponding result:

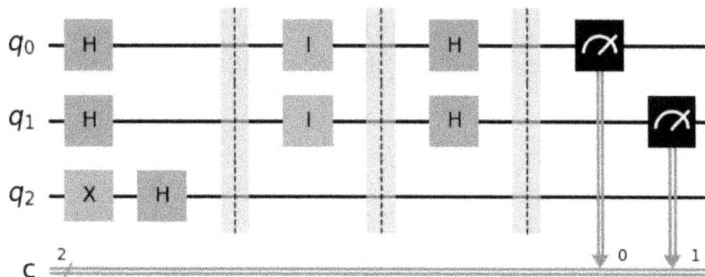

Figure 9.19(a): Circuit when Boolean function is constant

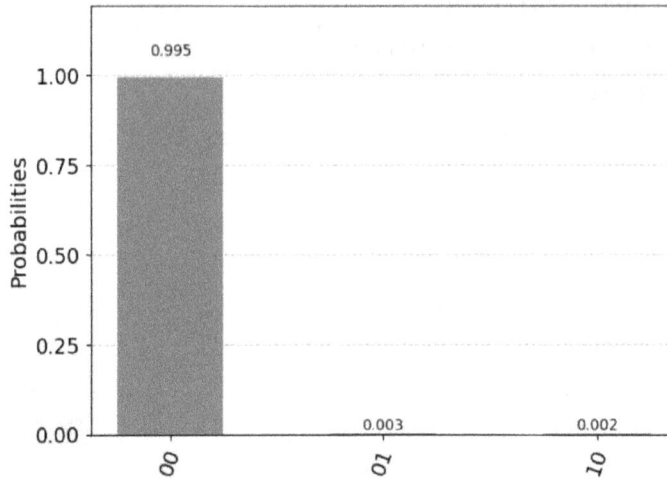

Figure 9.19(b): *Result of algorithm when Boolean function is constant*

Bernstein–Vazirani algorithm

The Bernstein-Vazirani algorithm is a quantum algorithm that was designed to solve a specific type of problem much more efficiently than classical computing algorithms. This algorithm was proposed by *Ethan Bernstein* and *Umesh Vazirani* to show the computational advantages of quantum algorithms over classical algorithms.

The problem involves a hidden binary string stored inside a box and the task is to identify the string using a quantum oracle function. In classical computing, the algorithm would need to query the Oracle for each bit in the string. Therefore, for a string of length n, it would take n queries to find the hidden string.

The Bernstein–Vazirani algorithm instead makes use of quantum parallelism, a property of quantum computing, and solves the problem with only one query to the Oracle, regardless of the size of the string. This is because the Hadamard transform creates quantum superposition by transforming a qubit's state into an equal probability distribution across all possible states. This superposition allows quantum computers to evaluate multiple possibilities simultaneously, enabling quantum parallelism. As a result, they can process a vast number of computations at once, significantly speeding up tasks compared to classical systems, which must evaluate each possibility sequentially.

Let us say there is a hidden string with n bits. There is an Oracle that implements a function $f(x)$ which returns just one bit → $\{0,1\}$, such that $f(x) = s.x\ mod\ 2$, where $s \in \{0,1\}^n$ is the hidden string, x is the input query, and $s.x$ is the dot product of s and x. The task is to find the value of that string s.

In classical computing (*Figure 9.20*), we can identify the information one bit at a time using the preceding oracle function. This can be done by assigning 1 to the first bit and 0s to rest of the bits in the input and query the Oracle. For example, assume that the hidden string is 011. The first query will be 100. The output of Oracle would be *s.x mod* 2 = (0.1 + 1.0 + 1.0) mod 2 = 0. In the next iteration, assign 1 to the second bit keeping rest of the bits as 0 in the query. Keep repeating this for all the n bits. *Table 9.1* shows the output for n=3. After all the iterations, the sequence of output is nothing but the hidden string, which is 011.

The problem with this approach is that the magnitude of time is $O(n)$, and it will take a lot of time for a large n.

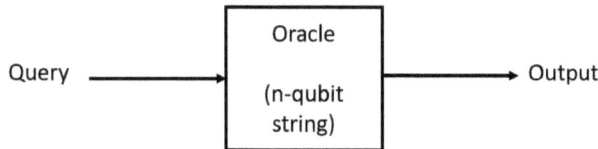

Figure 9.20: *Circuit for classical approach (Source: QISKIT Textbook)*

Query	S (hidden) = 011	MOD 2
100	100.011 = 1.0+0.1+0.1 = 0	0
010	010.011 = 1	1
001	001.011 = 1	1

Table 9.1: *Output of classical approach*

The Bernstein–Vazirani algorithm will solve the same problem with just one query to the Oracle, as shown in the following figure. Just like the Deutsch-Jozsa algorithm, we will use an ancilla qubit along with the n-qubit input.

Define a quantum oracle U_f that implements the aforementioned function f(x) such that it maps the input state $|x\rangle|y\rangle$ to $|x\rangle|y \oplus f(x)\rangle$, where f(x) = *s.x mod* 2, $|x\rangle$ is the state of the n input qubits, $|y\rangle$ is the ancilla qubit, and $\oplus$ is addition modulo 2. *Figure 9.21* represents the corresponding approach:

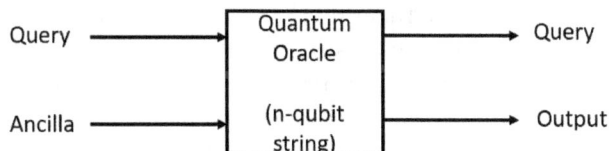

Figure 9.21: *Bernstein–Vazirani approach (Source: QISKIT Textbook)*

We will follow the flow of equations from Deutsch-Jozsa algorithm (previous section). The following is the equation from a previous section, when the Hadamard gates are applied on the n qubits from the output of Oracle:

$$H^{\otimes n} \left[\frac{1}{2^{n/2}} \sum_{x=0}^{2^n-1} (-1)^{f(x)} |x\rangle \right] \quad =$$

$$\frac{1}{2^{n/2}} \sum_{x=0}^{2^n-1} (-1)^{f(x)} \left[\frac{1}{(2^{n/2})} \sum_{y=0}^{2^n-1} (-1)^{x.y} |y\rangle \right]$$

Combining the two registers (query and ancilla),

$$|\Psi\rangle = \frac{1}{2^{n/2}} \sum_{x=0}^{2^n-1} (-1)^{f(x)} \left[\frac{1}{(2^{n/2})} \sum_{y=0}^{2^n-1} (-1)^{x.y} |y\rangle \right] \otimes \frac{1}{\sqrt{2}}(|0\rangle - |1\rangle)$$

Rearranging:

$$|\Psi\rangle = \frac{1}{2^n} \sum_{y=0}^{2^n-1} \left[\sum_{x=0}^{2^n-1} (-1)^{f(x)} (-1)^{x.y} \right] |y\rangle \otimes \frac{1}{\sqrt{2}}(|0\rangle - |1\rangle)$$

$$f(x) = s.x \text{ modulo } 2.$$

Therefore,

$$|\Psi\rangle = \frac{1}{2^n} \sum_{y=0}^{2^n-1} \left[\sum_{x=0}^{2^n-1} (-1)^{s.x} (-1)^{x.y} \right] |y\rangle \otimes \frac{1}{\sqrt{2}}(|0\rangle - |1\rangle)$$

$$= \frac{1}{2^n} \sum_{y=0}^{2^n-1} \left[\sum_{x=0}^{2^n-1} (-1)^{s.x + x.y} \right] |y\rangle \otimes \frac{1}{\sqrt{2}}(|0\rangle - |1\rangle)$$

$$= \frac{1}{2^n} \sum_{y=0}^{2^n-1} \left[\sum_{x=0}^{2^n-1} (-1)^{x.(s\oplus y)} \right] |y\rangle \otimes \frac{1}{\sqrt{2}}(|0\rangle - |1\rangle)$$

Measure the first register. The amplitude of first register for a given $|y\rangle$ is

$$\frac{1}{2^n} \left[\sum_{x=0}^{2^n-1} (-1)^{x.(s\oplus y)} \right]$$

Probability is $\left| \frac{1}{2^n} \left[\sum_{x=0}^{2^n-1} (-1)^{x.(s\oplus y)} \right] \right|^2$

When $s \oplus y = 0$, probability will be 1, and 0 otherwise.

$s \oplus y = 0$ is true when $s = y$. Therefore, the output of the circuit yields the secret string s.

The final measurement reveals the hidden string s directly because the quantum state is prepared in such a way that the Oracle marks the correct outcome. After applying the Hadamard gate, the algorithm creates a superposition of all possible states. The Oracle then flips the phase of the states corresponding to the hidden string s. These flipped states interfere constructively when the quantum state is measured, enhancing their probability of being observed. The states that do not correspond to s remain unchanged. These unmarked states interfere destructively, reducing their probability of being measured. Therefore, when the qubits are measured, the constructive interference of these marked states collapses the superposition to the specific state that corresponds to s, allowing it to be extracted directly with a single measurement.

Let us now look at the Python code that is run on ibm_osaka quantum computer:

1. Import the libraries:

```python
# initialization
from random import randint
# importing Qiskit
from qiskit import IBMQ, Aer
from qiskit.providers.ibmq import least_busy
from qiskit import QuantumCircuit, transpile, assemble
# import basic plot tools
from qiskit.visualization import plot_histogram
```

2. Generate a random hidden integer **s**:

```python
# Number of qubits used to represent the binary string s
n = 4 # number of qubits used to represent s
# Generate a random integer between 0 and 2^n - 1 (inclusive) to
# represent the hidden binary string
s = randint(0, 2**n - 1)
# Format the integer s as a binary string with n bits, padding with
# leading zeros if necessary
s = format(s, '0'+str(n)+'b')
print(s)
```

Result is 1011.

3. Build the circuit, call the Oracle, and measure the qubits:

```python
# We need a circuit with n qubits, plus one auxiliary qubit
# Also need n classical bits to write the output to.
bv_circuit = QuantumCircuit(n+1, n)
# Put ancilla qubit in a superposition state |->
bv_circuit.h(n)
bv_circuit.z(n)
# Apply Hadamard gates before querying the oracle
for i in range(n):
    bv_circuit.h(i)
# Apply barrier to visually separate sections of the circuit
bv_circuit.barrier()
```

```
# Apply the oracle
# Below line of code performs bit reversal to adjust for Qiskit's
# qubit ordering, which is in reverse order from the classical left-
# to-right representation. This ensures that the qubit states are
# correctly aligned with Qiskit's indexing.
s = s[::-1]
for q in range(n):
    if s[q] == '0':
        bv_circuit.i(q)
    else:
        bv_circuit.cx(q, n)
# Apply barrier to visually separate sections of the circuit
bv_circuit.barrier()
# Apply Hadamard gates after querying the oracle
for i in range(n):
    bv_circuit.h(i)
# Measurement
for i in range(n):
    bv_circuit.measure(i, i)
```

The following figure gives the overall circuit along with the Oracle interspersed between the two barriers:

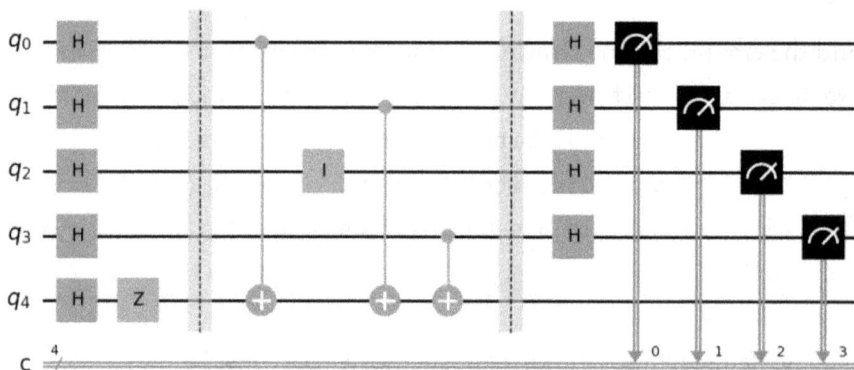

Figure 9.22: Circuit for Bernstein–Vazirani algorithm

4. Identify the least busy IBM Quantum computer and execute the circuit:

```
# Load the IBM Quantum account for access to the available resources
IBMQ.load_account()
# Retrieve the IBM Quantum provider for the specified hub
provider = IBMQ.get_provider(hub='ibm-q')
# Find the least busy backend that can accommodate the required
# number of qubits (n+1)
backend = least_busy(provider.backends(filters=lambda x:
    x.configuration().n_qubits >= (n+1) and
    not x.configuration().simulator and
    x.status().operational==True))
print("least busy backend: ", backend)
# Run our circuit on the least busy backend. Monitor the execution of
# the job in the queue
from qiskit.tools.monitor import job_monitor
# Define the number of times circuit will be run
shots = 1024
# Transpile the circuit for the specified backend with the highest
# optimization level
transpiled_bv_circuit = transpile(bv_circuit, backend)
# Execute the transpiled circuit on the backend
job = backend.run(transpiled_bv_circuit, shots=shots)
# Monitor the job status at 2-second intervals
job_monitor(job, interval=2)
```

5. Get the result, which is shown in *Figure 9.23*

```
# Get the results of the computation
results = job.result()
# Retrieve the counts of measurement outcomes
answer = results.get_counts()
# Plot a histogram of the measurement results
plot_histogram(answer)
```

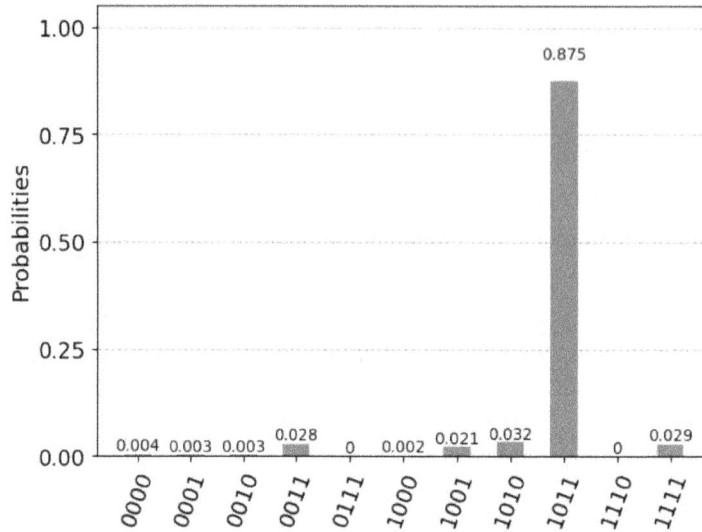

Figure 9.23: *Result from Bernstein–Vazirani algorithm*

As can be seen in *Figure 9.23*, probability of *1011* is the highest. It is nothing but the hidden string s that we originally started with. Since this is run on a real quantum device, few other occurrences are also seen due to noise. On a simulator, probability of measuring *1011* is 100%. Thus, this run aligns with the theoretical part of this section which determined that the probability will be 100% for a result y when it is equal to the hidden strings.

Conclusion

This chapter explored a few quantum algorithms where each algorithm demonstrated the potential of quantum computation to tackle problems much faster than classical computers. These algorithms demonstrated unique characteristics and potentials, further highlighting the diverse nature of quantum computing. Quantum algorithms have initiated a paradigm shift in computational power, unravelling potentialities for solving complex problems. Understanding and harnessing their full potential remains crucial for driving the next wave of technological breakthroughs. While the specific applications of these algorithms vary, they all leverage the unique properties of quantum mechanics to achieve significant speedups. Further research and development is crucial to refine these algorithms and discover new algorithms to pave the way for practical implementation on future quantum computing platforms. Quantum algorithms undoubtedly represent a new era, opening tremendous opportunities in the rapidly evolving field of quantum computing. The next chapter enumerates various use cases of quantum computing.

Multiple choice questions

1. **Which of the following best describes quantum phase kickback in quantum computing?**

   a. The transfer of energy from one qubit to another during measurement.

   b. The transfer of a phase change from a target qubit to a control qubit in an entangled state.

   c. The loss of quantum information due to decoherence.

   d. The creation of entanglement between two uncorrelated qubits.

2. **Which of the following statements best describes the advantage of Grover's search algorithm over classical search algorithms?**

   a. Grover's algorithm sorts data before searching, making it exponentially faster than classical algorithms.

   b. Grover's algorithm can search an unsorted database in linear time, just like classical algorithms.

   c. Grover's algorithm can search an unsorted database in approximately the square root of the number of steps required by classical algorithms, providing a quadratic speedup.

   d. Grover's algorithm only works on sorted data and is slower than classical algorithms.

3. **Which of the following statements best describes the significance of Shor's algorithm in the context of cryptography?**

   a. It provides a classical method for encrypting data using large prime numbers.

   b. It enables quantum computers to factor large integers exponentially faster than classical algorithms, threatening the security of RSA encryption.

   c. It guarantees the security of RSA encryption by making factorization impossible.

   d. It is only useful for small numbers and has no practical implications for real-world cryptography.

4. **Which statement best describes the advantage of the Deutsch-Jozsa algorithm over classical algorithms for determining whether a Boolean function is constant or balanced?**

   a. It can determine if the function is constant or balanced with fewer classical queries by random sampling.

   b. It always requires checking every possible input to guarantee the answer.

c. It provides a probabilistic answer that may be incorrect.

d. It determines with certainty whether the function is constant or balanced using only a single query to the function on a quantum computer.

5. **Which of the following statements best describes the main advantage of the Bernstein-Vazirani algorithm over its classical counterpart?**

a. It finds a hidden binary string using only one query to the oracle, regardless of the string's length, by exploiting quantum parallelism

b. It can solve any computational problem faster than classical algorithms.

c. It requires more queries as the string length increases, like classical algorithms.

d. It does not use quantum superposition or Hadamard gates.

Answer key

1. b
2. c
3. b
4. d
5. a

Questions

1. How does Grover's algorithm use quantum principles to achieve faster search, and what are its main components?

Answer: Grover's algorithm leverages quantum superposition, entanglement, and interference to search unsorted data more efficiently than classical algorithms. It consists of two main components: the Oracle, which flips the phase of the amplitude of the target state, and the Diffusion operator, which amplifies the amplitude of the target state. By repeating these steps about times (where N is the number of possible states), the probability of finding the correct answer becomes significantly higher than with classical search, making it especially effective for large, unstructured datasets.

2. Why is Shor's algorithm considered a milestone in quantum computing, and what impact does it have on RSA encryption?

Answer: Shor's algorithm is a milestone in quantum computing because it demonstrates that quantum computers can solve the integer factorization problem exponentially faster than classical computers, specifically in polynomial time689. This has a profound impact on RSA encryption, which relies on the difficulty of factoring large integers for its security. If a sufficiently powerful quantum computer were built, Shor's algorithm could efficiently break RSA encryption by quickly finding the prime factors of the large numbers used as encryption keys, rendering current RSA-based cryptographic systems insecure[689]. However, practical implementation is currently limited by the lack of large-scale, fault-tolerant quantum computers.

3. What is quantum phase kickback, and why is it important in quantum computing??

   Answer: Quantum phase kickback is a phenomenon where a phase change applied to a target qubit in an entangled pair is reflected back onto the control qubit, even if no direct operation is performed on the control qubit. This effect arises due to quantum entanglement and interference, and it plays a crucial role in many quantum algorithms (such as Shor's and Grover's algorithms) and quantum protocols, enabling complex quantum computations and operations.

4. How does the Deutsch-Jozsa algorithm use quantum principles to determine whether a Boolean function is constant or balanced, and how does this compare to the classical approach?

   Answer: The Deutsch-Jozsa algorithm leverages quantum superposition and interference to evaluate a black-box Boolean function for all possible inputs simultaneously. By preparing the qubits in a superposition, applying the oracle (which encodes the function), and then using Hadamard gates, the algorithm creates interference patterns that reveal whether the function is constant or balanced upon measurement. If all qubits are measured as 0, the function is constant; otherwise, it is balanced. This process requires only a single query to the function, whereas a classical deterministic algorithm would require up to $2^{n-1} + 1$ queries in the worst case to guarantee the answer.

5. How does the Bernstein-Vazirani algorithm achieve a speedup over classical algorithms in finding a hidden binary string?

   Answer: The Bernstein-Vazirani algorithm achieves its speedup by utilizing quantum parallelism, which allows it to evaluate all possible input queries simultaneously through superposition. By applying the Hadamard transform to the input qubits and using a quantum oracle, the algorithm encodes information about the hidden string into the quantum state. After just one query to the oracle, measuring the quantum state reveals the entire hidden binary string, whereas a classical algorithm would require n separate queries for a string of length n.

Join our Discord space

Join our Discord workspace for latest updates, offers, tech happenings around the world, new releases, and sessions with the authors:

https://discord.bpbonline.com

CHAPTER 10

Applications of Quantum Computers Across Industries

Introduction

Quantum computing is at the forefront of technological innovation, harnessing the mysterious and powerful principles of quantum mechanics to unlock a realm of possibilities previously out of reach. This cutting-edge technology promises to transform industries, offering the potential to revolutionize everything from cybersecurity to healthcare. In this chapter, we journey through the diverse and fascinating applications of quantum computing across multiple sectors, exploring how it is reshaping the world as we know it.

Structure

The chapter covers the following topics:

- Sector-wise applications of quantum computing
- Cryptography and cybersecurity
- Finance and risk analysis
- Pharmaceuticals and drug discovery
- Materials science
- Artificial intelligence and machine learning
- Logistics and supply chain

- Climate modeling and weather forecasting
- Healthcare
- Telecommunications
- Energy

Objectives

This chapter aims to provide a comprehensive overview of the revolutionary potential of quantum computing across diverse fields. Readers will explore its transformative applications, from enhancing cryptographic security and optimizing financial risk analysis to accelerating drug discovery and advancing artificial intelligence. The chapter will also discuss the role of quantum computing in solving global challenges such as climate change, sustainable energy, and efficient supply chain management. By the end of this chapter, readers will gain a clear understanding of the current landscape, future possibilities, and practical insights into the integration and implications of quantum computing in various sectors.

Sector-wise applications of quantum computing

The following are some of the sector-wise applications of quantum computing:

- **Cryptography and cybersecurity:** Quantum computing's ability to break traditional encryption methods poses both a challenge and an opportunity, prompting advancements in quantum-safe cryptographic techniques such as **quantum key distribution (QKD)**.
- **Finance and risk analysis:** Quantum computing enhances complex modeling and risk analysis, offering the potential to optimize investment strategies and market predictions with greater accuracy.
- **Pharmaceuticals and drug discovery:** Quantum computing accelerates drug discovery by simulating molecular interactions at a highly detailed level, aiding pharmaceutical companies in developing new treatments more efficiently.
- **Materials science:** Quantum computing supports the discovery and design of new materials with unique properties, advancing industries such as electronics, manufacturing, and sustainability.
- **Artificial intelligence and machine learning:** By processing vast amounts of data efficiently, quantum computing contributes to more powerful AI models and enhances machine learning capabilities.
- **Logistics and supply chain:** Quantum optimization algorithms improve complex logistics problems, reducing inefficiencies and streamlining supply chain management.

- **Climate modeling and weather forecasting:** Quantum computing enhances the processing of climate and weather data, leading to more precise forecasts and deeper insights into climate change mitigation.

- **Healthcare:** Quantum algorithms have the potential to revolutionize medical diagnostics and personalized treatment planning, contributing to more effective healthcare solutions.

- **Telecommunications:** Innovations in quantum computing improve network security and management, ensuring more reliable and secure communication systems.

- **Energy:** Quantum computing aids in optimizing energy grids, advancing sustainable energy solutions, and improving the efficiency of renewable energy sources.

Examples of real-world impact

Let us look at some examples of real-world impact:

- **Cryptography and cybersecurity:** Quantum computers can break traditional encryption methods, but they also enable quantum cryptography techniques like QKD, used by companies such as ID Quantique for ultra-secure communication.

- **Finance and risk analysis:** Banks like JPMorgan Chase are exploring quantum algorithms to optimize portfolio management and fraud detection, providing faster and more precise risk assessments.

- **Pharmaceuticals and drug discovery:** Quantum computing is accelerating drug development at companies like Roche and Google DeepMind, helping simulate molecular interactions at an unprecedented level.

- **Climate modeling and weather forecasting:** Researchers at NASA are leveraging quantum simulations to improve climate prediction models and understand the impact of climate change more accurately.

- **Artificial intelligence and machine learning:** IBM and Google are developing quantum-enhanced AI models that can solve complex problems faster than classical counterparts, revolutionizing fields such as natural language processing and robotics.

These examples illustrate the tangible progress quantum computing is making, and highlighting its potential to drive innovation and address some of the world's most pressing challenges.

Challenges and ongoing research

Despite its potential, quantum computing faces significant hurdles. High error rates due to quantum decoherence and noise remain a major challenge, necessitating advancements in quantum error correction techniques. Scalability is another critical issue, as current quantum processors have limited qubits and require substantial improvements in hardware design. Additionally, the need for robust quantum algorithms that outperform classical solutions in practical applications is an area of active research. Companies such as IBM, Google, and startups like Rigetti Computing are working on increasing qubit coherence times, developing more stable quantum architectures, and exploring hybrid quantum-classical approaches to bridge the gap between theory and real-world applications. Governments and academic institutions worldwide are also investing heavily in research to push the boundaries of quantum computing capabilities.

While quantum computing holds immense promise across these sectors, these challenges must be addressed before widespread adoption. The following sections will explore each sector in depth, addressing current developments, limitations, and future directions in quantum computing.

Cryptography and cybersecurity

Quantum computing research and its evolution in cryptography and cybersecurity are focused on both the challenges posed by quantum computers and the development of new, secure solutions to counteract these challenges.

Quantum computers have the potential to break widely used encryption algorithms, posing significant risks to data security. Key threats include:

- **Breaking traditional encryption:** Quantum computers have the potential to break widely used encryption algorithms such as **Rivest Shamir Adleman (RSA)** and **Elliptic Curve Cryptography** (ECC), which are based on the difficulty of factoring large numbers and solving discrete logarithm problems. Quantum algorithms like Shor's algorithm can solve these problems efficiently, compromising the security of data protected by these methods.

- **Need for quantum-resistant cryptography:** The emergence of quantum computing has spurred research into **post-quantum cryptography** (PQC), which focuses on creating cryptographic algorithms that are resistant to quantum attacks.

Let us look at research and evolution in quantum cryptography:

- **Quantum key distribution (QKD):** Leveraging quantum mechanics, QKD provides secure communication channels for encryption key exchange. Various companies and research institutions are working on QKD implementations. However, real-world adoption is challenged by factors such as hardware requirements, distance limitations, and integration with existing cryptographic systems. Additionally, QKD requires specialized optical infrastructure, making its deployment costly and impractical for widespread use. Furthermore, QKD does not solve all cryptographic challenges, as it primarily secures key exchange rather than encrypting bulk data.

- **Development of new algorithms:** Researchers are focused on designing quantum-resistant cryptographic algorithms that can withstand quantum attacks. These include:
  - Lattice-based cryptography
  - Code-based cryptography
  - Hash-based cryptography
  - Multivariate cryptographic schemes

Challenges in implementing post-quantum cryptography

Despite significant advancements, the implementation of PQC faces several technical hurdles:

- **Computational overhead:** Many PQC algorithms, especially lattice-based schemes, require significantly more computational resources than classical algorithms, impacting performance and efficiency.
- **Key size and bandwidth requirements:** Some quantum-resistant cryptographic algorithms require larger key sizes and increased bandwidth, posing scalability challenges for existing systems.
- **Compatibility with existing infrastructure:** Transitioning from classical cryptographic methods to PQC requires extensive updates to hardware and software systems, which may not be feasible for all organizations.
- **Security validation:** Ongoing research is needed to rigorously evaluate the long-term security of PQC algorithms, ensuring they are resistant to both classical and quantum attacks.

Standardization efforts in post-quantum cryptography

Given the urgency of quantum threats, global standardization efforts are underway to ensure a seamless transition to quantum-resistant cryptographic systems:

- The **National Institute of Standards and Technology (NIST)** is actively evaluating and standardizing PQC algorithms through its PQC Standardization Project. This initiative aims to develop robust cryptographic techniques suitable for widespread adoption.
- Various industry and academic collaborations are contributing to the development and assessment of these algorithms, focusing on performance, security, and practical deployment.
- International standardization bodies, including ISO and ETSI, are also working on guidelines to facilitate the adoption of PQC globally.

Industry contributions

Several technology leaders are driving research and development in quantum computing and its implications for cybersecurity. The companies leading the way in this sector are:

- **IBM:** IBM is actively engaged in quantum computing research and its impact on cryptography. Through platforms like the **IBM Quantum Experience**, researchers can experiment with quantum systems, including their cryptographic applications.

- **Google:** Google is exploring the cybersecurity implications of quantum computing and contributing to the development of quantum-resistant cryptographic algorithms.

- **Microsoft:** Microsoft's **Quantum Development Kit** allows researchers and developers to experiment with quantum computing, including its applications in cryptography and cybersecurity.

- **ID Quantique:** Specializing in quantum-safe security, ID Quantique is a leading provider of QKD technology and secure encryption solutions tailored for quantum threats.

Quantum computing is driving a paradigm shift in cryptography and cybersecurity. While it presents significant risks to traditional encryption methods, it also fosters innovation in secure communication and encryption techniques. However, challenges such as computational overhead, infrastructure transition, and security validation must be addressed to ensure the practical implementation of PQC. As research advances and industry leaders push for standardization, the future will witness the widespread adoption of quantum-resistant cryptographic solutions capable of withstanding emerging quantum threats.

Finance and risk analysis

Quantum computing holds the potential to transform complex financial modeling and risk management by providing significant computational advantages. Here is a brief overview of how quantum computing is impacting this sector:

- **Portfolio optimization:** Quantum computing enhances the efficiency of complex optimization problems, enabling the management of large, diverse portfolios while incorporating multiple constraints and objectives.

- **Derivative pricing:** By processing vast datasets and simulating financial models at unprecedented speeds, quantum computing allows for more accurate pricing of derivatives and other financial instruments.

- **Risk management:** Quantum algorithms can analyze large datasets and complex financial models, providing deeper insights into risk exposure and potential market fluctuations.

- **Fraud detection:** Quantum machine learning algorithms can detect anomalies in financial data more efficiently than classical methods, improving the accuracy and speed of fraud identification. For instance, quantum algorithms leverage pattern recognition and anomaly detection techniques that scale better with large, complex financial datasets compared to traditional statistical methods.

Let us look at research and evolution in quantum finance:

- **Monte Carlo simulations:** Quantum computers offer a significant speedup for Monte Carlo simulations, which are crucial in financial applications such as option pricing and risk assessment. Specifically, quantum amplitude estimation reduces the number of required simulations, accelerating convergence and enhancing accuracy.

- **Machine learning for financial predictions:** Quantum-enhanced machine learning improves market trend predictions and financial forecasting, enabling more informed investment decisions.

Industry contributions

The companies leading the way in this sector are:

- **Goldman Sachs:** Collaborating with quantum computing firms like D-Wave and IBM, Goldman Sachs explores quantum applications in portfolio optimization and risk management.

- **JPMorgan Chase:** Working closely with IBM, JPMorgan Chase is leveraging quantum computing for risk assessment, financial modeling, and portfolio optimization.

- **Ally Financial:** Partnering with quantum startups, Ally Financial investigates the use of quantum algorithms for financial services, particularly in portfolio and risk management.

- **BBVA:** The Spanish banking group BBVA is researching quantum computing applications in risk assessment and fraud detection, aiming to improve operational efficiency and decision-making.

- **Cambridge quantum computing (CQC):** A leading quantum technology company developing quantum algorithms tailored for financial modeling, optimization, and secure transactions.

Challenges and outlook

While quantum computing presents exciting opportunities for finance, several challenges must be addressed before widespread adoption:

- **Hardware limitations:** Current quantum computers lack the scalability and error correction needed for practical, large-scale financial applications.

- **Algorithmic maturity:** Many quantum algorithms are still in the research phase and require further refinement for real-world financial use cases.
- **Integration with classical systems:** Financial institutions must navigate the complexities of integrating quantum solutions with existing classical infrastructure.

Quantum computing is revolutionizing the finance sector by enabling faster and more sophisticated financial modeling and risk analysis. As research progresses, we can anticipate broader adoption of quantum technologies, leading to more accurate predictions, optimized portfolios, and enhanced risk management strategies. However, overcoming hardware and algorithmic challenges remains essential for achieving practical implementation at scale.

Pharmaceuticals and drug discovery

Quantum computing is poised to revolutionize pharmaceuticals and drug discovery by accelerating the development of new drugs and enhancing precision medicine.

Quantum applications in pharmaceuticals and drug discovery are as follows:

- **Molecular simulation:** Quantum computers can simulate molecular behavior and interactions with unprecedented detail by handling exponentially larger state spaces. This enables researchers to model drug-target interactions more effectively, improving drug design and development.
- **Drug design and optimization:** Quantum computing accelerates the identification of promising drug candidates by rapidly analyzing large datasets of molecular structures and properties.
- **Protein folding:** Predicting protein folding is crucial for understanding diseases and designing treatments. Quantum algorithms, such as the **Variational Quantum Eigensolver** (**VQE**), assist in accurately modeling protein structures, potentially leading to breakthroughs in treating conditions linked to misfolded proteins.
- **Precision medicine:** Quantum computing enhances precision medicine by analyzing a patient's genetic data alongside environmental and lifestyle factors. This enables more accurate predictions of drug responses and the identification of personalized treatment plans.

Let us look at research and evolution in quantum pharmaceuticals:

- **Faster drug discovery:** Quantum computing has the potential to reduce drug development timelines, which currently span decades, by enabling more efficient molecular screening and simulations. This also leads to significant cost savings for pharmaceutical companies.
- **Simulation of biological processes:** Quantum computers can model complex biological systems with greater accuracy, providing deeper insights into disease mechanisms and potential treatments.

Industry leaders and collaborations

Several major pharmaceutical companies are actively investing in quantum computing research. The companies leading the way in this sector are:

- **Pfizer:** Pfizer collaborates with IBM to explore quantum applications in drug discovery, focusing on molecular modeling and optimization.

- **GlaxoSmithKline (GSK):** GSK has partnered with Cambridge Quantum Computing to leverage quantum algorithms for molecular simulations and drug discovery.

- **Bayer:** Bayer is working with quantum computing firms to investigate quantum-enhanced simulations of molecular interactions, improving drug formulation and testing.

- **Roche:** Roche is researching quantum-driven advancements in personalized medicine, focusing on genetic data analysis for targeted therapies.

Quantum computing is transforming pharmaceuticals by enhancing molecular simulations, accelerating drug discovery, and enabling precision medicine. As pharmaceutical companies continue collaborating with quantum computing firms, drug development is becoming more efficient and precise, paving the way for faster medical breakthroughs.

Challenges and outlook

While quantum computing presents immense opportunities for pharmaceutical innovation, several challenges must be overcome before it can be fully integrated into drug discovery pipelines:

- **Hardware limitations:** Current quantum devices lack the necessary qubit stability, coherence time, and error correction required to simulate complex molecular systems at a practical scale. Near-term quantum hardware (NISQ devices) can only tackle small molecules or simplified models.

- **Algorithmic development:** Quantum algorithms for drug discovery, such as the **Variational Quantum Eigensolver (VQE)** or **Quantum Approximate Optimization Algorithm (QAOA)**, are still evolving. Many remain in experimental stages and require refinement to match the complexity of real biological systems.

- **Integration with classical systems:** Combining quantum simulations with existing classical bioinformatics, cheminformatics, and pharmaceutical workflows poses significant integration challenges. Hybrid quantum-classical systems must be carefully designed for seamless operation.

- **Talent and training gap:** The pharmaceutical industry faces a shortage of interdisciplinary professionals skilled in both quantum computing and biomedical research, hindering the pace of innovation and adoption.

- **Validation and regulatory approval:** Drug discovery and development are tightly regulated. Quantum-enabled discoveries must undergo rigorous validation and meet strict regulatory standards, which may slow adoption despite technological advances.

Quantum computing has the potential to dramatically accelerate and refine the pharmaceutical R&D process—from molecular simulations and drug candidate screening to personalized medicine and biological modeling. As partnerships between quantum technology firms and pharmaceutical companies grow, the industry is gradually moving toward a more data-driven, efficient, and targeted approach to drug development. However, overcoming current hardware, algorithmic, and integration challenges will be crucial to unlocking quantum computing's full value in transforming healthcare and therapeutic innovation.

Materials science

Quantum computing is revolutionizing materials science by accelerating material discovery and design. This technology enables researchers to explore new materials at an atomic level, offering unprecedented precision and efficiency. Key applications in materials science include:

- **Molecular and atomic simulations:** Quantum computers, leveraging principles like superposition and entanglement, can simulate the behavior of atoms and molecules with significantly higher precision than classical computers, which struggle with the exponential complexity of these systems. This capability allows researchers to develop new materials with enhanced properties, such as high-temperature superconductors and next-generation battery materials.

- **Designing novel materials:** Quantum simulations help scientists understand and predict the interactions of materials, aiding in the creation of substances with tailored properties such as superior strength, improved conductivity, or enhanced flexibility.

- **Predicting material properties:** By accurately modeling how materials respond under different conditions, quantum computing supports the development of efficient and sustainable materials, impacting industries such as aerospace, energy, and semiconductors.

Let us look at research and evolution in quantum materials science:

- **Accelerated research and development:** Quantum computing drastically speeds up material testing and prototyping by allowing accurate simulations before costly and time-consuming physical experiments. This innovation reduces Research and Development costs and expands the scope of material exploration.

- **Materials for quantum technologies:** Researchers are developing advanced materials tailored for quantum devices, including superconducting materials for qubits and novel compounds for quantum sensors.

The companies leading the way in this sector are:

- **IBM:** IBM Research is actively using quantum computing to simulate molecular structures and design new materials. One of their notable projects focuses on simulating lithium-ion battery chemistry to improve energy storage.

- **Google:** Google's quantum division has leveraged its Sycamore processor to study quantum phase transitions, a breakthrough that could pave the way for novel electronic and magnetic materials.

- **Microsoft:** Microsoft is researching topological qubits, which require specialized materials to improve quantum stability and error correction, potentially enhancing the scalability of quantum computing.

Real-world implications

The advancements in quantum materials research hold significant promise for various industries:

- **Aerospace:** Lighter and stronger materials could improve fuel efficiency and durability in aircraft and spacecraft.

- **Energy:** Enhanced battery technology and superconductors could lead to more efficient energy storage and transmission.

- **Semiconductors:** Quantum-designed materials could revolutionize chip manufacturing, leading to faster and more energy-efficient electronics.

Quantum computing is transforming materials science by enabling the precise simulation of materials at an atomic level. As research progresses, this technology promises groundbreaking advancements in energy, electronics, aerospace, and beyond. By overcoming challenges such as error correction and scalability, quantum computing will unlock new frontiers in material innovation, accelerating the development of next-generation technologies.

Artificial intelligence and machine learning

In the field of **artificial intelligence** (**AI**) and **machine learning** (**ML**), quantum computing has the potential to revolutionize data analysis, model training, and algorithmic efficiency. Here is a brief overview of how quantum computing is impacting this sector.

The following are quantum applications in AI and ML:

- **Enhanced data processing:** Quantum computing can process large and complex datasets more efficiently, potentially accelerating AI and ML applications.

- **Quantum machine learning (QML):** Quantum algorithms can improve machine learning models by introducing novel methods for optimization, classification, and clustering.

- **Model training and optimization:** Quantum computers can explore parameter spaces more effectively, enabling faster and more efficient model training and optimization.

- **Quantum neural networks:** Quantum computers can enhance neural networks by leveraging quantum properties such as superposition and entanglement, potentially leading to more powerful AI models.

Let us look at research and evolution in quantum AI and ML:

- **Hybrid quantum-classical models:** Researchers are developing hybrid models that combine classical and quantum computing, leveraging the strengths of both to improve AI and ML applications.

- **Quantum-assisted learning:** Quantum computing can assist in learning tasks such as feature selection, data classification, and anomaly detection, providing new insights and capabilities.

Quantifiable benefits

While quantum computing is still in its early stages, some research suggests that certain quantum algorithms can achieve speed-ups over classical methods. For example, quantum algorithms have the potential to process optimization problems exponentially faster in specific cases, leading to improved efficiency in ML model training and data analysis.

Industry leaders

The companies leading the way in this sector are:

- **Google:** Google is known for its work in quantum AI, exploring how quantum computing can improve ML models and processes. Their AI blog includes updates on their work in this field.

- **IBM:** IBM's quantum computing division collaborates with researchers to develop quantum-enhanced AI and ML models. They offer tools such as *Qiskit* for experimenting with quantum computing in AI applications.

- **Microsoft:** Microsoft is actively researching quantum computing for AI and ML, including the development of tools and frameworks such as *Q#* for building quantum algorithms.

Quantum computing is poised to transform AI and machine learning by offering new methods for data processing, model training, and algorithm optimization. However, challenges such as hardware constraints, algorithmic development, and cost must be addressed for its full potential to be realized. As research progresses, we can expect more practical applications of quantum-enhanced AI and ML, leading to more efficient, powerful, and innovative models across various industries.

Logistics and supply chain

In the field of logistics and supply chain, quantum computing offers promising potential to optimize complex operational challenges and improve efficiency across the industry. Here is a brief overview of how quantum computing is impacting this sector:

- **Route optimization:** Quantum computing can solve complex optimization problems, such as the traveling salesman problem, more efficiently, leading to better routing for delivery and transportation services.

- **Inventory management:** Quantum algorithms can help manage inventory levels by predicting demand and optimizing stock levels across warehouses and distribution centers.

- **Supply chain network design:** Quantum computing can assist in designing more efficient and resilient supply chain networks by considering multiple variables and constraints simultaneously.

- **Dynamic scheduling:** Quantum computing can optimize scheduling for production, transportation, and workforce allocation, leading to more efficient and flexible operations.

Let us look at research and evolution in quantum logistics:

- **Real-time decision-making:** Quantum computing can enable real-time analysis and decision-making in supply chain management, allowing companies to quickly adapt to changes and disruptions.

- **Risk mitigation:** Quantum algorithms can identify potential risks in the supply chain and provide strategies for mitigation, ensuring more reliable operations.

The companies leading the way in this sector are:

- **D-Wave Systems:** D-Wave has been developing quantum algorithms for logistics optimization, including route planning and scheduling. A specific example is their work on improving delivery efficiency by optimizing traffic flow in urban settings.

- **IBM:** IBM offers quantum computing services and solutions for supply chain optimization, including risk management and inventory planning. Their quantum-powered simulations help businesses predict supply chain disruptions.

- **Volkswagen:** Volkswagen has explored quantum computing for optimizing traffic flow and routing problems in urban logistics and vehicle distribution, demonstrating practical applications in reducing congestion.

Quantum computing is set to revolutionize logistics and supply chain management by addressing intricate optimization challenges more effectively. As research advances and partnerships between technology firms and logistics companies strengthen, we can anticipate significant improvements in supply chain efficiency, flexibility, and reliability.

Challenges and outlook

Although quantum computing offers transformative potential for logistics and supply chain optimization, several practical and technical challenges must be addressed before widespread implementation can occur:

- **Hardware constraints:** Current quantum processors are still limited in qubit count, coherence, and reliability, restricting their ability to handle large-scale, real-world logistics problems with the required precision and speed.

- **Scalability of algorithms:** Many quantum optimization algorithms, such as the QAOA, are still in early stages of development and may not scale effectively for complex, global supply chain networks involving thousands of variables.

- **Integration with classical infrastructure:** Supply chain systems are heavily reliant on mature classical software platforms (e.g., ERP, WMS, TMS). Seamlessly integrating quantum solutions into these existing systems requires robust hybrid architectures and interoperability frameworks.

- **Data quality and availability:** The effectiveness of quantum optimization heavily depends on the quality, granularity, and timeliness of input data. Many logistics networks still lack the data infrastructure necessary to support such advanced analytics.

- **Domain expertise and skill gaps:** There is a shortage of professionals skilled in both quantum computing and supply chain management, slowing down the translation of research breakthroughs into practical logistics solutions.

Quantum computing has the potential to significantly enhance logistics and supply chain operations by solving complex optimization problems faster and more effectively than classical systems. From route planning to inventory management and risk mitigation, quantum solutions promise greater responsiveness, resilience, and efficiency. However, widespread adoption will depend on overcoming current hardware limitations, evolving algorithmic robustness, and building hybrid systems that align with industry-specific operational needs. As the field matures and collaboration between quantum tech providers and logistics companies deepens, we can expect more adaptive and intelligent supply chain ecosystems powered by quantum intelligence.

Climate modeling and weather forecasting

In the field of climate modeling and weather forecasting, quantum computing presents opportunities to revolutionize how we predict and understand complex weather and climate systems. Here is a brief overview of how quantum computing is impacting this sector:

- **Data processing and simulation:** Quantum computing can handle vast amounts of climate and weather data quickly, enabling more accurate and detailed simulations of atmospheric conditions and climate patterns. Quantum algorithms have the potential to analyze intricate variables simultaneously, improving overall modeling efficiency.

- **Model optimization:** Quantum algorithms can optimize climate models by identifying the most efficient computational pathways, enhancing accuracy, and enabling more precise forecasts of extreme weather events and long-term climate trends. For instance, quantum-assisted machine learning techniques can refine parameter estimation in predictive models.

- **Long-term climate predictions:** Quantum computing can simulate complex interactions between atmospheric, oceanic, and terrestrial factors, leading to improved long-term climate projections. These simulations can provide insights into feedback loops, such as the influence of ocean currents on global temperature changes.

Let us look at research and evolution in quantum climate science:

- **Improved forecasting accuracy:** By enabling more efficient processing of large datasets, quantum computing can lead to significant advancements in weather forecasting accuracy. This can benefit critical sectors such as agriculture, transportation, and emergency management, where timely and precise predictions are crucial.

- **Climate change mitigation:** Quantum computing can support research into climate change by modeling the impact of various mitigation strategies. It can simulate the effects of carbon reduction initiatives, assess global temperature projections, and help optimize renewable energy deployment strategies.

- **Current research and challenges:** While quantum computing holds promise, there are challenges, including hardware constraints, the need for more robust quantum algorithms, and error correction in quantum systems. Research efforts are ongoing to refine these technologies and expand their applicability to climate science.

The companies leading the way in this sector are:

- **IBM:** IBM's quantum computing division is actively developing quantum algorithms for climate and weather applications, utilizing its quantum hardware and software to refine simulation models.

- **Google:** Google is leveraging its quantum expertise to explore applications in climate modeling, focusing on improving computational efficiency in atmospheric and weather research.

- **Microsoft:** Microsoft collaborates with researchers and institutions to apply quantum computing to environmental science, including climate modeling and sustainability initiatives.

- **Collaborations and Funding Initiatives:** Numerous collaborations between research institutions, government agencies, and private sector companies are driving advancements in quantum climate applications. Increased funding from governments and organizations is accelerating progress in this field.

Quantum computing is poised to significantly enhance climate modeling and weather forecasting by enabling faster and more accurate simulations of complex climate systems. While the field is still evolving, ongoing research and technological advancements suggest that within the next decade, quantum-enhanced models could lead to groundbreaking improvements in forecasting precision. As computational capabilities expand, we can anticipate better preparedness for extreme weather events and more effective climate change mitigation strategies.

Healthcare

In the field of healthcare, quantum computing is beginning to make a significant impact by offering innovative solutions for medical research, diagnostics, and personalized treatment plans. Here is a brief overview of how quantum computing is affecting this sector:

- **Genomic analysis:** Quantum computing can process vast amounts of genetic data to identify disease-causing mutations and optimize personalized treatments. For example, quantum algorithms can analyze genomic data significantly faster than classical methods, reducing analysis time from weeks to hours.

- **Medical imaging:** Quantum algorithms can enhance the quality and speed of medical imaging techniques, aiding in faster and more accurate diagnostics. For instance, research suggests that quantum computing could potentially reduce MRI scan times by 50% while improving image resolution.

- **Drug discovery and development:** Quantum computing accelerates the discovery and development of new drugs by simulating molecular interactions more efficiently. Quantum simulations can model protein folding and chemical interactions in ways classical computers struggle with, potentially reducing drug development timelines by years.

- **Optimization of treatment plans:** Quantum computers can help optimize treatment plans by modeling various scenarios and predicting outcomes based on patient data. This enables more personalized and effective treatment approaches.

Let us look at research and evolution in quantum healthcare:

- **Improved diagnostic accuracy:** Quantum-enhanced AI and machine learning can analyze medical data and images more precisely, leading to more accurate diagnoses. Studies indicate that quantum-enhanced models can improve diagnostic accuracy by up to 10% compared to conventional methods.

- **Personalized medicine:** Quantum computing enables the processing of individual genetic and medical data to tailor treatments to each patient's specific needs, making precision medicine more effective and accessible.

The companies leading the way in this sector are:

- **IBM:** IBM's quantum computing research includes applications in healthcare such as analyzing medical data, optimizing treatment plans, and simulating biological processes. IBM has partnered with pharmaceutical companies to accelerate drug discovery.

- **Google:** Google is known for its work on quantum computing and has explored potential applications in healthcare, including the use of quantum algorithms to analyze medical imaging data with enhanced precision.

- **D-Wave:** D-Wave collaborates with healthcare institutions to apply quantum computing to complex optimization problems, such as improving hospital logistics, resource allocation, and patient flow management in medical facilities.

Quantum computing offers groundbreaking opportunities in healthcare by providing the ability to process large datasets, simulate complex biological systems, and optimize treatment plans. By addressing current challenges and furthering collaborations between healthcare providers and technology companies, the future holds significant advancements in medical diagnostics, treatment options, and personalized care.

Telecommunications

In the field of telecommunications, quantum computing is emerging as a game-changing technology with the potential to revolutionize network security, data transmission, and communication protocols. Here is a brief overview of how quantum computing is impacting this sector:

- **Quantum key distribution (QKD):** QKD enables secure transmission of encryption keys over a communication channel, using quantum mechanics principles. This ensures that any attempt to intercept the keys can be detected, providing a higher level of security. However, QKD requires specialized hardware and is subject to distance limitations, which are ongoing challenges.

- **Secure communication protocols:** Quantum computing can enhance existing communication protocols and create new ones that are more secure against potential quantum attacks. These protocols leverage quantum entanglement and superposition for increased security.

- **Network optimization:** Quantum computing can optimize network management and routing by processing vast amounts of data more efficiently than classical systems. Examples include traffic congestion reduction and dynamic resource allocation in large-scale telecommunications networks.

- **Error correction:** Quantum error correction is critical for overcoming noise and decoherence in quantum communication. Research into quantum error correction codes, such as surface codes and bosonic codes, is essential for developing reliable quantum networks.

Let us look at research and evolution in quantum telecommunications:

- **Improving data transmission:** Quantum computing can enhance data transmission methods, making them faster and more secure. Recent research has demonstrated quantum-enhanced signal processing, which could lead to more resilient communication infrastructures.

- **Quantum networks:** The development of quantum networks is an area of active research, involving the construction of secure, quantum-based communication infrastructure. Entanglement-based networks, such as China's quantum satellite experiments (e.g., Micius satellite), have demonstrated the feasibility of long-distance quantum communication.

Industry leaders

The companies leading the way in this sector are:

- **British Telecom (BT):** BT has been working on integrating QKD in its network to enhance data security, particularly in secure government and financial sector communications.

- **Toshiba:** Toshiba is a leader in quantum computing research and is known for its advancements in QKD technology, including commercial QKD solutions.

- **Huawei:** Huawei is involved in research and development of quantum computing applications in telecommunications, including exploring quantum networks and secure communication protocols.

- **IBM and Google:** Both companies are pioneering quantum computing research, with efforts in quantum-safe cryptography and quantum networking technologies. IBM has developed quantum-safe encryption protocols, while Google's research focuses on error correction and large-scale quantum systems.

- **Startups in Quantum Networking:** Various startups, such as QinetiQ, ID Quantique, and Quantum Xchange, are actively developing quantum-secure communication solutions.

Recent developments

Recent breakthroughs in quantum communication include advancements in entanglement-based quantum repeaters, which extend the range of quantum networks. Research papers from institutions like MIT, Caltech, and the Chinese Academy of Sciences have explored scalable quantum network architectures and real-world QKD implementations.

Quantum computing is set to transform the telecommunications industry by providing more secure and efficient communication methods. As research progresses, innovations in secure communication, network optimization, and quantum networks will continue to emerge. The growing involvement of leading technology companies and research institutions underscores the accelerating momentum in this field, paving the way for a more connected and secure world.

Energy

In the field of energy, quantum computing has the potential to revolutionize how energy is produced, stored, and distributed by addressing critical challenges such as inefficiencies in energy grids, limitations in material performance, and the need for sustainable energy solutions. Traditional methods often struggle with computational complexity, whereas quantum computing offers unique advantages in tackling these large-scale optimization and simulation problems. The quantum applications in energy are as follows:

- **Materials for energy:** Quantum computing can help design and simulate new materials for energy production and storage, such as high-efficiency solar cells or advanced batteries, by accurately modeling quantum-level interactions.

- **Optimization of energy grids:** Quantum algorithms can optimize energy distribution networks by analyzing large datasets to improve grid reliability reduce losses, and improve overall efficiency in energy distribution networks.

- **Nuclear fusion:** Quantum computing can simulate complex nuclear reactions with higher precision, potentially accelerating the development of viable and sustainable nuclear fusion as a clean energy source.

- **Carbon capture and storage:** By simulating molecular interactions, quantum computing can aid in designing more efficient materials and processes for capturing and storing carbon emissions, which is crucial for mitigating climate change.

Let us look at research and evolution in quantum energy:

- **Simulation of energy systems:** Quantum computing allows for precise simulations of energy systems at a molecular level, offering insights into improving their efficiency and stability.

- **Optimization of renewables:** Quantum algorithms can enhance the integration and operation of renewable energy sources like wind and solar power into the grid, ensuring better load balancing and energy distribution.

Potential challenges

Despite its promise, quantum computing in energy faces limitations such as hardware constraints, error rates, and scalability issues. Current quantum processors are still in the early stages, and achieving fault-tolerant quantum computing remains a significant hurdle. Additionally, classical computing techniques are highly optimized, making it essential to identify specific energy-related problems where quantum solutions provide a clear advantage.

Industry leaders

The companies leading the way in this sector are:

- **IBM:** Engaged in applying quantum computing to energy challenges, including material discovery and grid optimization.

- **Google:** Researching quantum applications for energy optimization and advanced material simulations.

- **D-Wave:** Partnering with energy companies to leverage quantum annealing for optimizing energy distribution and supply chain logistics.

- **Siemens:** Utilizing quantum computing to model energy storage systems and enhance the integration of renewable energy sources.

Quantum computing is transforming the energy sector by enabling breakthroughs in materials discovery, energy grid optimization, and sustainable energy solutions. While challenges remain, continued research and development will determine how effectively quantum computing can address the pressing energy problems of the future.

Conclusion

The applications of quantum computing across various fields presents an exciting frontier of possibilities and potential breakthroughs. From cryptography and cybersecurity to finance, pharmaceuticals, and energy, quantum computing is transforming how we approach complex challenges and opportunities in each sector. This transformative technology is reshaping traditional industries, enabling us to model and simulate intricate systems with unprecedented precision. It turbocharges artificial intelligence and machine learning, leading to leaps in data analysis and algorithmic efficiency. It also revolutionizes logistics and supply chain management, optimizing global operations for a seamless future. Moreover, it aids in climate modeling, providing sharper insights for accurate forecasting and mitigation of climate change. In healthcare, quantum computing promises to reshape medical diagnostics and personalized treatments, revolutionizing patient care. Lastly, it brings innovations to telecommunications, transforming network management and enhancing communication reliability. As quantum computing continues to evolve, we stand on the cusp of a new era of technological advancements that hold the promise of profound impact on our world. However, realizing this potential requires ongoing research and development to overcome key challenges such as hardware limitations and scalability. Addressing these obstacles will be crucial in ensuring that quantum computing achieves its full transformative power across industries. The journey ahead is filled with excitement as we explore how quantum computing can push the boundaries of what is possible and revolutionize the way we live and work.

Multiple choice questions

1. **What algorithm is used by quantum computers to break traditional encryption methods such as RSA?**

   a. Grover's algorithm

   b. Shor's algorithm

   c. Dijkstra's algorithm

   d. Kruskal's algorithm

2. **In finance, what is one major benefit of using quantum computing?**

   a. Slower data processing

   b. Inability to model complex portfolios

   c. Improved risk assessment

   d. Limited scope in algorithm application

3. **How does quantum computing accelerate drug discovery?**

   a. By delaying molecular simulations

   b. By randomly selecting drug candidates

   c. By simulating molecular interactions rapidly

   d. By ignoring complex biological processes

4. **What type of problems can quantum computing optimize in logistics and supply chain management?**

   a. Simple inventory problems

   b. Low-level operations

   c. Routine tasks only

   d. Complex routing and scheduling problems

5. **In which field can quantum computing significantly improve network management and security?**

   a. Manufacturing

   b. Telecommunications

   c. Agriculture

   d. Tourism

Answer key

1. b
2. c
3. c
4. d
5. b

Questions

1. Explain how quantum computing can enhance machine learning and artificial intelligence algorithms.

   Answer: Quantum computing can enhance machine learning and AI algorithms by processing vast datasets quickly and efficiently, allowing for more complex models and better optimization. Quantum algorithms, such as Quantum Support Vector Machines and Quantum Neural Networks, can also improve the accuracy and performance of AI tasks such as classification, clustering, and neural network training.

2. Describe the potential impact of quantum computing on energy grid management.

   Answer: Quantum computing can optimize energy grid management by analyzing large datasets to improve the reliability and efficiency of energy distribution networks. It can also help integrate renewable energy sources into the grid, leading to a more sustainable and balanced energy system.

3. How can quantum computing contribute to climate modeling and weather forecasting?

   Answer: Quantum computing can process vast climate and weather datasets rapidly, enabling more precise climate modeling and weather forecasting. This can lead to better planning and responses to climate-related challenges, such as extreme weather events and long-term climate change.

4. Discuss the role of quantum computing in designing new materials for various industries.

   Answer: Quantum computing allows researchers to simulate and predict the properties of new materials at a quantum level, enabling the design of substances with unique characteristics. This can lead to innovations in industries such as energy, electronics, and construction, as new materials offer improved efficiency and sustainability.

5. What challenges might arise from the use of quantum computing in healthcare, and how can they be addressed?

   Answer: Challenges in healthcare include data privacy concerns, ethical issues related to personalized treatments, and the need for regulatory frameworks. Quantum computing has the potential to accelerate personalized medicine by enabling more precise and efficient analysis of patient data. However, the development and deployment of quantum algorithms in healthcare may require new regulatory frameworks to ensure ethical use and data security. Addressing these challenges will require careful data management, ethical guidelines, and collaboration between researchers, healthcare providers, and policymakers.

6. Name one quantum algorithm used for searching unsorted databases more efficiently.

   Answer: Grover's algorithm

7. What is one application of quantum computing in pharmaceuticals?

   Answer: Simulating molecular interactions for drug discovery.

8. How can quantum computing improve AI algorithms?

   Answer: By processing vast datasets quickly and efficiently.

9. In which sector does quantum computing aid in optimizing complex logistics problems?

   Answer: Logistics and supply chain management.

10. What is one benefit of quantum computing in finance?

    Answer: Improved risk assessment and portfolio optimization.

Join our Discord space

Join our Discord workspace for latest updates, offers, tech happenings around the world, new releases, and sessions with the authors:

https://discord.bpbonline.com

Index